To Jack
Merry Christmas '81!
From John

*See overleaf.* Ben Campanale at the Milwaukee Mile in 1938

# HARLEY~ DAVIDSON

## THE MILWAUKEE MARVEL

**HARRY V. SUCHER**

Foulis

Haynes

ISBN 0 85429 261 6

© Harry V.Sucher

First published **August 1981**

**A FOULIS Motorcycling book**

*Printed in England by the publishers*
**Haynes Publishing Group Ltd**
Sparkford, Yeovil, Somerset BA22 7JJ, England

*Distributed in North America by*
**Haynes Publications Inc**
861 Lawrence Drive, Newbury Park, California 91320 USA

*Editor:* **Jeff Clew**
*Cover design:* **Phill Jennings**
*Layout design:* **Lynne J.Blackburn**

# Dedication

Dedicated to the memories of Arthur Davidson and William S.Harley who, starting out with little more than an idea, and in the American free enterprise tradition, founded an organization that was to become of historical significance to American transportation.

# Foreword

Any Publisher who proposes to produce a factual and readable book on the early history of motorcycling in America at this late date must find an Author who is a motorcycle enthusiast, blessed with amazing perception, literary ability, and insatiable desire, before it becomes too late, to record for posterity this sector of American transportation history. He will need a number of old-time motorcycling friends, who, in turn have old-time motorcycling friends, engineers, mechanics and champions. Then, in order to get started, he must have the time, the available funds, the energy to write to, travel to, visit with and pick the recollections and brains of those few remaining 'old timers' (of which he himself will desirably be one) to collect and collate over a period of months and possibly years, the varied memories and opinions of informed, uninformed, prejudiced, or sometimes spiteful persons. Finally, and most importantly, he must wind up the job by 'sifting the wheat from the chaff', giving the benefit of the doubt to those deceased and defenseless persons, many of whose actions, while controversial, were of necessity created by the natural desire for economic survival.

The publisher of this book is fortunate to have as the Author, Dr.Harry V.Sucher of Garden Grove, California, who measures up to the features suggested in the above paragraph.

While I have not found it easy to agree with the opinion of all of Dr.Sucher's informants, which is quite understandable, he has done an excellent job of sifting the wheat from the chaff and has come up with a book which, in spite of the time lapse and the demise of practically all of the principals, matches or betters his 'Iron Redskin' book of a year or two ago, which covered in detail the founding and development of the Indian motorcycle, the great competitor that Harley-Davidson contended with all through the years.

My long-time personal association, friendship with, and admiration for Bill, Walter, and Arthur Davidson, Bill Harley and their sons and grandsons, and the previously inadequate record of their achievements, caused me to offer my co-operation to Doctor Sucher. I can recommend this book to all would-be and should-be owners, and to all the 'Old Timers' who like myself, even before the days of Mr.Ford's 'Tin Lizzie', enjoyed the thrill of twisting the right grip of a 'Silent Gray Fellow' on an open road, experiencing for the first time the never-to-be-forgotten thrill of the sport of motorcycling.

**Alfred Rich Child**

# Contents

# Author`s Preface

From the backyard of a modest home in Milwaukee, when the uncertain clatter of the first Harley-Davidson motorcycle first pierced the air, to the lusty roar of a modern chopper as it rockets through the streets of Las Vegas, Harley-Davidson has ever been a dominant force on the American motorcycle scene.

As one of the pioneers of the industry, Harley-Davidson experienced the initial triumph and then the near demise of American motorcycle manufacturing. In the period between the wars, the motorcycle became an insignificant entity within the domestic transportation scene, due to the complexity of certain socio-economic factors which we will examine. With their backs to the wall, the surviving makes struggled on, maintaining a brave front to the world, but perforce existing through subterfuge and deception. As an already controversial entity, the motorcycle industry, through its business relationships and marketing methods, became even more controversial. As the sole surviving member of that industry, (a remarkable achievement in itself), Harley-Davidson has lived on in the eye of the storm.

Strangely enough, the true story of the life and times of Harley-Davidson has never been thoroughly explored. Through the years we have been exposed to both the fictionalized and self-laudatory 'histories' published by the factory, as well as many unfounded excoriations by critics whose writings were based on unsound evidence.

It now appears that never before has the history of Harley-Davidson been subjected to professional journalistic research. The author hopes that this effort will fill this void, and at the same time offer an interesting portion of the saga of American transportation history.

*Harry V. Sucher*

10

# Acknowledgements

THEY SAID IT COULDN'T BE DONE. THE AUTHOR WAS WARNED BY COMPETENT advisers that to attempt the writing of the history of Harley-Davidson could only result in a dead end. No help would be forthcoming from surviving Company personnel, they said, nothing but adamant opposition to the telling of the REAL story of Harley-Davidson. But this proved not to be the case. The present executives of the AMF concern, now the present owners of the Company, were most friendly and co-operative. But the doomsayers were right in one respect: certain of the Company's old timers, including former President William H.Davidson, and certain surviving remnants of the old Milwaukee staff, gave official notice that they wanted no part of any such revelation. The traditional veil of silence that ever surrounded the internal affairs of the American motorcycle industry was still to be reckoned with.

But in starting the project, it was soon found that a vast store of information was forthcoming from many hundreds of people who were interested in seeing that this vital segment of American transportation history be recorded for posterity. These included past and present dealers, owners, and most fortunately, a large group of one-time Company employees. Added to these were surviving old time riders of Harley-Davidsons and other makes of American machines, as well as many former competition stars whose varied recollections and impressions could be distilled to provide the essence of the story.

In addition, certain elements of the history are autobiographical, as the author, a veteran motorcycle owner and rider, fortunately possesses a first hand knowledge of many of the events that took place, as well as personal experiences involving many of the various models that Harley-Davidson produced through the years.

Some of the more prominent people from the past whose contributions are gratefully acknowledged include Hap Alzina, Nelson Bettencourt, Floyd Clymer, Charles Cook, Joe Frugoli, Dudley Perkins, Angelo Rossi, and Claude Salmon.

At a later date there was Paul Albrecht, John and Jean Burdette, Skip Fordyce, Orrin Hall, Armando Magri, Frank J.Murray, Gene Rhyne, Joe Sarkees, Francis 'Shorty' Tompkins and John Underwood.

During the years when the author was actively engaged in collecting and restoring old machines, there was Bruce Aikin, the late J.Worth Alexander, Maury and Beverly Biggs, P.T.Boone, Russell Harmon, the late Elmo Looper, Sam Pierce, Bob and Pat Ross, Ernest Skelton, Bob Stark, and Gerald and Ted Williams. As such activities involve much sentimental interest, these people not only contributed much material assistance, but are revered for their warm personal friendship as well.

Former competition stars who added much color to the story include Bud Ekins, Fred Ludlow, Ed Kretz, and the late Joe Petrali. Former race mechanics whose help is acknowledged include the late Marvin 'Red' Fenwicke and 'Pop' Schunk, as well as the contributions of the late Joe Walker. The latter, a long time Harley-Davidson dealer, was not only a valued friend for many years, but generously allowed me to test ride various older model machines that passed through his hands, as well as ensuing later models as they appeared. I am also most grateful to his widow, Edith, for allowing me access to his extensive collection of private papers and Company literature and correspondence that made up his vast file of Harley-Davidson memorabilia.

I am grateful for the kind encouragement of Theodore A. (Ted) Hodgdon, one of the Honored Founders of the Antique Motorcycle Club of America, and Arthur Segal, a Past President. Also, I would like to thank Frank Conley, Secretary of the Classic and Antique Motorcycle Association, as well as Jeff Clew and Arthur Mortimer of the Vintage Motor Cycle Club.

A most outstanding contributor was Alfred Rich Child, the patriarch of Harley-Davidson, and a very wonderful gentleman who is now in his ninetieth year. Still an ageless and articulate individual, his keen mind provides a total recall of both his long time close association with the four Company Founders, as well as many others connected with Company affairs. The complex history of his representation and association with the Company in the Orient for many years is now fortunately revealed for the first time.

I am very appreciative of the assistance of William 'Bill' Dutcher, present Publicity Director of AMF-Harley Davidson, a member of the new generation of the revitalized Company, who generously provided photographs and other data concerning Harley-Davidson's ongoing manufacturing and marketing activities.

I am particularly grateful for the helpful advice of two very dear friends of many year's standing, Dewey Bonkrud and Johnny Eagles. Both are highly expert mechanics and practical engineers. Not only do I appreciate their valued friendship, but also their invaluable technical advice gained from their many years of practical experience and observation.

I am also indebted to my wife, Margery, who carefully typed and edited the manuscript, and offered her incisive comments as to its contents.

Not to be forgotten is my Editor, Jeff Clew, who is also the Executive Editorial Director of the publishers of this book. As a noted motorcycle expert and author of a large number of technical works on the subject, he is also a recognized historian in the field, and has had published a number of valuable works on the subject. Not only do I appreciate his warm personal friendship through the years, but also his helpful guidance and sympathetic understanding in the execution of a very difficult and demanding task.

Mention must also be made of the photographic artistry of George Hays, Ed Heslin, David Rose, and Alisha Tamburri who provided an outstanding group of illustrations. I am particularly grateful to the latter for her expert restoration of many of the older pictures for proper reproduction.

Harry V. Sucher
Garden Grove,
California 1980

# Chapter 1

# William S. Harley and the Davidsons

THE DIRECTION OF PUBLIC ATTENTION TO THE MOTOR BICYCLE IN THE USA CAME about in a somewhat indirect manner through the medium of professional bicycle racing which, at the close of the 19th century, was of great interest to a vast bicycling public. In certain competitive events held at the many indoor board tracks or velodromes located in the larger cities throughout the country, tandem machines propelled by two riders were used to pace or precede competitors in sprint events in order to 'cut the wind' or otherwise allow the racers to ride in their slipstream. This was to make for faster times and to give the effect of a more accurate or 'pure' indication of the rider's speed capabilities. Such tandem pacers had already been in use in Europe, and particularly in France, on some of the larger velodromes since 1894 or 95. A couple of seasons later, motor powered machines came into use, some being roadster-type powered bicycles, and some being rather large machines with big, slow-turning engines specially built for this purpose. Motor powered pacers were first seen in the United States in 1899, when a one-time bicycle racer, Kenneth Skinner, and the manager of bicycle racing events at New York's famous Madison Square Garden, imported about a dozen small De Dion type engines for this use. Various cycle mechanics adapted several tandem pedal pacers for this use, but reliability was sometimes a problem because an engine failure could terminate an event. A young bicycle mechanic named Carl Oscar Hedstrom made a name for himself at this point by refining and improving Skinner's engines for better performance and he designed and built his own version of a powered tandem. His efforts later resulted in the founding of the giant Indian motorcycle company.

During this period the several leading bicycle journals featured continuing articles on the progress of powered bicycle design, most of which was then taking place in England and Europe, although a few native experimenters had entered the field. The first American of note was one E.J.Pennington, of Trenton, New Jersey. In 1894 he had built a rather unorthodox machine based on pedal cycle frames but fitted with very large diameter tyres. A two cylinder engine was fitted on an outrigger frame behind the rear wheel, the drive to the axle being by means of a pair of cranks. While the machine could be made to run after a fashion, it appeared that its inventor was more of a promoter than an engineer. He endeavored to create a paper empire by offering large blocks of stock for public sale. After interest in the project in the United States was not forthcoming, he journeyed to England where he was able to found the Great Horseless Carriage Company through the co-operation of a bicycle financier, H.J.Lawson. The latter was able to sell about 100,000 worth of stock before the venture predictably collapsed in 1899.

In the meantime, the world wide bicycle boom flourished unabated, with hundreds of large and small factories operating at peak capacity. In June of 1898, the Waltham Manufacturing Company, of

Waltham, Massachusetts, makers of the famous Orient Bicycles, announced their intention of marketing motor bicycles. They had adapted their heavyweight roadster bicycle for the fitting of a small De Dion type engine built in France by the newly founded Aster concern, and proposed to name it the Orient-Aster. The first models were offered for sale in the spring of 1899. The Marsh Cycle Company of nearby Brockton built a similar machine, also powered with a De Dion type engine, which was first offered for sale in January of 1900. The following spring, Colonel Pope announced that proto-type motorbicycles were being tested at his Hartford factory. In the spring of 1901, Carl Oscar Hedstrom and George M.Hendee formed the Hendee Manufacturing Company, following the successful public demonstration of the former's prototype machine in Springfield. The E.R.Thomas Company of Buffalo, New York, announced the introduction of their soon-to-be-famous 'Auto-Bi' a few months later. By the turn of the century, the American motorcycle industry had become a reality.

Around the turn of the century, two young men who had been close friends since their early grammar school days in Milwaukee, Wisconsin, and who were both bicycling enthusiasts, turned their attention to the design of a practical motor bicycle. William S.Harley was born in Milwaukee in 1880 to working-class parents who had recently emigrated from England. The origins of the Harley family are somewhat obscure, but it is known that they came from the vicinity of Manchester. When young Harley had completed his education at the age of fifteen, he found employment as an apprentice bi-cycle fitter in a small cycle factory in North Milwaukee. He was described by contemporaries as having a natural aptitude for mechanics and, paradoxically, he was also interested in the out-of-doors, natural history, and drawing and sketching. Two years later he decided to broaden his technical capabilities by becoming an apprentice draftsman in a small metal fabricating plant in Milwaukee, where his boy-hood friend, Arthur Davidson, was also employed as a pattern maker. A year younger than Harley, he was the younger son of a family of three boys and two girls who had emigrated to the States from Aberdeen, Scotland, sometime in 1871 or 1872.

It is at this point that the true events of their mutual interest in the developing gasoline engine diverge somewhat according to several slightly differing accounts that subsequently appeared in Harley-Davidson Company literature in later years. The official version has been that their initial ex-periments with small gasoline engines were directly concerned with powering bicycles. However, two contemporaries of both Harley and Davidson independently told the author in the early 1950s that their first efforts were directed toward the development of small engines for powering rowboats. It seems that Harley, with his aforementioned interest in nature, was also a dedicated trout fisherman, and frequently, with young Davidson, fished many of the lakes that abounded in the Milwaukee region. As a powerboat could obviously vastly enhance a fisherman's scope of activity, it is not sur-prising that it should capture the young outdoorsman's interest.

It appears that with their preoccupation with gasoline engines, the two read all of the current literature on the subject they could lay their hands on, which included the leading scientific journals of the day, as well as automotive publications that were now becoming widely circulated, and material in the popular cycling magazines dealing with the now emerging motor bicycle.

Harley and Davidson's interest was also enhanced through their recent acquaintanceship with a newly-emigrated German draftsman who was employed in the same shop, one Emil Kroeger (or Kruger) who had in his possession some actual shop drawings of some small De Dion type gas engines acquired from the Aster concern in Paris, where he had lately been employed. It is known that the pair built three small prototype engines, the last being of sufficient power to propel a small rowboat, fitted with a propellor and installation equipment also built by the partners of their own designs. Unfortunately, no photographs or other specific details of their excursion into marine engineering sur-vive.

During the fall of 1900, Harley and Davidson next turned to the study of motor bicycle engines, and during the ensuing winter made the patterns for the castings of a small engine based on the Aster drawings with a $2\frac{1}{8}$ inch bore and $2\frac{7}{8}$ inch stroke. Working in their spare time during the evenings and weekends they assembled three or four of these engines and tested them in standard heavyweight, utility type, pedal cycle frames. Their main technical difficulties at this time appeared to be with car-buretion, and they finally settled on a primitive spray type instrument that offered little if any throttle control, limited engine speed variations being effected by altering the dry-battery-activated spark control setting. After much experimentation, a fairly satisfactory carburetor was subsequently evolved.

It was during this time that Arthur undertook another and unrelated after-hours venture (no doubt to earn extra funds to finance the engine experiments) involving the making of job patterns. This was in association with another young mechanic named Ole Evinrude, who was later to win fame and fortune as the developer and promoter of the first practical outboard marine engine.

As this was the day of the primitive 'clip-on' motor bicycle, Harley and Davidson had ample opportunity to observe the technical details of the various makes of machines already in commercial production. Some of these, such as the Indian, Marsh, Orient, Pope, Thor, and Wagner, to name the most prominent, were of fairly substantial construction. But as is too often the case when a new product is capturing public attention, about a dozen fly-by-night concerns were producing flimsy and inferior machines in order to make a quick profit.

Sometime during 1902, Arthur's 26 year old brother Walter, who had been an apprentice machinist in one of the railroad shops in Milwaukee, but who was then employed in its shops in Missouri, Kansas, and Texas Railroad in Parsons, Kansas, moved back to Milwaukee and secured a similar position with the Chicago, Milwaukee, and St.Paul Railroad. He had been in touch with the powerboat and motor bicycle engine experiments through correspondence with Arthur, and now offered to lend a hand with the project in his own spare time.

As the work advanced, the lack of suitable shop equipment at the Davidson family home at the corner of 38th Street and Highland Avenue made further progress most difficult. Fortunately, Harley was now able to secure the use of a small shop owned by a mutual friend of his and the Davidsons that was equipped with a small lathe and a drill press, together with a fairly comprehensive set of hand tools.

The first prototype model was finally completed early in the Spring of 1903. During the initial road tests the engine ran well and appeared to be acceptably reliable, producing a top speed of about 25 mph, but lacking sufficient power for serious hill climbing. During extended testing on the usual muddy and rutted roads of the Milwaukee suburbs, the weakness of the standard pedal cycle frame became all too apparent, with frame breakages, distortions, and the repeated failure of the steering head bearings.

The ancestor of the H-D big twins: The 1911 magneto-equipped twin.

Realizing the immediate need for a more powerful engine, Harley designed a new and larger model, following the now almost standard De Dion configuration, but with a 3 inch bore and a 3½ inch stroke, heavier castings and flywheels, and a swept volume of 25 cubic inches. After the drawings were made, Arthur again made up the casting patterns.

With a more powerful engine, fitted into another pedal cycle frame, chassis failures were intensified, and both Harley and Davidson at once agreed that in order to produce a practical machine, the whole had to be conceived as a motorcycle and not a converted bicycle. The new frame was a frank copy of the best in contemporary practice. It was brazed up from heavy gauge tubing, with a lengthened wheelbase to allow for a loop to house the engine case just ahead of the pedal bracket. The fuel tank was carried in the modern position on the top tube; the tool case and battery box being positioned on the frame to give the best balance. The fork, while unsprung, was made from extra heavy tubing and carried a triple crown, supported by extra heavy bearings and races in the head lug. The drive was by a flat leather belt, with a spring-loaded pulley as a tensioning device bearing against the lower run that was activated by a ratcheted hand lever. This last was a fitting common to nearly all the more successful contemporary machines, as it could be used as a primitive clutch when a momentary halt was expedient. It also helped when getting underway, which was accomplished by vigorous pedalling along with a gradual manual tightening of the belt.

The original and later enlarged shop housing the initial H-D assembly. It was situated at the rear of the Davidson home at 38th St. and Highland Avenue in Milwaukee.

While the belt drive in both flat and V type form was the drive fitting of choice in most pioneer motorcycles, exponents of chain drive were already questioning its efficiency, citing slipping problems when wet and the vulnerability of the necessarily large diameter rear wheel pulley to clogging with mud, which resulted in reduced tractive power on anything other than gentle gradients. On the other side of the coin, belt drive was cheap and economical to assemble. and provided 'soft' power through its flexibility that lessened the possibility of frame distortion from the torque of the engine. Then there was the added advantage that the manual control of slipping the belt through the use of the idler pulley could somewhat mitigate the 'all-or-nothing' speeds of these early machines that universally possessed a somewhat vague regulation of the engine revolutions. While some early contemporaries, such as Indian, Reading-Standard, and Thor fitted chain drives, early chains were prone to breakage under hard going, and the power transmission was somewhat harsh and led to much chain snatch at low speeds. It was not until friction discs and spring loaded shock absorbing devices came into being that chain drive became more satisfactory.

Harley and Davidson at long last found themselves with a machine which they considered suitable for commercial sale. The improved engine and drive train had proved sufficiently reliable after exhaustive testing, and the frame and forks appeared sturdy enough to contend with the universally bad roads then existing. Another point in question that was satisfactorily solved was the fitting of very sturdy wheels. Most pioneer designs featured heavy pedal cycle wheels which soon failed through fractured spokes and broken bearings. Harley had designed his own heavy duty type with large hubs and heavyweight annular bearings that appeared to last indefinitely if kept well greased. While the machine was not innovative in the fitting of the standard De Dion type engine or in its overall configuration, its massive components ensured that it would not disintegrate during the first few dozen miles of travel as would many of its contemporaries. It may well be noted that the rugged construction of the developed prototype presaged generally sturdy and heavyweight constructions that have ever been the hallmark of Harley-Davidson products.

In the beginning both Harley and Davidson had agreed that the new machine would be named 'Harley-Davidson', as confirmed both from their own later statements, and in the recollection of several contemporaries. The mention of Harley first was in recognition of his original concept of the overall design and of his development of the prototypes. The opinion was later reinforced by the other Davidson brothers who later joined in the formal founding of the company. In any case, the wording 'Harley-Davidson' was more agreeably euphonious than 'Davidson-Harley'.

Now that the ultimate design had been finalized, it was at once painfully apparent to Harley and Davidson that they lacked sufficient capital to undertake any semblance of commercial production. In fact, through economic necessity, they were still committed to their regular employment to pay their own living expenses, the whole project being a very limited 'backyard' type of venture.

At this juncture, the elder Davidson, William C., the Scottish immigrant carpenter, erected a 10 x 15 foot wooden shed in the backyard of the family home, which housed a lathe and a drill press, both bought second-hand, and powered by a small gasoline engine. The legend 'Harley-Davidson Motor Co.' was painted on the door as an optimistic announcement that a new name was being added to the ranks of American transportation history.

What with the completion of the prototype machine, Harley decided that he would greatly benefit from additional training in the formal study of automotive engineering. While it was obvious that he possessed the natural mechanical ability to create a practical motor vehicle, it was still more obvious, most of all to himself, that he could have arrived at his ultimate goal much more quickly had he enjoyed a more formal background in the subject. He was also rightly convinced that he could better serve the now infant company's projected future with a more solid foundation of expanded engineering knowledge. Therefore, in the fall of 1903, he enrolled in the Engineering Department of the nearby University of Wisconsin at Madison. With but meager cash reserves, he paid his expenses by waiting on tables at a fraternity house and undertaking small, part-time engineering assignments at local manufacturing concerns. In the meantime, Arthur carried on at home with the individual hand assembly of motorcycles, with the aid of a few part-time helpers who were paid a small salary on a piecework basis. When technical problems arose, Harley was able to advise his partner as his own knowledge progressed. Arthur built two motorcycles that winter to special order, the assembly being financed by charging half the purchase price as a down payment, with the balance on delivery.

With more orders being placed by interested customers, who had learned of the new make's reliability by word of mouth, Walter Davidson quit his job at the railroad shop in the spring of 1904 to devote his full time to motorcycle production. Up until this time, Arthur had been in full charge of the shop in addition to his regular employment, and both he and Harley agreed that another hand was needed if the project was to move forward. Also, with more orders coming in, it was now expedient to fill them as quickly as possible, otherwise the whole venture would readily die on the vine. The size of the shed was now doubled to 10 x 30 feet, and four part-time helpers were taken on to assist Walter in    17 machine building. Arthur, who still remained in his regular employment, now devoted all his spare time to sales promotion of the new machine. Three machines were built and sold during the summer and fall of 1904, five more being assembled during the following year.

It now became evident that the backyard shed at the Davidson home was too small to permit further expansion, so it was decided to purchase a factory site in the industrial area of Milwaukee. Still hampered by lack of working capital, yet with an inbred Scottish aversion to paying high risk interest rates to commercial banks, the partners were fortunate in being able to enlist the aid of a well-to-do relative. James McLay, a maternal uncle, who had emigrated to the States some years before the Davidson family, agreed to loan the money for the purchase of the land. At that time residing near Madison, Wisconsin, he had reputedly prospered handsomely in land speculation, and also followed the avocation of bee keeping. In due course a large lot was secured at the corner of 27th and Chestnut Streets, conveniently adjacent to a spur line of the Chicago, Milwaukee and St. Paul Railroad. The name of the latter street was ultimately changed to Juneau Avenue, giving it later world wide significance as the traditional home of Harley-Davidson. A small, two-storey wooden building was erected on the rear of the property which afforded a considerable expansion of working area. Production facilities were greatly enhanced with the acquisition of more tooling. The result was that 49 machines were built and sold to residents of the Milwaukee area during 1906.

This encouraging increase in sales prompted Arthur to at long last quit his job as a pattern maker and to devote his full time to sales promotion. During 1907 his efforts in canvassing individual potential customers as well as the inducing of several local bicycle dealers to take up franchises saw sales triple to 152 units for that year.

It might well be mentioned that while public interest in motorcycles had increased steadily since the initial appearance of the first pioneer machines at the turn of the century, their sales and marketing were as yet a somewhat uncertain proposition. By this time there were a number of fairly soundly conceived designs on the market and also a number of very inferior products. Some were placed on the market without adequate prototype testing, while others were cheap copies of already successful machines. As the extension of the bicycle, the earliest motorcycle dealers were quite naturally for the most part proprietors of established bicycle shops. While obviously thoroughly familiar with bicycle mechanics, only a few of these had little more than a rudimentary knowledge concerning the intricacies of the gasoline engine. Their ability to aid their customers in the upkeep or repair of their machines was frequently woefully inadequate.

On the other hand, the widespread public interest in the newly emerging automobile was of direct benefit to motorcycle sales, as most of the young men of the time, yearning for personal transportation, had not the means to purchase the former. The cheap mass-produced car had yet to appear on the market.

During the years of their prototype experiments, both Harley and Davidson had become well aware of the emerging problems of sales and marketing, and it was Arthur's early conclusion that the building of a strong retail dealer's organization to support any projected mass production of the product was essential.

The earliest successful motorcycle manufacturer to build a strong dealership was George M. Hendee of Indian, who had already gained much experience in the field as bicycle manufacturer. In the promotion of motorcycles, he not only relied on his own bicycle dealerships for a nucleus, but made sure that they possessed the mechanical aptitude to quickly adapt to the servicing and repair of motorcycles. Other early manufacturers who followed this same well tried formula were the Pope concern, already with a vast sales network of bicycle dealers, and the George N. Pierce Company, who shared the same background.

Arthur wisely followed these well-proven procedures in his promotional activities in the Milwaukee area. He was particularly careful to make a thorough investigation of a prospective dealer. He not only gained a first hand opinion of his personality, but could observe his work habits, his ability to handle customers, as well as the extent of his standing and reputation in his immediate community.

Now that he had thoroughly convinced himself that he had arrived at the proper formula for retail expansion, Arthur next suggested that the company be incorporated under the laws of the state of Wisconsin. Harley and his brother Walter immediately agreed to his proposal, and so on September 22, 1907, the Harley-Davidson Motor Company of Milwaukee became a corporate body. In the still infant organization, Walter was named President and General Manager, Arthur was Secretary and General Sales Manager, and the still absent Harley, pursuing his studies at the University, was named Chief Engineer and Designer, as well as filling the post of Treasurer.

In order to strengthen their manufacturing procedure, the eldest Davidson brother, William A., then thirty six years of age, was invited to join the company as Vice President and Works Manager. As expert tool maker and metal fabricator, and possessing an extensive practical knowledge of metallurgy, he had also accumulated valuable experience in shop practice as the toolroom foreman for the local

A representation of an early 1903 H-D single. Now on view in the Rodney C.Gott Museum at the AMF-H-D assembly plant at York, Pennsylvania.

repair branch of the Chicago, Milwaukee and St.Paul Railroad. Described as a large, heavily built man, slow of speech and deliberate of thought, he was known to possess the qualities needed to handle and oversee the activities of the usual rough-hewn, hard-drinking men that characteristically manned the industrial and manufacturing plants of that era. As a paradox to his later stature within the industry he remained a lifelong non-motorcyclist.

As an aside to William A.'s joining the company, the incident of his birth later became an interesting vignette of H-D history. Born in 1870, he was wont to refer proudly to close associates about his Scottish ancestry and to his birth in Aberdeen. In later years, copy writers for company literature solemnly affirmed that the Davidsons had all been born in the United States, specifically in Milwaukee. This somewhat trivial point became the focal point of testimony in a government tariff hearing some forty years later.

During the first year of corporate organization, titles meant little, with all of the partners lending a hand along with their staff in whatever undertaking demanded attention. In later years, all four were referred to in company literature as the Founders of the company, apparently as a courtesy to their joint participation in corporate organization that more or less officially marked the entrance of the company into the industry.

The machine with which the company now proposed to seriously attempt a penetration of the soon-to-be stormy American motorcycle market, was still the basic 1903 model that had been produced in very small numbers up to that time with but a few very minor improvements as indicated by trial and error in actual use. It was wisely decided to continue manufacture with a one-model program, in spite of the fact that most of the several dozen concerns now in the field offered different sizes of machine. Arthur was adamant in reminding possible critics that the present model was a sound all-around machine capable of a variety of applications and employment, and that concentration on one model rationalized manufacturing procedures and helped to keep costs and consequent retail pricing highly competitive. This proved to be sound reasoning, as what with many small and lightly financed manufacturers in the field, the building of too many diverse models often proved their undoing. Coupled with this, the science of costing, production control and marketing analysis was still highly underdeveloped.

To the bewilderment and confusion of potential buyers, the motorcycle market was overcrowded with a myriad of small manufacturers, many of whom were making extravagant claims for their products. Added to this, a brisk component part and supply trade had come into being, and it was possible at that time to purchase sufficient frames, forks, wheels, fuel tanks, and even several types of engines, often of doubtful quality, to actually assemble complete motorcycles. These were supplied by firms such as the Harry O. Geer Company of St. Louis or the Rochester Cycle Supply of New York. The availability allowed almost anyone who could purchase a few part sets to produce his own make with a few hand tools, with his own name affixed to the fuel tank. Mostly flimsy affairs, these were seemingly always able to attract a few buyers.

With an already established if limited reputation for building a sound machine, the infant company next grappled with the most pressing technical problem now facing the industry, namely that of front suspension. Almost without exception, the pioneer machines of the 'clip-on' era utilized conventional unsprung pedal cycle forks, with a single crown passing through the head lug. This, of course, made for a very harsh ride, considering the roads of the period, the comfort of the rider being inadequately taken care of by the doubtful resiliency of a standard bicycle-type saddle. These problems were later compounded by the increasing weight and the increased power of the more latterly developed machines. Perhaps the most serious complication was that the enhanced stresses and increased vibration syndromes made more imminent the danger of fracture of the fork legs from the molecular disintegration of the metal.

William Harley was evidently quite familiar with these problems, as the 1903 prototype model was fitted with very strong forks. Numerous other designers, such as Carl Oscar Hedstrom of Indian, fitted cartridge-type forks, as did some of his imitators, which offered a fair degree of spring travel. Their disadvantage, however, was the constantly varying wheelbase which made for uncertain handling on rough roads, and in cornering. Harley's answer to the problem was conceived while he was in his senior year at the University, and was ultimately based on the leading link principle. It consisted of a pair of solid unsprung legs supported by a triple crown lug at the steering head. The sprung legs were positioned just ahead and parallel to these, and were attached to the steering head above by a single crown just above the triple crown of the fixed legs. The two sets of legs were connected at the bottom by a pair of forged steel links to form the pivot joint. The sprung legs were joined over the top of the mudguard by a steel forging that formed a bridge. The spring action was controlled by four long coil springs enclosed within the tubes forming the moveable fork, the upper pair for load, the lower for rebound. The wheel axle carried just forward of the sprung blades lower attachment designated the descriptive term of the system.

The advantage of this arrangement was its rigidity, made as it was from sturdy heavy gauge components, low stress factors on the springs, adequate wheel travel on impact, and a non-varying wheelbase. While the device worked very well during the years when high speeds were not yet attained, certain deficiencies appeared during the classic era when high performance models were developed. The handling could become uncertain in the event of even slight misalignment, and a positively dangerous wheel wobble occurred in certain subsequent models. As the original design was carried forward on nearly all of the production machines for the ensuing four decades, it was this single feature that ultimately became the subject of perhaps more controversy than any other facet of H-D design.

With the formal incorporation of the company, it was now obvious that an effective advertising campaign must be instituted. The story is told that one Walter Dunlap, a member of a newly organized Milwaukee advertising firm of Klaus, Van Peterson and Dunlap, was contacted with this end in view. As neither firm was as yet in a strong financial position, the work was contracted for an a pay-as-we-go basis. The Company continued to retain this firm for the next fifty years, not only to provide media exposure, but in the preparation of catalogs and dealer aids as well.

Factory floor space was slightly enlarged in the spring of 1908 to 4,760 square feet, and production was tripled over the previous year with 456 machines assembled by 36 production employees. In order to keep abreast of the latest manufacturing methods, Walter Davidson enrolled in a local trade school to learn the latest test methods of heat treating metal, in turn imparting these to the production staff. He next journeyed to Chicago, in company with William Harley, to acquire the latest techniques of oxygen-acetylene welding, which were also incorporated into production.

Arthur had by this time traveled extensively throughout the Eastern United States demonstrating the latest H-D which now incorporated the new spring fork. Dealerships in New York, Chicago, Philadelphia, Atlanta, Newark, and other large cities had now been franchised. The West Coast was well covered by active dealerships in Los Angeles, San Francisco, and Seattle. With characteristic Scottish caution, he was careful to select only those to represent the company who, in his estimation, possessed the mechanical aptitude to set up and manage repair and service facilities, as well as the necessary business acumen to insure success in the venture. It has been reported that Arthur on numerous occasions expressed anguish that he often felt obliged to refuse certain H-D enthusiasts who clamoured for franchises but who in his judgment lacked the necessary qualifications properly to represent the company or service the product.

It was about this time that a range of bicycles was added to the line, the machines being built under contract with the H-D label and color by the famous Butler Brothers, who were wholesale suppliers located in Chicago. It was reasoned that as long as most motorcycle dealers also handled bicycles, the company could enlarge its representation and add to sales volume by supplying pedal cycles as well. As the large supplier could furnish the bicycles at a lower cost, and as the H-D Company had insufficient space to fabricate bicycles anyway, the arrangement proved both advantageous and profitable.

By this time there were about 36 significant motorcycle manufacturers in the United States. Indian, sparked by the able management of George M. Hendee, was the largest, and was complementing its expanding sales with continuous factory expansion. Excelsior, backed by the Schwinn Bicycle empire and Pope, with similar backing, ranked next, followed by Iver Johnson, Merkel, Reading Standard and Wagner, all of whom built good quality machines. The day of the flimsy 'clip on' was now happily past, and the motorcycle was at long last coming into its own as everyman's personal transportation, the cheap car as yet still in the future. Mechanical innovations such as the cam operated inlet valve and all-chain drive, together with reliable clutches, were now appearing, although most makes adhered to the V or flat belt drive. The motorcycle was still mainly a utilitarian vehicle, and H-D, whose origins lay within this concept, sought to enhance the ruggedness and reliability of their product. A commendable sidelight to this dedication was their desire to make the motorcycle more acceptable to the general non-motoring public, and to this end they endeavored to remove the main public objection to powered two wheelers: the usually offensive exhaust note. Even the earliest models were fitted with efficient silencers and in keeping with their now traditional light gray color, came to be known as 'The Silent Gray Fellow'.

In line with this early utilitarian concept of H-D machines, Arthur spent much time in canvassing various commercial and government agencies where the use of motorcycles could be applicable. In 1909 he attended the annual convention of the Rural Free Delivery Mail Carriers of America held that year in Chicago. Motorcycles had recently found favor in rural mail delivery, due to their economy and ability to negotiate the country roads of the period. Up until this time, Iver-Johnson, Jefferson, and the Wagner machines, all simple but sturdy conventional types with belt drive, had been the favored makes for this employment. Arthur took a demonstration machine to the meeting, which was favorably received, and the Advertising Department subsequently contracted for large advertising displays in the monthly *RFD News* magazine. These efforts resulted in H-D machines being purchased in large numbers by the mail carriers. Clarence Chamberlain, who was later to gain fame as a transatlantic aviator, was for a time a mail carrier in Dennison, Iowa, and rode H-D machines for several years. Other large commercial organizations, such as the Bell Telephone Company, who eventually put 700 machines into service, and numerous other public utility organizations and law enforcement groups purchased H-D machines.

While at its inception the motorcycle was essentially a utility vehicle, the growth of motorcycle sport was inevitable, due if nothing else to the inherent form of the machine. Even during the earliest pioneer days, sporting bicyclists and clubmen projected its suitability for competition events, such as

The classic photograph of Walter C. Davidson after winning the 1908 Long Island Endurance Run. The machine is almost identical to the first 1903 models except for the sprung leading link fork.

speed and reliability trials, endurance runs, as well as out-and-out racing. As early as 1903, members of the New York Motorcycle Club, first formed as an auxiliary to the New York Bicycle Club, met with members of the nearby Alpha Motorcycle Club to found the Federation of American Motorcyclists. It was projected that this organization could serve the interests of motorcyclists at the national level, as well as to organize and regulate various competition events in the future. While the foundations of a national organization were now formally inaugurated, it was not until 1908 or 1909 that the FAM had any real influence, when significant numbers of motorcyclists were active to give it impetus.

Up until this time, the H-D Company ignored all types of competition, although numbers of H-D machines were entered in various events by private enthusiasts. There are numerous accounts of H-D victories in early issues of bicycle magazines, most of which by this time contained a motorcycle section. Their successes were generally due to their inherent ruggedness and dependability even though they were certainly not the fastest when compared with contemporary makes. Many of these early speed or reliability contests were of the hare-and-hound variety. A pack of fast but not too reliable machines out-distanced the field at the start, only to be ultimately passed when stranded at the roadside by a plodding H-D.

In June 1908, the FAM announced the first large event of its kind to be held in the United States, billed simply as the 'Endurance Run'. Planned as a two-day affair, it was to start at Catskill, New York, proceed to Brooklyn, and finish with the 180 mile circuit of Long Island. It was at this juncture that President Walter Davidson decided that H-D could not afford to ignore any form of competition any longer, especially as the other factories were boasting of competition victories in the trade press. Feeling confident of being able to make at least a good showing, and with an eye to the possible advertising value, he shipped a standard model to New York as an official entrant. No less than eighty four riders representing twenty two makers of machines were flagged off at dawn on June 29th. Stiff gradients and badly rutted country roads eliminated nearly half the field by the first day. Walter was still in the running by nightfall, however, and the next morning checked out with the other survivors for the circuit of Long Island. Timing his arrival at the various check points with meticulous care, he successfully completed the run. When the final scores were tabulated, he was found to have made a perfect 1000 point record. As a complimentary gesture, the competition committee awarded him five additional points, making a perfect score plus five.

Not content with this outstanding victory, Walter remained in New York to compete in the FAM Economy Run which was staged the following week in a hilly country area adjacent to Roslyn, Long

Island. Walter again racked up a sensational victory, as with a quart of fuel in the tank, he won with a calculated 188 miles to the gallon average. Much was made of these two victories in the trade press, both for their own merits, but especially in view of the fact that it was the first time that the company had officially supported formal competition. Established dealers reported increased sales as a result, and several new franchises were awarded on the Eastern seaboard.

Meanwhile, back in Milwaukee, William Harley returned to the factory after graduating with honors from the University with his degree in Automotive Engineering. He was gratified that both sales and production had materially increased since the previous season, augmented in no small degree by the recent inauguration of the spring fork which greatly enhanced rider comfort. In the anticipation of further plant expansion, the Production Department personnel was expanded with the hiring of George Nordberg, an experienced tool and die maker, as William Davidson's production assistant. His association was almost immediately reinforced by the addition of another associate, one Frederick Barr, another competent machinist and shop expert. Both men were to figure prominently in H-D affairs for some years thereafter.

Harley's immediate plans now called for the updating of the original 1903 prototype machine which had been in continuous production for the past five seasons with but minor improvements. The new prototype was laid out with a longer and heavier frame, together with a strengthened spring fork, which increased the wheelbase from 51 inch to 57 inch. It also featured a larger single cylinder engine of 3-5/16 inch bore and a 4 inch stroke for an increased piston displacement of 35 cubic inches, still based on the original De Dion principle with an atmospheric inlet valve. The new engine was rated at 5 hp and now increased the top speed to 50 mph. Designated as the Model 5-35, it was to be introduced for the 1909 sales season.

Also subjected to prototype development was a new V twin model. The identical 5-35 cylinders were fitted, but with a slightly reduced bore to give it a rating of 7 hp. Belt drive was retained for both models, control still being effected by the standard idler pulley working against its lower run, just behind the engine pulley.

Then, as now, there was a constant search for more speed and power. What with the now substantial increase in motorcycle sales generally, the leaders in the industry rightly concluded that the vast distances and generally bad roads still in existence in most parts of the United States indicated the development of heavier and more powerful machines.

An interesting feature of the prototype twin was the fitting of a mechanical inlet valve. This fitting was a modification of the overhead De Dion type, the action being activated by a tappet running off a timing pinion in the engine case. The cylinders were set at a 45° angle, establishing the H-D commitment to this configuration in all subsequent V twins.

It was during this period that most of the American manufacturers of any consequence were offering V twin models, most of which soon centered on the single liter or 61 cubic inch displacement. Many subsequent American motorcycle historians somewhat lightly described the V twin configuration as the most handy expedient to produce a larger engine than the single cylinder type that would be most easily accommodated in the standard bicycle type frame still in use, but the arrangement had much to recommend it. With the addition of a mere 30 to 35 pounds of extra weight (the poundage of most of the single cylinder assemblies of these days), the hp output could be more than doubled. In addition, the relatively narrow angle of the cylinders allowed for a short manifold coupling for the carburetor intake, which simplified induction problems. On the other hand, the almost universal adoption of the V twin by American motorcycle engineers that set the fashion for the industry at once imposed certain technical limitations. The first was that the narrow angle of the cylinders made for an unequal firing sequence, that of 42, 45, or 50° plus or minus the 360° of crankshaft rotation that inevitably led to an inbuilt vibration syndrome that was almost impossible to counteract. In addition, the narrow cylinder angle reduced the possibility of a large cylinder bore, increased piston displacement and subsequent better power output until then being inexorably mated to lengthening the stroke. The ultimate result was that critical piston speeds of over 4,000 feet per minute were imposed on this type of engine. In practice, few V twin engines could be run at speeds much over 7,000 rpm without encountering critical inertial forces, and the American designers at once limited the ultimate power development by following this type of design. On the other side of the coin, the V twin engine showed remarkable torque development at very moderate engine speeds, characteristically in the 2,300-4,000 rpm range, which made for a slow turning, long lasting engine, that was better suited for usage over long distances and would provide a high mileage between overhauls as demanded by American operating conditions.

The prototype twin was subjected to thorough testing, and as cleared for production was finalized with an engine whose displacement was slightly enlarged to the now standard 61 cubic inch piston displacement. For the 1909 season a Schebler carburetor was used, a proprietory instrument fitted to most American motorcycles, to replace the former H-D type. The high production rate of the

Schebler carburetor allowed it to be fitted with a considerable saving in cost. Both the single and twin for 1909 were now fitted with a more gracefully contoured fuel tank formed of two halves that enclosed the top frame tubes, and all engine controls were of the Bowden wire type, enclosed within the handle-bars.

The company's official competition activities for that year included the entry of Walter David-son and three other riders, Lacey Crolius, Frank Ollerman, and Robert E.Underhill in the FAM-sponsored endurance run from Cleveland, Ohio, to Indianapolis, Indiana. All four experienced no mechanical troubles and ended the run with perfect scores, winning the Team Prize for the company.

By the summer of 1910, motorcycle sport had become a fixture in the motoring scene. Out-and-out racing events had been held in many of the short 1/8th and 1/6th mile indoor board tracks or velo-dromes that had been previously built for bicycle racing. As the power and speed of the racing motor-cycles increased, these proved unsuitable, if not downright dangerous. To improve matters, Jack Prince, the New Jersey engineer who had superintended the construction of many of the early velo-dromes, built now 1/4 or 1/3 mile 'motordromes' in most of the country's larger cities during the next decade. Racing circuits were established in various geographical sections of the country and a point system enabled regional championships to be established. As the motion picture was still a limited form of entertainment, radio was as yet undeveloped, and professional athletics were as yet not well organ-ized, motor sport contests were now at the height of their popularity, especially as both the automobile and the motorcycle were still somewhat of a novelty for most people.

Dirt track racing at many of the county fair horse tracks also became soaringly popular, as fair-attending patrons offered a captive audience to the race promoters. This condition also explains why road racing never became popular in the United States, as there was no practical means of crowd control to create a paying audience along a spreadout road course.

Motorcycle racing continued to gain in popularity, and the leading factories supporting it with both specialsed machines and paid professional riders included Excelsior, Indian, Pope, Merkel, Reading Standard, and Thor. Other than supporting endurance runs and reliability trials, H-D con-tinued to withhold support from this type of competition.

A 1910 H-D 9-35 Model single at the 1974 Classic and Antique Motorcycle club rally at Visalia, California. *(George Hays)*.

A 1910 9-35 Model in original condition from the Bud Ekins collection. The belt pulleys and belt are missing. *(Alisha Tamburri).*

To cater to the burgeoning interest in motorcycling, numerous trade publications came into being. During the pioneer era, most bicycle magazines featured sections devoted to motorcycling. Among these were *Bicycling World* which later sponsored *Motorcycling Review.* Then there was *The Motorcycle Illustrated* and *Motorcycling,* published in Chicago. *The Western Bicyclist and Motorcyclist,* published in Los Angeles, later became *The Motorcyclist,* and ultimately became the last surviving trade publication during the lean years of US motorcycling in the 1930s. During their heyday, all of the trade journals were well supported by the various motorcycle and accessory manufacturers through their voluminous advertising.

H-D continued their two model single and twin line through 1910 and 1911, but for the 1912 season an innovation offered for both models was the fitting of an optional all-chain drive, although the belt was still available for a couple of more years. Also, the single was now fitted with a mechanical inlet valve, already standard on the original twin, which offered the advantage of higher engine speeds and enhanced power development. This change in design, while still based on the pioneer De Dion-Bouton configuration, was now to be seen in several leading American makes, and with the overhead rocker mechanism, became popularly known as the 'pocket valve' type. The side-by-side valve arrangement, offered by Indian after 1915 along with other makes, became known as the 'flat head' — terminology which persisted in domestic parlance for many years thereafter.

In reference to the chain drive, William Harley, who had come to recognize its mechanical superiority, refused to incorporate it into his designs until he had perfected what he considered to be a reliable clutch. While some competitive designs had sought to eliminate the all-or-nothing aspect of the best drive by fitting various examples of the proprietory Eclipse clutch which was designed to be fitted to the engine pulley, it was of somewhat light construction and its longevity questionable. Harley's answer to the problem was the fitting of a sturdy multiplate clutch with some 76 square inches of plate surface, inside the rear wheel hub, which was activated by a rod and bell crank arrangement whose control lever was mounted on the right tank side.

To start the engine, the machine was placed on the rear stand and the engine cranked by turning the rear wheel with the pedalling gear. After warming up, the clutch was disengaged, and the machine was rolled off the stand. The rider then got under way by manipulating the throttle and clutch lever. The new clutch proved rugged enough to stand up to the demands of heavy start-and-stop traffic, and was a decisive factor in making the new model a popular seller, especially for commercial work. The new model was designated the 9-35 — the 9 referring to the chronological year of development, and 35 to the cubic inches of engine displacement.

Another 1912 innovation for the enhancement of rider comfort was the introduction of the patent 'Ful-Floteing' seat post. While the negotiation of rough roads, (usually the rule of that day rather than the exception,) had been lately aided by the now universal fitting of some type of spring fork, the usual bicycle type saddle offered but little resiliency to the rider's posterior. The new H-D system included the spring loading of the seat post with a 14 inch coil spring inside the seat tube, the usual saddle springs being retained for initial deflection and rebound.

In the meantime, Arthur Davidson had been devoting most of his time to the further building of a strong dealer organization. An additional intensive visit to the Far West during 1912 and 1913 resulted in enhanced representation in California, Oregon, and Washington, as well as in Arizona and New Mexico, where the possibilities of nearly all-season riding enhanced motorcycling popularity. The im-

An official Company photograph of the Founders, taken about 1910. From left: William A.Davidson, Walter C.Davidson, Arthur Davidson, and William S.Harley. *(The H-D Motor Company)*.

proved twin was especially popular in the West, due to the vast distances in that area. In order to improve communication between the factory and the dealers, a house organ called *The Dealer* was circulated in leaflet form. Hints on selling techniques were discussed together with lavish praise of the various features of H-D machines in comparison with other makes. Couched in rather quaint and florid Victorian prose, the effort was an initial attempt to standardize factory sales policies. Very few copies of this publication survive today, as a large supply of back issues surviving in storage at the factory were destroyed in 1926.

By 1913, motorcycling in the United States was approaching the zenith of its popularity. About 35 makes were represented, offering both touring and utility type machines, including a couple of well-designed fours, the Henderson and the Pierce, together with the previously developed V-twins and singles, and a few ultralightweights of the two and four-stroke type. Indian was still the acknowledged sales leader of the industry, producing over 31,000 of the 71,000-odd machines made that year. H-D was already mounting a strong challenge, however. In 1911, H-D had enlarged its factory space to 80,000 square feet, and with 480 production employees had assembled over 6,000 machines. With its now strengthened financial position through increasing sales, the management, overcoming their original aversion toward paying bankers' interest rates, obtained a substantial loan from Milwaukee's Marshall and Illsley Bank to effect this expansion. During 1912, the Company again increased its floor area to 187,000 square feet and with over 1,000 production employees on the payroll produced over 11,000 units.

Aside from the soaring popularity of motorcycle sport at the motordromes, board tracks, and county fair tracks, the motorcycle was now well entrenched in the transportation scene for both utility and commercial purposes. Although automobile production was steadily increasing, most makes were still too expensive for the man of average means. While Henry Ford had launched his immortal Model T in 1909, its production had not yet attained its later volume, and the selling price of $850 was still nearly three times that of the average good solo motorcycle. In addition, the sidecar was now coming into popularity, and for an additional $75.00 or so it could offer limited transport for the family man. Furthermore, the early automobile still offered a formidable mechanical challenge, both in operation and maintenance. A motorcycle, much less complicated and with exposed moving parts, remained as a less complex form of motoring.

While the H-D factory still declined to provide private owners with official sponsorship in competition, personal machines were now being entered by private owners in numerous endurance and road racing contests, often with very creditable results.

The San Jose California Road Race held on December 8th 1912, saw Ray Watkins and Ben Torres on standard twins fitted with Flexi sidecars, a proprietary make having a hinged chassis that allowed the wheel to bank with the machine on corners. Both contestants averaged better than 49 mph over a rain-drenched and very muddy course.

In the 3rd annual running of the Bakersfield California Road Race, Frank Lightner took another standard twin over a very rough course for first place, arriving at the finish nearly an hour ahead of the next competitor.

A prominent Eastern fixture in those days was the 225 mile Harrisburg to Philadelphia and return contest. Entrants included factory teams sponsored by Indian, Merkel, Pope and Thor. The private H-D entrants, again without any official support, totaled eight riders. All finished the course with a 1-2-3 win, all the others placing.

In the Fall of 1913, the first of a series of desert road races through the Southwest was scheduled under official FAM sponsorship. Announced as an endurance event, the course was laid out over what has been aptly described as the worst roads on the North American continent. The route selected was between San Diego, California and Phoenix, Arizona, approximately 445 miles. It followed the isolated desert tracks first travelled by the covered wagons of the pioneer immigrants 65 years before, the only really passable one being the last leg from Caliente to Phoenix, a distance of 94 miles. In addition to the almost impassable condition of the road, if it could be called such, the contestants risked hunger, thirst, heat prostration and possible death from exposure in case of a breakdown. There was also a real danger of annihilation at the hands of roving bands of renegade Apache Indians who still roamed the region, as well as from Mexican guerillas who often raided the isolated ranches north of the border to steal cattle. The coming contest was given much publicity in the trade press, and was the object of much comment in the general media. After all, the earlier frontier days were still a timely topic of general interest, as many people yet living had participated in the great westward migration as children or young adults.

The first race was planned as a three day event, starting on October 31st with overnight stops at Yuma, 116 miles from San Diego, Caliente, 110 miles to the east, the last leg being the 94 miles to Phoenix. Eighteen riders representing Excelsior, Harley-Davidson, Indian, and Thor were flagged off at 2 minute intervals from the public square in San Diego. The H-D riders, Arthur Holmes and Frank Meock, were the only private entrants.

The first fifty miles offered little difficulty, as the track here was in fair condition. Ahead lay the dreaded Mammoth Wash, the sandy desert area that was the graveyard of many immigrant wagons whose remains still could be seen. Cannonball Baker on his two-speed Indian was eliminated here by engine failure. His teammate, Paul Derkum, forged on, aided by the fact that he had cemented small section car tires on his wheel rims, and made the first leg to Yuma in 7 hours 11 minutes. He also was first into Phoenix, followed by Indian riders Ray Smith and Harry Weitzell. John Long, Excelsior, and Roy Artley, Thor, placed 4th, followed by Lorenzo Boido, Indian. Art Holmes and Frank Meock trailed in together in last place.

Much was made of the results in the trade press. It was pointed out that almost all of the machines finished, in spite of the severity of both the course and the heat. Indeed, the modern machines of today would be hard pressed to duplicate their performance under such arduous conditions. While Holmes and Meock placed last, they were severely handicapped by the fact that their standard machines were single geared. Both were quick to inform the factory of this fact, together with the

*June 1912*          *Cosmopolitan Magazine*

# This Harley-Davidson Does the Work of Three Horses

THE Home Telephone Company, of Portland, Indiana, say in part:—"*Used our Harley-Davidson Motorcycle in trouble Department for two months, doing the work of three horses. It has traveled 2,400 miles, has given entire satisfaction, and the expense of gasoline and oil is so small as to hardly be worth consideration.*"
*HOME TELEPHONE CO.*

We have a large number of similar expressions from Butchers, Grocers, Jewelers, Department Stores, Gas and Electric Companies, etc. These firms have found the Harley-Davidson the most rapid and economical means of delivery and transportation. What the Harley-Davidson is doing for them, it will do for you. THE

## Harley-Davidson

### Is the Most Desirable Motorcycle for General Use

**It is the Most Comfortable.** It is the only motorcycle built with a Ful-Floteing Seat. This seat floats or suspends the weight of the rider between 24 inches of concealed springs. These springs assimilate all the vibrations, jolts and jars.

**It is the Most Economical.** The Harley-Davidson holds the World's official economy record, established at the National F. A. M. Meet, July 3, 1908.

**It is the Most Reliable.** The Harley-Davidson is the only machine ever awarded a diamond medal and a perfect score of one thousand points with a plus five points additional for its super-excellent performance by the Federation of American Motorcyclists.

**It is the Most Durable.** Harley-Davidson Motorcycles sold ten years ago are still running and giving satisfaction.

**Easiest Starting.** It is the only machine fitted with Free-Wheel Control. This control permits starting and stopping by the mere shifting of a lever. In writing for catalog state whether for commercial or private use, and we will send additional data.

## HARLEY-DAVIDSON MOTOR COMPANY
### 249 B. STREET :: MILWAUKEE :: WISCONSIN

An example of the large scale advertising campaign launched by the H-D Company during 1911 and 1912.

opinion that their engines were somewhat short on power when compared to the others, although they ran faultlesly over the entire distance. Holmes, in later commenting on the lack of factory support, bitterly castigated Walter Davidson as 'too tight fisted to even offer to pay for their fuel, oil and tires . . . .'

H-D quite naturally received much publicity in regard to this and other contemporary contests, especially where private entrants often made a very good showing, even if first place wins were not forthcoming in all cases. As a paradox, the factory still piously proclaimed in their advertising that they did not support racing or competition in any form. In the September, 1913 issue of *Pacific Motor-cyclist,* it was stated in a full page advertisement — 'Don't blame us when Harley-Davidson wins a race meet, because we do not believe in racing. We do not employ any racing men. We build no special racing machines, but the results speak for themselves.'

This somewhat high-handed attitude quite naturally antagonized substantial numbers of H-D enthusiasts who were competition minded. They had lately been entering various contests at their own expense, without the usual complimentary spare parts, fuel, oil, and tires that were generously supplied to the entrants of other competing makes, who also often enjoyed the help of factory mechanics in preparing their machines. During the winter of 1913, a few franchised H-D dealers began offering certain subsidies out of their own pocket to mollify those riders who were helping to glorify the marque.

At the same moment, and as later events proved, it was during the Company's public protestations against participating in competition that the top management was actually debating the advisability of offering official support to racing. It was now all too apparent that a large segment of the motorcycling public was competition-minded, as witness the large crowds generally seen at most race meets, and whether or not the bread-and-butter roadsters resembled the racing machines, the name of a winner on the tank sides was a powerful sales stimulator.

According to the composite recollections of several veteran Company employees, Harley and the Davidsons actually decided to take affirmative action during the late spring of 1913. The erstwhile plodding H-D was at long last to be committed to the perilous arena of motorcycle sport. To implement this decision, William Harley as Chief Engineer, offered one William (Bill) Ottaway the position of Assistant Engineer in his department. Ottaway was then employed by The Aurora Automatic Machine Company of Aurora, Illinois, as Chief Engineer in charge of design and development in their Thor Motorcycle Division. A pioneer automobile and motorcycle owner, as a natural mechanic and practical engineer he quickly became a self-taught innovator in engine design and tuning. Joining the Aurora organization in 1909 following their emergence from the clip-on period, he was responsible for the development of the famous 'White Thors', which were not only respectable road machines but in racing form quickly made a name for themselves in the early motordrome and horse tracks. One of Ottaway's assistants in the engineering department was one Albert G.Crocker, a former student of automotive engineering at the University of Illinois, subsequently to be employed in a similar capacity with Indian, and a later figure in the motorcycle industry whom we shall meet again.

There has been much speculation among serious motorcycle historians concerning the relative positions of both Harley and Ottaway during this period of H-D history. As the original developer and later official corporate head of the Company's Engineering Department, Harley was quite naturally responsible for the development of the H-D motorcycle up to this point in time. On this basis, it would appear that he might well have had the technical ability to proceed with the subsequent evolvement of more powerful and sophisticated engines with which to meet the challenge of the now spirited competition activities within the industry. On the other hand, he has been described by contemporaries as a plodding and methodical technician, proceeding cautiously, and indeed, up to this point, still preoccupied with refining the original concepts of De Dion Bouton. Although capable of turning out refined creations built on the work of others, it is evident that he lacked that certain flair of originality that has historically accompanied the efforts of less orthodox but more flamboyant engineers. To his lasting credit, Harley was at least able personally to face his own limitations in the matter, and seek association with another designer who had, in four short seasons, made an enviable position for himself as the designer of potent racing machinery.

The story goes that Ottaway accepted the offer immediately, agreeing to limit his efforts to the improvement of the basic and well tried H-D engines, without the option of putting the factory to the expense of tooling up for entirely new designs.

While Ottaway undertook immediate experiments in the engine department with speed tuning, Harley set about the task of developing an improved transmission system. The single gear concept for a high powered heavyweight V twin that had become the accepted American motorcycle design was now obsolete, as no engine could be expected to make efficient use of its potential power development without change speed gears. Then there was the added onus that with the now growing popularity of the sidecar, the single gear could not be successfully applied where an extra load was imposed, without

A 1912 belt drive 35 cu.in. single in original condition. The Company now was manufacturing two models, with the twin in limited production. *(George Hays).*

lowering the sprocket ratios to the point where the overall performance would be nothing short of pathetic. Harley's answer to the problem was a heavyweight, cluster-type, two-speed gear located in the rear wheel hub, which was combined with his already successful clutch, whose efficiency had done much to enhance the make's reputation during the past two seasons. The gear was offered for both the twin and single cylinder models, and with characteristic H-D caution, single gearing on both was still available at the buyer's option.

In the meantime, sales were increasing, due to a growing public demand and an ever expanding dealership resulting from the tireless efforts of Arthur Davidson. Outlets were now to be found in most of the country's larger cities, and the New England area. Now the rest of the North Eastern states, once an Indian stronghold, were well represented.

Plant area was again expanded, with a rearrangement of production facilities under the capable hand of William Davidson, assisted by George Nordberg and Fred Barr, with an eye to an anticipated 30% increase in production.

An innovation for 1915 was the introduction of the step starter, which replaced the bicycle type pedalling gear. This consisted of a pair of pedals with their shaft inserted through the countershaft hub. With the clutch disengaged, the rider could start or restart the engine at rest without the need of dismounting and placing the machine on the rear stand. Another progressive feature was the fitting of a hand lever that was connected to the rocker-type foot pedal controlling the clutch.

The sidecar really came into its own during 1914, both to enhance the motorcycle's usefulness to the family man, as well as in numerous commercial uses with various types of box or platform bodies. As H-D did not then have the production space to inaugurate sidecar production, they negotiated an agreement with the Rogers Company, a Chicago-based manufacturing firm organized in 1910, to supply sidecars to the trade. H-D accepted their standard single seat body, but specified a specially-designed heavyweight chassis that was more rugged than Rogers' original type and carried the standard H-D front wheel with its extra heavy annular-type bearings. An initial order of 2,500 units for 1914 was increased to 5,000 in 1915, when Rogers augmented their somewhat limited production facilities to supply this order.

The cyclecar appeared on the American scene in credible numbers during 1914, inspired by the popularity of the motorcycle, and attempted to appeal to the buyer by offering a lightweight four wheeled vehicle possessing initial stability. All of the larger motorcycle manufacturers were approached at varying times by the embryo builders of such machines to supply them with engine and transmission units. Most of these were by this time running at full capacity to service their own market, and most of them, including H-D, declined.

In the Fall of 1913, H-D's management decided that their production was such that they could now attempt to enter the export market. American machines of their characteristic rugged design had already been well accepted overseas, starting with Indian, who had established a foothold in the United Kingdom in 1908, and was now well entrenched in the European and Australasian markets, along with lesser numbers of Excelsiors, Hendersons, and Popes. H-D's first efforts in this direction were made in England, where one Duncan Watson, a Scot whose family was already engaged in the import-export trade, agreed to set up a distributorship in London.

To facilitate the hoped-for expansion of these markets, an Export Department was set up, and was headed initially by one Eric von Gumpert, who is said to have had some experience in the field through former employment in an import-export firm in New York City. The story is told that the Davidsons, who were reportedly staunchly anti-semitic, questioned von Gumpert's ethnic background. When it was discovered, upon investigation, that he was a member of a solid German immigrant family with proper Milwaukee antecedents, his appointment was confirmed.

With the consummation of the export agreement with Watson, who immediately set up facilities in London as an initial retail outlet and service agency, the first shipment of machines was received in April. It is reported that sales were brisk from the start, as heavyweight American V-twins had already made a place for themselves in the United Kingdom. They proved popular with both fast solo riders as well as sidecar enthusiasts through their previous exposure to Indian machines imported by Billy Wells since 1908, as well as lesser numbers of Excelsiors. Watson also took steps to set up dealerships in Paris, Amsterdam, Brussels, and Copenhagen, but the outbreak of the World War and the almost immediate dislocation of shipping activities halted these efforts for the time being. In all, about 350 machines were received before the declaration of war in August 1914. While the improved 5-35 single cylinder model was made available, very few of these were sold, as most buyers of American machines were quite obviously V-twin enthusiasts.

In the meantime, Bill Ottaway was well on his way to improving the efficiency of William Harley's already well proved 61 cubic inch twin. With modifications in the porting of the exhaust and intake manifolds, altered combustion chamber contours, and improved valve action, a considerable increase in the power of the standard roadster models was achieved. Ottaway also spent considerable time in studying the possibilities of lessening the inherent vibration characteristics of the engines through both static and dynamic balancing of the crankshaft and flywheel assemblies. While it was, of course, impossible to overcome this built-in design weakness entirely, the engines ran more smoothly as the result of his efforts.

In addition, Ottaway designed a special racing model for limited production. Catalogued as the Model II-K, the many H-D enthusiasts who had longed for an out-and-out competition machine now at long last saw their dream come true. Fitted with the one-liter 61 cubic inch 'pocket valve' engine that was basically the standard H-D roadster engine, it featured special cams and special intake and exhaust porting. Mounted in a short coupled racing frame with 51 inch wheelbase, it followed the fashion of the day by having countershaft gearing, as no gearboxes were ever fitted to the early track racers. It weighed slightly under 300 pounds with a gallon of oil and 3 gallons of fuel aboard.

Ottaway subjected several prototypes to rigorous testing on out-of-the-way fairground horse tracks, paying particular attention to steering and handling characteristics. Old time employees in the Engineering Department have recalled that one of the first problems was the handling of the machine with the use of the now standard H-D pattern leading link fork. While no serious problems had been noted in previous roadster machines, whose top speeds barely exceeded 60 mph, the 90 mph plus speeds of the II-K were something else again. The first prototype machine was seen to take the rider into a tank-slapping wobble before it reached 80 mph. Ottaway at once suggested that a new fork be designed, and was heard to voice the opinion that a trailing link type be substituted. The Company's top management vetoed this suggestion at once, stating that any racing machine should at least incorporate all of H-D's traditional design features, and Ottaway had to content himself with further modifications to the rake, trail, bottom link configuration, and spring tension rates which, after considerable trial and error experimentation, at least partially corrected the trouble.

The Model II-K was now set to open a new and thrilling chapter in H-D history.

# Chapter 2

# Success and Disappointment

HARLEY-DAVIDSON'S FIRST BID FOR COMPETITION SUPREMACY CAME ON JULY 14th 1914, at the soon-to-be famous two mile country fair horse track at Dodge City, Kansas, a well-known frontier town of the old West, which was subsequently to become the Indianapolis of American motorcycle racing.

The course had been selected for a projected 300 mile classic the year before, when FAM President, Dr.W.S.Patterson and a group of fellow motorcyclists visited the area while en route to their annual convention in Denver, Colorado. Being impressed with both the suitability of the track and the high state of competition enthusiasm evidenced by two wheel devotees in Dodge City, the competition committee began making plans for the event to be held there the following year.

The first 300 Miler saw six makes represented: Excelsior, H-D, Indian, Merkel, Pope, and Thor. The H-D team consisted of Walter Cunningham, Paul Garst, Paul Gott, 'Red' Parkhurst, and Alvin Stratton, all mounted on the new II-K models, carefully selected from the twelve initial machines produced, and personally tuned by Bill Ottaway. Excelsior fielded its now famous 'Big Valve' racers, a pocket valve type with $2\frac{1}{2}$ inch valves developed the previous season. Indian relied on their very fast 8 valvers perfected in 1911 by Carl Oscar Hedrom, although they brought along three standard pocket valve machines as a reserve.

The race was flagged off promptly at noon under a strong summer sun, the 36 contestants being lined up in six rows of 6 machines for a rolling start, behind the pace car carrying Dr.Patterson, who held the checkered flag. Lee Taylor on a Flying Merkel blasted into an early lead which he held for the first sixty miles for a time of 51 minutes 39 seconds. Behind him by twelve seconds was H-D's Walter Cunningham, who clocked a blistering hour and 28 minutes for the first hundred miles, to pass Lee Taylor on the north turn. A stretched rear chain and a fouled spark plug put him out of action at the 181st mile, ending H-D's chances of victory as he was the only member of the team with sufficient lead to put him in position for a possible victory. Glen 'Slivers' Boyd, on a very fast 8 valve Indian, roared ahead to win at 68 mph, closely followed by Bill Briar on a White Thor, who was second, and Carl Goudy, Excelsior, finished third. While the balance of the H-D team trailed the back, they all finished the course, and Cunningham's early scintillating performance created much excitement in the crowded stands. An added interest was the first public appearance of the usually staid H-D machines in racing trim, and with special machines at that!

On November 26th the second annual running of the 300 Mile Savannah Road Race was scheduled, comprising 27 laps over an $11\frac{1}{2}$ mile circuit of varied curves and straights. H-D again entered six machines, ridden by Irving Jahnke, Maldwyn Jones, Alvin Stratton, Martin Schroeder, Ray Weishaar, and A.W. Yerks.

Schroeder took an early lead in the second lap, followed by Bob Perry, Excelsior, Earle 'Red' Armstrong on an Indian, who in turn was followed by Ray Weishaar and Erwin G. 'Cannonball' Baker on a stock Indian.

Lee Taylor, now with the Wigwam on an 8 valve Indian, took the lead at the 14th lap, and ran away from the field to win at 61 mph, garnering the $800.00 winner's purse. Joe Wolter, Excelsior, was a far second, with Irving Jahnke, H-D a close third, with his three teammates close behind. While victory again eluded H-D, they made a very strong showing that was not lost on the fans, and the sports writers noted it as a promise of better things to come from Milwaukee.

It was also noted that Bill Ottaway's careful team organization and attention to reduced pit stop time had much to do with H-D's excellent showing, a factor not heretofore too prominent in American track racing.

In the Fall of 1914, the Company announced an improved version of their past season's two speeder, now catalogued as the 'J' model, for the 1915 sales season. This new machine was to be the forerunner of their Big Twin 'Top-of-the-Line' model that would continue in production with but detail changes for the next fifteen years. While identical in most respects to the two-speeder, it now featured a rugged three-speed all-enclosed sliding gear-type transmission, with a sturdy multiple plate clutch mounted on the countershaft. While the former two-speed hub gear had proved acceptably reliable, its lack of a third ratio had somewhat limited full utilization of the engine's power band, particularly in sidecar work. Then, too, while the in-hub unit was not particularly heavy, its weight, combined with that of the standard heavyweight hub bearing assembly, produced a certain amount of rear wheel hammering, especially in the rough roads of the period. With the necessarily heavy transmission now mounted in a more conventional position just behind the engine, the overall weight of the machine was in better balance.

A 1914 61 cu.in. twin two-speeder from the Bud Ekins collection, picture taken at Visalia in 1974. Note the rod control mechanism extending to the gears in the rear hub. *(George Hays).*

Noting the problems that had been encountered in some contemporary makes with clutches of insufficient strength and consequent reliability, William Harley carefully considered this aspect of his new transmission system and experimented with several possible variations. He ultimately settled on a rather massive heavyweight multiplate design that closely followed that of the proprietary Bendix type that had been manufactured for some years as an accessory and could be adapted to the engine shafts of earlier belt drivers. When Ottaway, who had been closely following the proceedings, noted that Harley had incorporated Bendix's screw-type release mechanism, he suggested that this feature might entail patent infringement, as Victor Bendix of the Bendix Manufacturing Company had purchased the manufacturing rights the year before with the intention of incorporating the clutch into his own range of products. For reasons known only to himself, Harley was adamant concerning the finalization of his design as planned, but Ottaway's opinion was later vindicated.

The new model was well received, and with sales of over 8,000 machines in 1914, President Walter Davidson was confident that this could be topped in 1915.

The popular step starter was retained in the new model, as it worked well in conjunction with the new transmission. While the company had ordered 5,000 sidecars from the Rogers Company for the new season, they received only 3,000 units, due to production problems. H-D still lacked the floor space to add their own sidecar manufacture, concentrating their efforts on enhancing motorcycle production.

While a slightly updated 5-35 single was still offered, with both single gearing either by chain or belt, or the 1913 two-speed hub as an option for utility and commercial work, most of the production centered on the Big Twins, as American buyers now favored heavyweight models.

The 1915 three-speed model exemplified the more or less standardized heavyweight American motorcycle now produced by Excelsior, Emblem, Indian, Dayton, Michealson, Reading Standard, and others less prominent. H-D was in a very excellent competitive position at this point of domestic motorcycle history. Fabricated from the best of available materials, its products now earned a well deserved reputation for general excellence. With the improvements in engine design by William Ottaway, together with the lessons learned in speed tuning incidental to racing, the standard twin now developed 37% more power than previously, with enlarged breathing porting, improved valve action, and an enhanced lubrication system.

In spite of the generally high enthusiasm for motorcycling, production for 1914 dropped from a high of 71,000 units for the previous year to just under 60,000 machines. The onset of the war in Europe had shut off the supply of many components previously imported from overseas, such as bearing sets, magnetos, and certain cycle parts. The inevitable inflationary effect of war had substantially raised the cost of iron, steel, tires and other rubber parts, as well as electrical equipment. These factors, of course, forced an immediate rise in retail prices, which inevitably resulted in some buyer resistance, as wages and salaries had yet to keep pace with the inflationary spiral.

Another disquieting event in American industrial history was the recent raise in wages granted by Henry Ford to his many thousands of production employees, who were now paid $5.00 for a ten hour working day, double that formerly paid, as $2.50 per day had for years been the standard for industrial production workers. Ford's enormously growing production and his consequent profits not only enabled him to afford this increase, but he cannily envisioned that the repercussions from this move throughout industry would enable more working people to purchase Ford cars. His action, of course, brought forth a storm of protest from most of the country's industrial leaders, who condemned it as inflationary, socialistic, and a potent danger to the economic stability of the country. Nevertheless, most of them subsequently followed suit, and wages generally kept pace with inflation. This condition had a significant effect on the domestic motorcycle industry. Many of the smaller manufacturers who, through limited production, enjoyed only a regional market adjacent to their factories, were already feeling the effects of inflation on their production costs. The total effect was that many of these makes of acceptable quality and loyal popularity simply ceased their operations, or converted to other products more closely associated with the changing times.

William Ottaway's improvements to the new H-D machines created no small interest on the part of their chief competitors, Excelsior and Indian. The former introduced a new variation of their famous 'Big Valve' models, and Indian's Charles B.Franklin hurriedly designed a more potent side valve model to replace the original pocket valve design of their founder, Carl Oscar Hedstrom. The once plodding H-D utility type image was now changed to that of a high performance machine!

The Fall of 1914 saw the first formal organization of the American Motorcycle industry with the founding of the American Motorcycle Manufacturers Association having headquarters in Manhattan. Its Board of Directors included W.G.Schrack of Angola, New York, Arthur Davidson of Milwaukee, Thomas W.Henderson of Detroit, K.H.Jacobs of Middleton, Ohio, and L.D.Hadden, of Hartford, Connecticut. This body was later to become the American Motorcycle and Allied Trades Association.

On the competition scene, H-D inaugurated their opening challenge to their chief rivals,   35

An intrepid traveler pauses to check his route map. The machine is a 1914 two-speeder. Note the large Solar acetylene headlamp. *(The H-D Motor Company)*.

Excelsior and Indian, by entering the FAM sponsored road races scheduled at Venice, California, in the spring of 1915. As a small seaside resort town southwest of the city of Los Angeles, co-operative city officials agreed to close some of the public streets for the running of the event. Strong factory support included teams sponsored by Dayton, Excelsior, H-D, Indian, Pope and Thor. The H-D team was captained by an emerging midwest racing star, Otto Walker, and featured improved engines developed by Bill Ottaway the previous winter. Walker covered the 300 mile course through the city streets at an average speed of 68.31 mph, to win the $800.00 first place purse. His teammate, Red Parkhurst, was a close second. Carl Goudy and Bob Perry on Excelsiors were third and fourth. A new rider whom we shall meet again, the youthful Fred Ludlow, was fifth on an Indian, followed by Morty Graves, also Indian mounted, for sixth place.

On July 4th, the Dodge City 300 Miler saw twenty nine riders on seven makes of factory sponsored machines, representing Cyclone, Emblem, Excelsior, H-D, Indian, Pope, and Thor, lined up for the start. Don Johns, on a Cyclone of very advanced design, set a terrific pace at the start and nearly lapped the field during the first three laps. While still far ahead at the 101st mile, he went out with a broken chain, leaving Carl Goudy and Morty Graves on Excelsiors in second and third places. Ill luck felled both the Excelsior and Indian teams during the 90th lap, leaving Walker and his five teammates to finish the race, the Walker taking the checkered flag at 79.84 mph, nearly nine miles faster than the previous year.

In August, teams from Excelsior, H-D, and Indian met at Tacoma, Washington, for the inaugural race at the newly completed board track just constructed by Jack Prince. Earle Armstrong won the main event at 79.84 mph, closely followed by Otto Walker on his H-D, who crossed the finish line just a wheel length behind, and barely ahead of, Don Johns on another Indian. The thrilling duel of these three riders during the final laps had a capacity crowd on its feet at the finish.

The following September the H-D team, again headed by Otto Walker, joined Excelsior and Indian at yet another of Jack Prince's new board ovals at Maywood, a suburb of Chicago. Walker won a signal victory, this time riding the new famous II-K model, which was now fitted with a new prototype engine designed by Bill Ottaway featuring 8 valves. In spite of some handling problems, Walker's win at 89.11 mph was an all-time record on the boards up to that time.

The favourable publicity resulting from these outstanding racing successes was such that nearly all of H-D's dealers reported increased sales, and a production target of 15,000 units was set for the 1916 sales season. The standard single and twin models were now offered with full electrical equipment specially engineered by the Remy concern. In addition, the step start was eliminated in favor of a more modern kickstart mechanism enclosed within the gearbox. The emphasis was now on the V twin, with very few singles being produced, most of these being sold for commercial use, such as for mail carriers or public utility service.

The most important item of H-D's ever-expanding competition program was the development of the soon-to-be-famous Model 17 racing 8 valver. While Ottaway had been able to greatly increase the power of the basic pocket valve models, it was obvious that the ohv four-valve per cylinder could greatly enhance the breathing capabilities and provide more efficient combustion chamber configuration if both intake and exhaust valves could be positioned within the cylinder head, as already proved by Indian's Carl Oscar Hedstrom.

Under Ottaway's direction, several prototype engines were built and tested, but preignition problems and spark plug failures were encountered, even though the interior shapes of the cylinder heads closely followed profiles recently developed by Ricardo in his epoch making experiments in cylinder head design. After continuing difficulties, Ottaway finally suggested to Walter Davidson that the Company engage Harry Ricardo himself to facilitate the development of the new engine. The story goes that Davidson demurred, citing the high cost of Ricardo's round trip steamship fare from England, together with the fee for his services. He ultimately relented, however, when Ottaway pointed out that the $25,000 already expended on the preliminary development would be lost entirely unless winning engines could be forthcoming. After several weeks of experimentation Ricardo at last came up with acceptable results, the new engines turning out a credible 55 hp from the standard 61 cubic inch configuration. And this in 1915!

The limited production racers were offered in both single cylinder 30-50 cubic inch and twin 61 cubic inch models, the former being produced by merely deleting the front cylinder and altering the timing sequence. The machines were at first intended only for the factory team, but it was later decided to sell a few to specially favored private competitors who had already proved their ability. The number of these singles built is not known, but veteran factory employees have stated that about 30 of the latter were ultimately produced. Some have ventured the opinion that only a few were made as Ricardo, by prior agreement, was to receive a small royalty on each machine completed.

As Competition Manager, Ottaway now organized the factory racing for the coming Dodge City 300 Mile Classic. Captained again by Otto Walker, the lineup consisted of Harry Brant, Floyd Clymer, Sam Corrento, Harry Crandall, Paul Gott, Irving Jahnke, and Ray Weishaar. In preparation for the coming season, Ottaway, now assisted by E.E.Welborn, drilled his riders in team tactics, practiced pit stops wtih the factory mechanics who were to accompany them, and perfected the flag signaling system, all of which had already paid such rewarding dividends during the past season. Team members were groomed to a razor edge of tactical readiness by physical conditioning, and good food and regular hours were also demanded from each member.

In commenting on these events in an interview with the author in 1965, the late Floyd Clymer, who had won a place on the team through some local wins in his native Colorado a couple of seasons before, stated that Ottaway was a stern taskmaster, and demanded total co-operation from all team members during an intensive six week training period. In commenting on the machines themselves, Clymer stated that the Model 17 was almost identical to the II-K models that preceded it, except that the wheelbase was lengthened slightly to 54 inches. According to his statements, this change created a number of steering and handling problems, not only from the changed frame dimensions, but also from the increased weight of the new engines. As with the II-K, each rider encountered steering and handling problems at high speeds, which were dealt with in various ways. With some riders, moving the seats either backward or forward to alter the weight distribution appeared to correct most of the troubles, but in the end, Ottaway also increased the rake in the forks of all the machines. In his own machine, Clymer recalled that the compression springs were shortened to lower the position of the pivot, and with the wheel axle now slightly above it, high speed stability was improved. This modification provided the limited fork travel so necessary in high speed track work.

At the third running of the Dodge City Classic on July 11th, the local Chamber of Commerce and the merchants' association went all out to make the affair a gala event for an anticipated crowd of 30,000 visitors. The main street was decorated with flags and bunting, and a parade featuring several marching bands and military units was held just before the race. Several floors of Dodge City's largest hotel, The Harvey House, were set aside as the official race headquarters. Riders, team managers and their personnel, motorcycle manufacturers and accessory and tire suppliers were in attendance.

The official starter manning the pace car was T.S.Sullivan, Automotive Editor of the *Boston Globe* newspaper, who waved off the contestants at 11.00am. Otto Walker was a non-starter due to a sudden illness and Ottaway substituted twenty-one year old Floyd Clymer. While many in the crowd were somewhat surprised at the change in the line up, Clymer was not exactly an unknown to many fans, due to his many recent racing victories in the Colorado area. It was also rumored that he was soon to take up an H-D franchise in Denver.

On the first lap, Don Johns took an early lead on his Indian, but was overhauled by Clymer in the second lap. Johns dropped back to third when passed by Bob Perry on a very fast big valve Excelsior, but was forced out in the fifth lap by a broken valve. Clymer now widened his lead, with nineteen year old Irving Jahnke coming up from the rear of the pack on a signal from the pits to close in behind. Clymer stayed ahead for the first hundred miles, pulling Jahnke along just behind him in his slip stream, setting a new record of 83.62 mph for the first hundred miles. At the one hundred and first mile, Jahnke pulled ahead, acting on pit signals, as Clymer's engine was noted to be overheating. After that they changed places every few laps, until at the 150th mile the timekeeper announced that their elapsed times were identical.

Don Johns dropped out at the 200th mile with a blown engine, leaving Clymer and Jahnke to alternate between first and second place. Clymer ultimately dropped out at the 296th mile with a blown rear tire. Joe Wolter, Excelsior, was a distant second, with Ray Weishaar, H-D, third. Paul Warner and Gene Walker on Indians were fourth and fifth, with Morty Graves on an Excelsior trailing in sixth. Jahnke's winning speed was a record 79.79 mph, for which he collected $800.00 in prize money together with an additional $200.00 bonus for his lap times.

On July 25th, the H-D team entered the races at the newly-opened board track at Sheepshead Bay, Long Island, New York, winning first, second, third, fourth and sixth places. Don Johns, Indian's star rider of the season, was the only member of his team to finish in a place, garnering the fifth spot. Red Parkhurst, the H-D winner, made the very fast time of 89.01 mph, in spite of a pit stop to change a fouled spark plug, and a very unnerving speed wobble in next to the last lap which nearly brought him down. In the National Championship races held on the same course, M.K.'Curly' Fredricks, Bill Briar, and Alvin Barclay won all three first places for H-D at speeds of well over 90 mph.

Space considerations preclude further accounts of H-D's phenomenal successes during 1916, but suffice it to say that the team criss-crossed the country during the balance of the season to win no less than fifteen National Championships.

The late Floyd Clymer, in recounting his experiences with the H-D racing team, told the author that while the machines were in most cases only fractionally faster than those fielded by Excelsior and Indian, it was Ottaway's tireless attention to pit stop timing and constant drilling of the riders in track strategy and signal techniques that had the most critical effect on their continuing successes.

H-D's showing in the 1916 desert races were somewhat of a disappointment. H-D enthusiasts Harry Crandall and R.J.Orput requested, but were denied, any factory support, and entered the contest on their own 1914 two-speeders which had obvious limitations as to both power output and speed.

The race was flagged off at Springerville at dawn on November 6th, the riders being started at two minute intervals. Roy Artley was first into Flagstaff, closely followed by Alan Bedell. Jack Dodds limped in two hours later, having had to stop at intervals to clean sand from his carburetor. R.J.Orput, on his H-D, was reported as having been stalled somewhere behind, with a broken fork spring. Just before reaching Winslow, Cannonball Baker was closely following Harry Crandall on his H-D when the latter went over a rise and skidded to a fall in loose sand just over the crest. Baker put his machine into a slide to avoid hitting Crandall, and both went into a ravine. They managed to make minor repairs to their battered machines and carried on. Al Meacham was the next casualty, buckling his front wheel on a large rock. Bedell took a header over his handlebars when fouled in a deep rut, and cut his forehead severely, but managed to remount and carry on. Roy Artley finished first for a time of 13 hours 12 minutes. A rather bloody Bedell was second, with Joe Wolter, Excelsior, third, and Dodds, Indian, fourth. Indian took three out of the first four places, with a dejected Crandall and Orput arriving hours behind. Orput was heard to denounce bitterly the parsimony of the factory for not supplying three-speed machines, and reportedly soon deserted Milwaukee for the Wigwam.

1916 was a year of attrition for the United States motorcycle industry. While a large number of manufacturers showed machines at the annual Motorcycle Show staged in January in Chicago, most of

The immortal 'Red' Parkhurst at Dodge City, Kansas, in 1915. The machine is an updated K-11 Model fitted with William Ottaway's improved pocket valve engine. *(The H-D Motor Company).*

these did not continue with actual production. While this may appear as a paradox to the soaring popularity of motorcycling since 1910, with now more than 200,000 machines registered on the North American continent, the fall came not without reason. Most of the early manufacturers were lightly financed, and operated with modest facilities and with a minimum of tooling. This necessarily limited their production, and most of them were never able to expand to the point of gaining a substantial dealer representation. In fact, many of them appeared to cater largely to a local market. The European war had caused a dramatic rise in the cost of materials, many imported accessories were now unavailable, and labor was demanding higher wages due to the effect of the continuing inflation. Added to these problems was the fact that in those days the science of industrial management, techniques of marketing, internal cost and inventory control, the essence of successful manufacturing, was as yet undeveloped. Many firms producing sound machines were haphazardly organised and ineptly managed.

Indian, still the leader of the industry was in sound financial condition, due to its high production and still growing sales position. Excelsior, backed by the astute Ignatz Schwinn, and financed through his fabulously successful bicycle empire, was also quite secure. H-D, through its cautious development and conservative growth, and now enjoying an expanding sales position, was also well in the black. Much of its soundness was due to the production expertise of William Davidson, whose tireless search for greater efficiency and ruthless methods of internal cost cutting consistent with quality control, were now a byword in the industry.

Other than these leading concerns, now known in the trade as the 'Big Three', the second string manufacturers were far less fortunate. Pope, a once viable operation, integral with its parent automobile and bicycle empire, was now faltering due to managerial difficulties encountered following the death of Colonel Pope in 1910. The brilliant Merkel was foundering on problems of quality and costing control, and the management of Thor, somewhat disheartened by the defection of William Ottaway, were now showing more interest in their highly profitable home appliance production. Lesser concerns, such as Dayton, Minneapolis, Feilbach, Flanders, Yale, and others, simply expired due to a variety or combination of the causes mentioned. Other than the Big Three, the principal survivors were Iver-Johnson, a favorite with rural mail carriers, and supported by their extensive fire arms manufacture, Reading Standard, Emblem, soon to become an export-only operation, and Schickel, a 500 cc two stroke with a rather unconventional cast aluminum frame. With conditions of attrition, and with the very low production of the secondary makes, domestic production had now fallen to slightly over 50,000 units.

While some of the factory and sales personnel of the surviving factories were jubilant over the decline of competition, wiser and more knowledgeable people within the industry viewed their now thinning ranks with foreboding, and as a dire portent of things to come.

1916 also saw the first employment of motorcycles in the U.S. Army's combat units. In the spring of that year, the War Department dispatched a punitive expedition of about 20,000 men into northern Mexico under the command of General John J.Pershing, in pursuit of General Francisco (Pancho) Villa. A participant in the Mexican Revolution of 1910, Villa's military activities in the north were seen to get out of hand, and acting on his own initiative, he began raiding U.S. territory north of the border. His depredations ultimately included the attack on the town of Columbus, New Mexico, killing 19 Americans. Mexico's President, Francisco I. Madera, whose government forces were insufficient to cope with the wily ex-bandit, gave the US government permission to enter the country in hopes of capturing him. While Pershing was unable to find either Villa or any of his tattered army in the vastness of his own territory, the campaign was significant in that it was the first time that motorized units, including aircraft, trucks, automobiles, and motorcycles, had been used in a military operation in North America under actual combat conditions. Equal numbers of H-D's and Indians, together with lesser numbers of Excelsior big twins were employed, in both solo and sidecar form. These machines were standard roadster models, the only concession to military use being the fitting of slightly lower gear ratios. All the heavyweight twins acquitted themselves nobly, providing both adequate performance and dependability, often under appalling field conditions and with but minimum maintenance. It was this somewhat limited campaign that had much to do with revising the thinking of the US Army's General Staff concerning the mechanization of warfare, which heretofore had been based entirely on cavalry operations or horse drawn transport.

In the field of endurance runs, H-D's 1916 records were no less outstanding. In the FAM-sponsored 24 hour Poughkeepsie run, solo and sidecar teams of three entrants each won perfect scores for team prizes. In the Worcester, Massachusetts 24 hour run, two H-D sidecar teams won gold medals for perfect 1000 point scores. A 450 mile endurance run held in the vicinity of Omaha, Nebraska, sponsored by the FAM with trophies donated by the *World Herald* newspaper, saw H-D entrants winning first and second places. Eight out of ten H-D riders made perfect scores in the Portland, Oregon to Roseburg run.

In an attempt to publicize the all-electric Remy equipped models, H-D's factory sponsored team all featured this equipment in the 400 mile run. While the electric models had been introduced the preceding year, the reliability of the contemporary batteries were sometimes in doubt, and many veteran riders still preferred the reduced illumination of the well known Solar acetylene or in-unit carbide systems which, up to this point, had proved more dependable. Among the H-D competitors were Julian C. 'Hap' Scherer, whom we shall meet again, and A.W.Herrington, later to be associated with both the once famous Marmon car, as well as the Indianapolis speedway. He was, for a time, employed in the H-D engineering department.

A disappointing setback in August was H-D's failure to win the much publicized Pike's Peak hill climb, scheduled by the FAM a month after the official opening of the first passable auto road to the top of the 14,000 foot mountain. Excelsior, H-D, Indian, and Thor all fielded strong teams. In an all out effort, Indian mounted 8 valve track engines in roadster frames with three-speed gearboxes. It was Floyd Clymer, however, who stole the show, with an ultralight cut-down track frame and a specially tuned engine, made up especially for him by the local Excelsior dealer. The H-D contingent could take some comfort, however, by Van Vanderkoff and Harold Boyd winning the sidecar event in a specially tuned 1915 three-speed outfit.

In the Fall of 1916, Arthur Davidson announced that a new sales innovation would be the implementation of a new system of factory-dealer liaison by the division of the country into geographical districts, each with a factory represenative. These representatives would report directly to the factory concerning any sales or delivery problems encountered in the retail outlets. While this new policy would undoubtedly facilitate dealer factory communication more effectively, critics noted that it would at once tighten control of the H-D management over their dealers, as Arthur Davidson was already noted for keeping what is known as a very tight ship.

To this end, the often quaintly composed factory dealer communique, *The Dealer,* was withdrawn, and in its place, a new publication named *The Enthusiast* was published under factory auspices. It was sent broadcast to all registered H-D owners, including the dealers themselves, on an infrequent basis.

Former Enduro Champion and latter day motion picture stunt rider Bud Ekins with his 1915 'J'
Model. This was the last year of the step starter and the first year a three-speed transmission was
fitted. *(Alisha Tamburri)*.

Johnny Eagles (left) and Bud Ekins fire up the latter's 1915 'J'. The cloud of blue smoke indicates
that the total loss lubrication system is functioning satisfactorily. *(Alisha Tamburri)*.

In the Fall of 1916, all formal competition activities were suspended, both through the mandate of the FAM and through mutual agreement by the manufacturers, due to the increasingly troubled international complications brought on by the war in Europe. The position of the United States since the beginning of the War in August, 1914, was to remain neutral. In fact, President Woodrow Wilson in his 1916 campaign for re-election promised to keep the country out of the war. But the sinking of the Lusitania, followed by continued attack on American shipping by German U-boats, had aroused much sentiment for the Allied cause, augmented by the harrowing stories told by newsmen concerning alleged German atrocities against Belgian civilians. After his re-election in 1916, President Wilson received permission from a now compliant congress to place the country on a preparedness footing. As a result, a large number of manufacturing firms readied themselves to fulfill war department contracts for materiel.

After the successful demonstration of the motorcycle's role in the Mexican campaign, all of the Big Three's management held themselves in readiness to produce machines for the government, and instituted individual prototype experiments with military models.

It was this now sudden preoccupation with military machines, and the subsequent war department contracts consummated, that was to have a most significant effect upon the future of the H-D Company.

The Indian Company, whose fortunes since 1913 had come under the control of a non-motor-cycling board of directors who were more interested in profits than in the long term future of motor-cycling, decided at this point to go all-out in the securing of military contracts. They reasoned that it would be more economical to supply the armed forces than to continue to compete in the civilian market, for the duration of the war at least. To this end, and in an effort to corner the military orders, they offered government purchasing agents the opportunity to buy solo machines for $187.50, with $49.50 for sidecars. In addition, Indian boldly offered to supply 20,000 machines at this price. This price cut profits dangerously thin, and at the same time allowed no margin for the very real prospect that the inevitable war-time inflation could suddenly drive production costs higher.

H-D's management at once saw the folly of neglecting the civilian market, especially as they themselves were just now gaining a strong second place as compared with Indian. While the dictates of maintaining a patriotic stance in the matter precluded their seeking a unit price per machine or sidecar unit higher than that of Indian, they prudently made their offer on the supplying of 7,000 machines, projecting at the same time a 10,000 machine output for civilian consumption.

Accordingly, and while widely announcing H-D's contribution to the war effort, Arthur Davidson inaugurated a blitz sales campaign to recruit new dealers, especially in areas where Indian had been the strongest, and where motorcycle sales in general had been flourishing. As the supply of new Indian machines and accompanying spare parts now slowed to a trickle, not a few Indian dealers switched their allegiance to Milwaukee.

Late in 1917, H-D again offered 50% of their production to the government, which ultimately totaled approximately another 7,000 units, and received, together with Indian, a slightly better price due to the inflationary rise in production costing. At the same moment, H-D was able to more firmly entrench themselves in the civilian market at Indian's expense, and their 17,000 unit production for the 1916-1917 year enabled them to challenge Indian's usual annual 20,000 plus production that they had enjoyed for several seasons past.

The 'J' models were greatly improved, both in the military and civilian versions which were almost identical, largely as the result of the engine modifications learned from the past racing seasons. With new high velocity intake manifolds, altered cam profiles, strengthened valve gear, and a larger oil pump, about 25% more power was available. In addition, the front forks were improved with larger diameter tubes for greater strength, and better spring action. The clutch and gearbox were now fitted with heavier plates and enlarged shaft bearings. The appearance of the machine was enhanced by altering the dies that stamped out the fuel and oil tank halves, the slab sided razor edged profile seen since 1909 now giving way to a more pleasingly rounded shape.

As their contribution to the war effort, the American motorcycle industry supplied 15,000 H-D's, 2,600 Excelsiors, 41,000 Indians, and about 200 Cleveland lightweight two-strokes. In common with other types of war material produced in vast numbers, large numbers of these machines never reached the fighting front. Many machines which ultimately survived the hard usage of active service were left behind in vehicle dumps, a few of which later found their way into native civilian hands. Most of the machines remained in the States, where they were employed in training and staging centers. Most of the new machines received but not used were declared surplus, and came onto the civilian market through agents, who bought them in quantity through competitive bidding. Many of the machines which saw but limited service through these channels remained in active service for several years thereafter. Some of these could still be seen in daily use in stateside posts or in such far flung areas as the Philippine Islands or at the Panama Canal Zone until well into the 1930s.

In referring to H-D's role in the war effort, an anecdote often repeated with varying details in subsequent issues of the *Enthusiast* was how Corporal Roy Holtz, mounted on a sidecar outfit, was the first American soldier to enter Germany at the cessation of hostilities. With his company captain as a passenger, Holtz set out on a mission near the German border close to his base in northern Belgium. After a series of blunders where they lost their way during a heavy rain storm, they inadvertently crossed into Germany on November 9th 1918, and were immediately captured by a German patrol billeted at a farmhouse where they stopped to ask their way. They were released at noon on November 11th, with directions on how to return to their home base. Now united with their infantry unit, they re-entered Germany on November 12th, where a Signal Corps photographer snapped the now famous picture. Holtz remained in Germany with the army of occupation for another eight months, and his sidecar outfit reportedly gave flawless service during the balance of his tour of duty.

The maintenance of service motorcycles of all participating makes was under the direction of Thomas Calahan Butler, a member of Indian's sales force on leave of absence, who was said to have received his appointment from President Wilson. Butler recruited about 3,000 mechanics from the various factories, and several service departments were established on the East Coast. Only a small number of this force actually saw overseas service, however, as the war ended before the maintenance system had been fully organized. As an outgrowth of this effort, all of the Big Three manufacturers subsequently established their own service schools after the war to train dealers and their personnel. H-D's service school was under the capable direction of Joseph Ryan for some years thereafter. The rugged American V twins had established an enviable record of service under conditions of hard wartime use, giving outstanding performance in scouting and liaison assignments, as well as in dispatch carrying or in maintenance of telephone and telegraph lines at various points along the front.

By virtue of their somewhat limited war production and continued attention to the civilian market, H-D found themselves in a strong position at the close of hostilities, as their long-time rival, Indian, discovered their once strong dealer organization in disarray due to an almost total commitment to War Department contracts.

Arthur Davidson at once moved to strengthen his own dealerships by weeding out ineffectual or

A 1917 'J' Model sidecar outfit from the Bud Ekins collection. The sidecar bodies were built for H-D by the Rogers Company of Chicago. Their style was practically identical from 1915 through 1924. *(George Hays).*

non-aggressive outlets. He also stepped up H-D's traditional strong advertising policy by instructing the Company advertising agencies to contract for additional space in a variety of other than the usual trade journals, such as hobby and mechanics publications, hunting and outdoor periodicals, and other media particularly directed to youthful readers. He was able to implement his previous intention of stationing factory representatives in various regions of the country to keep in closer contact with the dealers.

Of signal advantage to the company's continuing good fortune was the knowledge and experience gained in the production department during the enforced pressures put upon it to supply both the military and civilian markets. Efficiency had been improved through the tireless efforts of William Davidson, together with enhanced quality control and continuing excellence of the product through the employment of advanced metallurgy. Production efficiency was also aided by the fact that the company was still concentrating on mainly a one model range. While the older type singles and twins with both single gears or the 1914 type two-speed rear hub were still available on special order, most of their ancillary parts were identical with the 61 cubic inch 'J' type. Of this, the two principal variations were either the magneto equipped 'F' models, or the fully electric 'J' with a generator battery system.

In a burst of optimism over the company's prospects of assuming a dominant role in the industry during the coming post war years, the founders decided to update their production facilities with the building of a vast new addition to the factory. With construction commencing in the late fall of 1918, the new quarters were ready for occupancy by April of 1920, and were laid out as an L shaped multi-story edifice affording a total of nearly 600,000 square feet of floor area. With working space for 2,400 employees in 96 departments, it now surpassed the Springfield plant built by Indian some years before as the largest motorcycle facility of its kind in the world. Overcoming their earlier reluctance to pay bank interest rates, the founders were said to have borrowed over $3,000,000 from Marshall & Illsley to construct not only the building itself, but to add nearly $500,000 worth of the latest type of machine tooling. The company was now in a position to double their present production to a total of 35,000 machines per year.

The industry was electrified in April 1919, when as a complete surprise an entirely new and radically different type of machine was announced by H-D. Designated the Model 'W', and called the 'Sport Twin', it was a rather small and compact machine on a 53½ inch wheelbase, weighing about 275 pounds ready for the road, and powered by a horizontally-opposed side valve engine of 37 cubic inches displacement, with an SAE rating of 6 hp.

A very rare 1917 'J' Model 35 cu.in. single as restored by Bud Ekins. In limited production through 1920, they were available on special order until 1922. They were mostly used in commercial applications. *(Alisha Tamburri).*

An electrically-equipped 1917 military 'J' Model in original condition from the Steve McQueen collection. The 61 cu.in. and later 1922 74 cu.in. 'Js' were identical in appearance from 1917 through 1924. *(Alisha Tamburri).*

A three-speed sliding gear-type transmission was mounted just behind and slightly to the rear of the crankcase, the primary drive being by helically cut gears to a multiplate clutch running in oil. The final drive was by chain completely enclosed in a dust-proof sheet metal case. The footboards, clutch and brake lever attachments were carried on brackets fitted to the bottom of an open bottomed diamond or 'Keystone' type frame.

A marked departure from the now traditional H-D leading link front suspension was the fitting of a trailing link strut braced fork activated by a single barrel coil spring attached to the head lug. The initial 'W' type featured magneto ignition, with an optional acetylene lighting set. Also offered later was a 'WJ' type with battery and coil ignition and electric lighting.

Frankly based on the contemporary English Douglas, whose several models of horizontally-opposed twins had been popular sellers in the United Kingdom and elsewhere for several seasons past, the new model was easy to start, possessed almost no vibration at any speed, and had a top speed of 48-50 mph, with a comfortable cruising speed of about 40. As subsequent performance tests were to prove, it was a machine that, under somewhat different domestic social and economic conditions, might well have become an economical everyman's motorcycle.

While the domestic industry had for the past several seasons concentrated almost entirely on filling the now well-established public demand for heavyweight V-twins, the new model was, of course, at complete variance with current fashion. However, some knowledgeable motorcyclists, highly placed within the industry, had been heard to question the general lack of mediumweight and more moderately powered models. While possessed of high power and with speed capabilities that usually far exceeded the road facilities extant at that time, most big twins were rather difficult to start and awkward to manhandle within a confined space. By necessity they attracted mainly speed enthusiasts who were perforce mostly athletic young men. The medium and lightweight utility type of machine would, of course, have had an appeal to an actually larger and more broad spectrum of the potential transportation market, if properly introduced and promoted. As a paradox, a recent attempt by the Indian company to penetrate this market with the ultralight two-stroke model K single and later a medium weight opposed twin Model O met with failure. This was in large part due to the new model's rejection by many of the Indian dealers themselves, who were big twin enthusiasts for the most part, and appeared either unready or unwilling to promote a new model within another segment of a previously untapped market.

On the other hand, the only enduring model to find favor with a rather limited utility market was the two-stroke Cleveland, launched in 1915. However, it had been marketed by established bicycle dealers and sporting goods or allied retailers, whose main preoccupation was point-to-point utility transportation and who had no interest in high speed travel or competition activities. Almost unnoticed by the general motorcycling public, Cleveland managed to produce and sell about 5,000 machines each year, half of which went to export markets.

H-D's top management must have carefully charted their course with the introduction of the W Sport Twin, offering a well made and substantial non-sporting type machine that was easy to ride and maintain. In its sales promotion, Arthur Davidson sought to interest certain potential dealers who were already known to be partial to the potentials of the utility market, coupled with an accelerated advertising campaign to acquaint the general public with a new type of motorcycle. To this end, he engaged one Walter Klemenheimer, a former newspaper advertising specialist, and Julian C. ('Hap') Scherer, a former sales manager for the Firestone Tire Company. The latter was both a pioneer motorist and motorcyclist and had already gone on record as favoring lightweight machines as the logical answer to the average man's transportation needs. Described by contemporaries as a genial and ebullient personality, he was apparently well fitted to fill the newly-created post of Publicity Manager.

An expert and experienced rider, Scherer immediately set out to prove the Sport Twin's mettle, setting some notable records. On June 21st 1919, he rode a factory-prepared machine from the Canadian border to Tijuana, Mexico, for a new Three Flag record of 64 hours, 58 minutes for the 1,689 mile distance. This bettered the previous time set by Wells Bennett on a 61 cubic inch Excelsior twin by 5½ hours.

The following Spring Scherer attacked the Denver to Chicago record made by Floyd Clymer on a Henderson Four in 64 hours for the 1,224 miles during May 1920. With the aid of Denver's enthusiastic H-D dealer, Walter W.Whiting, Scherer made the run in the opposite direction during the following month, beating Clymer's time by 16½ hours. H-D's advertisements in the trade press concerning this exploit pointedly emphasized that the Sport Twin had less than half the cylinder displacement of the Henderson. In all fairness, however, it must be pointed out that the roads of that day gave a medium weight machine a distinct advantage, providing its engine produced effective low speed torque (which the Sport Twin's did). Deep ruts, the presence of many large stones, viscous mud during rain storms, and the necessity for many off-the-road detours, all tended to put a heavyweight machine at a disadvantage under road conditions where full power could not be used, and the excess weight became an actual disadvantage.

Another well publicized performance of the Sport Twin was the ride of one Edwin Hogg, a leading naturalist and conservationist of the day, and one time disciple of the noted John Muir, on a survey trip through California's notorious Death Valley. Hogg's expedition was sponsored through the joint efforts of the Pacific Coast Borax Company, The Tonopah and Tidewater Railroad, and the Death Valley Railroad, who were considering the establishment of three resort hotels and rail lines to serve them in this scenic but extremely primitive area.

A most inhospitable region, Death Valley is a vast sunken area some 150 miles long and 10 to 40 miles wide, surrounded by granite mountains of 8,500 to 15,000 foot elevation. Arid and forbidding, with scant rainfall and summer temperatures of up to 140°F and few watering holes or springs, countless travellers have died of exposure and starvation within its confines since its discovery in the mid-1800s.

As an amateur motorcyclist dedicated to the lightweight concept, Hogg rightly concluded that a two-wheeled vehicle could better traverse the primitive trails of the region. After surveying the motorcycle market, Hogg purchased a Sport Twin from Harley Rathbun's San Bernardino agency which was then carefully tuned after its running-in period by mechanic Jack Fletcher. Starting from his home in Los Angeles, Hogg made the 1,200 mile round trip through Death Valley, completed his survey, and returned two weeks later. He reported that the Sport Twin performed faultlessly under extremely strenuous use, his only problem being with numerous tire failures that included wearing out of a set of them during the journey.

In the Spring of 1919, H-D renewed its export efforts in the United Kingdom, and the 1914 agreement with Duncan Watson was reactivated. The latter established a large salesroom at 74 Newman Street in London, and made plans to set up satellite dealerships in other areas of the British Isles. The actual details were worked out through the efforts of Eric von Gumpert, who was to reactivate the Company's export program now that the war was over. During the war effort, von Gumpert had been occupied as Traffic Manager, with duties involving the routing of dealers' machine and parts orders via the nation's now extensive network of railroads, which were then the only means of public, personal or commercial transport. Incidental to these duties, von Gumpert did not leave Milwaukee, but conducted his assignment through voluminous correspondence. An export branch was established in Australasia, to serve the Australian and New Zealand markets, which were finalized by Arthur Davidson himself on a personal tour to this area where he met with numerous prospective dealers and enthusiasts.

In the initial shipment of 50 machines to the United Kingdom, 15 were Sport Twins, which reportedly met with a good response from British buyers. They were to receive good acceptance from sales efforts in Belgium, Holland, and the Scandinavian countries, Norway, Denmark, and Sweden.

During the spring of 1919, the Company reactivated their now dormant competition program, under the continuing direction of Bill Ottaway, assisted by R.W.Enos, who now proceeded to organize what was to be perhaps the most formidable array of racing talent yet seen in the United States. Soon to be known as the 'Wrecking Crew', its more prominent members included Jim Davis, Ralph Hepburn, Walter Higley, Fred Ludlow, Otto Walker, and Ray Weishaar. All were skilled competition riders of proven abilities, and their formidability was enhanced by their expertise in team tactics and pit stop techniques, implanted by Ottaway and Enos.

Excelsior and Indian had also committed themselves to a strong post-war competition program, and together with H-D, were shortly to inaugurate the so-called Golden Age of motorcycle competition in the United States.

Indeed, all forms of motor sport were now recapturing the wide public interest that it enjoyed during the immediate prewar years. Both the automobile and the motorcycle were still a relatively recent development in the transportation field, and manufacturers of both supported competition activities to advertise their products. Then too, it must be recalled that during this period in history, professional athletics in general were as yet somewhat limited in scope. Professional football and basketball were as yet undeveloped, and the beginnings of professional baseball had just been given a

The classic photograph of Corporal Roy Holtz — 'The first Yank to enter Germany' — November 12, 1918. *(U.S. Army Signal Corps).*

setback and were tainted in the public mind by the Black Sox scandal in Chicago where an alert sports reporter exposed the fact that certain games were fixed for the benefit of certain gambling interests. The only other competitive sport to capture public attention was prize fighting, which often was too brutal for general public taste.

Most of the board tracks built just prior to the war had been rebuilt and repaired. Jack Prince, the principal builder, undertook most of these projects, as well as construction of a number of new tracks adjacent to several of the country's larger cities. In addition, many of the nation's hundreds of county fair horse tracks were altered to better accommodate auto and motorcycle racing.

The Wrecking Crew, now ready for the opening of the 1919 season, proceeded to duplicate their impressive 1916 record with an almost unbroken series of victories. 'Red' Parkhurst, a newcomer to the H-D team, won the 200 Mile International Road Race Championship at Marion, Indiana. Otto Walker headed the H-D team at Los Angeles Ascot Speedway on November 30th to win all three first places. At the next race, held on January 4th 1920, before a capacity crowd of 26,000 enthusiastic spectators, the H-D team took four first places in the 100 Mile Main Event. Walker, the winner, racked up

Two views of William Ottaway's 61 cu.in. pocket valve racer developed for H-D's post-WW I racing program. The prototype as shown was fitted with unsprung strutted girder forks. Subsequent machines were fitted with modified H-D leading link sprung types *(C.May)*.

a time of 77 minutes, 42 seconds, for a new course record of 77.25 mph. Hepburn, Parkhurst, and Ludlow captured all the succeeding places at speeds exceeding 74 mph.

As an interesting aside to these victories, an article in the *Western Motorcyclist* and *Bicyclist* described the extensive preparations carried out by Ottaway in order to save valuable time during pit stops. The mechanics had advance notice of individual rider's needs via a telephone line that extended along the track to a lookout. At the pits, quick axle release nuts facilitated 10 second wheel changes, along with special fuel and oil containers which allowed almost instantaneous topping up of fuel and oil tanks through extra large tank orifices. Pit stops also included a fresh pair of goggles for the rider, and a refreshing drink of water or fruit juice. After intensive drilling, such pit stops could be accomplished and the rider pushed off within 55 to 60 seconds.

During the early part of the 1920 season, the H-D racing team was provided with newly developed pocket valve engines which replaced the former 8 valve types. H-D's management reasoned that the advanced development of the standard roadster engine configuration could not only lead to enhanced performance of these models, but that potential buyers would be more impressed if the racing machines appeared to be using engines similar to types offered for public sale.

On January 11th, the H-D team swept the field at the 50 Mile Ascot Championships, with Walker again winning, this time at 80 mph, with team-mates Ludlow taking second, Parkhurst fourth, and Hepburn fifth.

Hap Scherer's Three Flag record of 1919 had just been broken by Cannonball Baker on a 61 cubic inch Indian Powerplus on July 15th, and a few days later it was broken again by Wells Bennett on a 61 cubic inch Excelsior, for a new time of 53 hours 28 minutes.

On September 15th, Al Hadfield, as a private entrant without factory support, riding a standard 61 cubic inch H-D standard twin, left the Canadian border at dawn, arriving at Tijuana 51 hours and 22 minutes later. This record stood for a year, only to be bested by Wells Bennett on an Excelsior, shaving Hadfield's record by 18 minutes. Hadfield again challenged this record in November, beating Bennett with a flat 49 hour run. This exploit was given much publicity by the trade press, as heavy rains slowed progress through Washington, Oregon and Northern California, necessitating much high speed running in central and southern California toward the end to make up for lost time.

As an aside to the numerous competitive long distance runs of the 1915-1920 periods in the transcontinental and Three Flag categories, it will be noted that H-D was never represented by the most famous of the long distance riders, namely Cannonball Baker. The author, who was researching various historical aspects of the American motorcycle industry during 1955 and 1956, interviewed Baker regarding this during Baker's visit to the West Coast for the annual meeting of the Trailblazers, an organization of pioneer motorcyclists. Baker said that he was in the habit of representing any make of machine whose manufacturer would offer $500.00 to $1,000.00 appearance money, together with a stipulated bonus for lowering the elapsed time of a previous run. He said that on two or three occasions H-D's President, Walter Davidson, contacted him about the possibility of setting up an attack on record runs for certain distances held by competing makes. In each case, Baker reported that Davidson balked at the paying of the appearance money, stipulating that bonuses be paid only if the run in question set a new record. As Baker's reputation was already well established, he insisted that an appearance fee be paid. Since the two could never come to terms, no agreement was ever consummated.

H-D offered three basic roadster models during this period: The magneto-equipped 'JF' with optional acetylene lighting, the electrically equipped Model 'J', and the Sport Twin. During the late summer of 1919, the Model 20 J was announced with the Company's own make of electrical equipment, featuring their version of generators, horns, batteries, and lighting sets. While the batteries were furnished by outside suppliers, the balance of the system was offered on the premise that Remy's equipment no longer measured up to H-D's standards of reliability. While this new policy freed the company's reliance on Remy, in reality their first units were not wholly satisfactory and many dealers were forced to supply Remy equipment to owners who experienced difficulties with the Company's own products. It was not until the fall of 1920 that the Company solved the problem of their ailing electrical units. It is said that a former electrical engineer in Remy's employ, one George Appel, was hired to superintend their improvement.

An important event in the history of American motorcycling in the summer of 1919 was the dissolution of the Federation of American Motorcyclists. Never a really strong organization, either numerically or financially even in 1916 when domestic registrations topped 200,000 machines, its strength was further eroded during the war years when most of its active members joined the armed forces. Indeed by the time the Armistice was concluded, FAM had lost fully half of its membership. Supported by a $2.00 annual subscription from members, often collected haphazardly through the regional chapters, its officers served on a voluntary basis, and in many cases were not reimbursed for expenses incurred in carrying out their duties.

The generally weakened condition of the FAM was first publicized in the trade press by Leslie D. (Dick) Richards, a pioneer motorcyclist Associate Editor of a leading journal of the day, *Motorcyclist and Bicyclist Illustrated* in the March 6th issue. Richards pointed out the general weaknesses of the organization at all levels, particularly in the matter of governing competition, which at this point was almost out of hand. He suggested that for proper functioning, a strong membership and efficient management were required if the interests of motorcycling in general were to be served by a national organization. It was also noted that with the general dissatisfaction with the present FAM, a splinter group on the West coast had recently been organized, known as the Federation of Western Motorcyclists.

Irwin D. Allen, of Akron, Ohio, the national President of the FAM, responded to Richards' comments through a series of letters sent to other trade journals. He admitted the current weaknesses of the organization, particularly in the areas of enforcement of competition rules, and the difficulty of carrying on FAM affairs generally in the face of declining membership and consequent impaired financial resources. During the course of his correspondence, he wrote that, in his opinion, if motorcyclists in general did not wish to support the organization in its present form, the formation of a new body was now most definitely in order, and that the present FAM management would be more than willing to step aside or offer to resign if such a step were considered necessary.

At this point, H. W. Parsons, the Editor and owner of *Motorcyclist and Bicyclist Illustrated*, published an editorial suggesting that Allen's suggestions should be acted on imemdiately in order to preserve a national organization dedicated to the best interests of motorcycling in general. Parsons then attended the annual meeting of the American Motorcycle Manufacturers Association, which was held in Chicago during the first week in July. He spoke at length on the need for a better organization, pointing out that among other matters, the chaotic lack of efficient enforcement of competition rules was now relegating such activities to an 'outlaw' basis, where much rule bending and gamesmanship were making a mockery out of motorcycle sport. He ultimately moved, and was seconded, that the manufacturers take over the functions of the FAM until such time as a new governing body could be organized. Parsons was promptly nominated and elected to serve as Chairman to carry out this edict. During subsequent meetings, and under the guidance of the Manufacturer's Executive Committee, the FAM was reorganized to form the American Motorcycle Association. It was originally intended to operate independently of trade influence, and to be a democratic organization, freely governed by officers elected from the ranks of the general membership.

At the annual Motorcycle Show held in Chicago in January 1920, the control of competition activities, the most controversial item within the membership of the former FAM, was placed in the hands of one A. B. Coffman, named as Competition Chairman. Although Coffman was a dedicated and capable administrator, and was able through herculean efforts to sort out and authenticate a large number of recent competition records, he was not popular with many of the members due to his alleged arrogant and dictatorial manner. He was replaced the following year by one Douglas Hobart, an Indian dealer in Hartford, Connecticut, who had at one time been employed in Indian's Engineering Department. He was shortly to serve for a time as the AMA's *de facto* President, and the official headquarters were moved to Hartford. In the meantime, Hobart received some strong support from many interested members in the final structuring of the AMA, especially from Dick Richards, who had now become Publicity Manager for the Indian company.

While the AMA was initially a private owner's organization, trade influence in various forms ultimately became an important factor in it, and its bearing on the subsequent turbulent history of American motorcycling will presently be noted.

During the early months of 1920, following the alleviation of the worst of the world wide economic chaos after the war, H-D became firmly established in the United Kingdom under the capable direction of Duncan Watson. It was about this time that Watson became Lord Mayor of London and was shortly afterwards knighted by King George V. While there was much enthusiasm among British riders for American heavyweight V twins, sales were modest due to the lower per capita income in the British Isles as compared to America. Regarded by most as a sidecar machine, many British sporting riders were quite taken with the high speed capabilities not found in contemporary domestic makes. A number of machines, many highly modified, began to make their appearance at Brooklands race track, where post-war speed competition was now in full swing. Prominent H-D enthusiasts included T. R. Allchin, Douglas Davidson (no relation to the Founders), Freddie Dixon, Frank Longman, and Claude Temple.

Davidson gained immediate notoriety for being the first British rider to attain 100 mph, although this record had already been established in the United States. His mount was one of two factory specials ordered from the factory by Duncan Watson for this express purpose, which were set up by Watson's mechanics in November 1920. In their original form, they were board track machines with short wheelbases and solid single gear countershaft drive, powered by specially tuned standard pocket

Two H-D riders duel on the famous Maywood Speedway near Chicago in 1920. Note the vast expanse of 2in x 4in laid-on-edge decking. *(C.May)*.

valve engines with polished manifold passages and high lift cam gears. During initial practicing, winter weather permitting, it was found that the short wheelbase frames were difficult to control on Brooklands' rough surface. The machines were disassembled, and during the winter, were rebuilt with standard wheelbase roadster frames, which proved more suitable. This change resulted in Davidson's subsequent record. Claude Temple, riding the second machine, rode in the famous duel with Herbert Le Vack on his well-known 1911 8 valve Indian factory racer. On April 29th, just 24 hours after Davidson's 100 mph run, Le Vack, on his Indian, topped Davidson's record with a timed speed of 106.52 mph.

The noted Freddie Dixon, long a Yankee big twin enthusiast, riding a 1916 board track type Model 17 with an 8 valve engine, nosed out I. P. Riddoch on a 994 cc Zenith Blackburne at the Clipson Speed Trials by over 3 mph, his speed being 101.12 mph. He subsequently raced the same machine at Brooklands, when, on October 20th 1923, he won the British Motor Cycle Racing Club Championship at 100.00 mph.

Claude Temple, for several seasons past a big twin enthusiast, had already duelled with Davidson for the 100 mph record, being beaten by only one-fifth of a second during the latter's classic run. He was still second best three weeks later, when on April 21st 1921, he again ran second to Davidson at the BMCRC meeting in the three lap Senior Race. He finally gained a signal victory for himself when he lapped Brooklands' giant oval at 90.09 mph, the first over 90 mph time recorded on this famous circuit.

During the Member's Meeting in July, Temple won the Five Lap Championship for the Club and the Harry Smith Cup at 91 mph.

With one of the new specially-tuned pocket valve engines just developed by Ottaway as a replacement for the Model 17 8-valvers, Temple raised the Classic Hour record two weeks later to 87 miles 922 yards. In September he recorded 99.86 mph for the flying start kilometer, at the same time making a mile record at exactly 100 mph.

These Brooklands records received much attention from the British motorcycle press, and did much to enhance H-D's prestige, as well as to bring about a healthy increase in sales, although due to economic reasons previously mentioned, American V twins could capture only a small segment of the English market. The big 'Yanks' were always the beau ideal of sporting riders and aspiring boy racers.

Meanwhile, back home in the States, the Big Three readied themselves for the 'Golden Age of American competition'.

On February 10th, and as a prelude to the 1920 racing season, Bill Ottaway, Racing Team Manager R. W. Enos, and Publicity Manager Hap Scherer, went to Daytona Beach, Florida, along with star riders Fred Ludlow, Red Parkhurst and Otto Walker, two mechanics, several 8 valve racers, a couple of pocket valve specials, and a bullet-bodied racing sidecar. Their object was to attempt to set some new straight-away records on the now famous sand course. Now that the Competition Committee of the newly organized AMA had established definitive racing categories, it was obvious that priceless advertising for the marque could be forthcoming if the projected records could be established.

Upon the party's arrival, the condition of the course was scarcely promising. Heavy storms had ravished the Eastern seaboard, unusually high tides had softened the sand, and a lack of sunshine left the outer surface mushy. In spite of this and in defiance of superstition, Ludlow made a trial run on Friday 13th, making a one-way kilometer run in 21.75 seconds for an average speed of 103 mph, a remarkable speed for a pocket valve engine. Bad weather prevented further runs until the 15th, when Red Parkhurst, on an 8 valver, averaged 110.94 mph and set up a five mile distance in 3 minutes 32 seconds. The following day, under drier conditions, he raised his mile time to 112.61 mph and the three mile time to 2 minutes 46 seconds. With the weather now clear, Parkhurst rolled the sidecar outfit, with Ludlow as his passenger, at 82.09 mph for the mile and 83.9 mph for the five miles.

While these records were impressive, and were substantially faster than any others racked up in the United States up to that time, they became open to question, even though timed by admittedly accurate Stewart-Warner timing devices supervised by an official of the Motorcycle and Allied Trades Association. They were all tabulated on one way runs, and not the up-and-back traverse of the course, as was the usual practice even in those days for the establishing of timed speed records. Enos and his assistants carefully surveyed the wind conditions before each run, and quite naturally ran with the wind in each case. It was for this reason, and the glowing reports of the so-called 'records' reported in current issues of the *Enthusiast* that the international body governing motorcycle sport, the FIM, did not accept them as official.

Before returning to Milwaukee, the mechanics carefully tuned a bored and stroked version of the standard 61 cubic inch roadster engine that now boasted 68 cubic inches, and Parkhurst made several test runs with it, although its times were not recorded. This was a prototype of the new 74 cubic inch 'J' engine that was placed in production in 1921, no doubt as an answer to Indian's 74 cubic inch version of the popular 'Powerplus' model announced a few months earlier.

In the meantime, board track racing continued to capture popular spectator interest in all parts of the country. Jack Prince had built several new tracks adjacent to many of the nation's larger cities, and huge crowds thronged the grandstands at the weekly or bi-monthly meetings held during the summer racing season. Board track racing is an extremely hazardous sport, and many thoughtful people were appalled at the increasing number of gory accidents now decimating the ranks of the popular ace riders. In many instances, both the national and local press attacked auto and motorcycle racing as a murderous spectacle. While large numbers of people were by this time avowed racing fans, the sport was producing a very definite negative attitude toward motorcycling in general. While the tracks offered the vicarious thrill of a gladiatorial contest, the spindly and overly fast racing machines, with their short fire belching exhaust stacks emitting clouds of pungent burned castor oil fumes, were scarcely calculated to inspire the fans to acquire a motorcycle for their personal transport.

Both trade and spectator interest in motorcycle competition narrowed somewhat after 1920, when Ignatz Schwinn formally announced that henceforth the Excelsior Motor Company was officially supporting no more competition activities. Its engineering department had developed a fantastically powerful ohc 61 cubic inch racing engine late in 1919, and had built about six machines, together with a spare engine for each, for use by the factory team. Their star rider, Bob Perry, was tragically killed while testing one of these machines at Los Angeles Ascot Speedway on January 3rd. The story is told that in his grief at receiving the news Schwinn, who had come to regard Perry as a son, rushed to the racing shop and smashed several of the spare engines with a sledge hammer. A single machine with a spare engine remained at large in the hands of Waldo Korn, who proceeded to ride it as a private entrant for two succeeding seasons.

Meanwhile, at Dodge City, now hailed by the trade press as the motorcycling Indianapolis, plans were being made to revive the formerly popular pre-war 300 Mile Classic. Traditionally held on July 4th, it was scheduled this year for the 5th, as the 4th fell on a Sunday and the Race Committee thought it best not to risk the wrath of the stern midwest fundamental religious organizations. The town readied itself for an anticipated crowd of 30,000 fans, and the streets and many of the shops were again decorated with flags and bunting. The factory teams and private entrants had arrived a few days earlier for practicing and review of the course, as well as a final drill in pit stop procedures.

On the day of the race, H-D's now famous 'Wrecking Crew' was ready for action, manned by Roy Artley, Leonard Buckner, Jim Davis, Ralph Hepburn, Maldwyn Jones, Walter Higley, Don Marks, and Ray Weishaar.

The official Indian Team consisted of Albert 'Shrimp' Burns, M.K. 'Curley' Fredericks, now riding for the Wigwam, Bob Newman, and Gene Walker.

The H-D machines were all of the pocket valve type, but Indian fielded two 8 valvers first raced in 1919, together with the new side valve specials designed by Charles B.Franklin. The race was started behind a pace car, which pulled off the track after the first lap, to a rolling start. Gene Walker blasted into the lead with his 8 valver, closely followed by Burns on a similar model, with H-D's Jones and Hepburn coming up behind. The leaders went to the pits in the 31st lap, and Jones took the lead on his H-D to set a new 100 mile time of one hour 11 minutes and 12 seconds for an 84.22 mph average. Jones went to the pits at lap 57, with Ludlow now going into the lead and into a seesaw contest with Burns for the next 80 miles. At Jones' pit stop, Higley and Davis alternated in the lead in response to orders from the pits, with Jones returning in the 267th mile to set a new lap record of 81.76 mph for the 300 mile distance. This shaved a few minutes off the great Ralph Hepburn's distance record hung up at the Ascot Speedway the preceding June.

Burns and Jones then alternated in the lead until both were stopped by blown engines. Davis took the lead at the 119th lap and held it to the finish, taking the checkered flag. He crossed the line 2½ laps ahead of Gene Walker, who was followed by Weishaar on his H-D for third place, with Speck Warner, Indian, fourth. Davis averaged 81.8 mph for a new record. Eleven laps were recorded at over 90 mph, with Bob Newman on one of the new side valve Indians topping the field with an incredible 96 mph run. The fastest H-D lap was by Weishaar at 92.25. The Excelsior contingent, all riding as private owners, now without factory support, failed to finish.

The National Motorcycle Road Race of 1920 held at Marion, Indiana, has been described by motorcycle historians as the last large event of its kind to be held in the United States. Road racing in this country had never been popular, as local prejudice against both the machines and the sport precluded closing public roads suitable for the purpose. Then too, such contests were never attractive to potential promoters, as it was next to impossible to control a paying crowd within any sort of enclosure that could afford a satisfactory view of the contest.

The Marion Chamber of Commerce, in anticipation of vast crowds visiting the city, donated $5,000 to help grade and repair the five mile course, and to lay a coat of dust-inhibiting oil on the surface. A visitor's bureau was set up to co-ordinate the filling of available accommodations, and much advertising space was purchased in various publications to announce the event. The city government also co-operated to the extend of adding $2,200 to the winners' purses, already subsidized by accessory manufacturers.

Under clear skies the race was rolled off behind a pace car, with Shrimp Burns on a side valve Indian jumping to an early lead within a few seconds. Clearing a small mound of earth at the foot of the stands with both wheels in the air, he blasted around the course in 4 minutes and .02 seconds for a new lap record of 77 mph.

The H-D team kept well behind, on orders from the pits, in order to save their engines for the finish. The five Excelsior riders, now riding as private entrants, all followed suit. Burns rode on at full throttle, and in the 13th lap set a new course record of 4.01. On the 24th lap he broke his chain, and Ray Weishaar of the Wrecking Crew took the lead. Burns soon returned with a new chain, and with another desperate full throttle ride managed to overhaul Weishaar, racking up a 75.8 mph average for the first 100 miles, the fastest speed yet recorded in the world on a road course.

On the 32nd lap Burns again lost a chain, the flailing end of which tore off his fuel pipe and grounded him permanently. Weishaar continued at a somewhat restrained pace, winning at 71 mph. Leonard Buckner on a side valve Indian was a close second, with Jim Davis, H-D, just behind. A trio of Excelsior riders finished almost in a dead heat for fourth, fifth, and sixth places. With an attendance of over 20,000 spectators positioned around the five mile rectangular course, AMA-sponsored road racing in America was not seen tor another three decades. Prize money of $1,000, $500, $300, and $100 was paid for the first four places, together with bonus lap money provided by accessory manufacturers. At the end of the race, Weishaar commented that he could have made better time had he not been afraid of blowing his engine or breaking a chain. William Harley and Arthur Davidson, together with a contingent of factory personnel, were on hand to applaud the winner, and all received the congratulations of Indian's General Manager, Frank Weshler, who was ever a generous loser as well as a formidable opponent.

That Fall, H-D machines swept the board at the National Championship Sidecar races held at Greeley, Colorado on September 18th to 20th. Lester Foote and Frank Kunce captured all eleven first places between them, with twenty major places. These victories were somewhat hollow, however, as neither Excelsior or Indian fielded factory-supported teams. The competition offered by the private entrants at the event was so futile that it was described as nothing short of pathetic by the trade press.

Motorcycling activities and registration of machines in proportion to the population since the end of the war was now centered in the Far Western and Southwestern region of the United States. This was due to the all-weather riding climate that usually prevailed, coupled with the fact that the vast distances prompted the need for private transport due to the lack of public facilities. While the

The immortal 'Wrecking Crew' at Dodge City, on July 4, 1920. From left: Maldwyn Jones, Fred Ludlow, Ralph Hepburn, Jim Davis, Ray Weishaar, Otto Walker, and Walter Higley. (C. May).

The new Juneau Avenue factory building nearing completion, in 1920.

Eastern part of the country had a vastly more dense population, motoring was usually confined to the spring and summer months due to the rigors of the climate. Up to this time, Indian was far and away the sales leader, largely due to the efforts of such aggressive dealers as Guy Urquehardt in San Diego, C. Will Risdon in Los Angeles, and Hap Alzina in Oakland. In addition, many smaller but equally successful satellite dealers were to be found in the smaller cities. Excelsior was also well represented, as were a few less prominent makes such as Reading Standard and the utility type Cleveland. H-D's interests were well looked after in the San Francisco Bay area by Dudley Perkins, but the situation farther south was less fortunate. H-D's representatives in both San Diego and Los Angeles were, for various reasons, delivering only a token number of machines. Arthur Davidson, in appraising the situation, ordered the company's Northwestern factory representative, Verne Guthrie, to round up new dealers for the area. The story goes that Guthrie had recently become acquainted with one Rich Budelier, a pioneer motorcyclist and presently an instructor in Economics at the University of Utah. Guthrie was somehow able to induce the latter to move to San Diego and take over the ailing dealership. Budelier, a genial six foot giant of a man with an engaging manner and a persuasive personality, while possessed of no mechanical ability, was able within a short time to make the San Diego franchise a resounding success.

In spite of substantial public support of motorcycle competition, members of the industry now noted with alarm the sudden drop in motorcycle sales during the 1921 season.

At the close of the war, both H-D and Indian, as the leading manufacturers, each had the potential capacity of producing 35,000 units per year. Excelsior, with somewhat smaller facilities, could assemble about 25,000 machines per year. The third string firms had possibly a cumulative capacity of turning out some 6,000 machines per year, which matched their somewhat limited dealer representation. But with a production potentiality of 100,000 machines per year, the industry actually shipped only a third of this at the year's end. H-D, with its giant Juneau Avenue complex now fully implemented, could ship only slightly over 17,000 machines in response to dealers' orders. Indian, the production leader for the last decade and a half, shipped only 19,000 machines, far below the 30,000 projection, most of these being their popular 37 cubic inch Scout.

Many of the industry's executives at once blamed the soaring production of the cheap car, which was now coming to the fore in the US transportation scene. Henry Ford's production of his immortal Model T was such that he could lower its price to $400 at the factory gate, and boast that the company was now adding one new dealership every day. General Motors Chevrolet Division halted production of the large 'Baby Grand' model, and a new small model appeared that sold for only $25 more than the Model T. The ebullient William Crapo Durant was shortly to introduce his Star car, which would add some three million units to the low cost car parade. With their modest prices and their dealer representation now blanketing the country, the family man promptly ignored the sidecar combination, and opted for the stability of four wheels, full weather protection, and four to five passenger carrying capacity.

While this turn of events had ominous portent, the factories themselves chose publicly to ignore what was happening, and continued to issue glowing releases to the trade press containing highly exaggerated production and sales figures. It may be recalled that flamboyant publicity for well over the past decade had now, by tradition, become an almost inseparable adjunct to the motorcycle industry. This trend was undoubtedly inaugurated by one John J.O'Conner, a turn-of-the-century bicycle racer with a flair for journalism and a long time friend of George M.Hendee. The latter had appointed him Indian's Publicity Manager in 1909, and his subsequent exaggerated Victorian prose was to regale the motorcycling public for the next two generations. Other company house organ scribes followed suit, and motorcycle reporting assumed the literary stature of a vaudeville handbill. O'Conner's florid pronouncements of Indian's excellence paralleled Biblical prophesies, and in H-D's house publication, *The Dealer,* were such masterpieces of hyperbole that most surviving copies were ashamedly destroyed by company orders in later years.

In addition, the trade press now assumed a head-in-the-sand attitude toward the motorcycle's falling popularity. With the alarming rate of attrition among its manufacturers since 1916, advertising revenues had dropped accordingly. Haunted by the spectre of declining circulation, they lived in mortal fear of antagonizing those firms who were left. Outside of a few cautious editorials commenting on the need in some areas for cleaner dealer premises and the use of more advanced sales techniques, the

Ralph Hepburn receiving the congratulations of his fans at his 1921 win at Dodge City. *(C.May).*

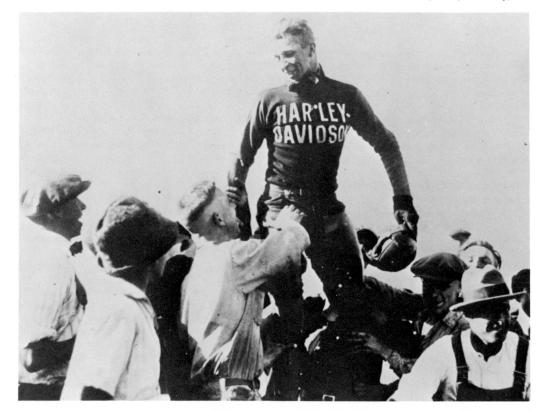

abrupt decline in motorcycle sales was never mentioned. Definitive or objective road tests of newly introduced models were never aired, and the offering of unsuitable machines or glaringly apparent faults in existing machines were suffered in silence. This state of affairs was particularly confusing to the possible aspiring novice buyer, who, in reading either company advertising matter or descriptions of currently offered machines in the trade press, could only conclude that the industry produced pluperfect machines. Added to this was the editorial inference that the American motoring public was on the verge of abandoning four wheels for two!

The only exception to this journalistic fairyland was the editorial offerings of H. W. Parsons, of *Motorcycle and Bicycle Illustrated,* the sole gadfly of the industry. He noted that the motorcycle was now no longer a medium of transport, and was becoming the toy of the wealthy sportsman. Due to the ever increasing costs of high performance machines, motorcycling was fast becoming an expensive form of entertainment. As an extension of this supposition, it was also becoming a 'gentleman's sport'. Shortly afterwards, Parsons emphasized how motorcycling was now appealing to an ever-shrinking minority. Compounding this problem, he became further concerned with the antisocial behavior of a growing minority within a minority, and was perhaps the first to express apprehension about motorcycling's potential image.

The artificial veil of silence thrown over the current state of the motorcycle market was at long last flung aside, not by the sycophantic trade press, but through the pages of a trade paper newly published for the benefit of the automobile industry. It came about when Norman G. Shidle, a young automotive engineer with a journalistic flair, founded in January 1919 a trade paper which he called *Automotive Industries.* Aside from his interest in the technical development of the automobile, he had recently become concerned with the problems of sales and marketing.

While automotive design and engineering improvements had done much to enhance the dependability of the post-war car, together with improved production techniques resulting in the registration of over eight million automobiles in the United States by 1920 (more than two thirds of all motor vehicles registered in the world), all was not well within a supposedly healthy industry. Nearly five hundred individual makes of vehicle were being offered to the market, yet the number of firms going into bankruptcy had become alarming. Most of these failures were due to the various manufacturers' failure correctly to predict the types and designs that would appeal to potential buyers.

In a series of articles, Shidle endeavored to point out the solutions to these problems through methods of marketing analysis, which were a forerunner of the science of market analysis which is today an integral part of all manufacturing endeavor. These articles also included data on setting up costing schedules for production planning.

At this point, Leslie D. (Dick) Richards, whom we have met before as the Associate Editor of *Motorcyclist and Bicyclist Illustrated,* filled the position of Publicity Manager for Indian in January 1920. Almost at once he became highly concerned with the problem of diminished motorcycle sales. An inveterate student of the transportation industry, he had lately been studying Shidle's articles on automotive marketing, and at length wrote him a letter suggesting that a similar inquiry be made into the motorcycle problem.

At the same time, and quite coincidentally, Hap Scherer, H-D's Publicity Manager, who was currently engaged in promoting the company's 37 cubic inch Sport Twin model, was also giving serious thought to the general public rejection of the motorcycle. It was later noted that Charles Cleland, Reading Standard's Publicity Manager, as well as the Publicity Manager of Excelsior, whose name is now forgotten, were exploring the same problem. During an interview in 1974, Richards told the author that Shidle had told him of his correspondence with representatives of the other factories during the summer and fall of 1920.

The upshot of the matter was that Shidle attended the National Motorcycle Show held that year in New York's Madison Square Gardens. During the ten day meeting he arranged a conference at the Algonquin Hotel with Richards, Scherer, Cleland, and the Excelsior representative. The object of the conference was to obtain from the various members of the industry certain data including recent production figures that comprised the number of units and types of models, together with their methods of projecting production, future sales prospects, and methods of determining material acquisitions. In return, Shidle and his staff agreed to conduct a marketing analysis for the benefit of the motorcycle industry. He also revealed that a member of his staff, one Raymond Prescott, was currently being subsidized as a student in advanced economics at Columbia University, probably the first scientific inquiry into domestic transportation marketing analysis.

During the course of the meeting, Shidle found that he was working in a rather sensitive area, as with the general declining motorcycle sales, each manufacturer had been careful to conceal actual sales or production figures, continuing to issue optimistic and highly exaggerated reports for the benefit of the trade press reporters.

While the motorcycle representatives were initially skeptical of Shidle's motives in the matter,

HARLEY-DAVIDSON WINNING ROCKY MOUNTAIN CHAMPIONSHIP OVERLAND PARK RACE TRACK, DENVER, COLORADO.

See photo caption on picture. *(C. May)*.

(for, after all, he had been originally preoccupied with their four-wheel competitors), his evident sincerity ultimately won their confidence, and all co-operated fully with his requests for information on their individual operations. At the same moment, all present agreed that for the time being at least, their deliberations must be kept secret, as if their respective factory top management were to learn of their divulging such data to one another or to an outsider, they would all no doubt be subject to instant dismissal.

Several additional meetings were held in various New York hotels that Fall, the motorcycle representatives journeying to that city on the pretext of other business commitments. After a few of such gatherings, the Excelsior representative elected to withdraw from the group, leaving Richards, Scherer, and Cleland to carry on.

Shidle's ultimate conclusions in the matter, aided by Prescott and the rest of his research staff, ultimately coincided with those already arrived at by Richards and Scherer, who had become warm personal friends. They concluded that the industry's emphasis on the heavyweight V twin models, together with extensive commitments to racing, had alienated the majority of potential American transportation buyers. The typical American motorcycle had grown progressively heavier, was consequently difficult to manhandle within a confined space, required much muscular energy to start, possessed an offensively loud exhaust note, and appealed almost exclusively to athletic young men whose interest was very likely to diminish with advancing age.

Shidle was particularly critical of the general emphasis on racing and competition, which, while enjoying a rather broad public appeal as a spectator sport to those craving thrills and excitement, had now firmly planted in the public mind the idea that motorcycling was essentially a dangerous undertaking. This simply led to the conclusion that most of the people attending race meets could never be

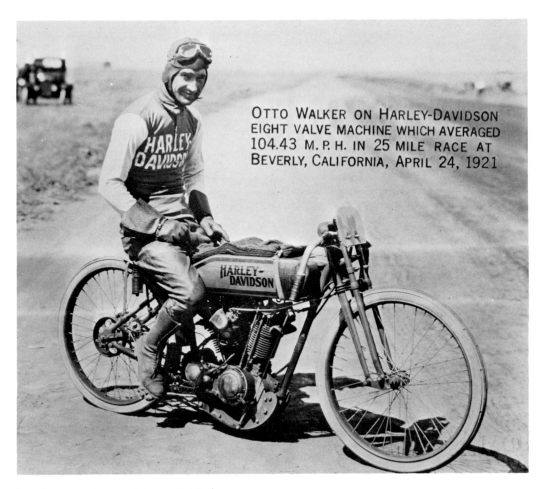

OTTO WALKER ON HARLEY-DAVIDSON
EIGHT VALVE MACHINE WHICH AVERAGED
104.43 M. P. H. IN 25 MILE RACE AT
BEVERLY, CALIFORNIA, APRIL 24, 1921

See photo caption on picture. *(C. May)*.

interested in the motorcycle as their own personal transport. The further conclusion was that a potentially vast market for low-powered, low-cost utility machines, originally the target of the turn-of-the-
century experimenters seeking to offer mass low cost transportation, had been totally ignored for at
least the past decade.

For the manufacturers whose representatives had participated in supplying data, Shidle and his
staff offered their confidential conclusions: H-D had an efficient production capability, enhanced by
their limited model variation, and a strong dealer representation; Indian suffered from a lack of co-
ordination between yearly sales projections and the acquisition of raw and component materials, but
also enjoyed a strong dealer representation; Excelsior offered limited production, but had the artificial
cushion of a vast bicycle market to offset any production inefficiencies; Reading Standard offered
nearly a dozen different models with a yearly production of under 2,000 units which seriously impaired
production efficiency and was further hampered by insufficient capitalization.

Shidle subsequently published these conclusions in a two-part article in his own publication,
*Automotive Industries*, without reference to his confidential meetings with the motorcycle representatives. Entitled 'Where is the Motorcycle Going?' copies were mailed for reprinting to the motorcycle
trade press. The first part appeared in his April 27th, 1921 issue, the second on May 4th. The only
motorcycle editor with the courage to reprint Shidle's article was H. W. Parsons, Richards' former
employer, of *Motorcyclist and Bicyclist Illustrated*.

Hap Scherer was particularly gratified at Shidle's conclusions, as he, like Richards, had for some
time been convinced that the domestic motorcycle industry had for too long been catering to a much
limited segment of the motorcycle market. His willingness to assume the position of Publicity Manager
at H-D was inspired by the hope that he could in some way focus public attention on the genuine merits

of the mediumweight Sport Twin model, which could have a broad appeal to people seeking dependable low cost utility transportation that was not related to high speed travel or competition activities. Since the introdution of that model, he had been able to convince H-D's management of the need to devote much space in the *Enthusiast* to articles on it, embracing touring and utility activities, as well as its suitability for both youthful and feminine riders. At the same moment, he felt somewhat reticent about revealing his part in Shidle's searching investigation into the matter, knowing full well of President Walter Davidson's almost paranoic aversion to any co-operation with competitors, even if such could be of benefit to the general industry.

Following the publication of Shidle's reports in his own publication, and the exposition of the same by Parsons, Richards decided to take a bold step and reveal the extent of his participation in the matter to his chief at Indian, Frank J. Weschler. After some deliberation the latter, although somewhat taken aback, gave him full authority to take over the management of Indians' material procurement facilities based on marketing projections, a move which was later credited with saving Indian during an extremely critical period of its survival history. Scherer, who had been in close touch with Richards since the meetings with Shidle, and after much soul searching, decided to take up the matter with President Davidson. In later years, Scherer revealed to intimates that Davidson's reaction was almost predictable. In a stormy session in his executive offices, he berated Scherer for acting without authorization from H-D's top management, for revealing critical company secrets, and for generally proceeding in a disloyal if not downright traitorous manner. Following a lively three-hour meeting, during which Scherer futilely attempted to defend his position and explain his concern for the current depressed state of the industry, he was summarily discharged with his salary terminated as of that date.

When word of the incident reached H-D's now widespread dealer organization there was much sympathy for Scherer's position in the matter. Not a few of the dealers who were aware of the industry's problems were in agreement with him, and all conceded that his promotional efforts on behalf of the company and in the promotion of the Sport Twin were all headed in the right direction. To add fuel to the fire, Scherer almost at once was offered the position of Sales Manager in Rich Budelier's newly organized dealership in Los Angeles, another controversial aspect of H-D history which subsequently will be considered.

As an aftermath of this rather turbulent affair, it will be noticed that in no subsequent issues of the *Enthusiast* are individual employees or their doings ever given undue exposure, the emphasis being on the activities of the Founders themselves. Brief personal items were allocated only to current competition stars, sales personnel or dealers, with no continuing coverage given to any individual. What with the sympathy within the trade for Hap Scherer, and the general consternation generated by his dismissal, the Company was apparently taking no chances on creating any more anti-heroes.

In spite of falling sales, the H-D Company entered the 1921 racing season with renewed efforts. Their first memorable win of the season saw the now immortal 'Wrecking Crew' become the first factory team anywhere in the world to win a contest at over 100 mph. This occurred at the new post-war Fresno, California board track, where both H-D and Indian fielded their best professional talent, riding ohv, side valve, and pocket valve machines. Out of four main events, Team Captain Otto Walker placed first, with his teammates taking nine out of twelve 1-2-3 places. Walker's wins were all run at speeds of well of 100 mph.

In the Fifty Mile Race, Walker, in a terrific burst of speed on the third lap, made the mile oval in 33 seconds for a time of 108.7 mph. His teammates all finished with 102-103 mph averages, as did second place winner, Gene Walker, on a side valve Indian.

A month later, on April 24th, Walker won the 25 mile race at 104.4 mph on the very fast Beverly Hills boards, with teammate Jim Davis a very close second. Davis went on to win the 50 mile race at 97.3 mph, with another teammate a fractional second, a machine length behind. Shrimp Burns, on a side valve Indian, won the fifteen mile Consolation Race at 102.5 mph.

At the fifth running of the Dodge City 300 Mile Classic, the three major manufacturers were represented, although the Excelsior contingent were now running as private entrants and had to supply their own fuel, spare parts, and pit organization. The track was opened for practicing a week before the race. Shrimp Burns racked up a new lap record of 1 minute 14 seconds, on an old 8 valve Indian at 97.4 mph, with a second lap in 1 minute 16.5 seconds, with most of his Milwaukee teammates turning out averages only fractionally slower.

Rain and thunderstorms muddied the track a couple of days before the race, but clearing skies and warmer weather soon dried it up, to the relief of all concerned. H-D's starting group now consisted of Jim Davis, Ralph Hepburn, Walter Higley, Fred Ludlow, Otto Walker, Team Captain, and Ray Weishaar. All were mounted on pocket valve machines, except Hepburn, who rode a specially tuned 8 valver.

Indian's team included Shrimp Burns, Floyd Dreyer, Curley Fredericks, Don Pope, Johnny Seymour, Hammond Springs, and Speck Warner.

Del Du Chene with his authentically-restored 1920 magneto-equipped 37 cu.in. horizontally opposed Sport Twin model. This machine is identical to one acquired by the author as a schoolboy in 1927. *(John R. Stinson).*

Excelsior was represented by Wells Bennett, Warren Cropp, Waldo Korn, Les Parkhurst, and Joe Wolter. All were riding rebuilt big valve models from previous seasons, as the fantastically fast ohc engines had been destroyed by Schwinn, and the few remaining examples had already exhausted their spare part supply.

The race was flagged off at 11.00 am, the riders pushing out in rows of four behind a pace car. Hepburn gunned his fantastically fast 8 valve H-D into the lead, and held a blistering pace through the 103rd mile, when he went to the pits for fuel and oil. Fredericks, Indian, and Cropp, Excelsior, with Otto Walker, had been dueling for the second spot, all well ahead of the pack in second, third, and fourth positions. Walker was now narrowly ahead during Hepburn's pit stop, but the latter pulled out to regain the lead position. Cropp and Fredericks next dropped out with blown engines, allowing Bennett, Excelsior, to gain a close second to Hepburn, making the best showing of the Chicago contingent. His advantage was short lived, however, as he went out in the 83rd lap with a dropped valve. Hepburn bored on to widen his lead to the finish, setting a new record of 87 mph at the 200th mile. Team Manager Ottaway attempted to flag Hepburn into reducing his speed somewhat to save his engine, but was ignored by the latter who forged on to ride a 103.5 mph 149th lap, the next to the last before he took the checkered flag. He finished twelve minutes ahead of Indian's Johnny Seymour who was second, with Ludlow, H-D, a close third, with Weishaar and Walker fourth and fifth just barely ahead of Indian mounted Don Pope.

T.R.Allchin and his modified 584 cc
Sport Twin at Brooklands in 1921.
With twin carburettors and increased
compression ratio he was able to
attain a speed of 68.90 mph. *(The
Motor Cycle)*.

Hepburn collected $1,300 in prize money, $1,000 for his win and the balance for record lap times. He also took the Schebler Carburetor Award for the winning machine.

The last big race of 1921 was the Grand National, held at the New York State Fairground track at Syracuse. It was here that Fred Ludlow made his name immortal in the annals of American racing by winning in one race the National Five, Ten, Twenty Five, and Fifty Mile Championships. Noting his faultlessly running engine, Ludlow was carefully shepherded through the pack by Team Manager Ottaway, aided in keeping his proper position by fellow members of the Wrecking Crew. At the proper moment, Ludlow forged into the lead, much to the delight of a capacity crowd who were on their feet for most of the contest. He racked up record speeds for the distance of 81.8 mph for the mile to 77.6 mph for the fifty miles.

While Ludlow had not been a consistent front runner in previous contests, he was a key member of the team through his faultless riding, and his ability, along with the others, to follow prearranged team tactics that made H-D the spectacular winner in most of the great races.

In spite of the sweeping victories achieved during the imemdiate pre-war and subsequent post-war racing seasons, and the invaluable prestige that inevitably resulted, H-D's management at last decided to terminate all official sponsorship of competition activities. It was all too apparent, then as now, that victories in any category of motor sport accrue to the organization willing to spend the most money, and the cost had been tremendous. The costs of the Company's final racing season were said to amount to about $200,000, comparable to a million dollars at today's reporting, with salaries of $15,000 to $20,000 for the star riders, as well as the mechanics' wages, the cost and maintenance of the machines, plus the expenses of travel and lodging while on the circuit.

It was also apparent that in spite of H-D's spectacular wins in most of the big national races, a total domination of the sport by one make was practically impossible. On the many hundreds of county fair horse tracks throughout the country, local Excelsior and Indian enthusiasts with either personal skills in speed tuning, or access to dealers or mechanics with such ability, racked up creditable victories. Then too, sectional loyalties were such that these competing makes might well dominate the market in any given area.

In a formal release to the trade press in December, President Davidson stated 'We find that we have become engaged in two distinct businesses at the factory: one the business of racing, with a complete separate organization, and the other the legitimate business of making and selling motorcycles.'

Chief Engineer Harley further elaborated on the change in company policy stating 'We found that instead of racing activities consuming only a small portion of the attention of the engineering department, the demands had gradually increased until it was all out of proportion to the results ob-

D.H.Davidson (no relation to the Founders) on this 989 cc H-D was the first rider ever to exceed 100 mph at Brooklands. The machine was originally fitted with a short wheelbase board track racing frame. When this proved unmanageable on the rough surface, a standard roadster frame was substituted. *(The Motor Cycle)*.

tained. With the new arrangement, the entire Engineering Department will be devoting all its time to the solving of production and engineering problems connected with the production of standard roadster machines, and the purchaser will benefit accordingly'.

It was emphasized, however, that a very limited number of racing machines would be produced for the benefit of qualified competitors, but without any official financial subsidizing of their maintenance.

The actual reason for the termination of factory-sponsored competition was, of course, the fact that sales had fallen to the point that only 11,000 machines were shipped in 1920, as compared to slightly over 17,000 ordered during 1917 and 1918.

William Davidson now streamlined the production lines for lesser production and better efficiency, trimming back the work force to about a thousand from a war time high of 2,500. The extra production facility adjacent to the main factory was now disposed of and the company tightened its belt for whatever might lie ahead. It was also coincidentally announced that henceforth the company would distribute no more bicycles, once thought to be an indispensable adjunct to a successful motorcycle dealership. As the bicycles had not been made in Milwaukee, but bought out from large manufacturing concerns such as Butler Brothers, the change saved the distribution costs, and these were now transferred to the Davis Sewing Machine Company, whose already intact bicycle subsidiary would now handle the spare parts for all machines formerly marketed under the H-D label.

The Indian company was in an even more dire situation. Its 1920-1921 production had now fallen to about 7,000 units, pathetically below the 20,000 figure of 1920. Due to the heroic efforts of General Manager Frank Weschler, the aid of Dick Richards' marketing and procurement date from the Shidle reports, and the popularity of Charles Franklin's immortal Scout, the company muddled through.

The Excelsior company merely cut back production on its once popular 61 cubic inch big twin, and concentrated on its newly-acquired four cylinder Henderson, which was now becoming the most popular mount for law enforcement use. Cushioned by its vast bicycle empire, the economic losses in motorcycle manufacture were scarcely noticed.

Cleveland, Emblem, Iver-Johnson, Reading Standard, and Schickel limped on with miniscule production, and an industry capable of producing 100,000 machines annually now turned out a bare 25,000.

The trade press continued to ignore the industry's crisis, except for Parsons' reports on the Shidle marketing survey. The only other exposure of the matter was from L.E.Fowler, an automotive engineer who edited the Chicago based *Motorcycling and Bicycling*, and who had designed the Cleveland 63 lightweight two-stroke in 1914. This was aired by means of an interview between Fowler and James Ward Packard, the then retired designer and one time Chief Engineer of the prestigious Packard Motor Car Company. Packard, who had been a pioneer bicyclist during the high wheel days, predicted not only a revival of interest in bicycling, but a possible vast market in lightweight utility-type motorcycles, provided they could be mass produced to sell at reasonable prices, be dependable, and above all, be easy to start. Prophetic words from an automotive pioneer, which would become a reality four decades later through the efforts of Japanese motorcycle engineers!

An unfortunate aside to the H-D Company's rather abrupt announcement concerning the termination of factory sponsored racing occurred at the State Fair races at Phoenix, Arizona in September. The Wrecking Crew had been sent to the Southwest following the Nationals at Syracuse, with high hopes of rounding out the season with another victory. While the team swept the field, as predicted, it now found to its consternation that the factory had not forwarded the necessary funds to pay for their train fare to their respective homes, as was the usual procedure. While the mechanics apparently had the means of returning to Milwaukee, along with the costs of shipping the machines, the Wrecking Crew, who were mostly lightly funded on arrival in anticipation of their usual salaries and expenses, now found themselves stranded. They were ultimately able to raise the train fare by pawning their watches and floating a small loan from the local H-D dealer. Varying reports of the matter were furnished in later years by surviving team members. Some have stated that President Davidson refused to accept collect long distance telephone calls in Milwaukee and that he ultimately dispatched a terse telegram, instructing them to return to their own homes without visiting Milwaukee!

Fred Ludlow, as H-D's top star at the termination of their official racing participation, was particularly bitter concerning the treatment meted out to him by Walter Davidson. A natural born rider, he was also a skilled mechanic and tuner, and had hoped for a future position with the company in the engineering department. Davidson had been noncommittal concerning his requests in the matter, but according to Ludlow he had not given a negative answer. After he had returned to his home in Los Angeles, Ludlow, with no other employment immediately in view, acquired a 'J' model sidecar outfit, together with some spectacular motion picture racing film footage, and toured the country giving film shows and lectures dealing with past racing seasons. Ludlow's presentation was generally well recieved, but on a subsequent trip to Milwaukee and a meeting with Walter Davidson, the latter castigated him quite severely concerning the subject matter of his films, stating that as much footage was devoted to Excelsior and Indian competitors as was allocated to H-D. In spite of Ludlow's protestations that any race by necessity featured competition, Davidson was adamant, and Ludlow hurriedly departed. He then defected to the Wigwam, to become shop foreman in C. Will Risdon's prosperous Indian agency in Los Angeles. He subsequently became a motorcycle traffic officer for the city of South Pasadena, retiring at the age of 60 in 1955. During the same period, he took part in various speed events on both Indian and Henderson machines, racking up numerous records that are still well remembered. At this writing he resides in a convalescent home in Pasadena, a much revered figure in American motorcycle competition history.

H-D engines and other components were utilized in two rather divergent efforts at producing cycle cars during the 1920-1921 season. The Grey Light Car Company, a miniscule operation in Denver, Colorado, built two prototypes of a light roadster fitted with H-D 61 cubic inch 'J' type engines and gearboxes and motorcycle wheels. Bearing a close resemblance to the later Austin Seven, it was rather heavily built to withstand the rough country roads of the Denver area. With 800 lbs of empty weight, it was of necessity geared rather low, and, while it ran satisfactorily, it proved to be too limited in overall performance to satisfy its buyers. The other effort took place in France, where Automobiles Rally, Colombes, Seine, put together a Bedelia type cycle car with a narrow wheel track and tandem seating. A standard 61 cubic inch 'J' type twin and gearbox were fitted, the final drive being through a pair of belts to the rear wheels. A somewhat archaic vehicle in concept, it gave way to a more conventional light car with a four cylinder water-cooled engine after three or four prototypes were built. The original components were purchased from H-D's Paris representative.

# Chapter 3

# The Roaring Twenties

AFTER A MINOR ECONOMIC DISLOCATION DURING THE FALL OF 1920 AND THE LATE Spring of 1921 due to a general reorganization of the country's post-war production facilities, the United States entered an era of almost unprecedented prosperity. Physically unscathed by the war, and sustaining but minimal casualties as compared with their European allies, the country had few problems in converting the economy to peacetime pursuits. With the rest of the world's producing nations still prostrate from the war's devastation, the United States quickly became the world leader in manufacturing. Yankee ingenuity now turned its attention to applying enhanced production knowledge to the development of new products for a seemingly inexhaustible consumer market.

The social order had also undergone rapid changes. Many of the young men who grew up in sectionalized rural isolation had gained new sophistication on foreign wartime assignments. Women now found a new freedom in the employment opportunities opened to them when male help was not available. Coupled with these factors, there was a growing public disillusionment with the government and political system when it soon became apparent that the 'war-to-end war' and 'peace without victory' was a myth when the realities of Versailles were critically examined. Added to this, the futility of attempting to legislate morality through the passage of the Prohibition amendment and the consequent growth of organized crime to supply the thirst for alcoholic spirits, further nurtured national disillusionment.

The newly inaugurated President, former Ohio senator Warren G.Harding, was a sensual man who was as corrupt as he was handsome. Succinctly he stated that 'normalcy' was now the order of the day, which was translated by the man in the street to mean the pursuit of happiness and the almighty dollar.

The most sought-after commodity, after a part of the general demand for time and labor saving household appliances was met, was now the automobile, as both an escape from isolation and to satisfy the natural human urge to travel. By 1921, over 400 distinct makes of cars weere on the market, ranging from undistinguished machines assembled from proprietary parts in localized areas, to the vast series production from industrial giants like Ford and General Motors. The former's production soon increased to the point where every other car on the road was a Ford, together with a host of small Chevrolets and a dozen lesser makes of similar size. With prices of such vehicles now hovering around $400.00 at the factory gate, the casual shopper for transportation would now no longer seriously consider the typical American motorcycle. This particularly applied to the family sidecar market, which disappeared almost overnight.

In consequence of this turn of events, the way in which motorcycles were marketed changed drastically. Following the 1913-1914 boom in two wheelers, many prospering dealers in the larger cities had acquired extensive and attractive premises, often rivaling those of adjoining automobile sales establishements. With the falling off of sales, not a few of these dealers dropped motorcycles in favor of cars. Other dealers, in being forced to operate on a reduced scale, left their large quarters in prime business locations in favor of smaller and less pretentious premises in less prestigious locations. Many dealers in smaller cities and towns found themselves forced into low rent unpretentious or even ramshackle quarters, which further diminished the marketing status of motorcycles.

As the motorcycle declined as a pure transportation entity, the character of the rider also changed. The typical motorcycle owner of the early 1920s was now more than likely to be a blue collar artisan or cowboy type, with a predilection for high speeds or adventure. He was complimented in some degree by a more prosperous, if iconoclastic sporting type, the thrill-seeking undergraduate, an occasional budget-minded commuter and, here and there, an adventuresome feminine enthusiast. Generally speaking, the riding of a motorcycle was now not considered to be entirely socially respectable. The scene was compounded by the rowdy speed demon who rammed a crowbar up his silencer system to destroy its effectiveness, and proceeded to further alienate the general public against motorcycling in any form.

Arthur Davidson, as General Sales Manager, was at once cognizant of the industry's mounting problems, and took steps to remedy them wherever possible. The obvious approach was to strengthen dealership representation. As all franchises were subject to yearly confirmation, wavering or ineffectual dealerships were cancelled, and more promising prospects were solicited to replace them. The regional Factory representatives responsible for covering the various geographical areas of the country were given crash courses in retail sales techniques and ordered to relay their knowledge to the individual dealers in their respective territories. Particular emphasis was directed toward encouraging individual dealers to clean up their premises, as too often new machines were displayed in windows so obscured by dirt and cobwebs that a prospective buyer could scarcely examine the machine displayed behind it!

While H-D production was concentrated on the now refined 'J' models, single cylinder Model 35 production having been terminated, much effort was also made to emphasize the Sport Twin, although much of its sales impetus was missing due to the loss of its most enthusiastic exponent, former Publicity Manager Hap Scherer. Orders were disappointing, in spite of its sales to such diverse non-motorcycling types as famous theatrical impressario, Daniel Froman, and Norway's dignified Crown Prince Olaf. Much space in the *Enthusiast* was devoted to its promotion, no doubt inspired by both the critical state of the motorcycle market and the admonitions of Dick Richards of Indian and the now absent Hap Scherer.

The 61 cubic inch 'J' model remained the backbone of H-D's sales efforts, and retained a hard core of loyal followers, mostly young riders in whose short span of memory the 'J' remained as THE classical H-D model. In response to the demand for more power, especially in heavy duty side-car or commercial box body outfits, a 74 cubic inch model was now offered. While it obviously offered an improvement for this use, its slightly higher top speed and enhanced low speed torque for faster acceleration was an immediate attraction to solo enthusiasts. The new model was also widely used as a sidecar outfit by transporters of illicit spirits, as such an outfit, in a good state of tune, could usually outrun pursuing law enforcement units who mostly used automobiles. It also offered strong competition to the newly introduced Indian Chief which, as a complement to the already popular Scout, was also a favorite transport in the now lucrative illicit liquor business.

As a paradox to the seriously depleted domestic sales, the American manufacturers, in the Big Three category at least, now found that their products were in strong demand overseas. While Great Britain up to this point was leading the world in the production of the largest number of makes and diversity of types, most were not generally suited to the stern demands of colonial service over bad roads in underdeveloped countries. The rugged Yankee V twins, with their massive construction and simple and easily maintained engines, fitted with rugged clutches and gearboxes, developed sufficient power to haul either a large sidecar or heavily loaded commercial body which greatly enhanced their usefulness. By 1924, fully 50% of domestic production of all makes was now allocated to overseas outlets. The Emblem Motorcycle Company, a relatively small concern with modest production facilities located in a small manufacturing facility at Angola, New York, now completely abandoned their domestic market, and dispatched all their production to Europe, where the make was particularly popular in Holland and Belgium.

As a paradox to their now weakened position in the industry, Indian's indomitable Frank Weschler announced that the company would continue to support professional racing competition. As a result, some of H-D's former stars such as Jim Davis and Ralph Hepburn, joined the Wigwam's contingent. For the following seasons, Indian quite naturally dominated professional racing competition, which was still centered on the country's numerous board tracks, even in the face of declining public support and the deteriorating condition of these vast timbered speed temples.

With the growing importance of the export market, H-D's top management turned their attention abroad. Eric von Gumpert, still technically the company's Export Manager but functioning as Traffic Manager, kept in close touch with company overseas operations, particularly with Duncan Watson. The latter, selling a substantial number of machines in the United Kingdom, within the limits of the British big twin market, had expanded his scope of operations by establishing dealer outlets on the continent of Europe and in the Scandinavian countries. The Jones Brothers of Christchurch, New Zealand, whose activities were enhanced by a favorable agreement with the factory negotiated by Arthur Davidson during a visit to New Zealand during 1920, had already established a viable dealership on that continent.

On the domestic scene, H-D was now the acknowledged leader, with a projected production of

Freddie Dixon with his H-D eight valve special. Assembled on a short wheelbase frame, Dixon rode it in the British Motor Cycle Racing Club meeting at Brooklands on April 23, 1923, winning three races, including the Three Lap Race at 94.5 mph. *(The Motor Cycle)*.

about 12,000 units for the 1923-24 sales season. Indian was second with a production of about 8,000 units, with Excelsior trailing with about 5,000 units, most of which were the steadily popular Henderson Four. Schickel and Iver Johnson had now almost retired from the struggle, with Cleveland and Neracar, a latecomer to the utility market, in very limited production.

In spite of its leadership in production, the dealer representation of H-D was virtually the same as Indian on the domestic scene, each now having about 1,100 dealers in the United States and Canada. H-D's excess production was allocated to the export market.

In line with the increasing importance of export sales, and with an eye to possibly bolstering the failing domestic sales of sidecar outfits, H-D's top management prevailed on the Rogers Company to build a widebodied sidecar body, capable of carrying not only two adult passengers, but an enhanced commercial load as well. The wheel track was necessarily extended to the then standard US automobile gauge of 56½ inches. While the enlarged body was favorably received in some quarters overseas, it was regarded only as a novelty on the domestic market, where it had the disadvantage of being difficult to handle at anything more than moderate speeds due to its wide track.

In the meantime, Arthur Davidson turned his attention to H-D's critical position in the now important Southwest and Far West markets, where the vast distances and all-weather riding conditions, not to mention the existence of a healthy number of sporting riders, was now absorbing fully one half of all domestic motorcycle sales.

It will be recalled that H-D's position in this area had been seriously weakened by inept dealer representation in both San Diego and the Los Angeles area following the war. The situation had been greatly improved in the San Diego area by the fortuitous appointment of Rich Budelier, but matters in Los Angeles were still critical, where C. Will Risdon of Indian, together with aggressive representatives of Excelsior, and to a minor degree, Reading Standard and a few other makes, were holding a wide sales lead.

The problem appeared to lie with the Appeal Manufacturing and Jobbing Company, which had held the Los Angeles franchise since early in 1918, and had fallen on evil days.

With no planned sales campaign, a refusal to purchase any local advertising, and a general lack of aggressive management, the concern was selling only a minimal number of machines in comparison to its competitors. A further impediment to success, although in no way their fault, was the presence, almost adjacent to the Main Street location, of several rather disreputable nonfranchise motorcycle repair shops which were repeatedly under surveillance by the Los Angeles Police Department for allegedly dealing in stolen machines and spare parts. As Sales Manager and titular head of the Company's dealer organization, Arthur Davidson was well aware of the problem, having made a personal survey of the situation during an inspection tour of the West earlier that Spring. In a subsequent meeting with factory representative Verne Guthrie, Davidson suggested that perhaps Rich Budelier

F. A. Longman, an H-D enthusiast, was a consistent winner in various Brooklands events from 1923 through 1926. *(The Motor Cycle).*

could be persuaded to move to Los Angeles. The Sales Department would, of course, revoke the Appeal Company's franchise in favor of Budelier, should he accept the proposed offer. To further implement sales on the West coast, the Company was already in process of negotiating an agreement with two warehousing facilities for the distribution of parts and machines. This was at once a departure from usual company practice of assembling and shipping machines and dispatching them from the factory only on dealer's orders. The new system would entail more expense in assembling and shipping machines before firm orders were received, but apparently the importance of the growing Western market was such that the Company considered it worth the extra capitalization involved. Agreements with the Santa Fe Warehouse Company in Los Angeles and the San Francisco Warehouse Company were consummated to receive and ship goods dispatched from Milwaukee.

It is reported that Budelier readily agreed to accept the Los Angeles dealership, as the largest city in prosperous California could most certainly offer more scope and opportunity. The now-booming San Diego franchise was then taken over by Roy Artley, the noted competition rider, and William J.Ruhle, a pioneer motorcyclist and a long time H-D enthusiast who was well acquainted in the San Diego area. Artley, coincidentally, was doubly related in law to Fred Ludlow, as the two had married sisters.

Budelier moved to Los Angeles, and after the Appeal Company closed out their operations, he opened up temporary headquarters at Main and Adams Streets, some distance from the notorious 'Motorcycle Row', and planned the construction of a large new facility. As a long time friend of Hap Scherer, and noting that he was now unemployed, Budelier immediately offered him the position of Sales Manager in his new venture. It has been reported by long time factory employees that Walter Davidson was so enraged that Scherer was about to rejoin H-D operations outside his immediate jurisdiction that he at once proposed to force Budelier to withdraw his job offer. It is also reported that Arthur Davidson intervened at this point, suggesting that Hap Scherer's popularity and broad acquaintanceship among H-D enthusiasts would be of significant benefit to the critical Western Sales effort.

Another significant milestone in this period of H-D history was the addition of Arthur R. Constantine to the Company's Engineering Department. Constantine was a graduate engineer who had lately been employed in the Development and Design Department of General Motors' Buick Division.

At this juncture, Alfred Rich Child enters the story; a most remarkable man whose subsequent connection with the H-D Company and whose later activities within the industry were to have a significant bearing on the course of the country's motorcycling history. He was born in Chichester, Sussex, England on May 20 1891, the son of a retired officer in the British Navy who had later returned to service with the Coast Guard. In common with many other sons of naval personnel, he had spent his early youth as a cadet in the Greenwich Royal Naval School, from which he had graduated in 1907. It was during this period that he first became familiar with motorcycles, as one of the instructors rode an early Ormonde machine. Following his graduation, Child's father proposed that he should apprentice himself to a corn broker, but young Child demurred at the confinements of a desk job and the limited future of an office clerk. The elder Child insisted, and in the ensuing family conflict engendered by his refusal, he ran away from home and took passage to New York City on a Cunard liner, working his passage as a mess steward. Arriving at his destination with but $3.00 in his pocket, he immediately obtained a job in an office building as maintenance man and elevator operator. Passing through a series of varied employments, he was, for a time, butler and handyman on the Long Island Estate of William Thaw, whose son Harry was involved in the noted shooting fray with architect Sanford White over the favors of Evelyn Nesbet, a well known New York courtesan. During this period, Child rode an early 'camel back' Indian owned by William.

Noting the lack of opportunity in being a servant, Child conceived the idea of establishing a travelling clothing supply and haberdashery business to serve the house staffs of the great Long Island estates, as their isolation and lack of transportation made it difficult for them to travel to stores. Child's transport for this enterprise was a 1914 H-D sidecar outfit, purchased from a dealer in New York City.

A short time later, soon after the start of the war in Europe, he obtained his first substantial employment as a petty officer in the US Coast Guard, based on his experience as a naval cadet. His initial assignment was aboard a cutter whose function was to carry personnel to board and search cargo and passenger ships leaving New York harbor for Europe for possible contraband that would aid the Central Powers, as even at this early stage of the war, US sympathies were for the Allies.

It was at this time that Child contracted a severe case of influenza, a world wide scourge of the later war period, and after he recovered sufficiently to return to duty, he was posted to the Passport Office. In those days the Coast Guard had the sole government jurisdiction not only for the issuing of passports, but also was empowered to collect income taxes from departing aliens who at that time were forced to declare any income derived during their stay in the United States.

It was in the performance of these duties that Child met David Weistrich, an English Jew who owned a wholesale bicycle parts supply concern in New York City. The latter urgently required a quick passport to enable him to make a trip to Holland to collect a $50,000 debt owed him by a firm in that country. As the proposed journey was most critical to Weistrich's fortunes, and as Child was able to expedite the clearance of his passport, the two struck up an immediate friendship. Noting Child's obvious executive abilities, Weistrich told Child to look him up following his return from Europe. Child joined the Weistrich sales force as a traveling representative in the late fall of 1918. His initial travels were scheduled through the Southern states, and Child elected to utilize a 'J' model H-D sidecar outfit which could also carry his samples. As Weistrich had, in the meantime, acquired the franchise for the wholesaling of New Departure coaster brakes and other bicycle parts, Child could now offer a broad line of highly saleable products. In addition, he carried a line of small oil lanterns made of copper, which sold for a dollar, and were very popular sellers where rural electrification was still two decades away. Then Weistrich became ill, and turned the management of the business over to his brother-in-law. Child recalls that he did not get along too well with the man, as the latter proposed to reduce his formerly lucrative commission agreement. Casting about for a new selling opportunity, and after some reflection, he decided to apply to the H-D Company for a sales position, being by this time favorably impressed with the ruggedness and dependability of their machines.

Child contacted the factory, and soon received a telegram from Sales Manager Arthur Davidson. The two ultimately met in the old Algonquin Hotel on 28th Street in New York City. Davidson was initially concerned about Child's ethnic background, particularly relating to whether or not he was Jewish! (Child still had his broad British accent.) Upon being assured of his pure Aryan background, Davidson next inquired whether his business and ethical concepts had been unfavorably influenced by his late connection with a Jewish owned firm, and if such might render him unfit to become associated with a strictly gentile-owned company. While this episode might appear preposterous in the light of today's racial and ethnic toleration, such was not the case in the United States in the early 1920's. As white Protestant Anglo-Saxon culture was predominant in America, most people were suspicious of foreigners, particularly following the victory of social radicals in Russia. The swarming ghettos of foreign races caused native apprehension in many of the nation's larger cities, particularly concerning the threat of job displacement. These emotions were heightened by the popular sentiment of isolationism following the war. The often prosperous foreigners, particularly Jews, were generally barred from membership in social clubs, country clubs, and many of the country's leading hotels and summer resorts. The reactivated Ku Klux Klan boasted over three million members, all dedicated to preserving the purity of America, and in some areas Jews, Catholics, and black people were subject to persecution. Henry Ford was soon to publish his infamous protocols of Zion, purporting to expose a widespread Jewish conspiracy to control the world's money supply. Racial and ethnic pejudice did not materially abate until well after World War II.

After some discussion, Child was able to convince Davidson not only of his pure Aryan background, but of his fitness to undertake a job, and he was put to work under Theodore A. (Ted) Miller, Arthur Davidson's assistant in charge of domestic sales. His first base of operation was from his home in Garden City, Long Island, from which he operated as a company Sales Representative and Area Supervisor for the States of New York, New Jersey, New England and Eastern Canada. Following this, he was reassigned to the Southern States. Child recalls that he was no doubt sent to this territory because of his previous experience in the area, and because H-D sales in the deep south up to this point had not been spectacular. As in the case of other factory representatives, he was provided with vouchers for his expenses for fuel, oil, food and lodging. With characteristic Scottish thrift, Arthur Davidson informed him that due to the exigencies of post-war inflation, the company was now forced to allow up to 80 cents a day for meals and up to $1.50 per night for hotel rooms, but in no case were these figures to be exceeded! Child's assignment was to personally call on the approximately 48 dealers presently franchised in the Old Confederacy, offer them help with sales promotion and sales techniques, and act to iron out any real or imagined problems they might have with their relations with the factory. He was also ordered to see to it that the dealers take delivery of crated machines languishing in railroad freight depots, as, in line with the company's strict pay-on-delivery policy, a sight draft from the local bank had to be presented to take delivery. It was his idea to take photographs of each dealer and his premises with his own camera, so the management could correlate their sales performance with their public image. This was a factor in determining the annual dealer review for the yearly franchise renewal.

In the Spring of 1921, Child was next assigned to Milwaukee, where he was still involved in the Sales Department, and he accordingly moved his family from Long Island to that city.

Arthur Davidson next projected a selling mission to South Africa, where Indian, and secondly Excelsior, were particularly strong, and where H-D's representation up to this point had not been effectual. Child, selected to make the journey, was provided with a new electrically-equipped 'J' sidecar outfit, fitted with a wide-bodied Rogers built unit for enhanced carrying capacity. He left Milwaukee early that Spring for New York, where he embarked on the Mauretania for Southampton. He first visited his parents in England, and then embarked on a Castle Line steamer, the Windsor Castle, for Capetown. His initial visit was with A.R.Callow Limited, who had taken a H-D franchise a year and a half previously, and to date had sold 39 machines, mostly sidecar outfits. Child remained in Capetown for a few weeks, aiding Callow to inaugurate a more aggressive sales campaign, which resulted in their selling more machines and enlarging their operation. He next journeyed to Johannesburg, calling on bicycle dealers in both that city and in adjacent territories. He recalls that his main problem was to locate such dealers with the requisite mechanical ability to undertake the service and repair of machines sold, which was a highly necessary adjunct to a successful dealership. Along the way, Child was able to undertake numerous sightseeing trips, implemented by the fact that Arthur Davidson had instructed him to stay at the best hotels and to entertain prospective dealers without reference to rigid economy, all backed with a $5,000 letter of credit from the Marshall and Illsley bank in Milwaukee. In this case, the traditional H-D Scottish thrift was subordinated to management's desire to appear before the South Africans as an outstandingly affluent organization.

Along the way, Child visited the famous de Beers diamond mine as well as the scenic Victoria Falls, and his subsequent travels through South Africa could provide enough subject matter for a separate book in itself. He traveled over nearly impassable or non-existent roads, sold 50 machines to a native dictator in Mombassa, and was transported over streams and rivers by large companies of native warriors, who carried the outfit bodily on a pair of long poles positioned under the sidecar chassis. After a series of incredible adventures which are now a part of Child's extensive personal memoirs, he ultimately arrived in Cairo, where he transhipped his outfit to Italy. In all, he booked orders for over 400 machines, and added a number of dealers to the Company's roster. In spite of his efforts, Indian continued to be the most popular big twin machine on the African continent.

Meanwhile, back at the factory, the H-D Company was in process of contending with the shrinking domestic market. The Company now had about 1,200 dealers franchised, producing about 11,000 machines for the 1921 sales season. Indian shipped about 7,000 units that year, due to numerous production and financial problems, but still serviced well over 1,000 dealers. While H-D led in production, its domestic sales still were about on a par with Indian, the difference being that H-D's export shipments to Europe and South America were ahead of the Wigwam. Excelsior was a poor third, with about 300 dealers who now concentrated on the four-cylinder Henderson. Cleveland, Iver-Johnson, Reading Standard, Shickel, and Neracar, the last a rather curious utility model with center-pivot steering, were still in evidence, but cumulatively sold only about 4,000 machines.

In order to beef up dealer confidence, H-D announced a general dealers' meeting to be held at the factory in the early spring of 1922. The event was billed as a dedication ceremony for the new factory, which in itself was a rather anticlimatic gesture, as he new facilities had been in operation for nearly two years. Invitations were extended to all dealers in the United States and Canada, but the bulk of the attendance was from the adjacent Midwestern region. Aside from a tour of the factory, whose production and assembly facilities were now drastically reduced, the general meetings were conducted in a large garage facility at the rear of the Juneau Avenue complex. The main conference featured the appearance of the Chairman of the Board of Directors of the Marshall and Illsley Bank, who in a somewhat florid speech, (the author's informant who was there states that in his opinion, it was written by the company's Publicity Department), extolled the merits of the Company and its products, and informed the assemblage that President Walter Davidson's credit rating was such that he could obtain a million dollar loan at any time by just signing his name for it. The meeting also featured the first official appearance of William H.Davidson, Vice President William A.Davidson's son, presently enrolled as a student at the University of Wisconsin in Business Administration, who gave an address on the promising future of the motorcycle industry.

The Company's labor force, now drastically reduced from the industry's salad days, consisted mostly of veteran employees from the Company's original incorporation in 1907, when production of H-Ds had begun in earnest. But few had been added since the drastic retrenchment a year or two before, and these only when needed through natural deaths or attrition.

William Davidson, always in charge of production, was ever the stern taskmaster, ruthlessly discharging on the spot any worker who was caught shirking his duties or whose efforts could not measure up to his exacting standards of excellence. On the other hand, any good worker who was experiencing personal, domestic, or financial problems, could find a readily sympathetic ear from 'Big Bill', as he was affectionately called. The latter always carried with him a sizable roll of money, and any worker in genuine need could always count on a $50.00 or $100.00 advance on his salary if the occasion demanded. These 'loans' could be paid back at the worker's option, but no formal demands were ever made for repayment. While the wages paid to H-D's production crew were always somewhat below that of the prevailing standard, they came to be a hard core of loyal enthusiasts whose term of service in many cases was measured in decades rather than years.

Claude Temple, a consistent winner at various Brooklands events. He is here seen winning the BMCRC Championship on October 7, 1921 at 92.37 mph. *(The Motor Cycle).*

The Company's sales efforts were now directed toward the refined electrically equipped 'J' model, lately offered in 74 cubic inch as well as the traditional 61 cubic inch categories. The Company had dropped the original Remy electrical equipment shortly after the war, not only to save the cost of buying proprietary equipment, but also to free themselves from dependence on outside suppliers. The first factory built units had in some cases proved unreliable, however, and many an owner had replaced factory equipment with still existing Remy components. The factory had made haste to rectify the matter, and by 1922 these were now functioning with acceptable reliability. What with the termination of factory-sponsored competition, the sales emphasis was now on reliability rather than speed, and the suitability of H-D products for individual transport, as well as commercial and law enforcement uses.

Touring articles were now featured in the *Enthusiast,* and they ran a series of continuing articles on the adventures of two ex-servicemen, or 'doughboys' as they were then called, Royal Gerberick and Roy Kerle, who with a 1920 electrically-equpped 'J' sidecar outfit covered 19,000 miles on a circuitous trip through the midwestern and western areas of the country. In spite of universally bad roads and a heavily overloaded outfit, the two intrepid travelers experienced but minimal mechanical trouble.

Meanwhile, H-D's management was in process of its continuing evaluation of the shrinking domestic motorcycle market. At midseason of 1922, President Walter Davidson ordered the phasing out of the production of the Sport Twin. Motorcycle historians have long speculated about the reasons for the dis-continuance of this very sound model. Outside of a few initial problems with overheating of the rear cylinder, which were solved by minor improvement to the lubrication system, the model had been eminently satisfactory within its sphere of employment. One logical theory is that the domestic middleweight market had up to that time been dominated by Indian's very popualr Indian Scout. While of the same cylinder displacement, its V twin configuration afforded it superior torque and pulling power, and its hill climbing abilities and top speed were somewhat superior to the 'W' as a result. Then too, it was of the now traditional American V twin design, where the former was of rather unorthodox type, to American riders at least. There was also a certain resistance to the model from the dealers themselves, already firmly orientated to heavyweight machines offering a high speed capability, and in many cases loath to promote a model that offered mild, but dependable performance to utility riders. Another possible alternative was the fact that H-D production was currently organized to manufacture the 'J' models, long the backbone of Milwaukee's organization, and the relatively low volume of 'W' production added to the costing that William Davidson was constantly seeking to rationalize.

While the machine was an attraction to schoolboys, rural mail carriers, cautious utility riders, and a few intrepid feminine enthusiasts, it was not a model that fitted in with the current high speed macho image fancied by the majority of fans who sought to emulate the racing star's image. Furthermore, its former principal exponent at the factory, Hap Scherer, was no longer engaged in promoting medium performance motorcycling on the West Coast. The Sport Twin was always more popular overseas than at home, being well accepted in England, Europe, Australia and New Zealand. The flat twin was already well thought of in these areas, where the type had been pioneered by Douglas as well as lesser makes. When production finally ended in 1922, about 6,000 units had come off the assembly lines. A few examples are known to have been shipped to Duncan Watson on special order during 1923 and 1924, presumably built up from remaining spare parts in stock. While the machine had created a mild sensation among utility riders a couple of years earlier, its death knell had probably been sounded by the cheap car, whose recent high production was now bringing vast numbers to the used market to sell at very low prices.

The author's first motorcycle was a weathered but sound 1920 'W' magneto-equipped model purchased in the Spring of 1927 in partnership with a schoolboy friend, who put up half of the $10.00 purchase price. A new set of spark plugs restored its inherent easy starting and smooth running capabilities, and it afforded many pleasurable short journeys into the countryside, adding much to the fascination of boyhood search for adventure. It was subsequently sold to make possible the acquisition of a more powerful 61 cubic inch 'J' model, which later added another facet to the author's H-D experiences.

In the Fall of 1922, Arthur Davidson and Indian's General Manager Frank Weschler inaugurated the first of a series of clandestine meetings between the top management of both factories.

The Temple-Anzani Special. The specially-designed 61 inch 998 cc ohc engine was fitted to a chassis built by the Osborne Engineering Company, utilizing many H-D parts. (*The Motor Cycle*).

The object appeared to be a general discussion of the many problems besetting the industry, but the main reason was to equalize the retail prices of their comparable models. While such agreements had long been illegal in business and industry under the Sherman and Clayton Antitrust Acts against restraint of trade, it was still an almost universal practice among like segments of American industry. While the Davidsons, with their usual Scottish caution, had ever been wary of any sort of fraternization with the personnel of competing companies, they had enjoyed a somewhat ambiguous relationship with Frank Weschler ever since he was Indian's unofficial manager in 1916. At all the big National Races since that time, when H-D was the more frequent winner, Weschler had always made it a point to cordially congratulate both riders and management on their victories. Then too, he had earned their natural, if grudging, admiration for his almost single handed heroism in saving the company during its dark days of 1921. With the current state of the motorcycle market, it now appeared expedient to at least remove any retail price differential between the two makes.

At the meeting in question, held in a suite in New York City's Astor Hotel, the author's informant, then a young member of the sales staff, stated that the two dined in private in an adjacent room. Savoring crepe suzettes and lobster thermidor in an atmosphere of somewhat strained conviviality, it was decided that as Indian had undercut by $5.00 on similar models in 1921, Indian would add a $5.00 premium to their 1922 models. It was then agreed that, henceforth, similar models in each case would carry the same price tag through a continuing yearly gentlemen's agreement.

By 1922, the more or less continuous attempts at long distance record breaking on the part of both car drivers and motorcycle riders had come to an end. By this time the surface of most of the principal continental and important regional routes had been improved to the point that ordinary travel had become commonplace. Through energetic lobbying on the part of various regional and national automobile clubs, the main transcontinental highway, now known as the Lincoln Highway, had been improved to the point that the adventurous motorist could now undertake its traverse without fear of

A 1926 Zenith-JAP Special at Brooklands. In common with many other large V twin Specials, this machine had fitted H-D forks. *(The Motor Cycle).*

either wandering from its well marked route, getting mired in axle-deep mud or sustaining physical damage from large rocks and boulders.

The principal long distance exponent for spectacular record attempts up to this period in US motoring history had been Erwin G. 'Cannonball' Baker, who had at one time or another ridden most leading makes of motorcycles as well as piloting several makes of popular automobiles over the country's nearly impossible routes. In the motorcycle sphere, at one time or another he competed for Ace, Excelsior, Henderson, and Indian, the notable exception being Harley-Davidson. In an interview with the author in 1957, when queried about this descrepancy, Baker stated that while he had several tentative contacts with H-D President Walter Davidson regarding both transcontinental and Three Flag record attempts on the West Coast, the two could never agree on Baker's financial terms for such appearances. Baker, after his reputation as a record breaker was well established, usually charged the sponsor of the make in question $1,000 for his appearance on the course, plus $25.00 per hour for each hour shaved from the current record. In his negotiations with Davidson, the latter demurred at the high initial fee, and instead countered with an offer of $250.00 for the appearance and $50.00 for each record hour. Baker stated that his own expenses for fuel, oil, and comfort stops en route at stated intervals usually cost more than this amount, mostly for fees for the persons involved in implementing them, and that Davidson's offer could give him only a modest fee for what was usually a herculean effort. It was for this reason that Baker never made any serious record attempts on H-D machines, as according to his own statements, Davidson was not sporting enough to invest any real money in Baker's now proven abilities of endurance.

An interesting footnote to long distance record breaking during the swashbuckling days of motorcycle was the experience related by Wells Bennett, the noted Excelsior exponent, incidental to his attempt in the early summer of 1921 to break the existing Three Flag record. Starting from the usual jumping off place at Blaine, Washington, he made phenomenal time from there through Oregon, due to unusually good weather conditions. His luck still held through California's great valley until he reached Fresno, when he was flagged down by a local motorcycle policeman for speeding. Bennett managed to put up bail to insure his return to fight the citation, but lost two valuable hours of riding time in the process. Upon reaching Bakersfield some distance south, he was again apprehended for allegedly exceeding the speed limit, and was incarcerated in the local jail for the night, obviously terminating his record attempt.

In later years, Bennett was fond of recounting this adventure, and offered evidence that the H-D dealers along the route from San Jose south had importuned the law enforcement officers to impede and ultimately to terminate his run, which was certain to have set a new running time.

During the 1923 competition at the great Brooklands oval in England, H-D entrants continued to rack up impressive records. On April 7th 1923, at a meeting sponsored by the BMCRC, Freddie Dixon won the Three Lap Solo Race on an 8 valve H-D Special, provided by Duncan Watson, at the record speed of 94.5 mph. That same Fall he won the 1,000 cc Championship Race with the same machine, at 100.10 mph. Taking it to France the month before, he had won the flying start kilometer record on the Bois de Boulogne at 106.8 m.p.h.

Brooklands speedman Claude Temple, during the early months of 1923, had put together a machine of his own design which he named the British Anzani Special, utilizing a specially built 998 cc 57 degree V twin with overhead camshafts. This machine, a wonder in its day at Brooklands, with H-D frame, forks, and wheels, hung up a number of speed records that stood for several seasons. This historic machine happily still exists in the hands of M.N.Mavrogordato, a British racing motorcycle enthusiast.

The high speed steering characteristics of earlier model H-Ds with their traditional leading link forks has long been a matter of controversy among motorcycle historians and vintage enthusiasts. Even the author has been preoccupied with the results of their effect on the early Brooklands record breakers. A more or less satisfactory answer to this question was ultimately forthcoming from the late Harry Coulter, a one-time mechanic who aided in the preparation of both H-D and other big V twins fitted with similar types of fork. In an interview with the author in 1959, Coulter stated that most of the H-D record breakers modified the steering geometry to form a greater rake at the head lug, and shortened the compression springs to bring the axle pivot well above its attachment to the fixed fork leg. This modification steadied the steering at high speeds, although it imparted a rather disconcerting roll when the machine was set to turn at speeds below 50 mph. While this effect could be of some consequence in touring or utility use, it was obviously unimportant at the 90-100 mph speeds attained in record breaking attempts.

A somewhat battered but mechanically sound 1924 magneto equipped 'J' model was the author's second machine, acquired in the summer of 1929 as the result of the sale of the originally owned 1920 Sport Twin. Purchased for $20.00, and enhanced by an $11.00 valve-and-ring overhaul by local Santa Rosa dealer Joe Frugoli's mechanic, Charles Cook, the machine provided many hours of pleasurable motorcycling adventure. In addition, it afforded first hand experience of the vagaries of H-D's classic steering at high speeds.

Somewhat north of the author's home in Santa Rosa, just outside the village of Cloverdale to the north, there was a long hill whose gentle gravel gradient provided a fairly smooth surface. Boy racers were wont to utilize this course, as it offered an enhanced simulation of motorcycle or car high speed capabilities. The author's 61, as overhauled and run in, had a top speed of about 64 mph. At this speed, the steering was steady. On the slight downgrade, at full throttle, this capability increased to about 72 mph, and at this rate of travel an annoying, if not dangerous, wobble made itself felt. A very slight acceleration then produced a tank-slapping gyration that was down-right frightening. The machine was subsequently examined by Dealer Joe Frugoli, who checked the frame and forks for cor-

John Cameron's 1920 eight valve Special. The engine was located in England, and John completed the machine with authentic period parts. *(George Hays).*

rect alignment, and found all in order. His ultimate suggestion was that the forks be dismantled and the compression springs shortened to decrease the angle of the bottom links, apparently even in those days the time honored cure. As the cost of this modification was $5.00, and the author was an impecunious schoolboy, the conversion was declined, and thereafter his riding was confined to speeds under 65 mph.

In the early spring of 1923, Indian's General Manager, Frank J. Weschler, journeyed from Springfield to Chicago, taking with him funds to pay off a short term loan negotiated from a bank in that city during one of Indian's recurring financial crises. As the Springfield banks had become somewhat wary of Indian, with their recent boom-and-bust history of performance, Weschler had been forced to travel far afield to raise capital to carry on operations. His terminus near Milwaukee then prompted him to arrange another policy meeting with H-D's management, subsequently held in the Blackstone Hotel, Chicago, on April 3rd and 4th.

With the usual price fixing on parallel models concluded, President Walter Davidson next suggested that another matter be settled, namely that franchised H-D and Indian dealers be forbidden to handle any other make of machine. Up to this time, it must be noted that some of the larger dealers handling both H-D and Indian frequently also held franchises for Excelsior, Cleveland, Iver Johnson, Reading Standard, and Neracar. While H-D and Indian were not particularly amenable to this arrangement, they often hesitated to interfere too far in the dealer's private affairs, especially if he had taken on either of the large manufacturer's makes after he had already undertaken business with other makes. Walter Davidson's reasoning and that of his brother Arthur was that with the critical condition of the domestic market, it was now illogical that the showrooms of the largest two surviving manufacturers should feature competitive machines. Weschler was reported to have disagreed, stating that

motorcycling in general might attract more potential converts if a wider choice of makes and models were available. The author's informant in the matter, a young clerk in Indian's accounting department who had accompanied his chief to Chicago, stated that Walter Davidson was adamant in the matter, and after a time, Weschler capitulated. The enforcement of the new edict was once placed in the hands of the regional traveling representatives of both factories, who would at once report any infraction of the ruling to the top management, so that the matter could be reviewed when the yearly franchise reviews came up. H-D, of course, would brook no flouting of their authority, but Indian's management sometimes looked the other way in cases where a few of their dealers had enjoyed previous successes with the Cleveland. The virtual phasing out of Excelsior's once-popular 61 cubic inch twin in favor of their more successful Henderson Four somewhat simplified the problem for both, as many new dealerships were being established to handle that model exclusively. H-D and Indian's enhanced 'gentleman's agreement' sounded the death knell of such marginal makes as Reading Standard,

Schickel, Iver Johnson, and pushed the mildly popular utility Cleveland out of the market. The clandestine Chicago meeting, while probably known to less than half a dozen people within the industry at the time, was ultimately to have far reaching effects upon the continuing decline of motorcycling interest in the United States.

All three of the domestic motorcycle factories now turned their attention to export markets, which were buying sufficient volume of production to ensure the survival of the industry.

# Chapter 4

# Oriental Interlude

THE EXPORT OF HARLEY-DAVIDSON MACHINES TO JAPAN AND THE ORIENT DURING the early 1920's involves a most complex set of circumstances, and therefore requires a separate chapter in itself. At the outset, it is sufficient to say that it was not only critical as a necessary adjunct to an export program necessary for the company's survival due to a depressed domestic market, but was also instrumental in Japan's development of its own future auto and motorcycle industries. It may be noted that Indian was already entrenched in Japan, with an active agency in Tokyo importing 600-700 machines per year, about 40% of them being sidecar outfits. Prince (later Emperor) Hirohito rode such an outfit for some years.

A handful of H-D machines were imported to Japan by the Army during the years 1912-1917, but, curiously enough, no spare parts were ever ordered. No doubt the Army officers involved believed quite literally the H-D advertising statements that their machines were largely trouble-free! Early in 1922, an import firm in Tokyo, Nippon Jidoshe K.K., headed by the young Baron Okura, which had been importing limited numbers of American automobiles since 1919, sent Milwaukee an order for a small trial order of 74 cubic inch 'J' model electrically-equipped machines in the Spring of 1922. During the following year they imported about a further dozen machines. During the following year they imported about a further dozen machines, ignoring company suggestions that they stock a few of the more critical categories of spare parts.

It was during this period that the Charles Cable Company, an import-export firm in San Francisco, wrote to Milwaukee stating that they were presently doing business with a merchant in Ulan Bator, the capital of Inner Mongolia. They suggested that if they could obtain the distributorship for all H-D products in Inner and Outer Mongolia, they would place substantial orders with the company, and pay against documents placed in San Francisco banks.

In the meantime, the Charles Cable Company placed some substantial orders for H-D machines that same year. Payments were made on delivery from funds deposited in San Francisco banks, and for some reason it was thought in Milwaukee that somehow the Charles Cable Company was supplying machines and other commodities to Ulan Bator. However, it soon became some cause for concern that no spare parts were ever ordered. Charles Cable insisted that the Mongolians had their own spare parts, although it was difficult to imagine that an area encompassed by the Gobi Desert and, under an economy based on the breeding of goats and camels, could possess machine shop facilities to carry on such work!

At this point, Alfred Rich Child, who had just returned from his epic journey on H-D's behalf through South Africa, was informed by the Company that he should soon be preparing himself for a survey of the Japanese and far Eastern situation regarding a potential motorcycle market.

On September 1, 1923, the Kanto or Eastern area of Japan was devastated by a catastrophic earthquake that killed or injured hundreds of thousands of people and left millions homeless. During this period, Charles Cable visited Milwaukee and had a conference with Eric von Gumpert, still H-D's titular head of the Export Department, but more properly functioning as Traffic Manager. Cable suggested that the time was ripe for appointing him H-D distributor for Japan, Korea, and Manchuria. On orders from management, von Gumpert informed them that at the moment, the Japan Automobile Company of Nippon Jidosha were the official distributors of the Company's products in Japan, and that pending a survey by Alfred Rich Child as Export Sales Representative, they would make no other appointments.

To further complicate the situation, in the Spring of 1924 the Congress of the United States passed a rigid immigration law severely limiting the immigration of Asiatics into the United States, which included Japanese. This was a tremendous blow to Japanese pride, and the Japanese Ambassador in Washington D.C. immediately demanded an exception to the ruling for his countrymen, on the threat of 'serious consequences'. When such a ruling was not forthcoming, violent demonstrations erupted in every Japanese city from Hokodate to Kagashima.

It was in this hostile atmosphere that Alfred Rich Child disembarked at Yokohama in July 1924, from the Canadian Pacific liner 'Empress of Canada', and registered at Tokoyo's Imperial Hotel. It became evident that Charles Cable had contacts in Japan as well as in Ulan Bator, as Child was invited a few days later to dine with the Baron Okura, who had been educated in both England and the United States, and spoke excellent English.

During the subsequent meeting with Okura, Child pointed out that H-D's management were dissatisfied with the sales results so far achieved by his staff of Nippon Jidosha, as well as their total disregard for the necessity for maintaining a stock of spare parts. Okura, on the other hand, continued to defend both his own and his employees' sales policies, and demanded that Nippon Jidosha be granted a continuation of their present yearly contract. After several futile attempts to resolve the matter, Child ultimately broke off all negotiations with this group.

It was at this juncture that an English speaking native named Yamada, who had once represented the Izu Peninsula Tea Growers as a lobbyist in Washington, introduced Child to one Genijiro Fukui, a US-educated individual who was one of the three founders of a now prestigious pharmaceutical manufacturing concern, the Sankyo Company Limited of Muromachi, Tokyo. Its President, Matasaku Shiohara, was presently in negotiation with Dr.Baekeland, the inventor of 'Bakelite', to secure the rights to manufacture products made from this material in Japan. During Child's conversations with Fukui, it was revealed that he and one Ichita Taguchi headed the Koto Trading Company, an import and export subsidiary of the Sankyo Company Limited.

It then became apparent to Child that Charles Cable had been secretly diverting some of the H-D motorcycle shipments, originally consigned to Mongolia, to Japan, and in effect 'bootlegging' them to the Koto Trading Co. right under Nippon Jidosha's nose, in spite of their so-called exclusive sales rights to act as H-D agents.

Perceiving the duplicity of the Koto organization, Child then opened negotiations with the three principals of the Sankyo Company in view of appointing them H-D distributors from Japan, subject to certain conditions which would be laid down by Milwaukee. It was obvious that in view of the earthquake devastated Japanese roads, a 1200 cc H-D sidecar, sidevan, or three-wheeled rear car would be for several years an ideal vehicle to use under these conditions.

During an exchange of cablegrams between Child and Milwaukee, it was decided that Child should be the titualar head of the agency, in view of the double-dealing that had been experienced between Cable and the Koto organization. During this time Baron Okura attempted to intervene on his own behalf, but was ultimately informed that his company would receive no more H-D machines. At this point, the three principals of the Sankyo organization were agreeable to the condition that Child remain in Japan to act as liaison between themselves and Milwaukee. To this end Child produced a letter of credit from the National City Bank of New York to cover the purchase of 350 Big Twin H-D machines, mostly with sidecars. Also included were $20,000 worth of replacement parts and $3,000 worth of dealers' repair tools. In addition, the whole transaction was covered by an agreement that Child would be the Managing Director of a newly formed 'Harley-Davidson Sales Company of Japan', his recompense to be 5% of the landed cost of all H-D products. The wholesale cost of the machines was augmented by freight, crating, and excise duties paid at the port of entry.

Following the consummation by cable of the details of his export agreement, Child sailed for the States on the Empress of Canada, whereon landing at Vancouver he met Arthur Davidson who was just returning from a sales trip to Australia and New Zealand. Arthur was justly congratulatory of Child's Japanese effort, as he had originally discouraged the initial sales attempts in that country due to the current anti-American sentiment following the Asiatic Exclusion Act.

Child met with the Founders in Milwaukee to finalize the details of the export of machines to

Ray Weishaar's 1923 61 cu.in. pocket valve racer. In original condition, it is a part of the Bud Ekins collection. Weishaar cut his name on the timing case cover. *(Alisha Tamburri).*

Japan. In August, 1924, he returned to Tokyo to organize the import machinery. He had previously hired Harry Devine, the factory H-D Parts Manager who had already enjoyed nearly twenty years of experience with the parent firm, to accompany him.

The H-D Motorcycle Sales Company of Japan, now its official title, set up headquarters in a rented building just off the Ginza at the Kyobashi crossing in Tokyo. One of the earliest native employees was Yamada, who became Child's right-hand man, along with Morikichi Sakurai who was not only a skilled mechanic but an ardent motorcycle enthusiast. Most of the subsequent staff became enthusiasts as time went one. Capitalization for the agency was provided by Genjiro Fukui of the Sankyo Pharmaceutical Company.

The first shipments of H-D machines to Kyobashi were the 1925 models as designed by Arthur Constantine, much to Child's peace of mind, as the earlier sheet metal soldered tanks from the flat tank era were prone to leak.

When the new bulbous tank models were imported during January 1925, there were few motorcycles manufactured in Japan, as at that time they had no such industry. Competition was provided by Indian, who were at this time marketing 800 to 1,000 machines per year. Various production and financial problems in Springfield had been making shipments somewhat erratic, however, and within a couple of years H-D imports exceeded those of Indian. Other makes concurrently being imported included AJS, Matchless and Norton from England, Husqvarna from Sweden, Moto-Guzzi from Italy, and after 1927, BMW from Germany. Realizing that the prime transportation requirement in Japan at this time was in the commercial sphere, Child wisely concluded that the rugged 74 cubic inch models could be best utilized as sidecar, sidevan or for the powering of rear cars. Morikichi Sakurai designed both the heavyweight and light duty rear cars, the latter for use with the newly introduced 21 cubic inch side valve singles in 1925-26.

Limited competition from a native manufacturer subsequently appeared in the form of a rear car powered with a 500 cc proprietary side valve engine supplied by J.A.Prestwich of Great Britain. Another contemporary Japanese firm entered the rear car field with an exact copy of the 21 cubic inch H-D design, built by a company that ultimately produced the contemporary rotary engine Mazda.

As the Sankyo Company's original activity was the manufacture of pharmaceutical products, it quite naturally participated in contract sales of these products to certain government agencies, namely the Army and Navy. Following up these contacts it also secured contracts for the sale of H-D motorcycles to the armed forces, and these machines became the standard military vehicles.

In addition, district police prefectures and the Post Office department purchased hundreds of H-Ds. Through the Outer Mongolian contacts, numerous H-Ds were sold to various Chinese and Manchurian War Lords, after 1929, such as Chang Tso Lin. His son Chang Hsu Liang, as well as Chiang Kai-shek, purchased as many as 200 machines at a time, mostly sidecar outfits.

A typical small town rural motorcycle dealer's premises in the deep South. This was apparently the time before H-D exerted its single-make mandate over their franchisees. *(Alfred Rich Child).*

A typical Southern sheriff with his trusty 'J' Model. Charged with suppressing the illicit liquor traffic, law enforcement officers frequently encountered rum runners using identical equipment! *(Alfred Rich Child)*.

As the business expanded, branch sales offices were opened in Osaka and Fukuoka in Japan, and Darien, Manchuria. In addition, a new four story structure was built in the Temeike district of Tokyo containing a large spare parts warehouse and service facility. This building was used until 1973 when it was replaced by a larger edifice. Spare parts distribution was handled from Tokyo, which allocated them throughout Japan and Manchuria, as required.

In addition, about 400 service and dealer outlets were established throughout the islands of Japan itself. Some of these were substantial operations, but the majority were characteristic Oriental single family enterprises, where the mechanic's family lived and worked in a one room makeshift building on dirt floors. Such was characteristic of all engine and mechanical repair work undertaken in the Orient during those days, and Child reports that it was difficult to induce the mechanics to utilize the conventional work benches that he later provided from company workshops.

Subsequent to the inauguration of H-D sales in Japan, Child made at least one journey a year to Milwaukee to maintain a close contact with the company, and to suggest improvements in shipping methods. A particular problem of this period was the rough handling accorded crated machines in transit, and Child had to insist on extra heavy packing of shipments to avoid damage, which in many cases in the past had been extreme. It was during this period that Child underwent treatment for a cancerous condition in the bones of his left hand. He was first treated in Milwaukee General Hospital, but shortly afterwards sustained an amputation in Saint Lukes Hospital in Tokyo.

A critical problem for all importers of American products into Japan arose in the Fall of 1929 when the yen, which, in 1924, was the equivalent of 49¼ American cents, suddenly dropped to 20 to 30 cents. This meant that the ultimate retail price of H-D machines would by necessity be doubled. In discussing this matter with the author in an interview in the fall of 1978, Child stated that this new state of affairs indicated that either the export of H-D machines to Japan be terminated, or else an agreement be effected with the Company whereby manufacturing rights to H-D machines be secured for Japan. Not wishing to give up his by this time lucrative business in Japan, Child conferred at length with the management of H-D for the securing of such rights, along with the necessary blueprints, material lists and specifications, heat-treating formulae, machine tool and die sequences, plus all other necessary data.

Sankyo's management at length agreed to Child's proposal, as well as offering the requisite financial backing, and Child set sail from Yokohama on the Asama Maru in company with Shiohara's son-in-law, who was to act as liaison representative for Milwaukee.

At the initial meeting in Milwaukee, the Founders were all skeptical of the engineering and mechanical abilities of the Japanese to produce workable copies of H-D machines, and further expressed their surprise at Child's temerity for suggesting such an undertaking. After some considerable negotiating, however, and no doubt motivated by the sudden inauguration of a world wide depression, together with the payment of $75,000 as a royalty, they agreed to conclude an agreement with the Sankyo group for the manufacture of H-D machines in Japan. The Company agreed to provide all necessary blueprints, material lists, metallurgy schedules, and all other directions for motorcycle manufacture, in return for an agreement that no Japanese-built H-D machines would be exported. It was also agreed that while tooling up for production, and prior to the actual manufacture of machines, Sankyo would continue to import and market the Milwaukee-made product.

As a part of the transaction, Child was able to hire Fred Barr, H-D's Assistant Factory Superintendent under George Nordberg, to supervise the setting up of Sankyo's manufacturing operation in Japan. Barr's title was now that of Chief Engineer, and he was offered a lucrative tax-free contract for three years. While Barr was a key man in the Milwaukee operation, Child believes that the Company was willing to let him resign due to the fact that they were already feeling the effect of the depression and were coincidentally cutting down on staff and production personnel.

Barr proved to be the key official in the new Japanese operation as subsequent events were soon to show. Together with Mr. A. Sakurai, Sankyo's first engineering supervisor at the Kyobashi crossing in 1925, Barr put together a group of capable young engineering personnel and mechanics who had friends and acquaintances on allied mechanical lines who ultimately became subcontractors to produce various component parts of H-D machines from the blueprints supplied from Milwaukee. These were submitted to the Shinagawa plant for inspection and evaluation by Fred Barr before their incorporation into prototype models for final testing before production was inaugurated.

In retrospect, and in view of the fact that in 1929 the Shinagawa factory was the very first complete motorcycle manufacturing plant in Japan, it may well be said that Sankyo's effort here was the forerunner of the great Japanese motorcycle industry which today dominates the world markets.

Incidental to the inauguration of Japanese production, the first shipments of the first of the initially ill-fated VL side valve 74 cubic inch models began arriving in Yokohama as per the original licensing agreement. Of the initial production of the first 1,300-odd defective machines, Child ultimately was obliged to make good some 73 units, the details of which unfortunate episode in H-D history will subsequently be described.

In the meantime, and while Barr was co-ordinating Japanese production of component parts, certain surplus machine tooling was purchased from the parent factory, some of which no doubt being declared surplus in Milwaukee due to the decline of US motorcycle production following the onset of the depression. Additional tooling was purchased from other US manufacturers, as well as from Germany, due to the favorable exchange rate.

No Japanese personnel were ever sent to Milwaukee for training in the factory's Service School, due to language difficulties. Additionally, none of the four Founders or any members of the Export Department's staff ever visited Japan, except for a brief visit from Walter Davidson, Jr., President Davidson's son, who passed through Japan on a brief pre-college tour before the Shinagawa factory commenced formal operation.

The only company representative to ever visit Japan before the consummation of the Sankyo agreement was Joseph Ryan, the Company Service and Parts Manager, who made the journey at Child's request in 1925 when Child requested some official aid in setting up his spare parts dispersal system incidental to his first export agreement with the factory itself.

As H-D machines fabricated completely from Japanese-made parts were not assembled and sold until early in 1935, Child continued to import substantial yearly shipments of Milwaukee-made machines. In recalling this phase of H-D history, Child told the author in 1978 that the existence of the continuing 5% landed cost commission from the factory on such shipments was a potent factor in his continuation of his 1924 export agreement.

During the early negotiations for Sankyo acquisition of H-D manufacturing rights, and in the subsequent complete manufacture of H-D machines in Japan, the H-D company carefully avoided any public disclosure of either their dealings with Sankyo or the fact that their machines were subsequently built under license by a Japanese concern. This was no doubt prompted by the growing awareness in the US of the buildup of Japanese military power, together with the general public disapproval of the Japanese military adventures in Manchuria.

As most motorcycle applications were still in the field of commercial transportation, most of the imported Milwaukee models were of the 74 cubic inch big twins, and 21 cubic inch and 30.50 cubic inch singles. These were shipped for adaptation to various types of Japanese manufactured rear cars, and consisted of complete machines, but with the rear wheel and mudguard omitted. The 45 cubic inch twin was not imported, as its general configuration and power development was considered not suited to rear car applications.

After the final production of Japanese H-Ds was finalized by 1935, and, as at this point, the Japanese engineering crew had production well in hand, Fred Barr's contract was terminated. He and

The Traffic Squad for the city of Wins on-Salem, North Carolina. Photograph taken by Alfred Rich Child when he was a traveling H-D representative for the Southern States. *(Alfred Rich Child)*.

H-D Export Manager Eric von Gumpert (center, hands in pockets) attends a club rally in Christchurch, New Zealand, in 1927.

his family were showered with expensive presents by Shiohara and Fukui, and they were presented with first class steamer tickets for a world tour that ended back in Milwaukee.

At this point in time, a problem in Japanese-Milwaukee relations appeared which presented diverse difficulties in the relations between Sankyo and the parent company. H-D had just finalized the design of their new cradle framed 61E model, a 61 cubic inch ohv model offering higher performance than the long popular VL side valve machines. The Founders now proposed that the Sankyo Company, together with the payment of a very substantial license fee, acquire the manufacturing rights of the new ohv model.

As Child was, and had been, importing substantial numbers of Milwaukee-built H-D machines, his own organization quite naturally received one of the first of the new 61E models. Child's son, Richard, took this machine on a 400 mile test ride to the south of the main island of Japan, and ultimately returned to report the journey as nothing short of a disaster. The engine constantly leaked oil, the ohv rocker mechanism required continual adjustment, and the valve springs remained intact for only limited mileages.

Alfred Rich Child, his wife, Eleanor, and children, with the 'J' sidecar outfit. *(Alfred Rich Child)*.

In due time improved examples of the 61E arrived in Japan, following the Milwaukee factory's strenuous efforts to make the necessary improvements in the initial production run of some 1900 machines. Many of these had shown valve gear defects, and were thoroughly tested by Child and his staff regarding their suitability for Japanese application.

It was ultimately decided that the new model was less suited than the contemporarily produced side valve models, which possessed more tractive power at lesser and more economical engine speeds and were more suitable for sidecar and rear car applications.

As the result of these conclusions, at a meeting in the Muromachi Sankyo Building, Mr.Fukui and a half dozen of the company's financial backers, together with a group of the auditors, finally decided against any further negotiations with Milwaukee regarding the obtaining of a license to manufacture the new ohv machines.

As a further development of this discussion, which had become somewhat heated, one of the auditors took it upon himself to send a cable to a Mr.Kusanobu, the New York representative of Sankyo Pharmaceuticals, and suggested that he proceed to Milwaukee and contact the four Founders to advise them that Sankyo would no longer finance future shipments of H-D machines to Japan if

Child were to continue as Company representative in that country. He was also to emphasize the fact that Sankyo was not at all interested in producing any of the new ohv 61E machines, but would continue to produce at the Shinagawa plant the well proved side valve (now UL Model) machines which were by this time well proved and more suited to Japanese conditions. It was further intimated that these were to be produced under the name 'Rikuo', literally translated as 'King of the Road'.

Kusanobu, acting now as Sankyo's agent, was well chosen as an emissary as he had been born in Canada, educated in the United States, had married a Canadian and was well versed in American business methods as well as having a command of fluent English. His approach to the Founders was not well timed, however, and after a stormy meeting during which the Founders firmly rejected his proposal, it was reported by a reliable witness that burly young Walter Davidson Jr. (the son of the late William A.) came near to ejecting Kusanobu from the premises.

In the meantime, Child was in continuous communication with Milwaukee and Arthur Davidson over his own status with the Company, as well as the marketing situation of Milwaukee-built machines. The ultimate decision was that the factory would terminate all its agreements with Sankyo and the Shinagawa operation, and that Child would now head a new sales organization with himself as exclusive agent, with his own sales office, spare parts depot, and shipping arrangements. In addition, and for the first time in H-D history, the factory agreed to ship machines and parts on open account, with payment due 90 days after landed delivery.

Child immediately established a new headquarters in Tokyo under the name 'Nichiman H-D Sales', which was now, of course, a distinctly separate organization having no connection with the Japanese manufacture of native-built Rikuos. At the same moment, Mr.Fukui remained on friendly terms with Child, and purchased several hundred sidecar outfits from him during 1936.

As an aside to this rather bizarre reorganization, Child was not offered any financial remuneration from Milwaukee for his efforts in the Sankyo negotiations, no doubt in view of the fact that he had prospered handsomely during the past decade from his original company association.

Child emerged from the new agreement as the exclusive H-D sales agent for the whole of Japan, Korea, North China, and Manchuria, with access to both the 74 and 80 cubic inch side valve and 61E ohv machines and their concommitant spare parts. In addition, Fukui, the former Tameike Sales Department Manager, continued to sell Milwaukee machines, which they purchased from Child, to fill out their Rikuo line.

This budding and profitable venture was suddenly terminated, however, when in January, 1937, the National Diet, by this time a puppet organization of the newly-emerging militaristic government of Japan, announced that certain import tariffs, motorcycles among them would increase from Y74 to Y560.

This incredible increase in import duty appeared to have resulted from a previous conference regarding the importation of motorcycles between Child and one Colonel Fujii, who acted as liaison between civilian manufacturers and the military procurement apparatus. Fujii had at that time advised Child to dispose of his Japanese assets, terminate his commercial activities, and return to the United States with his family at the earliest possible moment. He was further advised tht Mr.Fujii would now purchase Child's present stocks of machines and spare parts, as well as arriving shipments in transit. As a further means of expediting the liquidation of Child's holdings, Col.Fujii stated that the purchase could be made with gold US dollars, which at that point in time were very difficult to export from Japan.

Child's first reaction to this proposal was to refuse. By his own admission he enjoyed his life in Japan, had made many firm friendships, developed a keen interest in Oriental art, and owned three palatial homes located in Yokohama, Kamakura, and Karuiziwa. On the other hand, the now politically powerful military regime was in firm control of the government, and it was futile to contemplate that they would make any concessions to aid any single individual. He therefore closed out his business and sold his remaining stocks of machines and parts to Mr.Fujii, which included those both on order and en route to Japan.

In order to minimize the effect of the termination of his franchise, Child cabled Milwaukee the details of Colonel Fujii's ultimatum, and at the same time requested that they dispatch at once up to 300 more machines in addition to those already on order and en route. The management was justifiably cautious, however, and advised Child to liquidate his holdings now in hand with all dispatch. Child complied, and leaving his wife and children in his home at Karaizawa, sold the Kamakura residence, and set sail for Milwaukee. He had hoped to obtain a domestic position in the Milwaukee Sales Department, but on his arrival and following an interview with Arthur Davidson, the latter informed him that the Company had no such position to offer him. He further stated that as Child had already amassed a tidy fortune from his Japanese operation, he could scarcely be satisfied with a salaried position in the Company which of necessity could offer him only a comparatively modest return.

Child next obtained a position with the Bendix Manufacturing Company of South Bend, Indiana, as their Sales Representative for North China, on the basis of his wide knowledge and familiarity with general business and marketing conditions in that area.

Due to the militaristic makeup of the new Japanese government, the Sankyo Company was not able to negotiate a new contract with H-D for either Japan or Manchuria. The Shinagawa factory continued to manufacture Rikuo machines during the war and shortly thereafter, but production declined greatly after 1946. The company concurrently manufactured naval torpedoes shortly before the attack on Pearl Harbor, some of which no doubt were used against the US Pacific Fleet.

H-D's Oriental interlude and the complex details involving Milwaukee's connection both with Child and the Rikuo machines was never publicized, either officially or unofficially. Due to the general growing apprehension in the United States, both within military and upper echelon government officials, the company no doubt thought it expedient to suppress any details of their connection with the building of Japan's war machine. There are, in fact, perhaps only a handful of men yet living at this writing who are conversant with the true facts of the matter.

Child's son, Richard, who assisted him in setting up the Nichiman-Harley-Davidson import agreement in 1935 and 1936, founded the Balcom Trading Company after World War II, with headquarters in Takanawa, Tokyo, and is at this writing the sole importer of H-D motorcycles, along with German BMW automobiles. In spite of the present state of world leadership in motorcycle manufacture now enjoyed by Japan, several hundred Milwaukee-built H-Ds are sold in Japan each year.

Child's contribution to the transportation economy of Japan long before any such industries were ever developed in that country, his influence upon the ultimate domestic establishment of such industries, as well as his contribution to the survival of the H-D Company during the difficult years of the US motorcycle industry, well deserve to be remembered. According to Child's own records, his organization imported an average of 2,000 machines each year from 1924 through 1936. In addition, several thousand Rikuas were built during the latter period after 1930. Added to this should be the 800-1,000 machines per year imported into Australia and New Zealand. Thus, the total Japanese and Australasian sales formed a very important and vital part of H-D's continuing fortunes.

While Child mentions many problems with the H-D Company incidental to his import operations, in his reminiscences he recalls that the management was ever co-operative and, in every case, treated him fairly.

# Chapter 5

# Disappointment and Disaster

SINCE ITS EARLIEST DEVELOPMENT THE MOTORCYCLE SOON BECAME A PRIME TOOL of law enforcement. It was apparently first employed in the nation's larger cities to catch runaway horses, but soon figured in the apprehension of speeding car drivers, even in the days when the average automobile had the frightening top speed of 30 mph. Indian, as the earliest leader of the industry, reaped the initial harvest of law enforcement sales, to be challenged by Excelsior and H-D as soon as their production became significant. H-D began a vigorous campaign for the law enforcement business after 1912, and this was intensified during the post WWI days when their production ultimately equaled and then surpassed that of Indian. While large numbers of both 'J' type H-Ds and Indian Chiefs and Scouts were now utilized by various law enforcement bodies, most motorcycle officers preferred the four cylinder machines built by Excelsior, as well as the newly-introduced Ace. The obvious reasons were that the fours were less prone to vibration, started more readily and, for their day, had rapid acceleration. It was much less physically tiring to ride a machine that was inherently immune to vibration for an 8 or 10-hour shift. Consequently the Henderson, and latterly, the Ace, became the favorite police machines, at least in areas where the authorities involved in purchasing were willing to expend public funds for a somewhat higher priced machine. In some areas where, in those days, officers were allowed to supply their own machines for official use on a contract basis, fours were almost universally the machine of choice.

With the demise of the Ace in the Fall of 1924, through unfortunate financial difficulties suffered by their maker, Schwinn immediately increased Henderson production, as well as substantially raising its retail price, now that he had a monopoly on the type. H-D's top management, ever cognizant of the now critical motorcycle market, at once foresaw the opportunity to compete in a new, if limited market, with a four cylinder model of their own.

In a private meeting, the Founders at once decided that the Engineering Department should set about developing prototype designs of such a model. William Harley initiated a survey of the matter, and after some deliberation, suggested that an outside consultant more conversant with four cylinder design should be engaged to assist in the matter. While some of Harley's contemporary critics within the industry had in the past offered the opinion that the latter's engineering abilities extended but little beyond that of making minor variations in the original works of DeDion Bouton, it was at least obvious that his prompt seeking of outside advice had in the past saved the Company much valuable time in the development of new designs.

Everett O. DeLong, formerly in charge of Ace's Engineering and Design, and currently at liberty with the collapse of that Company, was retained as a consultant with a six month's contract. DeLong's retention was obviously a good choice. A graduate automotive engineer, he had at once developed an absorbing interest in four cylinder motorcycle design. He was fully conversant with the type, throughout its F.N-Pierce-Henderson evolvement, and had first attracted the attention of the industry with a 90 in V-type four that he had designed in collaboration with Cannonball Baker in 1920. A promising design that had actually undergone prototype testing in an Indian Powerplus frame, only capitalization difficulties had prevented its initial manufacture. He had next become Henderson's protegé, and had worked with Arthur Lemon in the Ace Company, where the two had turned out some rather potent competition engines.

DeLong readily accepted H-D's offer, and sworn to strict secrecy in the matter, was installed in an office in an out-of-the-way area of the factory. As a top secret project within the Engineering Department, only the principals, George Nordberg, and two other trusted members of the staff were aware of what was underway.

Proceeding with a strict admonition that the new design should be rationalized within the present production schedule as closely as possible, DeLong suggested that an Ace-type F head engine be fitted into the standard J chassis. The front down tube was cranked forward to follow the wheel arc, and a rectangular tubular frame was set horizontally to accommodate the engine case. As the design work proceeded, William Davidson at once rejected it on the grounds that such an engine would be too costly to produce, so the project only progressed through the preliminary drawings.

DeLong's next effort, with some help from Harley, was perhaps more practical from the production standpoint. Again based on the standard J chassis, it was fitted with what was in essence two J-type engines placed side-by-side, utilizing a common crankcase. Standard J cylinder assemblies were incorporated, but the barrels were sleeved down to produce an engine that was of about 80 cu. in. displacement. A slightly modified three-speed J transmission was fitted, the countershaft being extended on additional outrigger bearings to accommodate the slightly widened drive line to the engine sprocket. The standard J clutch was fitted, but with extra plates and somewhat stronger springs.

Both Harley and DeLong were now quite enthusiastic about the design's possibilities, both from its rationalized production capabilities, and for the fact that such an engine would undoubtedly have fewer cooling problems, long the inherent weakness of the more familiar in-line type.

In the ensuing conferences with the Founders, William Davidson again rejected the proposal, stating that production costs could well price the finished machine out of the market. While both George Nordberg and the other Davidsons were reportedly favorable toward the project, William was adamant, and the project was cancelled. It was later reported that the wooden mockup of the engine made by DeLong was hurriedly destroyed to erase all evidence of its projected development.

Veteran H-D employees have long speculated about the projected four affair and most especially concerning William Davidson's role in its rejection. Some members of the engineering department informed the Author in later years that, in their opinion, the V-four as designed by DeLong had distinct possibilities, both as to its superior cooling capabilities, and in its possible economies in manufacture due to its utilization of the currently produced 'J' cylinder assemblies. Others have stated that, in their opinion, more in-depth costing studies might well have shown that the model's production was economically feasible.

Other old time or retired members of H-D's engineering staff have stated that William Davidson's opinions carried great weight within the Company's hierarchy, both from his position as Head of Production, and his financial interest in the Company. It has been ascertained from numerous knowledgable sources within the H-D organization that, due to the original terms of their corporate agreement, both William J.Harley and the Davidsons shared equally in the profits of the Company. However, while the other Founders had seen fit through the years to invest a part of their earnings in other ventures outside the Company, William Davidson had reinvested all of his shares within the Company itself, and had by this means now become its principal share holder. Holding as he did now, a commanding financial position, it is obvious that his decisions regarding general company policy would carry great weight. In addition, William's preoccupation with production efficiencies was by now a traditional byword at H-D, and the emphasis on production of the 'J' model had enabled him to rationalize its manufacture to the point that a very high quality machine could be assembled to sell at a very competitive price. It is also known that William was also firmly opposed to diversification of models and the consequent production disruption, and it may well have been that this was one important reason for his rejection of the four. While the details of the many closed meetings held by the Founders regarding on going Company policy could never be publicly revealed, the matter of the four remains as a challenging mystery in the complexities of H-D history.

After his contract with H-D was terminated, DeLong was subsequently retained by Cleveland to update the somewhat archaic T-headed four-cylinder model manufactured briefly in small numbers by that company after they terminated production of their long popular two-stroke lightweight model. He designed two high performance models of advanced design, one of 45 cubic inches, which was later

Del Du Chene's
authentically-
restored 1926 Model
'B' single. *(Alisha
Tamburri).*

91

dropped to make way for a 61 cubic inch model that was capable of over 100 mph. This latter was a sensation during 1928 and 1929, but the Company's mounting financial problems due to its limited retail outlets caused it to suspend production after only a few hundred machines had been produced. DeLong himself was to die tragically a few years later, hopelessly insane from an inoperable brain tumor.

H-D's participation in competitive sport was severly curtailed after the close of the 1921 season due to the official termination of factory support. The disposition of the remaining factory-owned racing machines remains an historical mystery. Some accounts have it that the former Wrecking Crew members were allowed to purchase them for $1,500 each. Others state that the Founders presented some of them with their mounts as a gift. A few Excelsior riders did the same, in line with Excelsior's similar policy, but without factory support neither group was able to do much better than second or third place wins. Indian, under Frank J.Weschler's dedicated management, elected to continue the Company's traditional support of competition in the traditions laid down by Carl Oscar Hedstrom and George M.Hendee. Several prominent members of the Wrecking Crew, including Jim Davis, Curly Fredericks, and Ralph Hepburn, transferred their allegiance to the Wigwam, and cumulatively racked up a string of impressive victories during subsequent seasons.

The numerous board tracks near the larger cities continued to attract large crowds, as public resentment against such often gory spectacles was gradually waning. Wind and weather was now taking its toll of the vast wooden structures, and encroaching residential and industrial expansion were already forcing some of them out of the picture. The death of Jack Prince, their principal exponent and promoter, from a sudden heart attack, had now eliminated their repair and renovation. In addition, the position of the motorcycle in the transportation field was now further eroded by the fact that the Model T Ford, due to its overwhelming production, could advertise the retail price of its two seater roadster at $265 without an electric starter, the self-starting model being but $20 more in similar stark form at the factory gate. Chevrolet and Star, vigorously competing in the same market, were also being offered for a few dollars more.

In the Spring of 1924, William Ottaway's warning to William Harley regarding the latter's pirating of the basic design of the Bendix clutch came true when Victor Bendix, its inventor and President of the Bendix Manufacturing Company of Indianapolis, Indiana, filed legal action against the H-D Company, charging patent infringement. Following a couple of hearings in Superior Court, H-D, on the advice of Counsel, capitulated with a confession of judgement. They subsequently paid Bendix damages in the amount of what was reported as $18,000. H-D's Engineering Department then immediately revised the basic H-D clutch design to include a cam type release that differed sufficiently from the basic Bendix design to terminate the infringement problem.

In the early Spring of 1924, H-D's management decided that an updating of the now classic 'J' model was in order. While the 'J' model had been much refined during the decade since its inception, with many improvements to the engine that made the model a high quality product, its appearance

Geoffrey Hockley, a New Zealand enthusiast, restored this 1926 ohv BA single. The side and ohv models were identical, except for the engine. *(The Antique Motorcycle Club of America).*

Famed competition rider Eddie Brinck with his 1926 'Peashooter'. Note the Flying Merkel-type telescopic fork. *(C.May)*.

was still that of a somewhat spindly motorcycle little changed in appearance since 1914. In the meantime, Ace, Henderson, and Indian had gradually updated their styling to offer a more streamlined appearance, which was most definitely more attractive. Chief Engineer William Harley now commissioned Arthur Constantine to redesign the new venerable 'J', with strict orders to execute the revision with as little increase in production costs as possible. Under the stern eye of William Davidson, Constantine was able to modernize the silhouette of the 'J' with a minimum of structural alteration. The frame was lowered at the seat post, giving a 3 inch reduction of saddle height, and a somewhat bulbous two-piece fuel and oil tank configuration was instituted which supplanted the former, now archaic design. In addition, the mudguards were widened slightly and given somewhat deeper valances, resulting in a more modernized and attractive appearance.

Constantine, on his own initiative, also undertook two other projects, one on behalf of the Company, the other as a private venture, which were to have ultimate far-reaching effects on his own career in the domestic motorcycle scene. The first was the order for a specially-designed 74 cubic inch 'J' model for a local missionary and friend of his, home on leave from an overseas assignment. His friend had written a letter to the Company asking for a specially-designed machine which would include some type of cleats attached to the wheel rims to give him additional tractive power when riding the machine off the roads in desert sand. Constantine designed a special machine with cranked seat and chain stays which, along with similar alteration to the fork tubes, would permit the fitting of metal cleats to the wheel rims to obviate the sand problem. In addition to this special one-off model, Constantine also designed an entirely new motorcycle. Based on the standard 'J' model, it featured a lowered and more comapct profile on a 57 inch wheelbase, having redesigned front forks, and a new pocket valve engine with 45 cubic inch displacement. When he showed the results of his work to William and Arthur Davidson, the latter at once dismissed the proposed new model as an unneeded complication to H-D's standard 'J' production. The former condemned it as both an unauthorized undertaking and a waste of valuable company time. In the resultant recriminations, Constantine resigned from his position as an assistant engineer, and subsequently took a position in the Excelsior Company, which event was to later form a subsequent chapter in American motorcycle history which will be explored later.

Another complication in subsequent 'J' models was the traditional valve cam arrangement, which due to the increased power developed caused undue stress on the cam followers, which were activated by a single roller carried on a single outrigger bearing. The traditional configuration was subjected to much wear due to the side thrust imposed by the inlet tappets to the overhead intake valve. Practical mechanics almost immediately found a solution to the problem by fitting Indian cam followers, which had a forked arrangement subject to less wear, the assembly being slightly modified to fit the standard factory fitting. This practice at once caused much consternation at the factory, and the Engineering Department at once issued directives condemning their use, which was emphasized by the traveling factory representatives. Knowledgable tuners and many dealers' mechanics persisted in the matter, however, and the author has observed many old 'J' engines in the hands of antique 'J' owners still fitted with reworked Indian adaptations that were resurrected in later years! The Company attempted to solve the problem by increasing the thickness of the original cam followers, but the problem of side thrust and consequent rapid wear was never totally overcome before the 'J' was supplanted by the later 'VL' models.

Bill Minnick and his 'J' type racer with Flxi banking sidecar. *(C. May)*.

The H-D Company was forced to manufacture their own sidecar models in both the passenger and commercial box body models late in 1925 when the Rogers Company suspended their production. With the death of the company founder, B.F.Rogers, the concern was eventually sold by the heirs to one B.F.Leopold of the Eros Manufacturing Company, another Chicago-based company previously engaged in the fabrication of sheet metal products and other metallic extrusions. Walter Davidson had made a couple of attempts, after 1920, to force the original Rogers Company to agree to supply the H-D Company with sidecar units exclusively, the idea apparently being to give H-D a monopoly on the supply of Rogers' products during the general decline of the motorcycle market. Rogers had refused, as his organization had been engaged since 1914 in supplying such units to the general motorcycle trade, including Ace and Excelsior, which now also included the popular Henderson. The story goes that Rogers refused to comply with this request even under threat of having the contract with H-D terminated. The same ultimatum was extended to Leopold, who not only refused to comply, but shortly afterwards terminated all sidecar production in favor of more lucrative commitments outside the motorcycle industry. As a result, the H-D Company initiated production of their own sidecar units, and set up a separate production facility.

Due to the general decline in motorcycle sales, various accessory manufacturers producing such ancillary items as lighting sets, rear mudguard carriers, speedometers, spotlights, heavy duty electric generators, and other items, gradually disappeared from the market. In consequence, the surviving three manufacturers at once were forced to supply such items to their dealers. The H-D Company set aside a large wing of the factory for the manufacture of these products, and within a short time had the largest such facility within the industry. A separate retail catalog was produced to advertise accessory items, along with confidential wholesale price lists for the dealers. The factory representatives were continually urging the enhanced stocking of accessories, emphasizing that the 40% to 60% retail markup was an important adjunct to dealer profits.

At the annual sub rosa meeting between Indian's Frank J.Weschler and Arthur Davidson, held in the summer of 1924 at the Astor Hotel in New York City, the retail prices for the H-D's 61s and 74s and the corresponding Indian Chiefs and Big Chief models were set at parity.

During the Spring of that year, an unsubstantiated rumor circulating through the Big Three factories had it that an unnamed import-export concern in New York City had formulated tentative plans to import a line of lightweight utility and mediumweight roadster machines from England. It has been reported that neither the Excelsior or Indian management were greatly concerned about the matter, but that Walter Davidson immediately took steps to track it down. After numerous inquiries, he decided to launch a frontal attack on the possible threat of a foreign motorcycle invasion by contacting Wisconsin's senior Senator, Robert M.LaFollette, a long time leading figure in the state's political scene, concerning the current tariff situation on imported vehicles. He learned to his dismay that the Tariff Commission had set a rate on them at a minimal 5%, as up to this time the importation of foreign vehicles had been almost non-existent except for a few Rolls Royce cars. Before the Senator had time to follow through with Davidson's request, he died suddenly on June 10th from a heart attack. His seat in the United States Senate was then taken over by his son, Robert Jr., who was to continue the LaFollette dynasty in Wisconsin. The latter who was, coincidentally, a distant relative of the author, in recalling the incident in later years, stated that he had informed Davidson that it would require substantial political effort and the expenditure of a sizable sum of money to lobby the Tariff Commission into extending the rates on foreign vehicles, especially as there was presently not sufficient imports of such to offer a threat to the American industry. After some reflection, Davidson is reported to have abandoned his efforts to pursue the matter further.

Another interesting vignette of H-D history during these years was the matter of the Pacific Motors affair in Los Angeles, and the alleged role played in it by the now very active H-D representative in that city, Rich Budelier. To begin the story, it is a matter of record that Indian machines were first selected by the Purchasing Department of the City of Los Angeles for law enforcement use, and had been the sole make in police department work since 1920. After he revitalized H-D's role in Los Angeles, Budelier quite naturally sought to break Indian's monopoly. During the annual performance tests conducted on the San Bernardino highway, Budelier readied a carefully run-in 61 cubic inch 'J' model to enter the contest. Upon hearing of Budelier's intention, C.Will Risdon, of Indian, put his ace tuners at work on a 61 cubic inch Chief, which model had been selected during the two previous years by the motor officers as their favorite. This machine was carefully honed to perfection with assistance, we are told, from Fred Ludlow. The Indian attained a speed of 92 mph against a 69 mph from the H-D, and Risdon was soon gleefully affixing police insignia to 25 new Chiefs for their official delivery to the Department.

Shortly afterwards, Risdon announced his intention to retire, and a prospective buyer in the form of one A.F.Van Order, arrived on the scene. It seems that Van Order had lately been the Sales Manager for Budelier, being frequently seen about the city on a pristine H-D sidecar outfit. In his

Johnny Eagles with his 1926 JD. The machine is authentically restored except for the fitting of a 1929 front wheel with brake assembly to better cope with modern traffic conditions. *(Alisha Tamburri).*

representations to Risdon, however, Van Order stated that he had just been fired by Budelier for some trivial reason, and as a dedicated motorcyclist he was anxious to transfer his allegiance to the Wigwam. The story goes that Risdon was not entirely satisfied with Van Order's offer, but was finally persuaded to sell him the franchise on the strength of the fact that Van Order had established a holding corporation which he had designated as Pacific Motors, and which had substantial monetary backing. Van Order took over Risdon's extensive premises, which included several dozen new and used machines, a well equipped workshop, and a comprehensive spare parts inventory. Van Order's next step was to increase the fire insurance coverage of both the buildings and contents to its ultimate maximum. The following month, the entire premises was suddenly engulfed in a massive conflagration, it taking six engine companies several hours to extinguish the flames that leveled both the motorcycle shop and two adjacent buildings. At this point the story becomes somewhat confused, as varying versions of the incident have been related by early day motorcyclists, some claiming that it was Budelier himself who set the fire, others implicating Van Order. The author, who has delved into the matter for some years, has

Harvey Mummert's 1925-1926 ultra-light monoplane with a geared-down 61 cu.in. 'J' type engine.

Close up of Mummert's chain reduction propellor drive.

Darter Tiffany's ultra-light biplane fitted with a 61 cu.in. H-D engine.

come up with what may be the most authentic evidence from the statements of the late Harold McClellan, then an investigator with the Los Angeles Fire Department's Arson Squad. He told him in 1958 that his agency had received a call from one of Risdon's ex-employees, now working for Van Order, that he somehow suspected an imminent catastrophy, and he called the arson investigators as the fire started. Officers immediately launched an investigation, dispatching detectives to both Van Order's and Budelier's homes. The former was not to be found, the statements from his family being that he was out of town on a business trip. Another squad of detectives who entered Budelier's home found him in bed, but fully clothed and with his shoes on! The late J.Harold Louderback, then a young legal assistant in the Los Angeles County District Attorney's office, later stated that while both Budelier and Van Order were somehow involved in the matter, investigators could not turn up sufficient hard evidence to sustain criminal charges that would hold up in court. Louderback went on in later years to become a distinguished judge in the state's Apellate Court.

H-D was without competition in downtown Los Angeles for two years until Albert G.Crocker     97 came out west from Kansas City to activate a very aggressive dealership, although Indian was still well represented in the surrounding cities in the Los Angeles basin. Budelier continued to expand his own extensive dealership, and Van Order remained in various capacities on the fringes of the industry. He later founded the Trailblazers, an organization of pioneer motorcyclists that still holds annual meetings in the Los Angeles area.

The now updated 'J' was well received by H-D enthusiasts, not only from its somewhat moderniz-ed appearance, but from further improved cam and valve action and a larger capacity oiling system which enhanced its performance as well as its already well-deserved reputation for reliability. Company-built sidecar models in both passenger and commercial carriers were also offered, along with a wide two-passenger type based on the original Rogers design that was built in limited numbers for export use.

In the Spring of 1925 the export of American machines to Great Britain received a severe setback when the Chancellor of the Exchequer announced the imposition of a 33⅓% import tax on foreign motorcycles. Growing economic and labor troubles were said to have inspired this action, as the cur-rent government was attempting to stabilize domestic marketing conditions. Its effect was the almost immediate cessation of Yankee imports, and Duncan Watson terminated his operations by canceling his H-D franchise agreement. The factory maintained a small parts and service outlet in London until 1930 for the benefit of British enthusiasts, many of whom were still riding 1914 and 1915 models. Repairs and maintenance were subsequently undertaken by several specialist shops operated by en-thusiasts through the early 1930's. In later years, F.H.Warr, who maintained premises in the London suburb of Fulham, became H-D distributor for the United Kingdom, selling new machines thereafter in very limited numbers, as the artificially high retail price now mandated by the newly imposed tariff, plus the shipping costs, priced new machines out of sight.

During the mid-1920's the total motorcycle production in the United States was substantially less than 25,000 machines. H-D production leveled out to approximately 11,000 to 12,000 units per year, with Indian making from 6,000 to 8,000 and Excelsior turning out about 3,500, most of which were their still popular four cylinder Henderson. In most of these years, over 50% of all domestic production was exported to overseas markets.

With this state of affairs, dealer morale in many cases was at a very low ebb, especially in the smaller towns and cities. H-D's factory representatives were circulating through their various territories offering encouragement through suggesting new sales and advertising techniques. In addition the Company bravely continued its extensive national advertising campaign, not only in the pages of the now dwindling trade press, but in mechanical and hobby magazines, outdoor and nature publications, and occasionally in local newspapers. Perhaps the greatest problem the industry faced during these dif-

An authentically-restored 1927 JD from the Bud Ekins collection. The 'J' models were updated in 1925 by Arthur Constantine, and were identical in detail until 1930. *(Alisha Tamburri).*

Three views of the Juneau
Avenue factory complex
in the late 1920s.

ficult years was the public image of motorcycling as reflected in their often dingy and rundown premises. The factory representatives were constantly exhorting dealers to clean up and to refurbish these establishments, an often impractical suggestion in the face of limited sales.

The now static condition of the domestic market quite naturally weakened the position of the AMA, together with the fact that public interest in competition was waning, following the gradual deterioration of the board tracks. There was also a certain monotony in these contests, as Indian had by this time become the dominant make in such contests due to continuing factory support of racing. While motorcycle registrations still numbered about 150,000 machines throughout the country, only a minority of their owners were willing to pay the $2.00 yearly membership dues to support the organization. In the Fall of 1925, AMA President Douglas Hobart, called a meeting of the Motorcycle and Allied Trades Association in New York City, which included representatives of the Big Three manufacturers, together with the now decimated ranks of the accessory manufacturers and the tire companies. Stating the obvious lack of support from the general motorcycling public, Hobart pointed out that the AMA was now in the same unfortunate position that the former AFM had found itself following the war. After some lengthy discussion, it was decided that each of the sustaining M & ATA members should contribute funds to the AMA on a pro-rata basis, as it was now obvious that the AMA would otherwise collapse. This was finally agreed upon, but at the same time it was decided that the factories, both directly and through their dealer outlets, would continue to solicit support from motorcycle owners at large. Hobart resigned his office shortly thereafter to take up an Indian franchise, and George T. Briggs, President of the Wheeler-Schebler Carburetor Company, was elected from within the ranks of the M & ATA to take his place, serving until the Fall of 1928.

During this period, the Excelsior Company decided to re-enter its official support of competition in the 21 cubic inch class, at the urging of one Joseph (Joe) Petrali, a budding competition rider. At the same time, Indian expressed interest in this competition category, as they were then in process of testing prototype ohv versions of their 21 cubic inch Prince model, placed in production the year before. Hobart's last official act, on his own initiative, was to give official AMA sanction to the recognition of this new competition class. This greatly angered President Walter Davidson, as up to this point, H-D had no 21 cubic inch machines in production. It was later alleged that he concluded that Hobart, being an Indian enthusiast, had attempted to place H-D at a disadvantage. When H-D took the dominant role in AMA affairs in later years, Hobart's name and his role in AMA history was stricken from the organisation's official records.

In spite of H-D's withholding of official support of competition during these years, H-D machines continued to figure prominently in many regional competition activities. Many racing enthusiasts and clubmen determined to individually keep Milwaukee's flag flying, and many racing specials, mostly personally built up from stock parts, emerged from both dealers' shops or the backyards of mechanically-inclined enthusiasts. While H-D could quite naturally not challenge Indian in either the big National Races or on the boards, they racked up credible wins at rural county fairs and out-of-the-way horse tracks. As the now weakened status of the AMA did not give them the power to put an end to unsanctioned or 'outlaw' events, H-D was still a potent force in official competition.

It was during this period that H-D engines figured somewhat prominently in the powering of ultra-light aircraft. While the recent World War had given great impetus to aircraft design progress, most of the machines produced for the war effort were too costly to be maintained by either private owners or commercial operators. Added to this, most of their engines were designed with but a short duration service life, which added to their general unreliability. At the same moment, the availability of large numbers of war surplus aircraft at give-away prices had up to this time effectively strangled private efforts at instigating general aircraft manufacture. Then too, the highly publicized exploits of the wartime aces featuring the 'knights of the air' concept could scarcely be related to an interest in flying on the part of the ordinary citizen. Most of the aircraft observed by the general public during the immediate post-war era were the exhibition flights and stunts performed at county fairs or during the course of patriotic celebrations — scarcely calculated to impress the public that flying could be other than a daredevil undertaking.

In an effort to stimulate public interest in private flying and at the same time to encourage the development of low cost aviation, a newspaper in England, the Daily Mail, sponsored a design contest for ultra-light aircraft at Lympne Aerodrome in the south of England in the Summer of 1923. In deference to the total lack of suitable professionally-designed small aircraft engines, the power plants were limited to a cubic displacement of 750 cc, or 45 cubic inches, which could include the converted motorcycle engines already utilized by the early experimenters. While the overall results of the contest were inconclusive, the meeting attracted world wide attention among aviation enthusiasts. In the United States, numerous experimenters had already been at work, such as Etiene Dormoy, Ed Heath, B.H. Petienpol, Weston Farmer, and Jean Roche. In addition to these, one Harvey Mummert, an aeronautical engineer employed by the Curtis Wright Aviation Company, who was also an H-D enthusiast, was engaged in building a small wood framed, low winged monoplane with a 26 foot wingspan. For power, he utilized a converted 61 cubic inch 'J' model engine. Entering it in the National Air Races held in the Summers of 1924 and 1925, he managed to attain second place wins.

While V twin engines were generally not well suited to ultralight aircraft due to the characteristic uneven firing angle causing sufficient vibration to shake the light airframes to pieces after a few flights, Mummert's results were somewhat more satisfactory, as he statically and dynamically balanced his engine for the 1,600 to 1,800 rate of revolutions that gave optimum propellor efficiency. He later built a small racing biplane for Sarter Tiffany powered by an inverted 'J' engine which competed successfully in the 1926 National contest. Most subsequent light aircraft were powered with Henderson or Indian Four conversions, due to their smoother running capabilities.

Production of the only mildly successful domestic lightweight motorcycle, the Cleveland, was phased out by its makers early in 1925, supposedly to make way for the assembly of their projected four cylinder models. The management of Indian, with possibly some inside knowledge of Cleveland's plans, hastened to produce a 21 cubic inch side valve model which was designated as the 'Prince', its designer, Charles Franklin, basing it on contemporary English models.

H-D's management immediately rose to the challenge, and the Engineering Department was at once put to work to develop a machine of similar size. During the prototype development, an Indian Prince, as well as a 350 cc BSA and a New Imperial imported from England were secured for evaluation. The outcome was what was essentially a scaled down 'J' model with the option of two engine types: a 21 cubic inch side valve model designated as the Model 'A', and an ohv model of the same displacement designated as the 'AA'. The economy models without electric lighting were priced at $210 and $250 respectively. The all-electric 'B' and 'BA' models sold for $235 and $275. The machines were well-balanced, handled and steered satisfactorily, and were capable of top speeds of about 50 and 65 mph respectively. The patented H-D spring seat post afforded acceptable comfort for the rider over rough roads, much superior to that offered in either the now defunct Cleveland or the current Indian Prince.

The side valve 'A' model enjoyed mild popularity with utility riders, such as newspaper delivery carriers and Western Union messenger boys. The performance capabilities were, however, somewhat limited by the fact that if the machine was ridden for any length of time over 45 mph the cast iron piston fitted to the earlier model was prone to seizure, the usual result being a broken piston. Practical dealers' mechanics and backyard motorcycle engineers were quick to ascertain that the pistons of a once popular Oldsmobile automobile could be substituted for the genuine factory article, and prudent dealers usually stocked such as they could be sold to the usually impecunious schoolboys for $1.50, a distinct saving over the H-D retail price of $4.50. This glaring defect was somewhat of an anachronism, as the cylinder head had been designed for the factory by Harry Ricardo, who was paid a small royalty for each machine produced.

The ohv model was somewhat more successful, and offered more sprightly performance, with a 65 mph top speed, and could actually produce a steady 60 mph cruising speed without trouble, providing suitable roads could be found to maintain this rate of travel. The exposed rocker gear, which was provided with only sketchy lubrication, wore rapidly however, and required frequent adjustment to keep the engine in tune.

The inherent possibilities of both models for economical transport in the United States was somewhat blunted by the universal availability of serviceable used Ford and Chevrolet cars, which were then selling on the used car market for $50 to $75. While the fuel mileages of both the A and B models was fantastic, such economies were unimportant in an era when gasoline was sold for 18 to 20 cents a gallon.

The principal market for the new singles was, of course, overseas, although the increased import tariff in England effectively cut off the anticipated sales in the United Kingdom which H-D had hoped to penetrate on the strength of the already established position of the big twin 'J's. Both models were fairly well received both in Europe and in the Scandinavian countries, where the demand for economical transportation wss paramount due to the high price of gasoline. On the home front, dealer resistance was still a factor, as most of these were still big twin orientated and were not overly inclined to promote a model that did not offer excessive power and speed.

In the meantime, flat track racing, which had been initiated in New Zealand, became a popular spectator sport in both Australia and England, and eventually received mild recognition in the United States. The high performance 'AA' ohv single was a natural for such competition, and due to its small size and displacement was compared to the usual heavyweight big twins, to become known as the 'Peashooter'. In consequence, the factory now offered a lightened competition version with a shortened frame to reduce the wheelbase, together with strutted telescopic forks based on an earlier successful design by Joseph Merkel for his once noted 'Flying Merkel' machines. With a high power-to-weight ratio and in competition form having a weight of only 215 pounds, the Peashooter had good handling characteristics and made an enviable reputation for itself on the short tracks, both in Australasia and

The Model C 30.50 single. Known as the 'Baby Harley', its side valve engine of modest power output was mated with an ultra-heavy chassis shared with the newly introduced 45 cu.in. side valve. Its main sales were in the export market.

in the United States during the late 1920's. Its popularity was only eclipsed when later highly developed Rudge and J.A.Prestwich speedway specials finally surpassed it.

The ohv Peashooter received a well deserved notoriety in its own country, on both short tracks and as a hill climber. The new 21 cubic inch competition class, as approved by the AMA through the efforts of Douglas Hobart, became a show case for the H-D Company, as Indian reneged on its offerings in this class due to its very limited production of the 21 cubic inch ohv Prince Models, said to have been caused by the company's now current financial troubles. In consequence, H-D now swept the board in 21 cubic inch competition, through the efforts of Joe Petrali, whose role in H-D history will be subsequently discussed.

In the meantime, Excelsior scooped the industry with the surprise introduction of a new 45 cubic inch middleweight motorcycle which was named the 'Super X'. This new model was a twin, as the formerly popular 61 cubic inch model had been phased out two years before to make way for enhanced production of the Henderson Four. It featured both in-unit construction of the engine and gearbox through a geared drive, as in the popular Indian Scout, with the pocket valve arrangement of the classic 'J' H-D. The few H-D employees who had access to the company's drafting room immediately noted that it was Constantine's 45 cubic inch model that had been rejected two and one half years before by Walter Davidson, shortly before Constantine resigned from the Company. The new machine was somewhat dissimilar in that instead of the rather bulbous fuel and oil tank, it utilized mostly Henderson components, no doubt to rationalize production, the frame being shortened and its bottom modified to fit the twin's crankcase.

H-D immediately rose to the challenge by commencing prototype work on their own 45 cubic inch model, and Indian's Charles B.Franklin designed an enlarged Scout engine to also fill this category. Early day riders have stated that the 'X' proved to be a very potent performer, although the quality of its general metallurgical components was not up to that offered in H-D machines, and it possessed a somewhat less-than-rugged lower bearing assembly.

At the annual secret price fixing meeting between Indian's Frank J.Weschler and Arthur Davidson, held in 1926 at the St.Regis Hotel in New York City, the retail price of the Prince was raised from $185 to $195. The $210 price of the side valve Peashooter was dropped to the same figure. As the 61 cubic inch Chief had now been dropped from the Indian line in favor of the more popular 74 cubic inch model formerly known as the 'Big Chief', the retail price of this and the HD-74 model were set at a $325 parity.

In the Fall of 1926, for the 1927 sales year, H-D introduced a new ignition system that featured a field coil generator to dispense with the more usual distributor and utilized a single coil that fired the spark plugs on both ignition and exhaust sequences. Although this split the sparking output and often caused minor explosions within the silencing system if unburned residual gases were present, the system proved reliable and was subsequently fitted to later models. In addition, standard Alemite lubrication fittings were installed as a replacement for the now obsolete cup-type formerly used. This made for more effective pressure lubrication of critical bearing surfaces, but enabled the rider to service the cycle parts of his machine at automotive garages or service stations.

A surprise offering which was of signal importance to the many thousands of 'J' enthusiasts was the new 'JD-H' model which featured a 'two cam' exhaust and intake configuration for the valve mechanism in 1928. The standard 'J's of course, had long appeared with a single lobe arrangement for each cylinder, and while offering satisfactory power output, also somewhat limited the possibilities of more sophisticated tuning for high performance. In common with the sporting 'J' model offered in 1925, the option of smaller 25 inch wheels was available, giving a somewhat lowered center of gravity. But without a reduced arc to the mudguards from the standard design the descrepancy between the two produced a somewhat shortened appearance on the overall silhouette of the machine.

This 'Two Cam' model, as it came to be called, quite naturally was an attraction to speed enthusiasts. The position of the valve lifting mechanism was such, however, that a side thrust was imposed from the cam gear, which produced somewhat rapid tappet wear, although this was of small consequence to the average handy owner who was usually something of a mechanic who could effect his own tappet replacement with little difficulty. Its high selling price of about $375 was somewhat of a sales handicap as it represented a $50 premium over that of the standard model, this in the days when a dollar could purchase vastly more than it can at this writing.

The two cammer was in the ultimate sense a very satisfactory model, both in terms of performance and reliability, and it has often been described by experienced old time H-D enthusiasts as one of the best models the factory ever produced.

In the Fall of 1927, AMA President George Briggs called a special meeting of the M & ATA directors and informed them that he was unable to implement the proposed programs of the organization due to lack of proper funding. Contributions from ordinary private riders had fallen far short of the director's original projections, due to lack of support. Co-incidental to this major crisis within the AMA, a new member of the M & ATA now entered the picture in the form of one James A. (Jim) Wright, a dedicated motorcycling enthusiast who had just joined the Indian Company as General Sales Manager. His fortuitous appearance was due to shake up Indian's management, wherein one Louis J.Bauer had lately assumed control of Indian following the resignation of Frank J.Weschler. Wright, who was already aware of the AMA's mounting troubles, had lately written a letter to President Walter Davidson, suggesting ways and means of alleviating the present difficulties. In later years, an old time H-D executive, who enjoyed certain confidences with Walter Davidson, told the author that the latter at first was somewhat hesitant to meet with Wright, who was a newcomer to the industry as well as employed by H-D's principal competitor. But realizing at the same moment the urgent necessity for strengthening the national motorcycle organization in the face of the industry's critical marketing position, he agreed to meet with Wright at the Blackstone Hotel in Chicago. The results of this conference were that the two were able to arrive at an understanding regarding the need for both a concerted drive

Harley-Davidson's finest hour. The immortal 'Two Cam' JD and JDH 61 and 74 cu.in. models. Only their necessarily high selling price prevented them from being runaway best sellers.

to induce more private owners to join and support the AMA, together with the need for enhanced financial subsidization on the part of both the Big Three producers and accessory manufacturers as well.

At the same moment, Wright was placed in a somewhat embarrassing position. The Indian Company was now undergoing financial difficulties because of President Bauer's proposal to diversify and manufacture non-motorcycle products. This lessened his inclination to put up more money for AMA support. Angry at being forced to provide the extra funds for the AMA, Walter Davidson reluctantly agreed to increase H-D's subsidy. Therefore, H-D became in fact, the controlling contributor to the AMA. This resulted in abolition of democratic control of the organization, and enabled the H-D Company literally to dictate future AMA policy.

As an aside to Davidson's and Wright's deliberations, it was also privately agreed that Davidson would now back Wright as the next incoming President of the M & ATA, as Briggs was in process of resigning. It was also agreed that the two would continue to meet annually to fix prices as it had now become an industry tradition. Oldtime members of the M & ATA have stated that Wright's main qualification for this office, other than his wholehearted dedication to motorcycling, was that he was one of the few men within the industry who could get along with Walter Davidson.

Early in 1928, the 'J' models were further modernized by the fitting of a front wheel brake. This was an innovation on the part of the American manufacturers, and lately had been added to the newly introduced Indian Scout and Indian-Ace four. While foreign motorcycles had featured a front wheel brake for nearly a decade. American designers had been tardy in accepting the idea. As it was, Yankee riders in many cases viewed the matter with suspicion, many claiming disastrous results where the front wheel might lock up on sudden braking, especially in a skid. Not a few of these diehards simply disconnected the control cable on new models just purchased, and proceeded with the rear brake as of yore.

In the Fall of that year, the 'JD' was further improved by fitting a larger capacity oil pump which was now interconnected with the throttle, the effect of which was to force more oil into the engine as the speed increased. This new system was not entirely satisfactory, as over-oiling was often experienced, such as in the ascent of a long gradient, when plug fouling occurred.

Another addition was a somewhat strengthened frame, which was made substantially heavier by the addition of more gussets at strategic points, such as at the steering head and beneath the gearbox. While the improved 'J' was now some 100 pounds heavier than its 1914 ancestor, the engine turned out double the original horsepower through evolved improvements. The 74 cubic inch model was now almost universally preferred by domestic riders, the 61 being more favored by overseas customers where the price of gasoline was a factor.

In the Summer of 1928, two entirely new H-D models were introduced and this brings us to a complex and almost unfathomable period in the Company's history.

In an apparent attempt to gain the best of both worlds, H-D introduced a larger capacity single to complement its 21 cubic inch single which was popular overseas, and a 45 cubic inch twin which was to offer needed competition to both Indian's soaringly popular 101 Scout and Excelsior's new Super X model. In an obvious attempt to rationalize production, both models were to share the same frame and cycle parts, the only difference being in the size of the engine. Built to a 56½ inch wheelbase, the new model was basically a scaled down 'J', as redesigned by Arthur Constantine in 1925. The single, with a long stroke side valve engine that displaced 30.50 cubic inches, was similar to the 21 cubic inch model and was fitted with the same clutch and gearbox. The 45 cubic inch differed only as to the engine. The immediate problem of these models was that both weighed substantially over 400 pounds, which seriously taxed the performance capacity of the single, whose top speed was cataloged at 60 mph. At the same moment, the twin's long stroke motor, initiating the classic 2¾ x 3 13/16 inch cylinder dimensions, was long on torque but short on acceleration capabilities. This, coupled with a ⅞ inch carburetor and restricted manifold breathing, severely limited its performance capabilities. While the single possessed adequate torque, its Ricardo-type cylinder head at once proved susceptible to overheating when driven hard, with consequent piston seizure, coupled with the fact that it was harnessed to an overly heavy frame. Its performance was best described as mediocre. The twin was hampered by the fact that its torque development was somewhat high for being mated with a light pattern single cylinder clutch and gearbox, which impaired its reliability. The twin, as competition for the Indians and Super X's, failed miserably in this respect, as its top speed in original form was but 56 mph. In addition, its light pattern forks seemed insufficiently strong to cope with ordinary road shocks, and were subject to distortion on collision with curbs or rocks.

Its most glaring defect, however, was the shape of the down tube of the frame, common to its companion single, as its straight line offered no space in the twin for the fitting of the electric generator in front of the crankcase, the only position available. To correct this, the standard H-D generator, utilizing the now well-proved H-D field coil system, was mounted above the crankcase on the left-hand side and set at an angle parallel to the front cylinder. This became known as the 'three cylinder

The author after a test ride on Bud Ekins' 1929 74 cu.in. two-cammer. Note the twin bullet headlights, featured only on this year's model. *(Alisha Tamburri)*.

The author and photographer Alisha Tamburri with the 1929 two cammer. *(Johnny Eagles)*.

Harley'. This instrument was activated by a rather unorthodox bevel gear drive taken off one of the forward timing pinions, and was soon to show its weakness under hard driving.

A new lightweight sidecar was offered to complement the new model; a disastrous decision. The purchasing agent of the Department of the Interior was induced to supply twenty five 'R' model sidecar outfits for use by the National Park Service Rangers in both Yellowstone and Zion National Parks, to provide both handy and economical patrol units for the Rangers. The late Thomas L.Rasmussen, then a Ranger in Yellowstone, told the author in 1958 that the 45's were unable to develop sufficient power to haul a rider and passenger over even normal gradients. The sidecars were detached as a result, and the motorcycles were then employed as solo mounts, retaining their rather low sidecar gearing in order to negotiate the undulating terrain of the Parks.

The author was fortunate to experience some first hand observations of the model through his friendship with a schoolmate, Charles Cook, who was employed by the local H-D dealer, Joseph (Joe) Frugoli, as a part time mechanic. Frugoli ordered one of the early 45 models, intending it for use as his personal mount and as a sales demonstrator, as its $295 selling price was substantially lower than that of the now classic 'J' big twin. After setting up the machine and subjecting it to a brief breaking-in period, he found that its top speed was no more than 56 mph — nearly 20 mph slower than its intended rival, the 101 Indian Scout. Frugoli and Cook were able to coax a slight increase in speed after fitting a larger intake manifold and a larger carburetor, along with alterations to the cam profiles. After some 800 miles, the generator drive shaft broke, and Frugoli relegated the machine to storage, vowing to order no more 45's. It languished there for some years, being finally resurrected for a utility rider during World War II.

After numerous complaints from disgruntled dealers, the factory made haste to rectify matters by fitting larger carburetors and installing larger bearings in the generator drive shaft. While these improvements ultimately boosted the top speed to about 62 mph, many otherwise enthusiastic dealers and riders asked the factory representatives and management why the Engineering Department had not subjected the model to extensive road testing before clearing it for production. In the meantime, the appearance and usefulness of the machine was somewhat improved during the Spring of 1929, by fitting a somewhat larger fuel and oil tank with more pleasing lines.

In the meantime, President Walter Davidson, in a series of meetings with Indian's Jim Wright, now installed as President of the M & ATA, and the Executive Committee, finalized plans to implement the administration of the AMA. E.C.Smith, a casual H-D sidecar rider formerly employed as an automobile accessory salesman, was installed as Executive Secretary, with the head office of the AMA now based in Columbus, Ohio. Smith was to serve in this capacity until 1954.

The improved 45 now evidenced further defects in that its light pattern clutch and gearbox, transplanted to both the new 30.50 as well as from the current 21 single, showed certain defects under hard usage, a somewhat sad surprise to one time 'J' owners who had become accustomed to H-D drive train infallibility.

The new 'C' series single, also known as the 'Baby Harley', fared but little better on the domestic scene, as the mildly-tuned side valve engine developed insufficient power in its heavyweight chassis to offer much in the way of performance. While cataloged as a machine capable of steady mile-a-minute speeds, prolonged running at over 50 mph repeatedly caused overheating and consequent piston seizures. Somewhat of a mystery machine, it was apparently produced only in small numbers, most going to export utility markets. The Company's Far Eastern Representative in Japan, Alfred Rich Child, placed orders for substantial numbers of the single cylinder 'C' model, as its low speed torque characteristics were well suited for use in the commercial rear car units in Japan. Most of the machines were ordered without rear mudguards or wheels, but with a lengthened rear chain to facilitate this usage. The Factory kept the model in production until 1937, especially for Child's benefit.

The author has first-hand knowledge of but two of the 'C' models. One was observed in Claude Salmon's Oakland, California showroom in 1936 as a used machine said to have been lately brought to this country by an Australian immigrant. The other was in the hands of the late J.Worth Alexander in dismantled condition, and following his death in 1977, it passed to other hands as a basket case. It is currently awaiting restoration. H-D enthusiast Robert Ross, of Los Angeles, has related his utilization of an old stripped down 'C' model in the once popular desert races and enduros held in the Southern California area in the early 1950's. He has stated that while the engine was generally reliable and exhibited good torque characteristics in hill climbing, it overheated badly under full throttle running. The author has attempted several times to obtain data on the 'C's' history from the factory but encountered the usual H-D wall of silence. It may be assumed that the machine enjoyed but limited production, and that only a few models were ever sold on the domestic market. About a dozen 'C' models still survive, in varying states of original condition, in the hands of several members of the Antique Motorcycle Club of America.

Coincidental to the development of the new 'R' and 'C' models, a new 74 cubic inch machine was announced in August of 1929. An entirely new machine with heavier frame and forks and a lowered riding position, it was offered to supersede the venerable 'J' type, the mainstay of H-D production since 1914. Generally characterized by massive construction, the 'VL', as it was cataloged, weighed about 550 pounds with fuel and oil. The engine was of the side valve type, with a bore and stroke of 3 7/16 x 4 inches, and with a 5:1 compression ratio stated to produce 26 - 28 hp. Critics were quick to note that the total loss lubrication system was still fitted, albeit enhanced by a variable oiling system interconnected with the throttle, as in the last of the 'J's.

The reversion to the side valve type was thought by many knowledgable H-D enthusiasts to have been influenced by Indian's long standing success with that type. It was also much cheaper to manufacture due to the employment of detachable cylinder heads. The power output was hopefully to be enhanced by the utilization of combustion chamber profiles developed by Ricardo. The side valve design also facilitated maintenance, as decarbonization of the cylinder head and piston crown and valve grinding could be effected without having to remove the engine from the frame, a practice not possible in the former 'J' models. Motorcycle historians conversant with design evolution noted that the new engines marked the end of H-D's last direct connection with the configuration of De Dion and Bouton.

A further interesting innovation in the 'VL' was the fitting of quickly detachable and interchangeable wheels and the introduction of a more stylishly streamlined sidecar unit. This improvement was suggested a couple of years before by Alfred Rich Child, who had already noted that certain British-built competitors on the export market, such as the AJS, were already so fitted. In addition, provision was made for carrying a spare wheel on the back of both the passenger sidecar body as well as the various types of commercial bodies now offered.

When the first production examples of the 'VL's reached dealers' showrooms, many enthusiasts did not take kindly to the overall aspect of the new model. Conditioned as they were to the classic 'J', they noted at once that the new machine was not only about 100 pounds heavier than its predecessor, but that the power rating over the last 'J's had not been increased. In fact, the dealers and the factory were besieged by requests for the continued manufacture of the two cam 'JH' model, which not only represented the ultimate development of that type, but whose overall performance was still superior.

In addition to these first-hand criticisms, the first production 'VL's proved to be an almost fatal disaster. While a well-finished machine built from the finest available materials, the engine had been designed with inordinately small flywheels. Old time factory employees have reported that these had been fitted in order to produce more rapid acceleration together with higher revving capabilities, presumably to give the 'VL' a more competitive performance, in comparison with the highly popular 'K' model Hendersons and Indian Fours which were still the machine of choice with most law enforcement bodies.

An offside view of Bud Ekins' 1929 two cammer. Note the distinctive disposition of the push rods. *(Alisha Tamburri).*

While the 'VL' in fact possessed vivid acceleration up to about 50 mph, the power output subsequently fell off badly due to the reduced torque effect of the small flywheels. Hill climbing and load carrying ability were thus greatly impaired, and the overall performance with a sidecar unit attached could only be described as unacceptable. The author was fortunate to have the opportunity to take a ride on Joe Frugoli's first 'VL' which was to be used as a demonstrator. He noted at once that the performance was impressive up to speeds of about 50 mph. After that, the power curve fell off badly, and the engine vibration above that speed was of an intolerable teeth-loosening and wrist-shattering variety.

There was, of course, immediate consternation both among domestic and export dealers when the initial 'VL's were uncrated and given test runs. The factory was besieged with telegrams, cablegrams, and telephone calls inquiring why the model was placed in production without prototype testing, which would have certainly revealed its initial weaknesses. In addition, many of these communications elaborated on the general dealer dissatisfaction with the recently produced 45 twins, again asking why the factory was releasing new designs without subjecting them to even nominal road testing.

Old time factory employees have described both the consternation at the factory as well as the general chaos in the field. There is no record of any official communication to the dealers regarding the solution to the problem, but the factory representatives in each of the country's geographical areas immediately contacted the dealers under their jurisdiction to assure them that matters would be shortly rectified. The dealers were exhorted to remain loyal to the factory, and to assure their customers that H-D's management would make good the defects in design. Such prompt action on the part of the factory was, of course, most expedient, as many customers who had received initial 'VL's were now either demanding that their machines be turned in and their purchase price refunded. To further complicate the problem, many law enforcement buyers had canceled their orders after testing their machines, and a number of dealers terminated their franchises, either quitting the game or defecting to Indian or Excelsior.

The Engineering Department at once embarked in a round-the-clock crash program of building and testing a revised engine design, and within a few weeks finalized production of a new engine. The original small flywheels were replaced with those of larger diameter, necessitating the fitting of larger crankcases. The design was further re-engineered with altered cam and valve action. While these modifications resulted in an engine of more acceptable all-around performance, the larger cases now required a deeper frame loop to accommodate them, and a new design was hastily jigged up and assembled to replace the original.

The factory next notified their dealers that the revised component parts would be shipped to them without charge, with the mandate that the dealers dismantle the machines either already in customers' hands or on order and rebuild them at their own facilities. This, of course, meant considerable expense to the dealers, as anyone familiar with motorcycles is well aware that to completely dismantle and reassemble a machine requires a considerable amount of shop time. Dealers who were adamant in demanding further financial compensation for this work were summarily advised by the area representatives to comply with the Company mandate or surrender their franchises. A number of dealers, disgruntled by what they considered high handed and arbitrary treatment by H-D's management, did just that.

This debacle quite naturally cost the factory a great deal of money. The composite statements of several old time factory employees indicate that the Company ultimately was forced to make good on about 1,326 machines. It has also been reported that the $75,000 received from Alfred Rich Child for the rights to manufacture H-D's in Japan was soon exhausted, and that an additional $35,000 was allocated from Reserve Company funds before all the new parts were ultimately placed in the dealers' hands.

In addition, the factory was still besieged by numerous dealers and 'J' enthusiasts for the resumption of production of a limited number of these models, especially the popular two cam 'JH' model, of which only about 1,900 units were built during 1928 and early 1929. Management's answer was that as the production facilities of the factory had by now been changed over to assembling current models, it was economically impossible for them to resume 'J' production. Upon receiving this rebuff, many dealers and not a few riders who were implacable 'J' enthusiasts, ordered large quantities of spare parts, stockpiling them to service the many thousands of 'J's still on the road, and which remained in active service for another two decades.

Incidental to the revamping of the 'VL's, the frame of the 21 inch single was shortened and the saddle post was lowered to give a somewhat more cobby appearance. Production of the ohv model was terminated, although in deference to the latter's competition successes, a large quantity of spare parts were continued in production. In addition, the performance of the ailing 45 twin was enhanced somewhat by the fitting of improved cam and valve action, and a strengthening of the generator drive mechanism which was giving constant trouble.

Nels Groftholdt's authentically restored two-cammer. This machine is said to have once been in California State Highway Patrol service. *(George Hays).*

As an advertising gimmick in the Spring of 1929, the younger Davidson generation, Gordon, Walter, and Allan, were dispatched on a cross-country trip from Milwaukee to Los Angeles. Mounted on the improved and pristine 45 twins, and nattily attired in well-cut English-style riding boots and breeches, the trio set out from their home base, typifying clean-cut young America on two wheels. Veteran dealers and their mechanics subsequently reported that lengthy stops along the way for repairs and adjustment to their machines made the journey unduly long, and an extensive publicity campaign heralding the event was canceled.

The chaos at H-D was paralleled at Indian, where a quick succession of management changes to executives who were not interested in motorcycling almost wrecked the company.

During the same period, Excelsior made a surprising comeback in the middleweight twin market with Arthur Constantine's brilliantly redesigned 45 cubic inch Super X, which at once outclassed the similar H-D model, and offered strong competition to Indian's now immortal 101 Scout, as it had a top speed of 90 mph.

At the annual general policy and price fixing meeting between Arthur Davidson and Indian's Jim Wright held at Columbus, Ohio in the Spring of 1929, Davidson urged a strong reaffirmation of the formerly sanctioned agreement between the two organizations to mandate the retail sale of only H-D and Indian. An observer at this meeting reported that Davidson's emphasis in the matter was due to the motorcycle sales activities of one Reggie Pink, who had a modest establishment in the Bronx in New York City for the sale of British machines. Starting on a small scale in the Spring of 1927, he had been able to build up a successful business handling Douglas, Norton, Velocette, and Ariel machines. Although Pink had not been successful in establishing satellite dealerships, Davidson apparently considered his activities as a possible threat to present Yankee supremacy.

As a paradox to Indian's greatly weakened position in the late 1920's, their professionals swept the board in 1928 and 1929 by winning all of the big National races. In spite of hard times, Indian was able to scrape together enough funds to continue factory support of competition. However, Indian's    109

Robert Ross's 1929 74 cu.in. two cammer in its more familiar Western guise as a 'California Bobber'. *(George Hays).*

position in AMA policy matters was greatly weakened as their management was willing to offer only token financial support to the organization. As a result, H-D remained as the largest contributor, its majority funding being augmented by minimal support from a few accessory manufacturers and tire companies.

The late 1920's saw the emergence of the sport of hill climbing as a somewhat minor sporting fixture. Uphill races had long been popular in motorcycling circles, but later developments saw the contests relegated to unclimbable off-the-road gradients. H-D's C.W.Hemmis in the East, and Windy Lindstrom, Joe Herb, and later Joe Petrali and Sam Arena in the West, vied with Indian's 'TNT' Terpenning and Orrie Steele. Excelsior found a potent champion in Gene Rhyne, who won all the big Nationals for Super X in 1930 and 1931.

During the 1930's nearly every edition of the popular Fox and Movietone newsreels shown in motion picture theaters featured a 30 to 60 second sequence of daredevil riders climbing nearly perpendicular hillsides.

Most of the factories built a few special machines for such use, loaning them out to favored competitors who had previously proved their mettle on homebrewed machines. H-D produced a limited number of these interesting specials, some of which were designed for methanol fuels.

Surprisingly, 1929 turned out to be a banner year for the long-ailing domestic motorcycle industry, with a total output of over 31,000 machines. This was the industry's best year since 1919, when 62,000 units came off the production lines. Over half of this output was exported, however, and in proportion to population growth and now soaring automobile production, the industry assumed an even more redundant position in the domestic transportation field.

A further interesting facet of H-D history during the middle and late 1920 period was the gradual establishment of a company museum, featuring a collection representing a model of each machine ever produced by the company. Many of the earlier types were already in company hands from the numerous prototype experiments conducted by the Engineering Department. Later models were sometimes asembled from old parts still on hand, and some were acquired from dealers who had either owned them outright, or acquired them from various private owners. This collection has come to play an important role in securing for future generations a first hand view of domestic motorcycle history, and is presently housed in a special building at H-D's American Foundry complex in York, Pennsylvania.

Unlike Excelsior and Indian, H-D machines were never directly available for retail sale from a dealership within the Milwaukee factory complex. Such sales were by company mandate only from franchised dealers who did business on their own account. While it was always possible for a purchaser to travel to Milwaukee to take delivery of his machine, and save freight charges, the financial details were always handled through the rider's local dealer. As an encouragement to enthusiasts to visit the factory, guided one-hour tours of the plant were traditionally held twice daily, except for the annual vacation period in the late Summer, when production was suspended for about two weeks.

During the late 1920's certain events occurred on the international economic scene which caused further problems for the troubled domestic motorcycle industry. The United States, as has been mentioned, emerged virtually unscathed from the World War holocaust, and was almost at once able to concentrate on industrial development that made it the leading manufacturer of all manner of products. The resultant prosperity made it possible to retire all of the national indebtedness incurred in the war effort, and the country was enjoying unprecedented prosperity. Wage earners, professionals and business owners, not to mention the myriad of corporations, were prospering handsomely. The only exception to this happy state of affairs were farmers. The mechanization of farming brought about a large surplus of foodstuffs. This kept farm prices down, while the costs of operation advanced along with a continuing rise in inflation. As domestic agricultural producers were not then protected by tariffs, they were in constant competition with foreign products usually priced lower.

As a result, there was much pressure upon Congress, especially from the midwest farm bloc, to institute protective tariffs for the benefit of agriculture. This situation caused the drafting of the McNary-Haugen bill, named for its congressional sponsors. This bill provided, in addition to high tariff walls, price supports for domestically-produced footstuffs, together with government purchase of surplus food products for resale on foreign markets wherever a demand might be forthcoming.

As a politically expedient bill which enjoyed much popular support in both houses of Congress by large majorities, it was presented to President Coolidge in the Fall of 1926 for his signature. It was immediately vetoed by Coolidge, who was adamantly opposed to any government interference with private economic matters. The bill was subsequently presented to him 1927 and 1928, with the same result. But in 1929, it was presented to the newly-elected President Hoover, who had effectively made his promised acceptance of it an issue in his campaign, and it was duly signed into law with much popular acclaim.

The immediate result of this legislation was the instant retaliation by many foreign governments in the erection of formidable tariff barriers against the import of American manufactured goods. This state of affairs was particularly critical in the Australasian markets, where both American cars and motorcycles had enjoyed substantial sales during the past decade. Similar high tariffs were established throughout Europe, as many economists had already concluded that the growing influx of American goods had hampered post-war development of their own industries. The principal export markets remaining that offered favorable trading conditions to US products were South Africa, various South American countries, parts of Africa, Belgium, Holland, and the Scandinavian countries which up to this time had no significant vehicular manufacture.

Now faced with the curtailment of the crucial export sales, the American factories were forced to make the best of their domestic position, previously only marginal.

H-D's management, headed in this instance, by General Sales Manager Arthur Davidson, immediately sought ways and means to strengthen their dealership organization. A few incompetent and wavering individuals had their franchises canceled, and their places filled by more erudite and progressive individuals. The Factory Representatives for the various areas were given updated information on the latest marketing techniques, and were exhorted to do their utmost to stimulate their dealers' sales efforts. Particular emphasis was centered on the proper maintenance and cleaning up of premises, as dingy retail quarters were still the bane of both the domestic manufacturers.

In addition, H-D's management had been continually increasing the size and scope of their accessory department. Dealers were constantly urged to stock more of these items: rear carriers, leg shields, windshields, speedometers, saddle covers, spotlights, as well as a comprehensive line of clothing, all obtained by the factory through outside wholesale jobbers.

It was during this period that the factory put increased pressure on the dealers to handle only accessory items supplied through the Company, the factory representatives reporting to Milwaukee when dealers were not fully co-operative in this policy.

With the sudden curtailment of the export market, the matter of domestic sales to law enforcement bodies now received increased attention. While in the public mind the purchase of any particular make of vehicle for this use might tend to indicate that the make was chosen for its superior qualities, in actuality nothing could have been farther from the truth. A particular make was often chosen if the local dealer in question was willing to make a financial sacrifice to have his product receive the consequent advertising value, and at the same time satisfy the dictates of a tight-fisted government purchasing agent. In other cases, where certain local political considerations had to be met, two or three favored makes would be placed in service on a yearly rotational basis, and thus subjected to a ruinous trade-in allowance to make way for a successor. In some cases dealers or suppliers had to contend with whatever political connivance or corruption was going on in their particular area, and often scheming politicians or corrupt civil servants had to be paid off under the table to consummate a sale.

The Henderson and Indian Fours were usually the choice of the officers, and after the newly introduced Henderson 'K' models were much desired. In cases where the purchasing organization did not wish to pay the high prices for these models, the choice was then between the H-D 74 and the Indian Chief. 45 inch machines were employed in limited numbers for this work, but the higher powered models were generally preferred. A few Indian Scouts were used, but the H-D 45 was never favored, as, in its early years, it was scarcely able to overhaul the contemporary family sedan.

All things considered, the supplying of law enforcement machines was generally considered to be a somewhat less than pleasant aspect of the business, and was treated by most dealers as a necessary evil.

As the decade grew to a close, the dealer representation of the two larger factories was reduced to about a thousand retail outlets each. Excelsior, always the underdog, had less than two hundred, and emphasized the Henderson in sales promotions over their limited production Super X.

The era of the great motorcycling spectacles was now over, as the board tracks were gone, the last survivor being the vast oval at Rockingham, New Hampshire, which saw a few races in the Spring of 1929 before being dismantled that Summer.

While the past two seasons had seen a slight upsurge in motorcycle sales, impending economic events were now drastically to change any hopes of a still rising market.

# Chapter 6

# The Great Depression

THE WORLD-WIDE ECONOMIC DEPRESSION WHICH HAD ITS BEGINNING IN THE United States with the infamous Black Friday on Wall Street in October, 1929, produced a catastrophic impact upon nearly every inhabitant of the country. One third of the nation's work force, estimated at between 13 and 15 million people, ultimately found themselves unemployed. One third of the country's railroads were in bankruptcy, and over 5,000 banks failed. In the rural areas, farmers and others in related agricultural pursuits were particularly hard hit, and in some parts of the country over one fourth of the real estate was under foreclosure. With many people facing actual starvation, many counties and municipalities stretched their diminishing tax dollars to set up soup kitchens to feed the hungry and homeless. Countless business enterprises, both large and small, were failing everywhere, swelling the ranks of those already plunged into abject poverty. An inquiry into the causes of this tragedy are beyond the scope of this work, but it was largely the result of world-wide financial speculation and the attendant inflation in the decade following the close of the war. In the United States, the lack of any government control over the trading of stocks and securities enabled speculators to buy on margin, with as little as 10% of face value. The crash came when traders were unable to come up with enough hard cash to cover their purchases when the demand was made. The average citizen, generally unfamiliar with the laws of economics, at once blamed President Hoover and the Republican Party then in power. It was then inevitable that the voters next turned to the Democrat Party and Franklin D. Roosevelt, who proposed to lead the country back to prosperity by way of Keynesian Socialism already popular in both England and Europe.

The sales of motorcycles, in common with all other consumer goods, fell alarmingly, and, as a now historically marginal industry, probably suffered to a greater degree than many others.

While motorcycles were obviously capable of being operated much more economically than automobiles, they never attained the status of a depression vehicle simple because there was such a vast number of used cars now available at give-away prices. Model T Fords, which had accounted for nearly one half of the domestic production during the 1920's, now sold for from $15.00 to $75.00, according to condition. Originally high-priced cars such as the stately Packards, Cadillacs, Pierce Arrows, or Peerless's could be had for from $100 to $300 and most of these were junked when no buyers could be found. In addition, with gasoline retailing at from 15 to 20 cents a gallon, economical operation was never too much of a consideration in a country where thousands of producing oil wells were now capped in a vain attempt to keep the price somewhere near a profitable margin.

Motorcycle dealers in many of the smaller towns and cities simply disappeared. Some formerly prosperous dealers in larger trading areas made further retrenchment from the salad days of 1920, and moved to less favored business locations, where garages or other buildings could often be rented for $25.00 per month. Others survived by taking on additional lines of commerce, such as sporting goods, outboard motors, or became fix-it shops undertaking household appliance repair or saw filing. Both H-D and Indian, once united against such practices by their dealers, now looked the other way, as any outlet that placed an order for the odd new machine or who ordered a minimal trickle of parts and accessories was now an increasingly desirable asset.

At the same time, President Walter Davidson, through the factory representatives, bluntly informed the dealership that they could expect no help from Milwaukee, even if their survival was at stake. They were further informed that in the face of the country's mounting economic troubles, no-holds-barred competition tactics were now the order of the day, the target being their mortal enemy, Indian.

The grip of the H-D Company over their dealers' daily fortunes is well illustrated by the so-called Denver incident. This involved their long time retail outlet in that city, owned by one Walter W. Whiting, and was a lively topic of discussion among pioneer western motorcyclists for many years after. Whiting, a pioneer motorcycle enthusiast had taken the Denver franchise in 1918, following its relinquishment by Floyd Clymer, who had obtained it in 1916. Through aggressive sales campaigns, coupled with fair dealing, Whiting had built up a very lucrative business with one of the highest sales volumes in the West. His chief competitor after 1921 was Floyd Clymer, who had re-entered the motorcycle trade with both Indian and Excelsior franchises. Clymer subsequently allowed his agency to languish in favor of the promotion of his then famous hole-in-the-windshield automobile spotlight, and in 1925 it was taken up by Leslie D. Richards, one time Publicity Manager for Indian. Richards and Whiting, in spite of being business competitors, struck up a warm personal friendship, and worked together to promote the cause of motorcycling in the Denver area. Both acted as co-sponsors for a very active motorcycle club, and also promoted tours, picnics, and gymkhanas to which riders of all makes were cordially invited. In addition, both Whiting and Richards were lightweight enthusiasts, and unlike many of their confreres, made a special point of promoting this class of machine. Another motorcyclist, O. B. Senter, who as Whiting's Sales Manager, also joined to help inaugurate what was a mild boom in motorcycling in the Denver area. When the news of the Denver situation reached the ear of Walter Davidson, he at once took issue with Whiting over his close association with Richards, and through the district factory representative, Whiting was warned that his close co-operation with his competition was most definitely against H-D Company policy. When confronted with this news, Whiting defended his position by calling attention to his impressive sales record, together with the relatively large numbers of motorcycles registered throughout the Denver area and the state of Colorado. He said that, in his opinion, what was good for motorcycling in general was in the best interests of all concerned. A further complication to Whiting's difficulties with the H-D Company was Floyd

William Hoecker's authentically-restored 1930-31 DLD 45 cu.in. side valve model, first introduced for the 1929 season. Known as the 'three cylinder Harley', it was fitted with an unorthodox vertically-driven generator. *(Alisha Tamburri)*.

Close up view of the early DLD near vertical generator. Bearing failures were experienced under high speed running. *(Alisha Tamburri).*

Clymer, who proposed to again re-enter the motorcycle business following the now failing popularity of his automobile spotlight. As Dick Richards was presently the well-entrenched Indian dealer, the only other obvious alternative was H-D. Clymer, who by this time was well aware of Whiting's difficulties with H-D's management, proposed that the Denver franchise be taken over by himself. It was decided that the dealership not be under his own name, but in the name of H.D.Cooper, who had previously been associated with him in the spotlight venture, the financing to be provided by Clymer.

H-D's management at once revoked Whiting's franchise accepting, it is said, a substantial sum of money for the transfer to Cooper. An embittered Whiting, as the story was recounted to the author by Whiting's nephew in 1967, deserted the motorcycle trade in favor of the automotive accessory field. Cooper immediately zeroed in on Richards' Indian business.

At this point, Indian's financial difficulties were causing many embarrassing delays in the delivery of new machines and spare parts. Cooper capitalized on this situation to sell Indian parts at greatly reduced rates, from part stocks still held by Clymer from his previous Indian dealership, with H-D's apparent blessing. In spite of the fact that Whiting's former Sales Manager, O.B.Senter, defected from the H-D camp to accept a like position with Richards' Indian agency, Richards was forced into bankruptcy. This most unfortunate affair, still well remembered by surviving pioneer motorcyclists, while of momentary advantage to H-D's cause in the Denver area, aroused the ire of many right thinking motorcyclists as the news of the matter spread throughout the West. Both Whiting and Richards were well respected, and they received widespread sympathy in their resulting financial losses.

Ironically, Clymer realized only small financial gain for his efforts. He was shortly afterwards convicted in Denver's Federal District Court for mail fraud, and was sentenced to serve an intermediate term in Leavenworth Federal Prison.

The 1929-1930 period of domestic motorcycle history, aside from the ominous overtones of the impending economic depression, was a time of crisis for all three of the surviving manufacturers. H-D was still smarting from the technical failures of both the initial new 45 inch models, as well as the newly introduced 'VL's. Indian was tottering on the brink of financial disaster, both from the general decline in motorcycle sales as well as from the inept management of three successive presidents. Only the continued production of their 101 Scout and a continuing infusion of capital generated by West Coast distributor Hap Alzina kept it perilously afloat. Added to this, there were continuing rumors that Ignatz Schwinn, the eccentric founder of the bicycle empire and the owner of Excelsior, was now contemplating the termination of motorcycle manufacture due to its minimal profit picture.

This somewhat dismal picture was somewhat relieved when on April 23rd, 1930, an article in the *New York Times* announced that E. Paul du Pont, scion of the noted du Pont de Nemours family, had just purchased the controlling interest in the Indian Motocycle Company. This news was viewed with mixed emotions by H-D's management, as Indian's shaky financial position was public knowledge, and many well informed people in the trade had for some time considered that with Indian's expected demise, H-D would now become the only significant domestic motorcycle manufacturer.

At the outset, it was common knowledge that du Pont, while a sporting motorist and pioneer motorcyclist with genuine interest in keeping Indian alive, was also interested in utilizing a part of the company's vast unused facilities for the manufacture of aircraft engines, as he had lately developed a consuming preoccupation with aviation. It was also now evident that Indian was in a very sound financial condition, as the multi-millionaire du Pont was not only enjoying fabulous profits from his Ball

Actress-Photographer Alisha Tamburri after a test run on Bill Hoecker's DLD.

Grain Powder Company, but from his additional holdings in various du Pont de Nemours subsidiaries as well as his bulging portfolio of blue chip stocks and bonds acquired for him through his brother Francis I. du Pont, owner of a prestigious brokerage firm on Wall Street. When du Pont took control of Indian, the production of diverse products was discontinued, and the company's somewhat disheartened dealers were now assured that motorcycle manufacture would be the order of the day, and that every effort would be made to regain Indian's once formidable sales position.

With H-D's management now considering this new turn of events in relation to their own marketing position, the industry's picture changed again late in the following Spring with Ignatz Schwinn suddenly announcing that he was was terminating the manufacture of Excelsiors and Hendersons. The current economic depression and indications of its severity and long duration have long been reported by various motorcycle historians as being behind Schwinn's decision. Other events, however, which were to now directly concern the future fortunes of H-D, were a critical factor in the demise of Excelsior.

As it may be recalled, the noted Henderson Four had long been the favored mount of law enforcement officers, and its prestige was enhanced by the introduction in 1929 of the newly designed 'K'

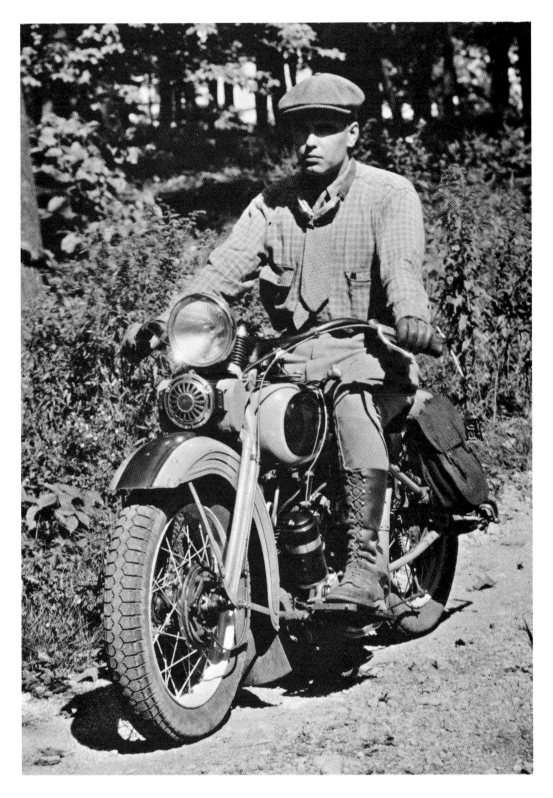

A youthful William Herbert Davidson, the son of Founder William A., winning the Jack Pine
Enduro on a 1930 DLD model.

models from the board of Arthur Constantine. These superb models, far and away superior to the contemporary Indian Four models which still utilized the only slightly updated 1919 Ace type engines, almost immediately accelerated law enforcement sales. Much of this added interest in the Henderson was quite naturally enhanced by the fact that many of H-D's law enforcement orders were canceled subsequent to the initial 'VL' fiasco, not to mention the added strengthening of Indian's position with their Four and Chief models for such use.

To further strengthen Excelsior's advantageous position in the matter, the canny Schwinn ordered accelerated Henderson production, and in an attempt to lower the somewhat non-competitive price of the new 'K' models made what proved to be a fatal blunder. The standard Splitdorf and Delco magneto and electrical systems were repalced in the Fall of 1930 with cheaper units, specially devised for the Henderson by some obscure manufacturer.

With outstanding law enforcement orders throughout the country, estimated by old time Excelsior employees as being nearly 450 units, an order for 150 machines was placed by the purchasing department of the State of California, for its State Highway Patrol. This large order, obtained by devious means, as described in the author's companion book on Indian, the *IRON REDSKIN,* was no more than delivered when Schwinn's fatal decision began to have its telling effect. The cheapjack magnetos were prone to cause misfiring during high speed running, and the generators were unable to function properly if the lighting sets, red warning spotlights, and sirens were operated simultaneously. California State Highway Patrol Chief, E.Raymond Cato, at once contacted Schwinn, and threatened legal action against Excelsior unless the ailing ignition and lighting systems of the initial 75 machines were replaced. Schwinn at once contacted the five principal Henderson dealers in the Los Angeles basin, where the first increment of Highway Patrol machines was in use, but to his consternation, all refused to participate in any validation of the usual factory guarantees regarding faulty factory equipment.

At this point, an Excelsior factory representative made a hurried trip to Los Angeles, and after a futile attempt to enlist Henderson dealer support in the matter, effected a contractual agreement with one Harley Rathbun, a San Bernardino H-D dealer, to replace the ailing electrical units on the initial 75 Highway Patrol Hendersons. Rathbun and his brother were long time H-D enthusiasts and dealers in the Los Angeles basin, and currently held franchises in Los Angeles, Santa Ana, and San Bernardino.

When the H-D factory got wind of the matter, they immediately contacted Rathbun, officially advising him not to enter into any contractual agreements with Schwinn, stating in effect that it was not proper for an H-D representative to pull Schwinn's chestnuts out of the fire. Rathbun's immediate reply to these top management directives was that in the face of the current depressed state of motorcycle sales, he was not about to turn down a somewhat lucrative repair contract, even it if were outside his usual H-D sales and service activities. Noting that Rathbun was adamant, and no doubt taking into consideration that Rathbun and Rich Budelier were the most prominent H-D sales representatives in the critical Southern California market, H-D's management relented and no official reprisals were instigated against Rathbun. As a matter of record, Rathbun ultimately repaired only about half of the ailing Hendersons, and many of these were later condemned out of service by the California State Highway Patrol. Rathbun later sold a number of these as second-hand machines. Of the twenty or more 'K' model Hendersons still existing in the hands of antique enthusiasts in the Southern California area, most are relics of Excelsior's California debacle.

Following the cessation of Excelsior production, the limited domestic market was at long last reduced to two manufacturers, who, during the ensuing decade, became locked in what became a fratricidal war rather than normal marketing competition.

E.Paul du Pont's acquisition of Indian had put the company back on its feet. This laid to rest the rumors that the Wigwam was shortly to suspend production. It was not only backed by du Pont's vast industrial empire, but benefitted from his general interest in sporting motoring. William Crapo (Billy) Durant, the ebullient automotive pioneer who had originally formed General Motors, only to have it wrested from him by E.Paul's uncle, Pierre S.du Pont, told the author in an interview shortly before his death that E.Paul du Pont's interest in motoring, together with his inherent pride in his present financial successes, would have never allowed Indian to fail, no matter what its depression losses.

At the same moment, the H-D Company, while currently enjoying the largest domestic production, and possessed of a strong background of financial solvency, had never been favored with any such outside cushion of financial reserve, and its only cash surpluses through the years had been accumulated by internally generated profits.

With the indeterminate position of Excelsior, it now appeared that the battle lines between Milwaukee and the Wigwam were shortly to be drawn. Whatever private thoughts the Founders may have had regarding the matter will, of course, never be known, but it was subsequently reported that there had been much jubilation among some of H-D's factory personnel in prospect of the industry

Two views of an interesting one-off Factory Special. A 30.50 cu.in. ohv road racing machine exported to Japan. It featured dry sump lubrication and was intended for use with blended fuels. None were available in the USA.

becoming a one-make monopoly. The new strength of Indian now changed the picture, together with the fact that the number of domestic dealers handling both makes was nearly equal, and domestic sales showed H-D held but a slight edge.

With the new turn of events, several old time H-D dealers have recalled that sentiment against du Pont was running high at Milwaukee. There were reportedly widespread derisive allusions to him as 'that New Jersey Jew', a patent misnomer as du Pont's ethnic background was Aryan French, and his historic home was in the state of Delaware.

Whether the Founders approved of these slanderous allegations is not a matter of record, but it is well known that the factory representatives in the various regions of the country put increasing pressure on their dealers to intensify their sales efforts in order to swamp the competition. Dealers were urged to junk any over-age Excelsiors or Indians that might come into their hands, either through trade-ins or outright purchase. It has long been a rumor, though unsubstantiated by any surviving documentary evidence, that any H-D dealer junking such machines could receive a $20.00 cash rebate from the factory, provided that the machine's registration papers were surrendered to the factory representative.

President Walter Davidson now conceived another sales campaign to strengthen H-D's position in the alarmingly shrinking law enforcement market. It was to make available to qualified buyers the Police Model 'VL' at a knock-down price of $195.00, only slightly more than its net production cost,

119

A limited edition 45 cu.in. ohv road racing machine intended for the European market only. None were available in the USA.

together with the trade-in of any other machines on hand, whether H-D, Indian, or Excelsior's Henderson. Furthermore, such sales were to be made directly from the factory by special sales agents, in itself a complete reversal of the company's lifelong policy of retailing machines only through their regular dealers. In addition, any and all of the trade-in machines were to be summarily junked. When the news of this proposal reached the dealers, there was a natural storm of protest, as these now beleagured individuals were being bypassed by the factory sales, and would not receive the usual dealer's markup. The factory representatives attempted to placate the dealers with the assurance that they would continue to receive the usual factory co-operation in the servicing and upkeep of whatever Police Specials were sold in their respective areas, but most of the dealers remained unmollified. Several cancelled their franchises, as many of them were by this time in straitened financial circumstances. A limited number transferred their allegiance to Indian, as the still popular 101 Scout was now being produced in slightly greater numbers due to Indian's revitalized management.

In spite of strong dealer protest, the program was carried on for another six months, and it was noted that several hundred machines of competing makes were junked in the process. While the company momentarily enjoyed a sales victory, the general bitterness within the trade, and indeed the revulsion felt within the company's own dealer organization at the cold bloodedness of the program, caused President Davidson to reluctantly terminate the offer.

Motorcycle historians are in almost universal agreement that it was this single episode in H-D history that precipitated the bitter war between the two factories that was most harmful to the whole domestic motorcycling movement, and of ultimate detriment to the progress of the industry as a whole. The country's Indian dealers were quite naturally outraged, especially as many aged but still serviceable Indians were reduced to scrap. The situation was particularly unfortunate at the retail sales level. Competitive dealers in the same or adjacent cities and towns, who had once enjoyed at least friendly rivalry, were often no longer on speaking terms. The effect upon private owners was even more tragic. In many cases a distressed rider requiring such necessities as lubricating oil, a tire or an inner tube or even a spark plug, would be refused service by the dealer of the opposite make.

The impact on club activities was also most unfortunate. Many such organizations, their numbers already decimated by the growing depression, were forced to disband, as the owners of the two rival makes now refused to meet or ride with their opposite numbers. In some instances, one-make splinter groups were formed from former members of formerly congenial clubs. Fights often resulted when they encountered their opposite numbers at race meets or even along public roads. Many thoughtful riders deserted motorcycling in disgust, and the public image of the sport, already somewhat tarnished, hit a new low.

The seemingly paranoic hatred on the part of H-D's top management, and especially that of President Davidson, for any competitive make of motorcycle, has long been the subject of speculation by both riders and motorcycle historians. Much of it was known to have centered on E. Paul du Pont, who was erroneously dismissed by some as a richly endowed dilitant playboy, when in realty he was a shrewd businessman and a highly knowledgeable industrialist. Also, the Davidsons may have harbored the somewhat natural resentment by people of working class backgrounds for those of inherited wealth and position. Coupled with this, there was still the rankling matter of the initial technical failures of the newly introduced 45 inch twin, and the disastrous debacle of the early 'VL' models. In addition, the now discontinued 'J' models still enjoyed a loyal following who had yet to accept the 'VL', and the factory was still being besieged by requests to resume production of the immortal two cammer 'JH'.

The ohv 'Peashooter' flat track racer. It was widely used in US events during 1928 through 1934. It was ultimately outclassed by the more refined English JAP machines.

With the depressed state of the industry, most of the once popular trade magazines had folded. The sole survivor by 1931 was the *Pacific Motorcyclist and Bicyclist*, which was now known as *The Motorcyclist*. Its new owner was one A.E.Welch, who had purchased the publishing rights for a mere pittance, and found that the general circulation had fallen to 15,000 copies per year. Even at a nominal one dollar per year subscription price, few riders appeared to support it.

Concurrently, the position of the AMA became reduced to pathetic proportions. With declining rider support, Secretary-Manager E.C.Smith eked out his own and the organization's existence from a handful of private owners' membership dues and from the very minimal donations now emanating from the trade, operating his office in Columbus almost singlehanded.

Due to the economic stress of the times, motorcycle competition was but a shadow of its former greatness. The great board tracks had all disappeared. Any thoughts of reviving them were now dashed by the final public rejection of their gory spectacles, and there appeared to be no promoters left with enough money to finance such contests. Dirt track racing events appeared sporadically at various county fair grounds, and were more often than not of the unsanctioned 'outlaw' variety, due to the impotent position of the AMA, whose once active Competition Committee now had no funds to furnish referees for such contests. Flat track racing was still mildly popular, riding on impetus derived from Australia and New Zealand, and was still drawing crowds in impoverished Great Britain. Its survival was no doubt largely due to the fact that a track could be prepared on any handy field by a few hours work with a road grader.

In spite of hard times, the Founders decided that H-D should re-enter the competition field, at least on a limited basis, by utilizing its still popular 21 cubic inch 'Peashooter' model that was racking up impressive records in Australia, New Zealand, and the United Kingdom. Up to this time, the 21 inch class had received but scant attention from either American competition riders or from the AMA. What action there had been was mostly dominated by H-D, as Indian had produced but few such models, and only during 1926. They decided to revive the class, and the now nearly powerless AMA Competition Committee readily assented, apparently to offer the sport and the public at least a token revival of American motorcycling's past glories. The H-D factory now hired a single professional at the munificent depression salary of $40 per week, one Joseph (Joe) Petrali.

This remarkable man, who was single-handedly to offer so much color to subsequent motorcycle history, was born February 22nd 1904, in San Francisco, California, the son of Italian immigrants. The family moved to nearby Sacramento in April 1906, just days before the tragic earthquake that leveled San Francisco. Young Joe's childhood interest in things mechanical was sparked by a neighbor, Dewey Houghton, a local cycle mechanic who owned a 1910 belt drive 30.40 cubic inch Flanders single. Sensing Joe's engrossing fascination with the machine, Houghton allowed him to clean it periodically, as well as to observe and later assist in its constant tuning up and overhaul. Along the way he frequently took young Joe to see such major pioneer competitors as Don Johns and Ray Seymour race at the old Sacramento Fair Grounds. At the age of 12, Houghton allowed him to ride the Flanders, and the following year Joe was able to persuade his father to allow him to purchase a well worn Hedstrom Indian 30.50 single.

A 1930 factory built 21 cu.in. hill climber. It was built for Herb Reiber, who was joined a year later by Joe Petrali.

A 1923 'J' type hill climber ridden by Oscar Hostetter in AMA events during the 1928-1931 seasons. Note the strutted front forks.

Abandoning any thoughts of higher education, Joe next went to work at Archie Rife's Indian agency, where Rife was amazed at Joe's natural mechanical ability. During slack times at the shop he allowed Joe to convert his own machine to racing specification, and he entered several novice and club competition events at the local fair grounds. He later won an economy run for single cylinder machines, covering 176 miles on a gallon of fuel, which made the 1918 National Record book.

Still running his Hedstrom single, he competed with much success in many of the outlaw events being held at various county fair tracks throughout Northern California. His many victories came to the attention of Jud Carriker, Santa Ana Indian dealer and the factory's West Coast Competition Manager, who attempted to secure for him a factory racer from Springfield. Due to Indian's post-war financial difficulties, no new racing machines were then being assembled, although Frank J. Weschler was aware of Petrali's budding potential as a competition star. Upon the tragic death of Shrimp Burns at Toledo, Ohio, in the early Spring of 1920, Weschler shipped his machine to Carriker for Petrali to enter the board track racing, which was opening in Fresno for the 1920 season. Carriker decided to experiment with alcohol fuel at the opening event, there then being no restrictions against its use, in order to give his protégé at least a fighting chance against the formidable factory-sponsored H-D Wrecking Crew, which that season consisted of Jim Davis, Fred Ludlow, Ralph Hepburn, Otto Walker, and Ray Weishaar.

In recounting the events of that day to the author in an interview in 1968, Petrali recalled that his carburetor had not yet been correctly adjusted to alcohol fuel. While his 8 valve engine ran erratically, he was able to work well up among the leaders early in the contest, and the now alarmed members of the Wrecking Crew maneuvered their machines to box him in. Through heroic efforts and a hair-raising burst of speed, he was able to finish second, a truly magnificent achievement for a 16 year old novice.

That Winter, Indian's Kansas City distributor, Albert G. Crocker, made Joe a most lucrative offer to work for him in his shop, his fame as a mechanic already established, and Joe moved to that midwestern city.

In the Spring of 1921, the first big National Race that brought him instant fame was on the great board oval at Altoona, Pennsylvania. Although billed as a starter, he was unable to enter, as by some mixup his machine had been shipped to Pittsburgh. H-D's great Ralph Hepburn, who fell during practice and injured his hand, noticed young Joe sitting disconsolately by the pits. He generously offered to let Joe ride his 8 valver and offered him a 50-50 split on any winnings he could garner. The machine had thrown Hepburn when the rear wheel locked up as its engine seized, so Joe, then totally unfamiliar with either the standard 'J' model H-D's or their special 8 valvers, quickly dismantled the engine and

123

converted it to run on high test tetraethyl lead aviation fuel, a small supply of which H-D entrant Eddie Brinck had just obtained from the nearby Wright Aviation Company airfield. Although Brinck and some of the other Indian riders had originally considered using this fuel, they decided, just before practicing got underway, that it was too volatile and dangerous and did not attempt to have their engines adjusted for its use.

Joe converted Hepburn's engine and at the same time cured its overheating problems in time for the first race. When the main event was started, Jim Davis blasted his way into an early lead, but dropped out on the 11th lap due to a broken valve, but not before he had lapped the field. Eddie Brinck took the lead on his Indian, and Joe worked his way up behind him. In a terrific see-saw battle that brought the crowd to its feet, Brinck took the lead in the north turn. In his intense concentration, Joe had overlooked the fact that Brinck had lost two laps during an enforced pit stop to change a front wheel, and did not notice the checkered flag. After completing the two extra and unneeded laps at breakneck speed, Joe coasted into the pits in a state of exhaustion. It was only then that he realized that he had won!

Joe received Hepburn's congratulations, and left immediately for Kansas City. In the meantime, H-D factory officials attempted to contact him in the pit area after the race, in hopes of signing him up as a rider, but no one appeared to know that he had left abruptly. When they ultimately traced him to Kansas City, they were unaware of his association with Crocker. He finally agreed to ride for them on a part time basis, as H-D, of course, no longer fielded factory teams. Crocker generously allowed him to continue in his present position as his Shop Foreman, servicing and repairing Indians, although he was subject to some criticism by neighboring Indian dealers for keeping Joe in his employ.

Joe next purchased an 8 valve from the H-D factory, his machine being built up from remaining parts in the Racing Department. He raced all through what limited events were scheduled during the 1925 season. He received strong competition from Indian, who were still officially supporting racing. The only concession the H-D factory offered was free spare parts and pit crews, where needed.

Joe's first big victory for H-D as a contract rider was on the very fast fairground track at Laurel, Maryland. He won the Ten Mile event at an elapsed time of 109 mph, and hung up a new record for the Twenty Five Miler. A naturally gifted rider, he was now rated as a top racing star, having at one time or another bested such outstanding contemporaries as Eddie Brinck, Jim Davis, Curly Fredericks, Bill Minnick, and Johnny Seymour.

At the close of the 1925 season, H-D decided to withdraw their previously limited support for competition, and Joe subsequently established a connection with Excelsior. While Schwinn had immediately terminated all factory-sponsored competition at the time of Bob Perry's death at Ascot in 1920, Joe felt that he might somehow persuade the latter to sponsor limited competition in the 21 cubic inch class in which the lower power and lightweight machines were far less hazardous to ride than the more usual 61 twins. Joe also wished to work with Arthur Constantine who, since his discharge from H-D, had headed Excelsior's Engineering and Design Department. During the initial conference at Chicago with Schwinn and Constantine, Schwinn expressed his confidence in Joe's competition and design capabilities, and agreed to offer limited sponsorship in the development of a new 21 inch class racer.

Constantine immediately set to work, and with considerable help from Joe, produced a very fast racing prototype. Before all the bugs had been worked out of the new design, the big initial competition event of 1927 was held at Springfield, Illinois. With the new Excelsior not yet ready to race, Joe accepted an offer from Indian to ride one of their specially prepared ohv 21 cubic inch Prince models, in company with Eddie Brinck and Al Pechar. Pechar had just returned from a very successful tour of New Zealand and Australia, where he had hung up several new records. A last minute addition to the team was the redoubtable Bill Minnick.

On the first lap of the race, Brinck went wide in the first turn, caromed off the fence, and went down just ahead of Joe. In the resulting crash, Brinck was killed instantly with all of his neck vertebrae fractured, and Joe sustained his first major competition injuries, a broken jaw, nose, and collarbone.

He made several spectacular victories during the ensuing season, and next joined H-D when the Excelsior factory closed in the Summer of 1931. For several seasons thereafter, he functioned as H-D's one-man competition team, competing in numerous races and hill climbs on the now immortal 'Peashooter'.

The year of 1931 opened with continuing economic stress, as the full effect of the depression was now felt world wide. The current H-D model range for 1931 was to be carried on in limited production for the 1932 sales year. The 21 and 30.50 cubic inch singles were continued unchanged. The now improved 74 cubic inch Big Twin was also carried forward, with minor improvements to the lubricating system and the fitting of a more massive clutch assembly. This model had by this time gained general acceptance through its improved performance and reliability, although it was still not wholly accepted by many dyed-in-the wool 'J' enthusiasts.

Windy Lindstrom, West Coast hill climb expert, with his factory built ohv model. Indian fans were amused at the fitting of the trailing link forks.

The ill-fated 45 was now redesigned, with a new engine that carried the generator in the more conventional position, just ahead of the crankcases, and was driven by the valve cam mechanism. It featured a new and heavier frame to fit the contours of the new engine, together with heavier forks which were seldom prone to misalignment. A further improvement was the fitting of a heavyweight gearbox and clutch assembly, these no longer being shared with the two single cylinder models. Offered as the 'D', 'DL', or 'DLD' model depending on whether it was in commercial, touring or sporting state of tune, its performance was still somewhat less than spectacular, although it has been described as being able to overtake the popular Model A Ford sedan. A rugged and reliable machine, it was still overshadowed by the Indian 101 Scout, which was discontinued for the 1932 season in the interest of rationalized production.

As a paradox to the continuing bitter rivalry between the two barely surviving factories, and the unrelenting savage enmity for the Wigwam on the part of President Walter Davidson, representatives of the two factories met that fall in New York's Waldorf Astoria Hotel for their annual price fixing meeting. The assemblage was reported as being somewhat gloomy, following a meeting of members of the directors of the M & ATA the day before in which the country's economic trends were under serious discussion. Present were General Sales Manager Arthur Davidson, together with his opposite number, James Wright of Indian, and along with each were a couple of trusted associates. In assessing the general condition of the market, it was mutually agreed to set prices of all machines at rock bottom levels. The H-D Big Twin and Indian Chief were priced at $320 at the factory, the H-D 45 and Indian

Bud Ekins' 1931 74 cu.in. VL model. The first 1326 machines built had to be dismantled and fitted with improved engines when the original design showed insufficient power. *(Alisha Tamburri).*

Scout at $295. As Indian presently produced no singles, the $195 and $235 prices of the two H-D singles were not at issue. James Wright made a confidential announcement that Indian was provisionally planning to market a 30.50 cubic inch twin the following spring, and Arthur Davidson then suggested that it should be priced at $250. Wright acceded to the fairness of this suggestion, but stated that the final costing estimates had yet to be made.

A surprise visitor at the meeting was Indian's President E. Paul du Pont, who arrived at the suite of rooms reserved for the occasion where the dinner was already in progress. Declining an invitation to break bread with the assembled guests, he began addressing the meeting with tight lipped restraint, his subject being the bitter competition between the two organizations which had lately reached almost untenable proportions. Addressing his next remarks to Arthur Davidson, he castigated him for the Big Twin sales campaign in the law enforcement matter, and stated that it was a flagrant abrogation of the former gentleman's agreement between the two factories to fix prices in advance of each sales season. He further warned that all parties concerned should continue to use great care to ensure the complete secrecy of the meetings. He said that if the knowledge of the meetings ever leaked out, all parties concerned would be subject to Federal prosecution. He next went on to express indignation at the fact that certain H-D factory personnel had characterized him as a despicable 'New Jersey Jew', and that he greatly resented such implications as being both insulting to himself and other allied du Pont organizations.

The author's informant, who was present at the meeting and who recalled its details in an interview in 1961, stated that Davidson was abjectly speechless during and sometime after du Pont's restrained but impassioned utterances. After several minutes he appeared to have somewhat recovered his composure, and spoke briefly in defense of his company's actions in the matters in question. He stated that H-D had recently been in critical financial straits, not only from the rapidly worsening depression, but had also suffered heavily in both the 45 twin and 'VL' debacles. He further pointed out that his company had not the financial backing of any related corporate organizations as did du Pont, and that H-D faced further marketing problems with the threatened loss of additional export markets due to present world wide economic conditions. He was next reported to have offered his personal apologies to du Pont for any alleged personal insults through company channels, and further stipulated that any future price fixing agreements between the two companies would be honored without any reservations. He added that he hoped that the present recriminations in the matter would be both forgiven and forgotten. du Pont then reportedly shook hands with Davidson, extended his own assurances of future friendship and co-operation together with his own personal regards, and immediately left the meeting.

A 1931 21 cu.in. single in original condition. This machine, found in Australia, had been fitted with oversized tires, English-type bars, and an Amal carburetor and controls. *(Alisha Tamburri)*.

Arthur Davidson's apprehension regarding the immediate future of the American motorcycle industry's export market soon proved to be well founded. A 10% import tax on all motor vehicles was imposed by all of the British Commonwealth nations in the spring of 1932, which included Canada and Australasia. This action was initiated by pleas from Great Britain who, as the mother country, solicited co-operation in its now most critical economic situation to institute a 'Buy British' program. As American machines had long been exported to these areas in substantial numbers, the added tax posed a formidable marketing barrier.

It was about this time that H-D engines again became associated with the ultra-light airplane movement when one Lester (Les) Long, an enthusiast from Beaverton, Oregon, built up an engine utilising 1924-1927 'J' cylinder and piston assemblies. Mindful of the inherent unsuitability of conventional V twin motorcycle engines for their use, Long devised a horizontally-opposed twin, using crankcases of his own design, fitting an oil pump and other ancillary fittings from readily available stock automobile parts. The result was a well-balanced engine that displaced 80 cu.in, the result of fitting a specially fabricated crankshaft that gave a slightly than longer stock 'J' stroke. Turning out about 30 hp and with the ability to spin a 5'2" propellor at a useful 2750 rpm, the engine provided a much needed power plant for light airplane design that heretofore had needed to make do with less satisfactory engines.

Long made a tentative appointment to meet with President Walter Davidson to discuss the possibilities of its limited production by H-D. In later years, Long stated that Davidson in the end refused to meet with him, citing the press of more important Company matters. In the end, Long made up about 50 engines, both in his own shop and through castings being ordered and fabricated by other enthusiasts. A few of these engines still survive in the hands of ultra-light airplane enthusiasts.

In contrast to the doom and gloom of 1932, H-D machines in all models were now offered in a series of attractive color combinations, a distinct departure from the former olive or Brewster green which had been the rule ever since the close of the first World War. This not only added a more stylish touch to the machines, but also offered additional competition to Indian, which by this time was, quite naturally, using various color combinations featuring du Pont de Nemours paint.

By 1933, the economic plight of both the United States and the entire civilized world had reached its lowest ebb. Newly elected United States President, Franklin D. Roosevelt, a Democrat, was swept into office by a disheartened electorate with an overwhelming majority, on the promise that the New Deal could solve the nation's ills. Roosevelt promptly assured the American people that all they had to fear was fear itseif, and subsequently dragooned a compliant Congress to authorize the inauguration of a vast network of government agencies to control all phases of the nation's economic life. For the next

127

Somewhere in China. Motorized units of Generalissimo Chiang Kai-shek's Eighth Route Army with VL sidecar outfits. Note the left-hand fitted sidecars. *(Alfred Rich Child)*.

two years, the country flirted with national socialism, the more flagrant aspects of which were declared unconstitutional by a conservative Supreme Court, whose tenure of appointment harked back to the days of more orthodox free enterprise.

During the late Spring of 1932, H-D introduced their Servi-car, a three wheeled rickshaw-like vehicle that was a frank copy of the rear car commercial units already produced for nearly a decade in Japan and the Far East. H-D's version was based on the currently produced 'D' model 45 cubic inch twin, fitted with a low compression commercial-type engine, a car type rear end with a differential axle activated by the extended final chain drive of the motorcycle.

This type of machine was pioneered in the US by Indian, when Charles B.Franklin designed several prototype units based on the 101 Scout. The initial employment in the United States was aimed at the automotive repair and service market, as the machine, named the Dispatch-Tow, was used to pick up and deliver automobiles for repair or service, the motorcycle unit being towed behind the car on a tow bar. As Indian suspended production of the 101 late in 1931, H-D remained as the sole manufacturer of these useful units until 1935, when Indian introduced a new Scout model.

The Servi-car not only filled the original automotive purpose of the original Dispatch-Tow, but soon found favor as a law enforcement unit to enforce auto parking time in congested urban areas. The officer assigned to this duty could proceed at low speeds through municipal parking areas with time limit mandates, marking the rear wheel of the parked cars with a chalk fitted staff. On the return time check, vehicles already marked could be issued citations for overtime parking. The machines could be readily and safely operated by otherwise non-motorcycling personnel, often feminine officers, giving rise to the popular appelation of 'Meter-Maids'. The Servi-car also found favor with commercial operators requiring light delivery duties, and were very effective in other utility use under low temperatures, snow and ice.

During 1933, the domestic motorcycle industry produced a total of 7,418 machines, 5,689 of which were built by H-D. The dealer representation of both H-D and Indian now stood at about 800 outlets each. Both companies sold about the same numbers domestically, H-D's disproportionate share being shipped to export markets still enjoyed in South America, Japan, and to a lesser extent in Spain, Germany, the Low Countries, and Scandinavia.

During the Spring of 1933, H-D's position on antisemitism was again aired in the Zimmermann affair, centered in Rochester, New York, a highly controversial issue long debated by pioneer motor-cyclists in the Upstate region.

Harry A.Zimmermann, an early day motorcycling enthusiast and one time Pope exponent, obtained an H-D franchise in 1922 through the offices of the area factory representative, who was later thought to be either oblivious of the fact that Zimmermann was Jewish, or somehow inexplicably unaware of long established Milwaukee policy in the matter of excluding Semites from participation in company affairs. Reportedly an individual of pleasing personality, Zimmermann had, by shrewd business tactics, coupled with innate attributes of honesty and fair dealing, built up a thriving business in the Rochester area. His particular interest had lately centered on the high performance two cam 'JH' models after their introduction in 1928. He subsequently sold a number of these superb models to sporting enthusiasts, as well as a few sidecar units based on this model and used by rum runners transpor-

The H-D-Indian hybrid. This 1929-1931 Excelsior Super-X was originally designed by Arthur Constantine as a prototype H-D just before his discharge by President Walter Davidson in 1925.

ting illicit liquor landed on New York's North Lake shore by high speed motor launches based in Canada. As the potent 'JH's could easily outdistance the stodgy Fords and Dodges then utilized by local Treasury agents, even when somewhat penalized by sidecar gearing and a heavy load of bottled spirits, their high speed performance soon became a local legend. Only after Treasury agents were able to secure a pair of the magnificent Model K Lincoln Police Flyers were any of the rum-running Harleys apprehended.

Zimmermann, in the meantime, had enjoyed the dubious distinction of not only selling and servicing the night running "JH's', but later maintained them for the Treasury agents, who used them in their law enforcement activities after they had been legally confiscated.

The story is told that an unnamed deposed Excelsior agent had coveted Zimmermann's franchise for some time, and ultimately approached Milwaukee for information concerning the present status of Zimmermann's franchise. Whatever the facts of the latter's ethnic background, or what previous exceptions H-D's Sales Department may have taken to his conduct of his dealership will, of course, never be known. It was alleged that the Company instituted an obstructive campaign against Zimmermann, old time riders of the Rochester area reporting that his orders for spare parts and accessories began going mysteriously astray, with orders for even new machines being delayed for no accountable reason. In addition, the factory was also alleged to have ceased to answer his correspondence, and the area representative no longer made his usual personal calls. After some three months had elapsed, and with no possibility of redress apparently in sight, Zimmermann regretfully terminated his franchise and almost immediately secured the representation of Indian, as there was at that time no Wigwam outlet in the Rochester area.

Zimmermann's initial motorcycle dealership had been opened under the registered name of 'Rochester Harley-Davidson Company'. With his assumption of the Indian franchise, Zimmermann saw fit not to change the title of his business, and casual callers not familiar with Zimmermann's past difficulties with H-D were now amazed to enter his premises and to encounter a showroom full of gleaming red Indians!

H-D's management was almost immediately apprised of the matter, and through the offices of their legal counsel, filed a lawsuit against him and in their pleading, they sought to forbid him to use the H-D name henceforth in any manner.

The matter subsequently came to trial in the Superior Court of Monroe County. Upon hearing the evidence presented, Judge Callahan ruled in favor of the defendant, stating that Zimmermann had entered into his original franchise agreement in good faith, and that if H-D chose to terminate the agreement, as a Wisconsin-based organization, they had no further legal connection with Zimmermann who operated his business in the state of New York, and that he was free to conduct his business under any name he chose.

During the Winter of 1932 and 1933, Indian offered H-D strong competition in the miniscule utility motorcycle market by introducing the Pony Scout, a small twin of 30.50 cubic inch displacement which, while introduced at an initial retail price of $225, was ultimately offered at $195, abrogating the previous year's price fixing agreement between H-D and Indian. While H-D's management was somewhat perturbed at this model's introduction, it was by this time painfully obvious that American riders had already rejected the single as being both too lightly powered and not in keeping with the established macho image of the fast and rorty big twin machine that was long the established model on the North American continent. Most of H-D's singles were sold on the export market, the 30.50 being imported by Alfred Rich Child in Japan in fair numbers to power his now popular line of commercial rear car models.

During the Winter of 1933, the officers and Directors of the M & ATA and the AMA met in Columbus, Ohio, to discuss the current dire state of motorcycling. With registrations for the whole North American continent at an all-time low of 96,000 machines, sales of new machines, due to the now devastating effect of the depression, were at an all-time low too. Motorcycle sport was now almost nonexistent. Professional racing was almost at a standstill, with H-D's Joe Petrali the sole surviving $40 per week employee carrying the flag for that class of competition. What with Excelsior out of the picture, and Indian no longer supporting professional riders, H-D's domination of the 21 cubic inch class was indeed a hollow triumph, as competition in this category was relegated to occasional appearances of one make.

After some discussion, it was ultimately decided that a whole new set of competition rules be promulgated, emphasizing the role of the private owner as a competitor in rather mildly conceived sports events.

Competition was divided into three categories, with Class A and B designating professional riders employed by factories, and Class C to include private owners. In order to compete in this class, a private owner was mandated to ride his machine in street trim to competition events. At this point, the headlight and rear tail light, which nominally included the hinged rear mudguard section, could be removed, along with the chainguard, and the entrant could then proceed with whatever type of competitive event was being staged. (Most privateers in practice habitually rode without a front fender). Stringent rules were laid down forbidding the radical alteration of engine specifications from stock specification, and competitors were barred from transporting their machines to competitive events by truck or trailer.

In addition, a new (to the US) type of sporting event was the English-type trial, introduced to the AMA Competition Committee by Theodore A. (Ted) Hodgdon, Indian's resigning Advertising Manager. This provided a sporting alternative to the more casual private owner who was not interested in high speed events, and indeed, could be entered without recourse to removing any of his machine's standard fittings.

By common consent, the AMA Competition Committee also decided that most of the Class C events be tailored to the use of 45 cubic inches in machines, an emerging popular class. It came within the purchase limitations of depression riders, which also more or less mandated a milder power output as compared with the more formidable 61 cubic inch class which, in the public mind, had already been established as capable of lethal top speeds. In this latter class, and including 74 cubic inch models, now the standard US big twin, certain other mild competition trials and hillclimb events were also undertaken.

This new official AMA sports classification was entirely in accord with H-D's Management wishes, as in their improved 45 cubic inch model they now theorized they had a production machine capable of competing with Indian's 101 Scout.

In addition, the country was again re-districted into various geographical competition areas, with an official referee with broad discretionary powers to both conduct and enforce the newly instituted rules of competition. In the practical sense, this latter innovation ultimately proved to offer some additional advantage to H-D, as in advancing the greater share of financial support to both the M & ATA and the AMA, the majority of the district referees were H-D enthusiasts. While many of these officials tended to handle competition matters fairly and objectively, certain favoritism and gamesmanship ultimately worked to H-D's competition advantage in future years, as will be seen.

The now burning question of the fratricidal warfare between H-D and Indian and its obvious detrimental impact on motorcycling as a whole, next occupied the attention of Arthur Davidson and Indian's James Wright. Noting that club life, the life blood of private motorcycling, had been unfortunately affected, the two agreed in a later private meeting that steps should be taken to calm the seriously troubled waters. AMA Secretary Manager, E.C.Smith, was next dispatched, riding an H-D Big Twin sidecar outfit supplied by H-D, on a truce-making tour of the country with the intent of remedying the situation. Smith accordingly set up in advance a series of meetings with the various once-active clubs across the country, and was ultimately successful in reactivating a number of them, even though their loyalties were divided between the two competing makes. His journeys were also oriented toward making the membership of each club 100% sustaining members of the AMA. His main selling point was that an active but mild competition program, including participation by each individual club member, could do much to resurrect renewed interest in the movement as a whole. While his efforts were generally successful, some riders remained unconvinced, pointing out that Smith was a life long H-D enthusiast and that most of the District Referees were H-D oriented.

As a further step in an attempt to strengthen the AMA, and to save money as well in very difficult times, the *Motorcyclist* magazine was designated as the official AMA publication. Those riders contributing the nominal $1.00 per year subscription fee would now receive an AMA membership card.

While the AMA was quite obviously a non-democratic trade-dominated organization, most club members at least saw the wisdom of having some sort of national motorcycling body, and in the end both the AMA and club activities received a needed shot in the arm.

During the deliberations of the AMA Competition Committee, a somewhat obscure and brief ruling was placed on the books that allowed 30.50 cubic inch ohv machines to compete on equal terms with side valve 45 cubic inch models, provided that their compression ratio was not over 7.5:1. This was a somewhat left-handed offer to include the very limited number of English machines then in the hands of American riders (probably not over 250 examples) and in later years this became the subject of most bitter controversy.

In the Fall of 1934, the single cylinder models were no longer shown in the domestic catalogues. A limited number of side valve 21s were manufactured for the export market until 1936, however, and fair numbers of the 30.50 model were exported to Japan for the benefit of Alfred Rich Child where they mostly formed the motive power for his specially-fabricated rear car units. This was carried on until 1937, when Child was forced to terminate his activities there by the newly instituted militaristic government. Emphasis was now on the 74 cubic inch Big Twin and 45 cubic inch models. Furthermore, the Servi-car and various sidecar models, both passenger and commercial, were emphasized. In

A VL rear car as manufactured in Japan for commercial use. The machines were ordered without rear wheels or mudguards, but with extra length rear chains. *(Alfred Rich Child)*.

An enclosed VL rear car as built for the Tokyo Branch of the Singer Sewing Machine Company. *(Alfred Rich Child)*.

A VL box-bodied rear car used by the National Cash Register Company's Japanese sales outlet.
*(Alfred Rich Child).*

addition to detail improvements in the lubrication systems and drive trains, the appearance of the
machines was enhanced by the fitting of more pleasingly contoured mudguards, in line with current
automotive practice. A new Big Twin model was announced with the enlarged piston displacement of
80 cubic inches, effected by slightly increasing the bore of the standard 74. This latter was marketed
primarily as a law enforcement model, together with a comprehensive line of extra equipment from the
Accessory Department, such as heavy duty spotlights and sirens.

By this time, the Big Twin 'VL' model had evolved into a very rugged and dependable machine,
easily started by means of its improved field coil generator which proved very reliable and was admirably suited to both private and commercial uses. For 1935, a four-speed transmission with optional
three forward speeds and reverse for sidecar use was offered, although most dealers held back on offering orders for this due to persistent rumors of a new Big Twin model that might leave them with an extra spare parts demand.

The idea of the extra displacement of the new 80 model was generally well received, as it offered
a slight power advantage in serious hill climbing as well as an edge for heavy duty sidecar work. Its
drawback, however, was a somewhat enhanced vibration problem due to the inherent imbalance of the
V twin configuration.

While now an admirably rugged and trouble-free machine, the Big Twin was still possessed of
one serious weakness, namely the very real possibility of overheating and piston seizure during prolonged full throttle running, especially during high summer temperatures. While the improved 'VL' was
said to have a slight top speed advantage over its traditional rival, the Indian Chief, the latter appeared
to be less susceptible to overheating, a telling factor in law enforcement use during high speed highway
pursuit of speeding motorists. Although the Chief, especially when fitted with the still optional
magneto, was a formidable competitor, it was almost impossible to start during cold weather unless
parked in a well-heated garage overnight.

Due to slightly improving economic conditions, H-D production for 1935 totaled 10,398 units, a
marked improvement over the 7,897 figure for the previous year. The sales improvement was due to
enhanced export markets, mostly in Japan, South America, Southern Europe and Australasia.

In an attempt to revive the now flagging interest in professional Class A, flat track racing, H-D's
engineering department brought forth another 'Peashooter' type model fitted with a 30.50 cubic inch
engine. A frank copy of the contemporarily successful J.A.Prestwich-engined models (more simply
known as JAPs) its development was largely the work of Joe Petrali, who designed and tested the new
engine largely on his own time. He was encouraged in the effort by President Walter Davidson, who
now hoped for a more potent machine to compete with the current crop of JAPs and Rudge Specials

which had lately dominated flat track competition. Petrali recalled to the author that Davidson had offered him a $1,000 bonus to oversee the design and limited production of H-D's entrance into the now popular 500 cc class. About a dozen machines were ultimately built in the racing department, but several bugs appeared and the machine's performance in the initial events entered did not prove encouraging. Walter Davidson subsequently ordered their production terminated, citing financial reasons for not subjecting the prototype design to further development. Petrali somewhat bitterly recalled later that Walter Davidson refused to pay him the previously stipulated bonus, again calling attention to the financial exigency of the times.

H-D production now centered on three twin models, the updated 45, the familiar 74 cubic inch VL, and the new 80 cubic inch twin, which was identical to the 74 except for the bored out cylinders. In addition, a line of sidecars and various commercial sidecar bodies were offered, as well as the Servi-car. In regard to the 74, H-D enthusiasts were now saying that it had taken the company five seasons to develop the 'VL' to the point that it could perform as well as the now defunct 'J' models. 'J' enthusiasts still referred longingly to the now immortal two cam 'JH'.

With an encouraging upturn in the nation's economy, H-D somewhat enhanced their advertising program, as well as both the content and distribution of the *Enthusiast* magazine. In addition, the activities of the accessory department were enlarged, and an important item was the introduction of the 'buddy seat', an elongated saddle that accommodated two riders. The passenger's feet were provided for by the fitting of either extentions to the rear of the footboards, also a new accessory item, or by means of a pair of foot pegs that could be bolted to the lower frame rails. This arrangement not only offered a safe riding position for two riders, but added the zestful possibility of very close contact between the driver and wife or girlfriend. In addition, the area over the rear wheel was clear for the fitting of either a rear carrier or saddle-bags, or both, and opened up enhanced possibilities for carrying luggage on extended tours.

Sporting motorcycling received a welcome infusion of renewed interest as well as providing some interesting competition to H-D in the 45 cubic inch class with the introduction of Indian's newly designed Sport Scout in the fall of 1934 for the 1935 sales season. While the late lamented 101 model had been dropped from the line for 1932, it was still the machine of choice for the majority of sporting riders. The new model was of approximatley the same size and weight as the H-D 45, and was possessed of a somewhat better speed potential due to its shorter piston stroke with consequently wider bore.

With a slight increase in public motorcycling interest due to the now encouraging economic upturn, the AMA Competition Committee now planned a somewhat expanded program of National Races in the early spring of 1935.

As an opening event, and with perhaps an attempt to revive the early post-war glories of the Marion Road Races, the Committee selected a fast road course at Camp Foster, an inactive military base near Jacksonville, Florida. Billed as a 200 Mile National, it was the first long distance event of its type since 1920. The course was eminently suitable, as it was fenced in to allow for crowd control, insuring a paying gate for the expected 10,000 spectators, as well as a reasonably safe road surface. In addition, it was also to serve as a showcase for the newly revised competition Class C rules that mandated the entrance of nearly stock machines.

A heavy duty VL rear car with artillery-type wheels. *(Alfred Rich Child).*

An elaborate VL rear car conversion with enclosed cab and car-type steering wheel controls. *(Alfred Rich Child)*.

A large field of 68 riders was flagged at noon on February 24th, a most unseasonably hot day under the blistering Florida sun. As the only domestic makes entered, H-D and Indian were evenly divided, together with single entries by riders of Ariel, Norton, Rudge and Velocette.

Red House, of Washington, D.C. took an early lead on his Sport Scout. A formidable contender, he was touted as a sure winner, but a blown tire in the 23rd lap of the 1.6 mile course ended his ride. Bill Carpenter, of Lancaster, Ohio, next took the lead on his H-D, and began a give-and-take battle with Rody Rodenburg of Indianapolis on a Sport Scout. The two switched first and second positions several times, with Rodenburg blasting into the lead at the finish when Carpenter ran out of fuel in sight of the finish.

To add color to the affair, National Class A Champion Joe Petrali acted as the official referee, with Indianapolis auto racing star 'Wild Bill' Cummings as the starter, and Cannonball Baker acting as one of the judges. Creditable rides were also made by an up and coming H-D star from San Jose, California, Sam Arena, as well as R.D.Johnson, from Savannah, Georgia.

Rodenburg's winning time was 3 hours, 51 minutes 31 seconds, with Carpenter just 6 seconds behind as he coasted across the line with a dead engine. A significant third place winner was George Pepper, of Belleville, Ontario, Canada, who was 2 minutes behind the winner on a 500 cc ohc International Norton. His remarkable performance was not lost on the large crowd of spectators, most of whom were unfamiliar with foreign machines. It also added further laurels to Norton's already distinguished position in international races, although the United States was now fully isolated from such competition.

At a subsequent meeting of the AMA Competition Committee, President Walter Davidson is reported to have urged that International Norton models should henceforth be barred from Class C Competition. He was subsequently overruled by the majority led by James Wright, who cited the fact that Pepper's machine came within established Class C specification, both as a catalogued model, and present state of tune. He further argued that with only five known International models being extant on the North American continent, such action would not only be unsporting but would amount in the public's eye as an overkill.

A few critics were quick to note that in the race report appearing in a subsequent issue of the *Motorcyclist* Pepper's closely placing 3rd was carefully glossed over, its focus being mainly in the tabulation of the various rider's times at the end of the article. When queried later about the matter, the then Editor, Chet Billings, was reported to have succinctly stated that as the presently official AMA publication, the magazine was mainly concerned with promoting 'American' motorcycling!

Numbers of American big twins saw military service in the Spanish Civil War. H-D had already become well established in Spain, with franchised dealers in Madrid, Seville, and Barcelona. Machines already in military service were used by both sides, with numbers of civilian models being impressed for whichever side was able to commandeer them. As the war was viewed with much apprehension, through the intervention of both Communist Russia and Fascist Germany, neither faction received much sympathy either in Europe or in the United States, all observers seemingly aware of the war's ominous import. It is probably for this reason that both American factories did their utmost to conceal the fact that their machines were being used in the conflict. A 1933 'VL' gained some notoriety, however, during the famous siege of the Alcazar. It was here that several hundred Loyalist military cadets were besieged for several weeks before being annihilated by Franco's forces. With its rear mudguard and tire removed, the machine was attached to a belt which activated an electric generator to supply lighting throughout the ancient fortress. As the machine was necessarily clamped in a stationary position, the engine was cooled by directing air to the cylinders by means of two household electric fans. The author has in his possession, among his considerable collection of H-D memorabilia, a newspaper photograph of this machine, which is unfortunately now too faded for photographic reproduction.

The Class C competition category was by this time receiving increased attention from many otherwise casual riders, as Class A racing was now all but dead. Most of the latter events centered around certain of the larger county fairground circuits, and were limited to the 21 cubic inch 'Peashooter' class. These events were dominated by H-D's sole professional, Joe Petrali. After his peak year of 1931, he was still a high point winner from 1932 through 1936. H-D's performances were almost a one-make show, as Indian virtually abandoned this class in favor of the further development of their Sport Scout for the more popular Class C competition. Aside from Petrali, Lou Balinski and Fred Toscani were active with their 'Peashooters', and received limited factory support for their efforts.

In the earlier days of Class C competition, H-D's 45s were more often than not outclassed by Indian riders. The discontinued 101 was still the favored sporting mount, as it could be stripped to weigh less than 300 pounds, and was equipped with magneto ignition as standard equipment. The H-D was not only heavier, but was further handicapped by not having magneto ignition available, and was forced to assume the weight penalty of a coil and battery. In addition, H-D's condensers were prone to over heat and fail under prolonged high speed running. Many enthusiasts wired up their condensers in series, and fitted a series of switches which would enable them to activate a new one when a failed unit cut out in a hard run. The long stroke H-D motor was unable to turn as fast as the Indian, which had a more equal configuration, although the torque output of the former was formidable once the revs had been built up. To counteract this disadvantage, some enthusiasts blanked out second gear, and thus could move into top gear from low without having to drop revs while going through second. The Sport Scout's engine could run even faster than the 101, which was of great advantage when coming out of a turn. Whatever the differences, the countless dirt track and TT duels between the two makes was the lifeblood of American motorcycle competition for the next two decades.

The AMA Competition Committee attempted to continue the enforcement of the strictly stock mandate for Class C Competition, but it appeared that by common consent, both factories soon abandoned such restrictions, and the AMA looked the other way.

In conjunction with the saga of H-D's 45 competition, and in the gradual development of H-D engines into more potent competitors, the marque's racing fortunes became explicitly interwoven with the career of Tom Sifton. An early day H-D enthusiast, noted for his mechanical skill, he became a sub-dealer in San Francisco in 1929 under the sponsorship of Dudley Perkins. He next obtained his own full dealership in nearby San Jose in 1933. Becoming increasingly involved in competition, in common with most dealers of those days, Sifton set about to breathe life into the admittedly anachronistic 45 engine.

It is by this time an almost legendary fact in motorcycle history that it was more often than not a practical engineer outside the factory that really made the make go. Ariel had its L.W.E.Hartley, Rudge its Roland Pike, Indian its Red Fenwicke and Pop Schunk, Norton its Francis Beart; and so it was that H-D had Tom Sifton.

By what alchemy these mechanical geniuses were able to breathe more life into powerplants not of their own original design, has long been a matter of historic speculation. It may well be that development engineers grow stale on a project perhaps too long on a drawing board. Or it may well be that long periods in the forest blot out the sight of the trees. At any rate, Sifton, by extensive modifications to porting, valve action, and other details, was ultimately able to make the long stroke 45 into a frequent winner.

The first competitor Sifton sponsored was Louis Guanella, who soon made a name for himself in the far west circuit, followed by Sam Arena, who was ultimately to become one of the most noted H-D contestants in the middle and late 1930's. He was able to mount formidable opposition to Indian's legendary Ed Kretz, who usually swept the board if his hell-for-leather riding style didn't blow his long suffering engine. Sifton importuned the factory to modernize and update the 45, but met with a cool reception from both William H.Harley and William Ottaway when he suggested that a modernization was in order. Sifton retired to his shop, and ultimately came up with a machine that enabled Sam Arena to win the Oakland 200, clipping 17 minutes off the previous record into the bargain.

In again referring to Sifton's wizardry, most H-D riders were convinced, mostly through sad experience, that one couldn't run an engine wide open for a whole lap without snapping the throttle shut at least twice to bring oil up into the cylinder walls. Sifton experimented with various oil control piston rings and eventually came forth with a lubrication system that would allow the cylinders to run wet. Critics, noting Arena's wide open running, warned Sifton that if he were not ordered to slow down, he risked certain seizure. Sifton's answer was, to himself at least, that if Arena slowed down, the clandestine oiling system would allow too much oil to come up and foul the spark plugs!

Sifton ultimately came into much conflict with H-D's management in the late 1930's when their Racing Department was in process of developing their later standard WR racer. Through direct contact with the factory representatives in person, the factory practically demanded that Sifton make known to them his heretofore secret modifications. It was alleged by H-D management that Sifton was conducting a competition with Sifton rather than H-D machines. The latter, however, remained adamant, and he did not reveal his tuning secrets to the factory until 1947, the year Sam Arena retired and took over Sifton's San Jose dealership.

H-D's official position in the matter of Class C competition remained critical during the late 1930's, due to the pre-eminence of Indian's Sport Scout. Rollie Free, a veteran Indian dealer in Indianapolis for many years, told the author in 1976 that following a spectacular race meet in that city in 1936 that ended in a sweeping Indian victory, a group of H-D factory personnel approached him to find out just why the Sport Scout could be tuned to deliver such outstanding performance. In the course of the meeting, held in an opulent Indianapolis watering place, the latter recounted both their problems in developing a really potent H-D racer, and their inability to persuade Tom Sifton to reveal his tuning secrets. Free related that he was able to both commiserate with them in their dilemma, accept their hospitality with grace, but at the same moment reveal none of his own private knowledge of just how the Sport Scout was tuned by knowledgable mechanics to deliver its winning performances.

Persistent rumors within the industry regarding experimental work at Milwaukee regarding the introduction of a new model H-D finally came to light in the spring of 1936 with the announcement of an entirely new model, the 61E, a massive V twin with overhead valves. The new machine, which bore no direct relationship to the previous 'VL' series, featured a cradle-type frame with twin down tubes, heavier forks, and incorporated a number of innovative features to both current H-D practice and to contemporary American motorcycle design. While maintaining the bore and stroke of 3 5/16 x 4½ inch stroke of the classic 61 cubic inch 'J' models, the new engine featured overhead valve configuration that doubled that engine's hp output to 36. With a compression ratio of 6:1 and a top gear ratio of 3.73 to 1, the theoretical top speed was projected at well over 90 mph. In addition, the new engine featured dry sump lubrication, already seen on Indian, and long a standard item on foreign designs. At last it brought H-D into the middle period of the twentieth century.

In addition, a wide ratio four-speed gear box with gears in constant mesh, coupled with a new massive multiplate-clutch mechanism, was to carry on H-D's established reputation of a trouble-free drive train. The overall appearance of the new model, which weighed slightly over 600 pounds with fuel and oil aboard, was enhanced with the fitting of an entirely new streamlined fuel tank, in two halves, the lubricating oil being carried in a gallon capacity tank fitted behind the seat post.

As the first domestic machine ever to be offered with overhead valves, the 61E featured push rods of unequal length running off a single lobe from the timing chest.

While ostensibly the work of H-D's design department, headed by William S.Harley and augmented by the efforts of Bill Ottaway, much of the practical development was effected by Joe Petrali and Hank Syvertson, a long time member of the Racing Department. In addition, much of the testing of the initial prototype models was carried out by William Harley's son, William J. The latter, born in 1912, had joined the Company at the age of 19. Expected to prove himself, he was started at the bottom as an apprentice. He also studied engineering at the University of Wisconsin, as his father before him, and gained his degree in 1935. While his formal duties were now that of a draftsman in the engineering department, he had much to do with the road testing of the two 61E prototypes. In later years, he confided to intimates that the latter models required extensive modifications to the original

The standardized VL rear car with optional all-weather enclosure. *(Alfred Rich Child).*

The three wheeled Servi-car introduced in 1932. The small town petroleum products outlet advertises regular and high octane gasoline at 18 and 20 cents per gallon.

Official factory photograph of a 30.50 cu.in. short track machine as originally designed by Joe Petrali.

steering ge<      >try, as he narrowly missed several crashes when testing the new model in extensive runs in the country adjacent to Milwaukee.

While the new model appeared basically sound, there were certain defects in the ohv system which were found to leak oil excessively. Petrali, who was well aware of these problems, told the author in 1968 that he cautioned H-D's management not to release the new model for production until the matter had been solved. President Walter Davidson, however, had set the target date at June 1936, and gave the go-ahead for production in spite of Petrali's warnings, the outcome of which will be subsequently discussed.

Concurrent to the development of the 61E, Petrali conferred with President Walter Davidson concerning the problem of updating or improving the current 45 model to make it more competitive with Indian's Sport Scout model, which by this time had proved itself to be a definitely superior machine. He suggested that the company take the initiative in bringing out a high performance ohv model, which would entail the design of an entirely new engine. His reasoning was that the H-D Company, due to its majority financial support of the AMA, could now dictate a new set of competition rules in the 45 cubic inch class that could not only obtain AMA approval of such a new model for Class C competition, but could force Indian to redesign their Sport Scout in order to compete with H-D. President Walter Davidson's answer was that the cost of such a project would probably entail the expenditure of at least $100,000 and with the present state of both the general motorcycle market and the company's current financial status, it was out of the question. He further stated to Petrali that the project could be instituted only if Alfred Rich Child could be induced to purchase the manufacturing rights of the 61E for this figure.

In the meantime, under the direction of William A.Davidson, the 61E was placed in production, and of a total of 8,879 machines projected for production in 1936, 1,926 were of the new model. While the 61E was basically a sound and rugged machine built from the best available materials in the time tried H-D tradition, early models showed certain defects in the valve gear. These included valve spring breakage, insufficient lubrication for the rocker mechanism, from massive oil leakage from the rocker boxes and subsequent loss of correct timing sequence with a resultant loss of power. The author, as a young man, recalls being allowed a test ride on Joe Frugoli's personal 61E which had been ordered for demonstration purposes. While the machine in the author's opinion offered decidedly better performance than the last 'VL' models, even including the briefly produced 80 inch model, upon his returning the machine to the shop he noted that his legs from the knees down were heavily saturated with lubricating oil.

With the official announcement that the 61E was a high performance machine of advanced design, (at least as far as the American market was concerned), many dealers were somewhat hesitant initially either to order the new model or to unconditionally recommend it to favored customers, due to their unfortunate experiences with the early 45 and 'VL' models during 1929 and 1930. When the obvious defects of the new ohv valve model became painfully apparent, both dealers and knowledgable riders again questioned the factory's judgment in releasing a new design for production before all the bugs had been thoroughly worked out.

In commenting upon this most critical phase of H-D history, Joe Petrali told the author that while he had had much to do with the basic design of the 61E, he had certain reservations regarding the ultimate reliability of the first prototype models. He then suggested to President Walter Davidson that more time be allotted to further testing with a view to correcting these faults, and that any official announcements regarding the release of the model for sale should be held in abeyance until such had been completed. Davidson's reply was that what with the relatively large sums of money that had already been expended on prototype development, the company was now forced to place the model on the market in order to recoup as soon as possible.

While the sychophantic motorcycling press, now solely represented by the AMA-backed *Motorcyclist,* offered lavish editorial praise to the 61E without reference to any concommitant road tests, its debut was somewhat overshadowed from an almost unexpected quarter.

Albert G.Crocker, whom we have met before as a one time colleague of William Ottaway's in the old Thor organization, had for the past few seasons been building a limited number of Class A speedway machines for use on short tracks. What with the recent ascendancy of the more highly developed JAP and Rudge-engined machines, he had ceased assembly of the latter to concentrate his activities on the production of a machine that had long been an unrealized ambition: a high performance heavyweight V twin the classic Yankee tradition. The result, with the collaboration of another heavyweight enthusiast, a practical engineer and skilled mechanic, Paul A. Bigsby, was a rather noisy and hard-to-start rorty big twin that offered sensational performance. Due to its more nearly 'square' bore and stroke configuration, moderate weight for its size and rather 'tall' gearing, its 100 mph plus top speed was at least ten miles better than the well tuned Big Twin H-D's and Indian Chiefs. During the initial speed trials held on the old Lake Muroc race course in the Spring of 1936, the newly-introduced Crocker beat everthing in sight. With the local sensation created by the new make, the *Motorcyclist* was literally forced to publish a graphic report of its achievements.

Old time H-D factory employees and dealers in various discussions of the matter through the years have attested to management's chagrin over both the results of Crocker's efforts and the attendant, though somewhat grudgingly accorded, publicity. Their subsequent reaction to the matter ultimately took a somewhat surprising turn, which we shall see.

Following the natural disappointment of many H-D dealers and riders over the initial shortcomings of the 61E, the Engineering Department at once inaugurated a crash program to rectify the matter. The metallurgy of the valve springs was improved, and a new supplier ultimately provided more long-lasting components. The rocker gear was redesigned for improved oiling capabilities, together with an improved bearing arrangement. Repair kits containing the new parts were dispatched to the dealers, with instructions to make good on any of the initial 1,900 machines that showed defects.

As a publicity stunt, and in an effort to publicly demonstrate the capabilities of the 61E, plans were formulated to attack the existing straight-away mile records long held by Indian rung up on the famous beach course at Daytona. Hank Syvertson of the Racing Department, with the help of Joe

Another version of the 1934 short tracker from the Bud Ekins collection. Note the Merkel-type forks and the similarity of the engine to the contemporary JAP design. It was quickly outclassed by the latter's later models. *(Alisha Tamburri)*.

Petrali, built up a special machine around a stock engine. Modifications included twin carburetors, a high tension magneto, increased compression, modified breathing capabilities, and high lift cams. Set with a high 3:1 top gear ratio, the machine was calculated to show a top speed of 160 mph. To reduce weight, a special frame of lightweight tubing was built up and high pressure racing tires were fitted, the wheels being provided with faired aluminum discs. A streamline tail section, reminiscent of contemporary racing car practice, extended from the rear of the saddle to cover the rear wheel.

After a number of studio pictures of the machine were taken by the Publicity Department photographer, including several with Petrali aboard wearing a clean white shirt and necktie, the 61, along with a stripped stock 45 inch model supposedly tuned to Class C rules, was loaded on a truck for the trip to Daytona Beach. A three mile course had been laid out under the direction of John La Tour, who had recently acted as the official timer for Sir Malcolm Campbell's recent record race car runs on the same stretch. One mile was used to get up speed before hitting the trap for the record, the third mile being required to bring the machine to a stop.

On March 13th, defying superstition, Petrali warmed up the 45 and made several runs through the course. What with problems experienced with carburetion and burned out spark plugs, the best average was a somewhat disappointing 102.04 mph. The 61 was next rolled out for a preliminary run, 141

Two views of Edward Carlson and his 1934 74 cu.in. VL. 1940 and later 16 inch rear wheels were often fitted to give a softer ride. *(George Hays)*.

but when a speed of approximately 100 mph was reached, the machine suddenly became unmanageable. Hoping that a quick burst of speed might correct the difficulty, Petrali opened the throttle, whereupon the front wheel started to aviate, and at the same time swung back and forth over the
course. Due to his consummate riding skill, Petrali was able to wrestle the 61 to a standstill. Noting at
once the unfavorable aerodynamic qualities of the wheel discs and tail fairings, Petrali ordered the pit
crew to remove them. In stripped condition, the machine now stayed on course, and three full throttle
runs were made, the best average being 136.18 mph, for a new record. This was a rather hollow
triumph, as it was only 10 mph faster than Johnny Seymour's 1932 record time made on a modified
board track Indian racer with a slightly modified 8 valve engine that was one of six assembled by the
factory in 1924.

While the H-D factory quite naturally made much out of the victory, it did not mention in the
publicity reports that the machine did not make its record run as a streamliner. Only one photograph
of the 61 on its actual running run was surreptitiously taken by a local newspaper photographer. The
actual machine is presently on view at William Tuthill's Museum of Speed at Daytona Beach.

In commenting on the matter in an interview with the author in 1967, Petrali stated that in his
opinion the 61 would have performed much better if it had been lighter, as even in stripped form it
weighed nearly 400 pounds, some 125 pounds heavier than Seymour's earlier Indian. He also was of the
opinion that if it had weighed 100 pounds less, it could have been fitted with taller gearing, and might
then have attained the 150 mph figure envisioned by President Walter Davidson. The latter's hopes for
this speed were centered on his offer to Petrali of a $1,000 bonus if he could reach this figure. Upon his
return to Milwaukee, Petrali attempted to induce Davidson to award him at least half of the promised
bonus, citing the problems experienced with the machine and his near disaster when the machine went
out of control. Davidson was adamant, however, and no bonus payment was forthcoming.

In the Fall of 1936, the now venerable 'J' model was retired from Class C competition in the TT
and hill climb categories by a change in the rules mandated by the AMA Competition Committee,
which effectively barred the model from future events. This action was, of course, instigated by H-D's
top management, which now decided that for too long the 'J's' had overshadowed the 'VL's', which
were now to be superseded by the 61E and the soon-to-be announced 'U' series. While no official announcements were forthcoming from the factory, the Competition Committee announced that
henceforth pocket valve engines and machines with exposed external compression type rear brakes
were to be barred from competition. This arbitrary action quite naturally angered the many die-hard
'J' enthusiasts, including its two leading exponents who had already racked up an impressive set of wins
during the past several seasons, Hap Jones and Fred Toscani. These two, in company with a number of
other sporting 'J' enthusiasts, were particularly chagrined, as they had collected an impressive array of

The Buddy Seat. An important adjunct to
social motorcycling.

The crash guard as pioneered by H-D in the
mid-1930s.

# FINEST MENS' AND LADIES' RIDING BREECHES
## POLO STYLE WHIPCORD
### *Dark Oxford or Police Blue*

Our leader in riding breeches. The nifty Polo Style is dressy. Here is a strong closely woven pre-shrunk cotton whipcord material that wears like iron. Double thickness on inside of knees and seat. Five roomy pockets. Sizes 28 to 40 in standard lengths, 30 to 38 in extra longs, 28 to 32 in extra shorts.

|  |  | Code |
|---|---|---|
| 11097-34—Oxford Whipcord | $3.95 | bykah |
| 11097-35—Police Blue Whipcord | 3.95 | byepr |

*Polo Style Breeches*

*English Military Style Breeches*

## ENGLISH MILITARY STYLE

Style plus utility. The last word in style and quality—these extra high grade, part wool breeches will appeal to the most critical buyer. Made from a new closely woven tan material, both distinctive and long wearing. Full grain leather facings are used at the knees. You cannot duplicate these high quality breeches at our low price. Sizes 28 to 40 in standard lengths, 30 to 38 in extra longs, 28 to 32 in extra shorts.

|  |  | Code |
|---|---|---|
| 11099-X—Tan only | $7.50 | bajox |

## MEN'S WHITE OR BROWN SUMMER WEIGHT

These light, summer-weight gabardine breeches are styled after a popular pattern, they are neat and attractive. Made of the best pre-shrunk, washable material. Five pockets. In white or rich brown. Available in sizes: 28 to 42 waist in standard lengths: 28 to 38 waist in extra shorts; 28 to 36 waist in extra longs.

|  |  | Code |
|---|---|---|
| 11094-36—White Gabardine | $3.75 | byede |
| 11098-36—Brown Gabardine | 3.75 | byeef |

## CLASSY LADIES' BREECHES and JODHPURS

Just what the girls want—classy, light-weight breeches or Jodhpurs to better enjoy the thrills of motorcycling. Made of pre-shrunk, washable gabardine. Double seats and knees with buttons at knee on breech. Either breeches or Jodhpurs are attractively styled, beautifully fitting, excellent tailored garments with high-rise back and liberal waist and leg outlets. All points of strain reinforced for longer wear. Available in standard lengths only. Sizes 24 to 34 waist measure.

*Jodhpurs*

*Ladies' Breeches*

|  |  | Code |
|---|---|---|
| 11092-36—Ladies' White Riding Breeches | $3.50 | byczy |
| 11093-36—Ladies' Rich Brown Jodhpurs | 3.75 | byeab |

## GENUINE HORSEHIDE

Leather riding breeches were made originally for the competition rider, as they are quite a protection against injury in case of a spill.

These well tailored horsehide breeches are really weather-proof. They are made from fine, soft, black, front quarter horsehide and are fully lined. Have five pockets and belt loops.

|  |  | Code |
|---|---|---|
| 11068-X—Black Horsehide Breeches | $12.50 | bahio |

## HIGH GRADE RIDING BOOTS

The field boot style, as illustrated, is the style desired by motorcycle riders. The lacings at the instep and the calf make it easy to put on and take off this style of boot. We can supply dress boots or ladies boots on special order, but the field boot is the most practical and is carried in stock.

Harley-Davidson boots are made from high grade calfskin that will give long service. They are fully lined and have excellent soles. Can be supplied in sizes 6 to 12, and all standard widths. Get your proper measurement from your shoe dealer. Stocked in black only.

|  |  | Code |
|---|---|---|
| 11090-34—Field Boots | $12.25 | buryh |

5

machines and spare parts, mostly of the two cam 'JH' type. Jones subsequently abandoned Milwaukee in disgust, and shortly afterward joined forces with Indian by taking a dealership in San Francisco. This action also removed the surviving Super Xs that were still active in Class C competition, as their pocket valve engines and rear brakes were identical with H-D 'Js'. As highly tuned Xs, many with strengthened lower ends were ever formidable contenders in any sort of competition, H-D's management, working through the AMA hierarchy, must have felt greatly relieved in disqualifying them.

The introduction of the 61E was followed that fall by two newly designed side valve machines, the 74 and 80 cubic inch 'UL' and 'ULH' models. These were practically identical to the former as to cycle parts, and in addition were fitted with a circulation oil pump and dry sump lubrication, the oil being carried in a four quart tank under the saddle, as in the 61E. In contrast with the early teething troubles of the latter, these two 600 pound heavyweights proved entirely successful from their beginning. They were further distinguished by the fact that they were probably the most rugged, durable, and trouble-free motorcycles ever produced by the American industry. They had the added advantage of being quickly and easily serviced, as a top overhaul, only required after high mileages, could be effected without removing the engine from the frame. With their massive high torque engines that turned out well over 30 hp at moderate revolutions, both models were well suited to heavy duty sidecar or commercial use. While their fork geometry was such that they steered somewhat heavily, they could be easily handled in city traffic as their massive multiplate dry type clutches could be slipped without harm, and even prolonged operation in this use produced but little wear in the mechanism. In addition, their fuel consumption was moderate if cruising speeds were held below 60 mph.

While well accepted by American riders, they were particularly successful on the export market, being utilized mostly for sidecar or commercial sidevan uses. Due to their ruggedness and longevity they were also popular for law enforcement use. They found almost universal acceptance by the Government of Mexico, as well as in various countries in Central and South America in military and constabulary units. Their ruggedness and low maintenance costs were advantageous, particularly in areas where highly skilled mechanics were lacking, as well as the fact that they could stand up to misuse and abuse meted out to them by inexperienced riders.

In short, the 'U' models offered a broader based appeal than did the high performance 61E, and their only real weakness was their inability to stand up to high speed running, especially in hot climatic

The 1936 VL 80 cu.in. model with four-speed transmission, the last year of the VL. The police accessory group is shown.

conditions. If operated at speeds over 70 mph, the cylinders and heads were much more prone to overheating and distortion, usually resulting in piston seizure. They suffered in comparison with the contemporary Indian Chief, their main competitor, as the latter's combustion chamber profile and cooling fin designed by James Hill appeared better able to cope with high speed operation. On the other side of the coin, Indian's oil immersed clutch and archaic sliding gear transmission suffered greatly in comparison to H-D's new heavyweight constant mesh gear set and multiple dry plate clutch configuration.

The 45 cubic inch model 'D' was also updated for 1937, and was fitted with the same mudguards and fuel tank pressings of the larger twins to rationalize production. In addition, its engine now had improved cooling and lubrication with the fitting of dry sump oiling, the latter being carried in a chamber in one of the tank halves. While the high compression engine option offered to riders seeking mild sporting performance gave somewhat more spirit to the formerly sedate model, its advantage was somewhat offset by the increased overall weight of the machine, which was now well over 500 pounds in road-going trim. It was no match for the more highly developed Indian Sport Scout and its appeal to sporting riders was further diminished by the fact that due to H-D's big twin parts sequence so that it was not possible to easily 'stroke' it to an increased piston displacement. On the other hand, its lower bearing and flywheel assembly was more rugged than that of the Scout, and practical mechanics almost at once began adapting these parts to the Scout engine, which then resulted in a highly potent machine with the displacement increased to 52 cubic inches.

A further weakness of the new model, especially when fitted with the high compression engine, was that under fierce acceleration the single frame tube that supported the engine base was prone to flexing and many riders found that this distortion caused the outer run of the double chain drive to run off the sprockets. The diameter of the tube and the thickness of the mounting flanges were inceased the following year in hopes of curing the trouble, but this was only partially successful. While a cradle type frame, such as seen in the current big twin models, would have undoubtedly corrected the fault, the resultant weight penalty would have been formidable in a machine already overly heavy for its power development. Nevertheless, the 45 remained as a popular utility mount for many riders, as well as for elderly or feminine types who did not opt for high performance and appreciated its easy starting capabilities as well as its usually unfailing reliability. It was widely exported to many undeveloped countries for utility or commercial use. It was also seen as a military mount, particularly in countries where universally poor roads ruled out high speed travel. In the United States, its most familiar guise was as the basis for the popular Servi-car, widely used as a commercial carrier or in law enforcement traffic and parking control.

The Winter of 1936 and 1937 saw the nation's industries encountering increasing problems with labor. Sociological historians may recall that the labor union movement had gained impetus during the closing years of the 19th century and the opening years of the 20th. Public sympathy was aroused with the exposure of the often appalling working conditions and low wages suffered by many of the production workers following the rise of industrialism in the United States following the Civil War. The problem was complicated by the hordes of immigrants that had been allowed to enter the country from Europe with the blessings of the industrialists who foresaw the need for a vast pool of exploitable labor. With the leadership of union organizers such as Samuel Gompers and John L. Lewis, trade unionism gained strength after the First World War, but much ground was lost during the depression when jobs were scarce and the general economic picture was such that any employment offering even minimal wages was at a premium. In 1934, the Populist President Franklin D. Roosevelt induced a compliant Congress to pass the Wagner Labor Relations Act, which encouraged union organization among workers, and which could now offer the hope of raising the then current 30 to 35 cent hourly stipend.

In the Midwest, and subsequent to the passage of the Wagner Act, several drives were instituted by union organizers to recruit members, one of which was led by one Charles Travis, one of the founders of the United Auto Workers. After some resistance, he was able to organize General Motors workers in 1935, and shortly afterwards, Chrysler. The giant Ford Motor Company was a much tougher nut to crack, as old Henry had long been an ardent foe of unionism. Union organizers fought a number of pitched battles outside the Dearborn plant, and two young labor organizers named Walter Reuther and Charles Frankenstein were badly beaten in one encounter with Company police units. After Ford ultimately capitulated, other related and sometimes unrelated manufacturers such as Caterpillar Tractor, John Deere, Libby-Owens Ford, and International Harvester, recognized the United Auto Workers as their labor bargaining agent.

The organizers next turned their attention to H-D, whose management had been historically opposed to unionization ever since the Company's incorporation in 1907. On the other hand, H-D had never held to a policy of sweatshop labor, and had habitually paid production workers from 40 to 75 cents per hour, according to their skills and abilities. As Head of Production, William A. Davidson, as has been seen, ran a very tight ship, but his paternalistic treatment of his work force and his sympathy

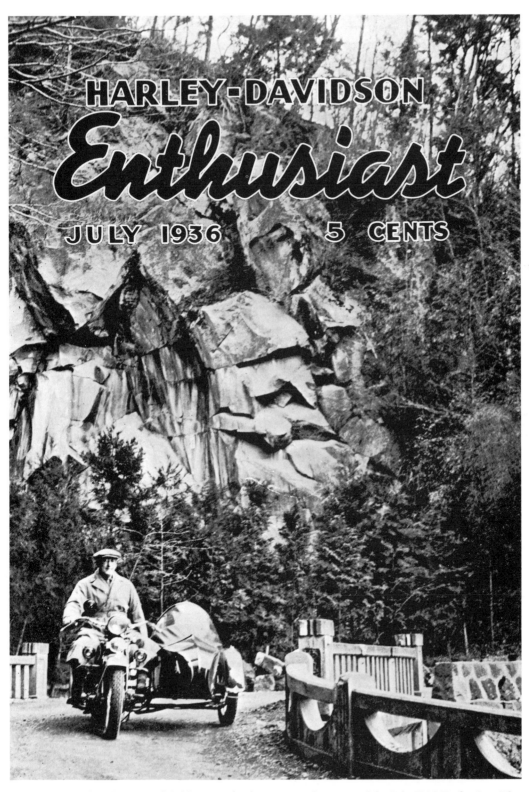

Alfred Rich Child, the perennial sidecar enthusiast, graces the cover of the July 1936 *Enthusiast*. The scene is typical of the Japanese countryside.

for their personal problems engendered a strong feeling of camaraderie and company loyalty. It has often been stated by many veteran H-D employees that while many of them could command slightly higher wages elsewhere in the Milwaukee area, their loyalty to 'Big Bill', the H-D Company, and the product, made it unthinkable for them to remotely consider any other employment.

At the same moment, the feeling for unionism was growing, and in the Fall of 1936, Walter Reuther ordered union organizers posted at the gates of the Juneau Avenue plant to hand out leaflets and otherwise announce that H-D workers were now being solicited to demand a union shop.

During this campaign, William Davidson tended to ignore the matter, sure of the loyalty of his staff. When warned of the dangers of possible impending violence, he shrugged the matter off with the terse statement: 'Let them try'.

The matter dragged on throughout the Winter, but events came to a head in the early months of 1937 with William Davidson's sudden failing health. A large, hearty man, with an appetitie for good food and drink, his weight had at long last attained rather alarming proportions. Shortly afterwards he sustained painful swellings in his lower legs which made mobility difficult. Early in March, he was confined to the hospital for several weeks, and was subsequently released by his doctors on the condition that he confine himself to his residence and make substantial efforts to reduce his weight. He patently ignored this advice, continued to consume his usual generous intake of food, along with his daily ration of strong German lager beer supplied to him by his lifelong friend, Fritz Gettelman, the brewmaster of a local brewery, for which Milwaukee was long justly famous. Late in March he was again confined to hospital, but in spite of intensive treatment his legs continued to swell alarmingly. At length gangrene set in, and in a desperate attempt to save his life, both legs were amputated. He never regained consciousness after this surgery, and died April 21st, 1937, in his 67th year. Mourned by his family, his brothers, company associates, dealers and H-D enthusiasts, his passing marked the end of yet another era in American motorcycling history.

The contributions of William Davidson to H-D's ultimate success were most substantial. In charge of production ever since the formal incorporation of the company, his previous knowledge of industrial procedures and general plant management were of inestimable value during the critical years when the company sought to penetrate an already well established industry. His competence in this field enabled the company to build a superior product, with Davidson's practical knowledge of materials and metallurgy, as well as to efficiently produce the products at rock bottom costing. It was this factor that enabled H-D to survive during an era when the often sound designs of the originator foundered on the inability of plant managers to translate them into production realities. While Davidson was known to be ruthless when it came down to the ultimate control of production line procedures, this factor, combined with his intimate knowledge of the materials involved, enabled H-D to produce a superior product at a competitive price.

It has further been noted that in addition to his initial ability to translate the original sound designs of William Harley into a practical product, his influence in design development and much of overall company policy was also due to the fact that of the four Founders, he held the largest individual block of company stock. While the others invested much of their individual profits back into the company, they also purchased shares in other enterprises unrelated to the motorcycle industry. Not so with William Davidson, whose sole efforts were orientated toward the company itself. A somewhat plain and rough hewn man, who was more at home on the production line than in the boardroom, his personal influence through the first three decades of the company's existence was perhaps greater than that of any of the other Founders.

In the interim following Davidson's death, William Ottaway took over production supervision. Faced with reorganizing and updating these facilities, together with the ever increasing pressure from the union organizers, and now abetted by certain of the younger members of the production force who favored unionization, Ottaway capitulated, and the company at long last signed an agreement with the United Auto Workers Union to submit to collective bargaining.

In the meantime, the local Milwaukee press, in reporting the progress of the proceedings at the H-D factory, noted that certain of the production staff favored unionization. While the media was now able to generate some public sympathy for the union, in the now highly industrialized state of Wisconsin, there was little enthusiasm for organized labor's victory. As a result of a series of meetings between union representatives and H-D's top management, there was an increase of 15 cents per hour for production personnel, along with certain fringe benefits. The consequent rise in production costs was reflected in a 10% increase in the retail price of machines.

Incidental to these events, the company's management next retaliated against certain members of the production force who had, in the later and more critical bargaining procedures, voted for unionization. Most of these were either relatively recently employed or apprentices, and were thus in the younger age group. In open defiance of the recently negotiated union contract most of these dissidents were at once discharged. Among them was one Johnny Speigelhoff, a Milwaukee resident

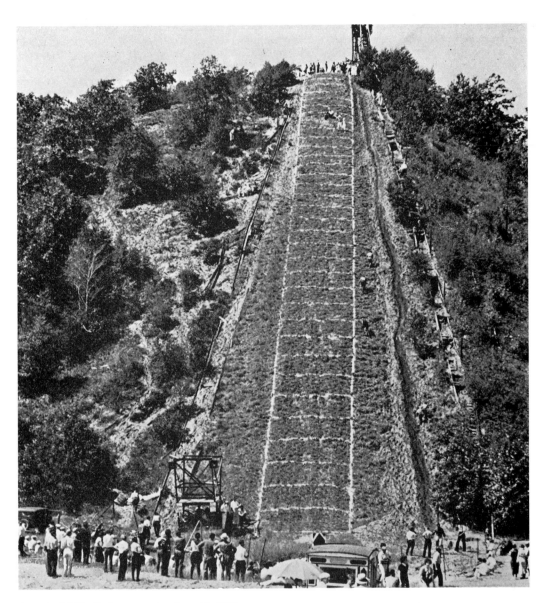

A typical hill climb course in the mid-1930s.

who had lately gained recognition as a formidable competition rider. He almost at once obtained employment as a mechanic at a nearby Indian agency, and for the next decade figured prominently in motorcycle sport on an Indian Scout.

Following this rather critical period in H-D history, veteran factory employees subsequently reported that never again did the former happy family atmosphere pervade the production department. The now mandatory presence of union stewards induced a somewhat dampening effect on the former spirit of camaraderie.

During the Summer and Fall of 1937, a series of articles in the *Enthusiast* offered tributes to William Davidson's many contributions to Company progress. It was pointed out that under his direction the factory's tool fabrication department produced nearly all of the necessary tools, jigs, dies and other equipment used on the production lines. The factory was also provided with over 100 automatic machines that produced various sizes of screws and bolt stock, and that other similar devices could turn out stock bars up to 4 inch in diameter. Other machines turned out various sizes of roller bearings in the millions. A giant hundred ton press, twenty feet high with eight foot wheels, could be inter-

149

changeably fitted with the various dies that stamped out fuel tank halves, mudguard shells, tool box and oil tank components, as well as the various sizes of sprockets. A number of the famous Bullard Multimatic machines were also utilized which carried out numerous individual machining operations automatically.

In the General Inspection Department, sample parts from each production run were checked against Rockwell Hardness in tempering. Bearings were checked to one ten thousandth of an inch, gear teeth being checked to half this gauge. Gear pitch was checked to one thousandth. As a master check on all inspection procedures, a set of the famous Johansen measuring blocks were utilized, which insured accuracy to one millionth of an inch.

In spite of the employment of such sophisticated machinery, visitors to the plant familiar with industrial production procedures often noted that the overall operation was a curious mixture of both ancient and modern. After component parts were fabricated and stocked, much of the final assembly was carried on by somewhat laborious hand fitting. Much of this work was effected by veteran craftsmen working in various small cubbyholes throughout the plant.

The H-D Company was long noted in the industry by its almost complete manufacture of all component parts. The management cited that supply difficulties had been experienced in former years when outside contractors, such as those furnishing electrical equipment, sometimes failed to make deliveries on time as promised, thus delaying production and order filling.

In common with most vehicle manufacturers, H-D assembled machines only on orders received, following the customer's orders to the dealer as to model, paint finish options, and accessory groups. This practice facilitated the saving of storage space, as large numbers of finished machines would have taken up much floor room.

During the mid-1930s, transcontinental record breaking again became popular, although the presence of much improved road surfaces now made it a much less heroic undertaking. In the Spring of 1934, Randolph Whiting on an Indian Chief set a new New York to Los Angeles record of 5 days 3½ hours. With no immediate challengers, Whiting broke his own record the following year, this time on a Sport Scout, racking up an impressive 4 days 19 hours. That Fall, Earl Robinson, the very enthusiastic Detroit H-D dealer, riding a specially tuned 45 model, made the 3,005 mile run in 3 days 6½ hours, an average speed of 39 mph. His record was shortly afterward challenged by Rody Rodenburg on a Sport Scout, who shaved 7 hours off his time in June 1936, averaging 42.9 mph.

A new transcontinental sidecar record was hung up for H-D by two experienced enthusiasts, William Connelly and Fred Dauria, in October 1936. Both had independently attempted solo crossings the Spring before, on 74 inch VL machines, but each had been put out of the running by both illness and mechanical troubles before reaching the Mississippi River. In order to insure success, they decided to team up on a sidecar outfit, and selected one of the new 1936 'U' models for the attempt. Their exhaustive preparations included the fitting of an auxiliary 15 gallon fuel tank in the sidecar to extend their cruising range, along with carrying numerous spare parts and extra tires and tubes. The total weight of the outfit totaled nearly 1,800 pounds, which cut their top speed to about 58 mph. Over the great plains country they cruised flat out, averaging 52 mph. To reduce fatigue, each drove 300 mile segments, with fuel stops scheduled at 600 mile intervals. H-D dealers along the route kept their shops open to provide both food and fuel.

Starting as they did rather late in the season, the pair encountered freezing weather over the Rocky Mountain passes in Wyoming. Halting briefly in Cheyenne to replace their now nearly bald tires and to obtain new spares, they next encountered unseasonably hot weather in Western Utah and Eastern Nevada. This caused their engine to vapor lock, and the subsequent fuel starvation reduced their top speed to 30 mph. Cooler weather corrected the problem about 100 miles east of Las Vegas, and as they sped into the suburbs of Los Angeles, they were met by a contingent of Los Angeles motorcycle officers who escorted them to the Selig Zoo, the official termination point, where an AMA timer clocked their finish. Their elapsed time was 69 hours 46 minutes for the 3,100 mile distance, nearly two hours off the previous solo record, with an average speed of 45 mph. Their record was not broken for another twenty years, until John Penton, on a BMW, set a new time of 52 hours as a solo entrant in the Summer of 1959. In the absence of other sidecar challengers, Connelly and Duaria's record still stands in the sidecar category. At the finish, their outfit was somewhat travel stained, but in generally good mechanical condition with the exception of some corrosion of the exhaust valves. Much was made of their very creditable exploit, both in the pages of the *Enthusiast* as well as the trade press. Their record was even more impressive when viewed as a private effort without any factory sponsorship. It also provided much well deserved publicity for the stamina of the now 80 inch model, which was to be continued the following season as the new 'U' cradle frame model.

In the Fall of 1936, Fred Hamm, a Pasadena motorcycle police officer who was both a long time H-D enthusiast and a physical culture devotee, broke the Three Flag record previously set by Paul Rameley on a 21 'Peashooter', ten years earlier. For his run, Ham selected a new 74 inch side valve

Joe Petrali and Jim Davis (both mounted) together with their pit crew at Syracuse, New York, where the former won the National Dirt Track Championship in 1936. Famed tuner Hank Syvertson at left.

The start of the 1936 Dirt Track National, with winner Joe Petrali.

model, and after a careful 1,200 mile break-in period, prepared to assault the record from the Canadian end of the course. Making the northward journey in leisurely fashion, he selected his route and made arrangements with dealers along the way to supply food, fuel, and spare parts if needed.

The return run for the record was started at Blaine, Washington, which was situated on the International border. He started at 3.00 am, in order to provide two days and one night of riding. Clad in leather breeches and jacket to combat the cold in the Washington mountains, he was able to average 50 mph for the first leg of the journey. Shedding these for the heat of California's great Central Valley, he was plagued by great swarms of insects which literally plastered the front of his machine, otherwise proceeding without incident. On the final stretch from Los Angeles to Tijuana he was escorted by San Diego H-D dealer, Roy Artley, himself a record breaker of an earlier era, who mounted a similar model. His elapsed time was 28 hours 7 minutes, some 10 hours off the old record. He experienced no mechanical troubles other than a broken throttle cable, the sturdy side valver never missing a beat for the entire distance.

Hamm's next triumph for himself and H-D was the racking up of numerous new AMA records for a non-stop 24 hour run at the Muroc dry lake course on April 8th and 9th 1937. This time he selected a new 61E ohv model, which was prepared by Pasadena H-D dealer Bill Graves after a careful 1,200 mile break-in period. The latter installed factory supplied improved ohv fittings and springs and a reworked oiling system to correct the earlier 61E faults. Hamm was determined to make the run as a solo undertaking, and already in superb physical condition, he underwent further taining by swimming several hours each days before the event. With his machine tuned to stock specification his only modifications were the removal of the front mudguard to enhance the flow of cooling air to the front cylinder and the addition of a specially-designed shroud to cover the carburetor air intake to keep out the fine sand of the lake bed. His efforts at preparation were aided by the advice of Fred Ludlow, the well known H-D racing star of an earlier era, who was now a motorcycle officer in the Pasadena Police Department.

The course was laid out in the center of Lake Muroc, a five mile circle outlined with both flags and flare pots for day and night running. While the smooth surface was ideal for safe high speed travel, the 2,680 foot altitude presented carburetion problems with 100 plus degree daytime temperatures and below freezing nights. At Ludlow's suggestion, Hamm fitted a buddy seat which enabled him to 'tuck in' his considerable bulk, and he commenced his tireless circling of the course. Stopping only for fuel, oil, and drinks of fruit juices, he managed to cover an incredible 1,825 miles during the 24 hours for an elapsed time of 76.02 mph and 83.25 mph for actual running time, setting 43 new AMA records in the process.

The 61E ran faultlessly during the grueling 24 hour run, requiring only a replacement of the rear chain at the 1,400th mile that was effected within a three minute pit stop. Much was made of Hamm's exploit, both in the pages of the *Enthusiast* and in the trade press. It was not only a tribute to Hamm's superb physical endurance, but also did much to enhance the somewhat original tarnished image of the 61E now fitted with improved valve gear.

As an indication of slightly improved economic conditions, H-D production rose from 8,879 units in 1936 to 11,674 in 1937. But the relatively soft state of the domestic market was emphasized by the fact that the combined output of both US factories for both years was but 13,907 and 17,704 respectively. Of these totals, over 50% of the output was exported.

The late 1930's saw an encouraging resurgence of motorcycle club activities, which were subjected to continuing attention by AMA Secretary Manager E.C.Smith through orders of the M & ATA's Board of Directors. Some of the clubs in the larger cities saw a membership of owners of both H-D's and Indians, together with a few surviving Hendersons and Super X's. In centers of smaller population, the clubs tended to be more of the one-make variety, dependent upon the willingness or ability of the individual dealers to offer support to owners of their own particular make of machine. The heavyweight models tended to be the favorites of clubmen, as these machines were better suited to long distance rides and offered the option of inviting wife or girlfriend, as well as being able to carry the requisite amount of luggage.

The touring family-oriented clubs, which usually had substantial numbers of sidecar enthusiasts, generally tended to favor H-D machines, while the sporting type clubs more often than not were mainly composed of Indian Scout owners who favored competition events as opposed to touring. In any case, the predominant machine was usually a big twin, now fitted with a dualseat, windshield, saddle bags, luggage carrier, together with whatever extra lighting and accessories the owners elected to install. Such machines later became known as being 'Full Dress', or 'Dressers', as opposed to those who favored stripped down sporting machines, usually of 45 inch displacement. Whatever the individual club's orientation, the AMA endeavored to see that all members were AMA affiliated, and as such received designation as an official AMA group.

It was during this period that the H-D Company enhanced its advertising program, and augmented the size and content of the *Enthusiast*. This was in direct competition with Indian's counterpart, *The Indian News*. Both companies engaged photographers to attend various club runs and contests to take pictures for future publicity and advertising campaigns, the latter then being made available to both the dealers and the trade press. It was usually a source of amusement at large motorcycle gatherings to witness the photographers persuading owners of the competing makes of machine to form into individual groups for such picture taking.

The editors of each house organ quite naturally gave exclusive prominence to their own make. Important regional sports events or big National races were featured only if the marque in question was the victor. By seemingly mutual consent, the opposite competitor was never mentioned by name. Tabulated race results at the end of each article inevitably left a blank space whenever the competitor was involved. A casual extra-terrestrial visitor from Outer Space, if he chose to investigate the current motorcycle scene, could well conclude that there was only one make of American motorcycle, depending upon which house organ he happened to peruse!

Another facet of this now somewhat amusing situation was that in the tabulation of official AMA records, precedence to H-D wins and placings was often noted, due to the fact that that company, through its top heavy financial support, historically dominated AMA affairs. Critics have been quick to note that upon close analysis, Indian wins or close placings in many cases were either distorted or omitted entirely from official tabulation. Indeed, much of the historic antagonism between enthusiasts of both makes can be traced to H-D's domination of AMA affairs. This rather unfortunate situation had its origins in the selection of the official referees and competition officials who, in a majority of cases, were H-D enthusiasts. In all fairness, it must be stated that many of these men went out of their way to be both objective and fair in conducting competition meetings, though there were many cases where this was not so. In recounting motorcycle history of an earlier era, many veteran riders have cited cases where, in some instances, a Sport Scout could lap the field, but then be awarded second place upon the citation of an obscure rules infraction! Several pioneer riders of the Midwest have recalled the July 4th race meet at Des Moines, Iowa, in 1936, where a Sport Scout and a resurrected Super X lapped the field in a twenty five mile main event race, only to be awarded second and third places behind an H-D due to an obscure technical infraction of the rules called by the referee. It was this sort of gamesmanship that often precipitated near riots at racemeets, and further tarnished motorcycling's image as a roughneck sport.

The four Founders inspect one of the first ohv 61E models to come off the line. *(H-D Motor Company)*.

A factory-built 45 cu.in. ohv hill climber as used in the West during 1934 through 1940. The engine is the same type as noted in the 1930 European Road Racer. *(Alisha Tamburri).*

In the Fall of 1937, and in an effort to correct this often unfortunate situation, a number of Indian dealers, together with a few of the more prominent Indian competitors, approached AMA President James Wright, Indian Sales Manager, concerning the problem of the imbalance of H-D enthusiasts filling official AMA competition committees. Wright's answer was to bring the matter to the attention of his boss, Indian's President E. Paul du Pont. The crux of the matter was, of course, H-D's overwhelming part in AMA financing, which had overshadowed that of Indian ever since 1929. The substance of their deliberations was never officially revealed, but Wright at length did report back to his Indian cohorts that du Pont remained adamant in his refusal to increase the amount of Indian's AMA subsidy. Some years later, however, in 1943, after Wright had resigned from the Indian Company, he revealed some of the details of the matter to a close personal friend, the late Paul A. Dunlop. Dunlop informed the author, in an interview in 1959, that during Wright's discussions with du Pont, he told Wright that he considered Indian's $20,000 per year AMA subsidy more than adequate, and that he was not prepared to increase it. He is reported to have further stated that with the acknowledged competition superiority of the current Sport Scout models over the opposite H-D model in the Class C category, he felt that this fact could well counteract H-D's advantage in having a preponderance of their own adherents in the AMA competition hierarchy. While Wright was not in total agreement with du Pont's conclusions in the matter, it was his own opinion that du Pont was still harboring hostile feelings toward H-D's top management in countenancing the attitudes of some of their employees in the 'New Jersey Jew' affair, and he was not prepared to enter into any negotiations with AMA's Competition Committee regarding changes in current AMA policies. Wright further stated that du Pont, while still vitally interested in Indian's welfare as its President and principal stockholder, was at the same time much preoccupied with the management of the Ball Grain Powder Company and his other industrial holdings which were then providing him with very substantial profits, not the case with his Indian interests. The total extent of H-D's financial subsidy of the AMA has, of course, never been revealed, but a composite summation of the reports of various former H-D employees indicate that it was, through the 1930's, at least $75,000 per year. The upshot of the matter was, as variously reported by old Indian enthusiasts, that Indian competitors received somewhat of a vicarious thrill in winning many events through the sheer merit of the Sport Scout, in spite of the fact that in certain of the competition events, they entered with the knowledge that the referees and officials were prejudiced against them at the start.

The almost traditional two make monotony that had pervaded the domestic motorcycle scene was somewhat relieved in the mid-1930's by the very limited appearance of a few British machines. Many of these were supplied by Reggie Pink, the Bronx entrepreneur, who imported small numbers of Ariel, Douglas, Norton, Rudge, and Velocette machines since 1927. His clientele appeared to represent a limited number of affluent enthusiasts who also favored foreign automobiles of the sporting type, which appeared in miniscule numbers during the depression days. In 1936, William E. Johnson, a Pasadena, California motorcycling enthusiast who was a successful attorney, established Johnson Motors, which imported Ariel and Triumph machines. Encouraged by his initial efforts, Johnson then established a branch outlet in San Francisco. His successes with such imports was largely based on the prowess of Edward Turner's noted Speed Twin, which offered outstanding performance in a machine that was essentially no larger than the standard British single, and which had created no little interest in its home country where the single had long reigned supreme. In addition, he offered the Ariel Red Hunter model, a mediumweight single which could often show a clean pair of heels to heavyweight domestic 'V' twins, although its longevity suffered from excessive high speed running. Jack Frodsham, an expatriate Englishman, opened a Velocette dealership in Los Angeles in 1935, and the rather surprising capabilities of the 21 cubic inch ohc KSS model were an eye opener to enthusiasts who formerly considered the 'one lunger' as a novelty not well suited to serious motorcycling.

While the scope of the foreign invasion was initially minimal, a grand total of 67 machines being imported during 1936, both domestic factories, in line with their traditional on-going gentleman's agreements, officially reminded their respective dealers, both from direct factory communication and through their traveling representatives, that under no circumstances would either of them countenance any of their franchises taking on sales agreements for any other makes.

At the same time, the H-D Company announced to both their dealers and customers that an expanded range of motorcycle accessories as well as clothing items were now to be offered from the Accessory Department. They also informed the dealers, through traveling factory representatives, that only accessories and sundry items obtained through factory sources could be sold by franchise holders. While this now established policy was, of course, a ploy to enhance the company's monopoly over their dealership's retail outlets, it was also obviously calculated to keep out any possible competition from foreign motorcycle accessory items that might somehow penetrate the American market along with the entrance of foreign machines.

A departure from H-D's ironclad ruling regarding the handling of other manufacturer's products, was the company's attitude toward the emergence of a limited number of motor scooters in the late 1930's. The most prominent were produced by the Cushman Motor Company of Lincoln, Nebraska, who for some years marketed a line of powered two wheelers, together with those built by Salsbury, Powell, Gladding, and a few other more obscure makes. A number of dealers, especially in the larger cities, handled some of these products, with the apparent blessing of both H-D's management and the ever-watchful factory representatives. While the domestic scooters of those days were basically somewhat crudely conceived, and rather indifferently powered with small industrial type, four-cycle, air cooled engines built by Briggs and Stratton or Lauson, they represented basic transportation at a $75 to $150 initial cost, a figure no conventional motorcycle of even primitive type could hope to match. Many dealers quite rightly theorized that they could very well give aspiring but impecunious schoolboy riders their first taste of motorcycling. As most states in those far off days allowed driving licensing to youths at the age of fourteen, the lowly scooter was usually the first powered vehicle purchased by adventurous newsboy types.

In contrast to their almost amused tolerance of the scooter, H-D's management was now thoroughly irritated by the justly-famous Crocker motorcycle. Based and sold in its greatest numbers in its home Southern California area, it continued to attract more than passing attention by its stellar performances, particularly at the usual speed trials continually being held both formally and informally at the Muroc dry lake course. Old time Crocker enthusiast Herbert Fagan relates countless incidents where the Crockers regularly beat specially tuned H-D and Indian Chief Big Twins in such trials, usually winning with a 10 to 15 mph edge. By the Spring of 1938, Crocker's miniscule production totaled but 36 units, and this in its second season of manufacture.

In casting about for ways to deal with this upstart in high performance motorcycling, President Walter Davidson, with the somewhat guarded advice of the Company's legal counsel, decided to explore the possibilities of bringing suit against Albert G.Crocker for patent infringement, the object being to put him out of business.

Accordingly, on March 7th 1938, Joe Petrali, together with an un-named factory mechanic and a commercial photographer named Austin Barnes met in a small automotive garage located in Chicago's south side under Walter Davidson's orders. Their mission was to dismantle the engine, clutch, and transmission of a 61 cubic inch Crocker that had been borrowed for the purpose, to ascertain if any of the Crocker's design features in any way resembled any aspects of the regularly produced H-D machines.

One of the first 61Es to arrive in Japan is delivered to a Tokyo enthusiast. Alfred Rich Child at right.

In recounting the details of this rather bizarre event to the author, Petrali stated that he remembered the machine as being finished in black with red trim, and that it carried a very low engine number, being described as a 61 cubic inch model purchased by a Midwest enthusiast sometime during the month of January 1938. The appropriate engine parts were dismantled and Barnes took a number of photographs, which were then forwarded to Milwaukee for evaluation. The Engineering Department ultimately reported that the Crocker's internal parts did not resemble those of H-D in details, but only in principal, and that in their opinion, there was no plagerization or copying of H-D's design. The Company's legal counsel, who was in close touch with the proceedings, concurred in this opinion, and Walter Davidson is reported to have at long last abandoned, if somewhat reluctantly, his plans to file a patent infringement suit against Crocker.

While following the advice of the company's legal counsel in abandoning his formal attempts to eliminate the Crocker, its continuing presence still rankled Walter Davidson. The following year, he unofficially informed both the Budd and Kelsey-Hayes concerns, then the principal supplier of domestic motorcycle wheel rims, that if they continued to supply such to Crocker, the H-D Company would subsequently cancel their contracts and undertake to build their own. Whether these companies took Davidson's threat seriously is not known, but at any rate they informed Crocker of the situation after supplying him with some sixty sets of rims. What alternatives were offered are today not known, but henceforth riders ordering Crockers were advised to bring along their own rims, purchased as a part item from some sympathetic H-D or Indian dealer.

As Crocker was now fitting Linkert carburetors to his currently produced machines, which for some seasons past had been fitted to some H-D models, the Company issued the same warning to Linkert, as it had to Budd and Kelsey-Hayes. According to a number of veteran motorcyclists, Linkert chose to ignore this edict and H-D, in spite of this, continued to fit Linkert units.

By a strange turn of fate, the author acquired a somewhat derelict Crocker from a Midwestern collector, R.J.Hicketheir, in 1967. In original condition, it carried black paint with Chinese red trim, and bore engine number 31. Joe Petrali subsequently came to the opinion that this machine was in fact the same one that was the subject of his examination twenty nine years before, especially as it was reported to have originated in the Chicago area and was registered in the State of Illinois.

At the close of the 1937 season, H-D's line of big twin machines was perfected to the point that it formed the main basis for H-D production for the next three decades. The 61E, following the correction of its initial faults, later became known as the 'FL' or 'FLH' model. In modifying its initial ohv mechanism its once potent top end performance was reduced somewhat, due to the adoption of an altered cam profile. Old time riders have reported that the later 'FL's were more sedate, but vastly more reliable. The rugged side valve models continued to be popular sellers, both at home and overseas, their dependability enhanced with detail improvements to the electrical and lubrication systems. Perhaps the outstanding feature of both types was the literally indestructible clutch and gearbox assemblies which made them outstanding in continuous heavy traffic work. While the side valvers were still vulnerable to piston seizure under prolonged high speed running, the 'FL' and later high compression 'FLH' models were not, and came into wide use in law enforcement, not to mention their appeal to the more sporting riders and distance tourists.

The updated 45 model still had limited appeal, but had some adherents in the utility field. Its chief domestic role now appeared to be as the basis for the Servi-car. In addition to the four twin models, the usual range of passenger and commercial sidecar types were carried forward each succeeding year.

The domestic American big twin, whether H-D or Indian, had by this time attained a state of reliability which was at least equal to, and in many cases better than, that of the contemporary automobile. Vast mileages could now be covered with but routine maintenance. In fact, the enthusiast could now plan a transcontinental journey with the expectation of an uninterrupted trip, except for perhaps one oil change and a couple of adjustments to the rear chain. Added to this, the Big Twins had the ability to carry a passenger with comfort and safety on a dual seat, together with space in the long wheelbase for necessary luggage.

The 1936-1937 61E, 45 inch and 'U' models featured a new type chronometric speedometer which was fitted integrally with an attractively streamlined instrument nacelle placed over the forward portion of the fuel tank halves. This not only afforded a more attractive fitting than the former accessory-type Corbin instrument that was carried on a protruding bracket, but was much easier to read under way due to a much larger diameter face. While the instrument was acceptably accurate as to recorded travel, it was characteristically adjusted at the factory to an optimistic speed setting and ultimately gave rise to the somewhat derisive 'Harley Speedometer' appellation. The author, who in later years acquired a pristine 1950 'FL' model, was quick to note that in the upper speed ranges his instrument was about 13 mph fast, a timed 75 mph being indicated as 88 mph. An inquiring letter to the factory elicited a somewhat vague and ambiguous reply, but a later conversation with a factory rep-

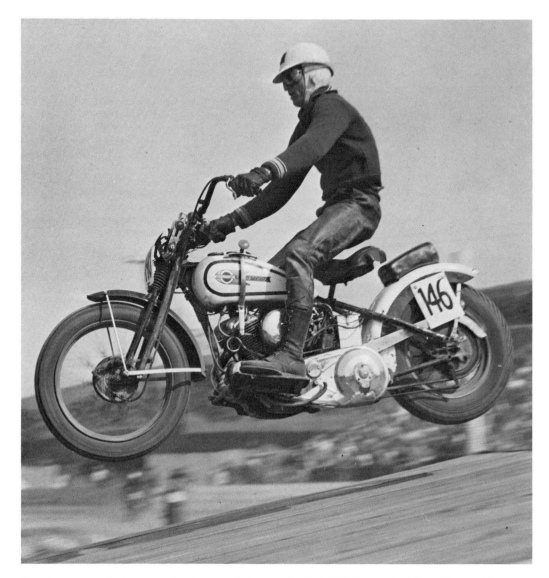

Don Ferra takes the jump at the Los Angeles's Lincoln Park TT Course in 1936. The machine is an 80 cu.in. VLH. *(Robert McGill).*

resentative brought forth the somewhat reluctant comment that the practice was a definite safety factory. In essence, a speed enthusiast who noted a 100 mph speed on the clock was officially being protected from himself and his own folly with a more realistic 86-87 mph. In addition, the high compression 'FLH' models, in the days of the classic leading link fork, could often exhibit an alarming speed wobble at 90 mph plus travel, and the indication of a 100 mph speed on the clock would usually satisfy the most rabid aspiring boy racer, as well as minimizing another controversial aspect of H-D design.

An interesting aspect of middle and late 1930 period motorcycling was the two-wheeler interest of many of Hollywood motion picture stars in Southern California where much of the country's interest in the sport was centered due to the all season riding potential. Much publicity was centered on the participation of such virile actors as Clark Gable, Ward Bond, Keenan Wynn, Robert Taylor, and Randolph Scott, together with a number of leading directors such as Victor Flemming, as well as lesser lights in the film making community. Beverly Roberts, a current B-grade thriller actress and 45 twin rider was featured in several issues of the *Enthusiast*. A favorite ploy of Hollywood press agents was the posing of some budding starlet astride a motorcycle, the pulchritudinous effect being emphasized, though the girl in question often appeared fearful, even on a stationary machine!

The most prominent Hollywood rider of the era was undoubtedly Clark Gable, then at the height of his popularity and fame as Rhett Butler in the epic 'Gone With The Wind'. A UL and FLH enthusiast, Gable purchased his first UL from Budelier in the Fall of 1937. He once informed a friend that he rehearsed his movie lines while enjoying leisurely long weekend country rides in the Southern California area.

H-D machines did not enjoy as much feature film coverage as did Indian, due no doubt to the indefatigable Floyd Clymer, Los Angeles Indian dealer, who made various Redskin models available as either outright gifts or on a no-cost loan basis to the leading studios. This obvious advantage was somewhat tempored by the fact that on occasion H-D enthusiasts among film production crews often made their own personal machines available for certain picture sequences where traffic scenes were featured. It is reported that Rich Budelier once approached President Walter Davidson regarding Company subsidization of a number of H-D models for loan or gift to film companies for such use, citing the incalculable publicity for the marque, together with the possibility of neutralizing Indian's already overwhelming exposure through Clymer's efforts. Davidson is said to have expressed disapproval of Hollywood's 'extravagant goings-on', and declined to expend company funds on such frivolity!

In the late 1930's the H-D Company inaugurated a program to foster closer relations between the factory and its dealers by organizing regional H-D dealer's associations throughout the geographical areas of the United States. One of the objects, as President Walter Davidson was quoted as stating, was "to discourage any H-D dealers from fraternizing with Indian people." Another advantage to the Company was that a ready made captive audience was available on the occasion of the meetings to push advanced sales techniques and to further reinforce the philosophy, in the minds of the dealers at least, that H-D produced the country's pre-eminent motorcycles.

While the Company was only able to sponsor twice yearly meetings in each locality, it offered a golden opportunity for the factory to reinforce 'brand name' loyalty.

One of the most notable money making schemes in the retail sale of used motorcycles, and a most potent factor in dealer survivorship in depression days, was that of the 'stripping' and re-equipping of such machines. This practice involved the removal of the usual 'dresser' accessories, such as windshields, spotlights, dualseats, saddle bags, and other extras, and the machine was displayed in stripped condition with the standard solo saddle in place. As many riders now subscribed to the 'dresser' mode, in most cases they would then purchase the standard accessory items from new stock as extras. The equipment removed from the later model machine was then kept on hand, usually in a back room, for sale to the purchaser of an older used machine who wished to conform to the contemporary style. The factory also encouraged this policy, as they profited from accessory sales to the tune of at least a 40% markup on wholesale costs to dealers, with the latter enjoying the same benefit from their retail markup. The accessory market, just before WW II, was such that special competition classes for 'dresser' machines became an almost standard club event in meets where H-D machines were the most popular. This was the so called 'Best Equipped' machine, which could well mean that some enthusiast attached some two hundred pounds of extra spot and tail lights, various sorts of luggage carriers, mudguard moldings, various chrome plated novelties, and other bric-a-brac, the whole festooned with a myriad of small colored electric lights that gave the total effect of an over-decorated Christmas tree.

The Professional or Class A competition category was almost non-existent since the inauguration of Class C competition, except for the sponsorship of the 21 'Peashooter' that was ridden by the country's sole surviving factory rider, Joe Petrali. He won almost all of the events in this class that were held concurrently during the big AMA national races. His usual opponents were Fred Toscani and Art Schaeffer, riding similar Indians. What with factory support, professional mechanics, and his own tuning ability, victory was almost always a foregone conclusion. In addition, the Indian contingent was forced to compete on ten year old machines, the engines of which had undergone but scant refinement before the factory terminated their limited production in 1927. According to a veteran Indian employee, Indian had decided some time before to concentrate their main engineering improvements on the very successful Sport Scout, rather than on a racing version of the single which had long been out of production.

Petrali's wins during his professional competition career were impressive. He was high point man in the AMA record books from 1931 through 1936. He was National Hill Climb Champion from 1932 through 1938, riding various factory-built specials. In these far western meets, he had in his pit crew, an enthusiastic teenager, one Earl Flanders who, later in post WW II years, owned a highly successful BMW dealership and large motorcycle accessory business. More recently, he has been prominent in the affairs of the Trailblazer's organization, and has also long been a member of the AMA Competition Committee.

A very rare 1937 45 cu.in. model from the Steve McQueen collection. Note the sports-type handlebars and period cowhide saddle bags. *(Alisha Tamburi)*.

A posed studio portrait of Joe Petrali and the 61 ohv Special built by himself and Hank Syvertson for an attack on the World's Land Speed Record at Daytona Beach, Florida. The photographer insisted that Joe wear a white shirt and necktie! (*H-D Motor Company*).

Early in 1938, the AMA Competition Committee decided to suspend Class A activities due to lack of public interest. It was further mandated that the main emphasis should be on Class C as this group, made up mostly of private owners, was quite naturally the largest, and included Novice, Amateur, and Expert categories. Petrali, who was by this time receiving a salary of $240 per month, met with President Walter Davidson and proposed that he be tendered a new position in the Experimental Department, along with a substantial increase in pay, recalling Davidson's refusal to make good on his promised bonuses for the design of the 1934 short tracker and his appearance on the 61E Daytona Special. Davidson countered with an offer of employment in the Experimental Department, but refused either to increase the pay rate, or to pay any bonuses. Following a somewhat stormy confrontation between the two, Petrali, with no little bitterness, resigned from the Company immediately. Shortly afterwards, he entered a few Class C races on the West Coast on one of Tom Sifton's famous modified 45's. After a series of creditable victories, he hung up his goggles for good after missing death by inches during the Oakland 200 Miler when Dick Ince, on another H-D, skidded in front of him and was instantly killed, going through the fence. He next became associated with Art Sparks, at Thorne Engineering, where his vast mechanical knowhow was valuable in the building of race car engines. His work with Thorne was subsequently noticed by the famous Howard Hughes, who put him in charge of his flight services and service management at his Culver City, California plant. Petrali learned to fly at once, and in later years regaled audiences with tales of Howard Hughes's eccentricities, like being aroused in the middle of the night to fly to Phoenix, Arixona for a hamburger! In all, he was with Hughes for about ten years, and flew with him in the one and only hop the famous 'Spruce Goose' ever made over the Long Beach harbor in 1947. He later became the Chairman of the Certification Committee of the United States Auto Club, and at one time or another certified most of the land speed record attempts at Lake Bonneville, Utah, as well as those held in other parts of the country. He also, on occasion, acted as an official timer for both the AMA and the international FIM.

Petrali ever enjoyed the reliving of his competition days, and was a frequent speaker at various motorcycle clubs, as well as at meetings of old timers, such as the annual dinner of the Trailblazers. He once told the author that the most fearless rider he ever competed against was Jim Davis, and that his most formidable hill climb opponents were Indian stars Howard Mitzell and Orrie Steele. He died suddenly in the Spring of 1974, as the result of a cerebral haemorrhage said to have been caused by a

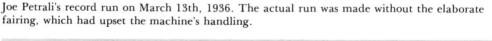

Joe Petrali's record run on March 13th, 1936. The actual run was made without the elaborate fairing, which had upset the machine's handling.

heat stroke sustained in the excessive temperature at a speed trial at Lake Bonneville. Mourned by all motor sports enthusiasts, he was truly one of the all time immortals of competition motorcycling.

The principal motorcycle events of the later 1930's were, of course, in Class C, and the far-sightedness of the AMA Competition Committee in establishing the Novice-Amateur-Expert categories paid off in bringing aspiring stars along in an orderly manner. After 1936, National AMA competition was largely dominated by the great Ed Kretz, Indian's star rider, whose unconventional but spectacular hell-for-leather riding style created a new era in American two-wheeled sport. In recounting the competition events of the period, most old timers agree that Kretz's winning of any contest was assured as long as his machine held up, but in many cases he was simply too much for his mount.

Kretz launched his spectacular career by winning the 200 Mile National, then held at Savannah, Georgia. Babe Tancrede, a seasoned H-D competitor from Rhode Island, a pre-race favorite, gave Kretz strong competition, along with veterans Ted Edwards and Ray Long. A surprise top finisher was George Pepper, the Canadian ace from Toronto, riding a 500 cc ohc Norton International. In keeping with the now established AMA position in regard to denigrating foreign competition, the report of the event in the *Motorcyclist,* still the official AMA publication, limited mention of Pepper's victory to the summary column at the end of the article!

H-D's racing star in the Class C category who ran Kretz a very close second in riding ability was Sam Arena. Surviving old time competitors, including Kretz himself, rate Arena as a very close contender. In addition, he was more versatile than Kretz, as he also excelled in hill climbing and Class A short track competition.

Starting out as a young boy with a bicycle powered with a Smith Motor Wheel, Arena progressed through the usual series of derelict motorcycles until 1933, when his budding mechanical ability won him a job, (this in the depth of the depression), at $18.00 a week as an apprentice mechanic at Tom Sifton's H-D shop in San Jose, California. With a 500 cc ohv flat track special obtained for him from the H-D factory by Sifton, he entered the limited professional B Class events for such competition on the short flat tracks then becoming a mildly popular spectator sport on the West Coast. After many consistent wins of the 1/5th mile ovals, he was transferred to the A Class, and was next awarded his soon-to-be-famous 79 competition number. In his first major TT race, which was held incidental to the 1934 Southern California Gypsy Tour at Lake Tahoe, he won handily on a stock machine over a large field of experienced riders.

Receiving some factory support in 1935, he entered a number of the big Nationals, and won many creditable victories in Class C on a potent 45 inch that had been tuned with uncanny skill by the wizard of San Jose, Tom Sifton. Sifton was already well into his perennial love-hate affair with the factory. As he adamantly refused to co-operate, the factory in the light of his remarkable results dared not cancel his franchise and the matter was shelved for the next decade.

Back to Sam Arena who, late in 1935, signed with Putt Mossman for a season for flat track racing in New Zealand and Australia, where he enjoyed much success. He returned to the West Coast the following year for another season of short tracking, and next rejoined Mossman in England where he was a member of the latter's team at Hackney Wick.

Again returning to the States in 1936, he rejoined Class C competition and was able to garner several second and third places in the big Nationals. He attained further triumphs in 1938, where he racked up consistent weekly wins at the Neptune Beach TT course. At the final big Pacific Coast event of the year, the Oakland 200 Miler, he not only won but broke all existing records in the Class C 100 and 200 Mile category. His average speed was 83 mph, 9 mph over the record!

In 1939, he was well on his way to winning the Daytona 200 Mile classic when a fall on the south turn filled his carburetor with sand and put him out of the running at the 183rd mile, the noted Ben Campanale then being the winner.

Returning to the Bay area, he entered the night races at the San Francisco motordrome, and was a consistent winner both there and at Neptune Beach in the B Class. He took second place at the Oakland 50 Miler, as well as being top man from 1939 through 1941 in the Professional B Class hill climbs. In these he competed against such well established local H-D stars as Joe Hern, of Modesto, and Windy Lindstrom of San Jose. He won 26 of such local events in both the 45 inch and 80 inch categories.

In 1940, the AMA Competition Committee chose to encourage Class C hill climbing, as it widened the field to more aspiring amateurs and made for larger cards of entrants. Special engines requiring blended fuels were now barred, as were special rear wheel traction devices. Arena shifted his interest to this competition, and was a consistent winner in events scheduled at the better known contest hills adjacent to Berkeley, Watsonville, Fresno, San Jose and Skyline.

He continued his short track racing as well, regularly sweeping the field at Sacramento, Riverside, and other West Coast courses. His only injury to date was a broken arm, sustained at Lakeport where he laid his machine down to miss a fallen competitor.

The author with his authentically-restored 31 Crocker. Both he and the late Joe Petrali believe that this was the same machine dismantled by the latter in Chicago in 1938, under orders from Walter Davidson who was contemplating a patent infringement action against Albert G.Crocker. *(George Hays).*

A blown tire cost him the Oakland 200 Miler in 1940, as did a similar incident at Hollister, where a win would have given him permanent ownership of the trophy. During this season he was also a regular entrant on the half mile tracks at Galt, Dixon, and Emeryville, where he was a consistent winner with almost monotonous regularity.

It was Arena's good fortune to sustain a miraculous escape from critical injury or death in August 1941, at the Oakland 200 Miler which saw perhaps one of the most tragic accidents in the annals of American motorcycle competition. Ed Kretz, flogging his Scout along at his usual blistering pace, had already lapped the field, and was well ahead at the 38th lap. Tommy Hayes, H-D star from Texas was second, and Kretz, coming up behind him, had just opened his throttle. At that moment Hayes overtook H-D mounted Ben Campanale in the north turn, but entered the corner too fast. Swinging to the outer edge of the track from the centrifugal force of his full throttle turn, he hit a rough area and was thrown from his machine, dying instantly from the impact. Campanale, immediately behind him, also went down, but at this moment, Hayes's riderless machine, its throttle still wide open, charged into the gap. All three riders following Kretz, John McCall, Jimmy Kelly, and Sam Arena, all H-D mounted, entered the resultant pile up in 1-2-3 order. McCall was killed instantly, and Kelly and Campanale each spent nearly a year in the hospital suffering from multiple fractures and extensive internal injuries. Arena was unhurt through some miracle, and was able to remount his machine and carry on. Trailing Kretz, he caught up with the latter just 32 miles from the finish when Kretz sustained a broken rear chain, and, in spite of a buckled rear wheel, Arena came in 7th.

Still undaunted, Arena entered other California flat track races with continuing success, together with numerous B and C Class hill climbs during the same period. At the TT race at Lodi, which proved to be the last pre-war competition meet, he took first in all events.

While the Indian Scout appeared to have a definite edge in various competition events during the late 1930's and early 1940's, just before WW II, the net results, as gathered from a myriad of reports on the sporting events of the period, saw both makes nearly equal as to wins. As the majority of the contests were in the Class C category, and as most of the riders were in the Amateur class, reaching for Expert status, their cumulative riding abilities were roughly equal. The overall results were greatly affected by track conditions, as county fair horse ovals were more often than not in rough and rutted condition. Then there was the matter of the degree of tuning skills available to the riders, whether performed by themselves, by either a local dealer or an independent handy mechanic. Added to this was the often reported gamesmanship on the part of a local AMA official, who more often than not was prejudiced in favor of H-D, although the odd Indian devotee with similar proclivities was not unknown. While the general run of competition under the prevailing Class C rules has been described by knowledgeable critics as somewhat ragged, the system was at least sufficient to keep the flag flying in the days when US motorcycling was far and away a minority sport.

One of the more significant reasons for the lack of general public knowledge of domestic motorcycle affairs or a recognition of its sporting events was the lack of any effective press coverage. Motorcycle historians have lately pondered over the possible reason the AMA hierarchy never made a conscious effort to hire public relations representatives, or to make any visible efforts to interest the leading sports reporters of the day in motorcycle affairs. Local news coverage of club events, social meetings, rallies, field meets, or any other such activities was never given, even in areas where motorcycling was mildly popular.

As far as the big National races were concerned, even these were limited to a few lines buried somewhere in the back pages of the sporting section. The only front page references appear to have been in cases where some bloody traffic accident involving motorcycles occurred, often with an editorial comment on the dangers of riding such vehicles. This most unfortunate situation is today considered by some historians to be responsible for the inferiority complex of the management of the surviving factories and translated itself into an almost paranoic fear of publicizing their minority position within the otherwise burgeoning transportation scene. It was almost as though the factories withdrew into their own cocoon of endeavor, and took their devotees with them. As it was, the average rider of those days often appeared as a defender, rather than an advocate, of motorcycle ownership.

On a happier note, the motorcycling scene was enlivened by the activities of a limited number of

John Coursey and his authentically-restored 80 cu.in. ULH model. Considered by motorcyclists as the most durable machine ever built, it was also the favorite of Mexican and South American Army and constabulary units. *(George Hays)*.

motorcycle drill teams that made their appearance in various parts of the country. The most noted was the organization sponsored by a popular motion picture star of the day, Victor McLaglan, who originally financed the formation of one as an outgrowth of his sponsorship of a horseman's troupe of parade riders. Its usual complement was about thirty six riders, elements of which performed various maneuvers in groups of sixteen to twenty four. Offering precision drills in often intricate patterns, the performances provided safety for the participants as no high speed stunt type riding was allowed. To join the troupe, an applicant's riding skills were carefully evaluated, and a criterion for membership was the ownership of a big twin H-D machine painted in black-on-white police colors. The H-D machines were selected as standard, as the oversize dry plate clutches enabled faultless low speed control. The troupe was featured in many parades as well as sports events and other civic gatherings in the Southern California area. The troupe remained active until the late 1940's.

The Nobles of the Mystic Shrine, an elite order of the Masonic Fraternity, formed numerous drill teams in several of the country's larger cities, largely patterned after the original McLaglan concept. Most of these groups also used H-D big twins. Another group of noted H-D riders were the famous drill unit from South of the border, the Mexico City Police Team.

This troupe, already well known in Central America, made several trips to the States to exhibit their talents at various holiday events. These organizations formed an effective showcase to exhibit the better aspects of motorcycling, and were popular favorites wherever they appeared. In recent times many of the old time drill units have faded from the picture, largely due to the increased cost of the machines, as well as the spiraling promotion expenses of staging such events. A leading survivor of these spectacular units is the Cossack Drill Team based in Seattle. A group of H-D enthusiasts, some of the members perform on meticulously restored class 'VL' models.

Another organization of private riders that brought much-needed glamor to motorcycling in the late 1930's was the Motor Maids of America, a feminine contingent of motorcyclists organized by Verna Griffith. Chapters of this body, who immediately gained recognition as an officially chartered AMA group, were formed in many of the larger cities of the country. Most were organized as auxiliaries to already established AMA clubs, although a few were formed as autonomous bodies. As the founder, Verna Griffith was an H-D enthusiast, and her cohort and later perennial National President was Dorothy Robinson, the wife of the popular Detroit H-D dealer, Earl Robinson, the tone of the Motor Maids organization was largely orientated toward H-D machines, although a few rode Indian Sport Scouts. Aside from their attractive appearance in smart uniforms at club outings, Gypsy Tours, and holiday celebrations, they commanded much attention from their ability to handle their heavyweight mounts. The fact that a petite 100 pound rider could readily start a 600 pound 61E or side valve 'U' model was a lasting tribute to the efficiency of the H-D field oil generator ignition system.

Motorcycle sales to law enforcement organizations received increasing attention from both of the surviving factories after 1930. The Henderson and Indian four cylinder models were the machine of choice in most of the larger cities, such as New York, Chicago, San Francisco, Oakland, Vancouver, and New Orleans due to their smooth running capabilities and general suitability for suburban patrol duties. While the 'K' model Henderson was eminently suited to the needs of long distance highway patrol duties due to its ability to maintain high speeds under the stress of long pursuits, the Indian Four, still carrying its 1919 Ace type engine was not, and for such duties the less costly big twins, both H-D's and Indian Chiefs were found to be far more suitable. The H-D Company's Sales Department developed a particularly aggressive campaign to penetrate this market, and as a result, by the end of the decade, the nationwide sale of H-D's topped Indian in this field by about two to one. H-D's selling emphasis was that their indestructive heavyweight clutch and gear box could stand up to more hard usage than the oil-immersed opposite on Indian, still fitted with the obsolete sliding gear arrangement.

H-D's factory representatives were given special training at the factory into the intricacies of promoting and consummating law enforcement sales for the benefit of the dealers in their respective areas. What many of the dealers were often to learn, however, was that the ultimate sale of any type of law enforcement vehicle was always involved in political gamesmanship. The transaction almost always meant dealing through corrupt politicians or avaricious tenured civil servants who inevitably demanded either a financial kickback or other special favors. The traffic officers who rode such machines often further complicated the picture by demanding special favors from the dealers who supplied the motorcycles, expecting them to service and maintain them. Often they requested goggles, gloves, or other riding equipment, which were to be supplied free of charge and billed to the regular service cost. In some cases, the officers were enthusiasts who also owned private machines, and the dealer was often expected to maintain these as well and add the charges to the law enforcement maintenance. While the dealer in question could invariably count on a steady source of income from the after sales service, many of them rightly concluded that having to deal with law enforcement bodies, as well as the often corrupt administration governing them, was in the end not worth all the complications involved.

Another ploy in law enforcement sales was the inclusion of specifications of either make into the

Ben Campanale, who won the Daytona Classic for Milwaukee in 1938 and 1939.

Another late 1930s Champion, Paul Goldsmith.

One of the most versatile of H-D's 1930s stars, Sam Arena was at home on either the track, TT course, or at hill climbing.

A 61E 'Knucklehead' as a 'California Bobber' — the forerunner of the post-war 'Chopper'. *(George Hays).*

procurement ordinances that set forth the type of machine that could be presented to the so-called competitive bidding system which was a part of most law enforcement charters. This practice, if it could be initiated, could assure the continuing purchase of the same make of machine. For instance, if the official specification for a machine called for in the bidding were described as 'a 74 or 80 cubic inch 'V' twin American-made motorcycle with a four speed transmission with left handed gear shift mechanism and right hand throttle control', it was obvious that only H-D machines could be offered. The H-D Company is said to have inaugurated this practice in the late 1920's. Dealers who possessed some local political influence, were urged by the factory representative to take advantage of their situation to see that H-D specifications were written into purchase ordinances. The factory's legal department also stood ready to offer both help and advice in giving effect to this intent. This is most probably the reason why H-D machines were predominent in law enforcement use throughout the country after 1935, although some large cities whose law enforcement organizations favored Indian, had similar ordinances favoring that make. H-D's notable failure to penetrate both the city of New Orleans and the State of Louisiana is a case in point. Indian's pioneer dealer, George Gonzales, who owned extensive sales premises on New Orlean's famous Canal Street, had in the early 1930's forged a strong political alliance with the notorious Governor, Huey P.Long. Gonzales's power was such that Indian specifications in both state and municipal ordinances effectively kept H-D out of the bidding. Gonzales continued his association with other members of the powerful Long family for many years afterward, and it has only been in relatively recent times that an H-D dealer could hope to prosper in the State of Louisiana!

H-D's signal advantage throughout this morass of political intrigue, was the fact that its massive dry plate clutch and rugged transmission was more suited to standing up to the hard usage meted out to the drive train under continuous service than was the oil-immersed clutch and archaic sliding gear transmission traditionally fitted to Indians.

In 1940, H-D, in common with Indian, offered the option of 16 inch wheels and 5 inch section tires on all models, the former 18 inch x 4 inch or 4½ inch type being retained if desired by individual customers. This new feature, together with H-D's effectively sprung seat post, made for an exceptionally smooth ride. On the now generally smooth highways, the actual need for a sprung rear end was all

Bud Ekins' 1940 61 EL. This was the first year of the optional 16 inch wheels and 5 inch section tires. *(Alisha Tamburri).*

but eliminated. On the other hand, many enthusiasts claimed that the larger diameter tires made the handling and steering less accurate, especially at high speeds. H-D's management, through confidential instructions to the factory representatives, put the word out to the dealers that the new tires could make for a much safer machine, due to the lessening of road shocks, and that H-D's now traditionally 'fast' speedometer aided in this premise by making the rider think he was going much faster than he actually was. The high speed wobble still encountered with the now classic girder fork, appeared now to be less of a problem. In the case of the 45 inch model, the new option added a further weight penalty, although the softer ride was an attraction to utility riders as well as export buyers who still had to contend with inferior road surfaces.

The retail selling price parity between H-D and Indian now tended to be somewhat divergent, due to the fact that Indian's model range had become more extensive. Their Four now sold at nearly $1,000, with the 30.50 Junior Scout offered at a modest $250. H-D's ohv 61E retailing at $475 had no counterpart with Indian, whose side valve 74 inch Chief was now $400. H-D's 74 inch side valver had a similar price tag, the 80 inch being $25 higher. The H-D 45 and Indian's Sport Scout continued at parity at $325. It has been reported that Arthur Davidson's last price fixing meeting with Jim Wright was held in Columbus, Ohio, incidental to a meeting of AMA officials to discuss general business matters.

It was during this latter period that individual brand name loyalty for either make had progressed to the point that a few dollars difference in cost became less important. At any rate, the economic picture of the country had now vastly improved. Times were generally better, as unemployment was lessened, due to the inflationary effect of the war in Europe. The United States at long last was enjoying a modicum of prosperity, not from the complex planning of a socialized government, but from external economic forces from abroad.

Domestic motorcycle production had become somewhat stabilized during the late 1930's. H-D's production of 8,158, 8,312, and 10,461 for the years of 1938, 1939, and 1940 almost paralleled that of Indian. The loss of H-D's production lead was no doubt due to their now shrinking wartime export market, although the domestic industry was still exporting about 50% of its output. The United States showed a national registration of 126,233 machines in 1939, which was only a slight increase over the 96,401 figure reported in 1935. These figures attest to the gradual decline of motorcycling interest throughout the decade, as the overall population of the United States had increased by one-third since 1930, and automobile registrations during the same period had tripled. There were now so few motorcycles amid such a vast horde of automobiles, that in the minds of many motorists, the motorcycle was now almost wholly associated with law enforcement.

At the same moment, American motorcycling was characterized by a very loyal, if small, following. Each factory kept in close contact with its respective adherents through their individual house organs. Each still quite naturally offered its own version of the motorcycling picture, reporting only sporting events where the make in question won, and totally ignoring those in which it did not. 'Brand Name' loyalty was paramount, and any defection to the rival make was the epitome of heresy. The *Motorcyclist* continued to offer bland platitudes concerning the joys of the sport, but without any objective policy regarding the road testing of the limited range of machines offered. News regarding the activities of a corporal's guard of dealers handling foreign machines was actively suppressed, as were their wins in field trials or club sporting events.

A pleasant adjunct to the end of a somewhat gracious decade as far as motorcycling was concerned was the club activities. Many of these, often sponsored by H-D dealers, stressed the family aspect by including many mixed social events as well as weekend picnic type outings. The emphasis on 'well equipped' machines that were sometimes overloaded with useless accessories, at least led to the criterion of clean, well-silenced machines. Most of the clubs adopted smart uniforms, mandatory at all club functions. Such activities did much to enhance the public image of motorcycling, as did the commendable policy of sponsoring or assisting in local charity drives or in acting as police auxiliary units or search and rescue teams in times of natural disasters.

To aid in sales, H-D sponsored a finance facility, officially known as the Kilbourne Finance Company, along with an auxiliary company that specialized in motorcycle insurance. Up to this time, the public image of motorcycling had been such that no usual bank or finance company would consider the public financing or insuring of machines. These organizations' activities quite naturally aided the sales picture, and dealers were extended further help by being able to finance the flooring of new machines through the Kilbourne organization.

The position of the clubs was strengthened by the fact that District AMA officials offered aid in either the formation of new groups or the strengthening of those already in existence. In return, all club members were expected to join as individuals. While some grumbled about the non-democratic character of the AMA and its trade management, it was generally conceded that the AMA was the only viable force in holding organized motorcycling together.

Robert Ross's superbly-restored 1940 61 EL sidecar outfit. This model is fitted with the 18 inch wheels of past models.

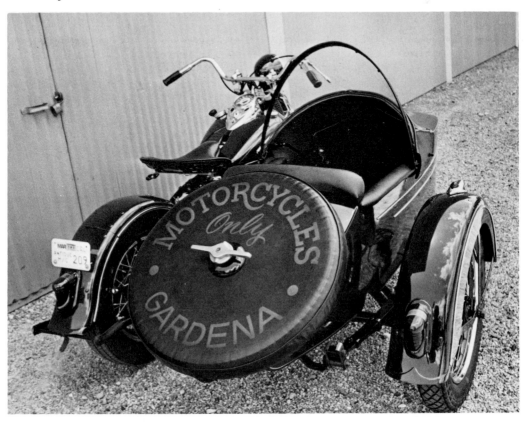

The sporting side of motorcycling during the late 1930's continued to attract a dedicated, if limited, following. Numerous clubs were formed whose membership was made up of sporting types, the majority favoring the Sport Scout. A serious impediment to enhanced public recognition of motorcycle sport was the general lack of publicity in the news media accorded to race meets, hill climbs, TT events and other competition. When approached about the matter on several occasions by concerned AMA members, President Jim Wright simply stated that a lack of funds prevented the implementation of a full scale publicity department within the AMA organization. As Indian's E. Paul du Pont had already gone on record as refusing to augment his company's minimal AMA contribution, coupled with President Walter Davidson's adamant stand against increasing H-D's already majority contribution to the organization's treasury, no effective steps were then taken to obtain expanded press coverage. It was later reported that Executive Secretary E.C.Smith, acting on orders from Davidson, shortly afterward informed the AMA Directors that organized American motorcycling existed principally for the benefit of its card carrying members, and that an extended publicity campaign would cost too much for the AMA's current financial resources. With this head-in-the-sand pronouncement, American motorcycling further retreated into its own inbred sphere of activity. While some of the big National races received limited space in some of the larger newspapers, most regional or local events were largely unreported.

The Class C sporting scene during the 1940-1941 season was largely dominated by the spectacular performance of the now legendary Ed Kretz. While he was more often than not a non-finisher, due to his explosive riding tactics which led to mechanical failure of his Sport Scout, his hell-for-leather tactics made him a first rate crowd pleaser. He was especially popular with the non-riding spectator contingent that had at long last found motorcycle racing as a new diversion. A popular sports rider of the day once reported that Kretz was a sure winner in any contest entered, providing his machinery held out, and the only question was who might come in second! Kretz relates that on numerous occasions he was approached by Milwaukee to desert the Wigwam and ride for H-D. He remained a steadfast Redskin, however, until Indian's last days. While his loyalty in this regard was unquestioned, there was also in the back of his mind the memory of the somewhat cavalier treatment that Walter Davidson meted out to such past heroes as Fred Ludlow and Joe Petrali.

In the Fall of 1940, H-D announced a 74 cubic inch version of the 61 cubic inch 61E that was now known as 74F, although the original version was still continued in the line. The new model, indistinguishable from its parent machine except for the engine, gained its increased displacement through cylinder enlargement by boring and stroking, the new configuration measuring 3 7/16 by 3 31/32 inch. Developing 45-48 hp on standard fuel, it was capable of a top speed of close to 100 mph with 3.73 solo gearing.

The new machine was quite naturally welcomed by speed enthusiasts, and sidecar owners at once noted its enhanced pulling power, especially in steep gradients. 61E enthusiasts were quick to note that the larger displacement machine was noticeably less smooth than its parent, and the characteristic rocking couple of the latter could at some engine speeds be most pronounced.

As H-D now entered a new decade, its products can well be stated as representative machines of their type; they were exemplary models of the American big twin concept. Built of the finest materials, with proper attention to rust proofing (long a bugbear of motorcycle finish), they bespoke both quality of product and meticulous attention to detail. With continually improved refinements in both lubrication and electrical systems, they offered automobile-type dependability, and usually required but three-kick starts in any weather, provided the correct drill was carried out to set them in motion. The now standard American control system of foot controlled clutch and hand controlled gearchange, later to be the source of much adverse comment, proved to be more than adequate for proper control of the massive drive train that was itself now a legend of dependability. Built without visable changes from 1938 through 1948, this series of machines, in the opinion of many veteran enthusiasts, implemented the so-called 'Golden Age' of H-D perfection. Many meticulously restored machines of this vintage are still providing their proud owners with yeoman service, and bring eight or ten times their original price when bought on today's market.

The last pre-war sporting event of 1941 was the 200 Mile National. This premier feature, inaugurated originally at the big county fair horse track at Savannah, Georgia in 1934, was moved to Daytona Beach, Florida, in 1937. The course was rather unorthodox, in the annals of American competition at least, as it offered a combination of both sand and road racing. The long legs of the track consisted of a portion of the beach, connected at either end by steeply banked turns to a rather uneven road course that was surfaced with clay and asphalt. The AMA Contest Committee decided that such a speedway could offer a more challenging terrain than the more prosaic horse tracks, and the road type course could produce higher speeds.

If the new course was an innovation compared to the classic American broadsliding style of competition, the results of the contest to both the AMA hierarchy and American motorcyclists alike were even greater, as it was won by one Billy Mathews, of Ontario, Canada, that country's budding racing star, on a single cylinder 500 cc ohc Manx Norton model.

The story behind Mathews' spectacular win is no less interesting. Motorcycling and motorcycle racing in the United States had long been almost completely isolated from International competition. There had never been an interchange of racing talent, and American competition affairs were totally divorced from the FIM ever since 1923, when Indian's British importer, Billy Wells, was removed as their representative to the international body. The foreign racing scene was never reported in the AMA-controlled *Motorcyclist* magazine, and American motorcyclists were for the most part simply unaware of foreign motorcycle affairs, or that the Norton marque had for some years been pre-eminent in international as well as British competition.

Mathews and J.M.McGill, Norton distributor for Canada, were, of course, keenly aware of the international competition picture. They also knew that the AMA and H-D, who controlled it, were dead set against either the importation or even the recognition of any type of foreign machine. When Mathews, intent upon invading the US with a British machine, signified his intention to McGill, who had provided him with official help in his Canadian conquests, McGill, after some reflection, declined to offer help for the Daytona challenge. McGill reasoned that with both popular and official sentiment being hostile to any foreign entry into the American motorcycle competition bailiwick, it would be virtually impossible for Mathews' entry to be accepted in the first place. Added to this, was the expense of transporting both men and machines to Daytona, as well as their maintenance while there.

After some further soul searching, Mathews decided to enter the contest as a private entrant, bearing the expense himself. Accordingly, he sent his official entrance declaration to the appropriate AMA officials, and much to his surprise, was accepted. The late Jack Halford, an immigrant Englishman who was once connected briefly with Reggie Pink's New York import organization and who was at the time well aware of the situation, told the author in an interview in 1964, that the AMA Contest Committee, who, for some inexplicable reason, were unaware of Norton's prowess in international racing, refused to take Mathews' entry seriously. Noting in Mathews' declaration that more than fifty International Nortons had been previously manufactured and sold, (an AMA rule for entering any make of machine) his entry was duly accepted. The Contest Committee's thinking was no doubt further influenced by the fact that foreign machines had never been able to make much headway on the domestic competition scene.

Up to now, it may be remembered that American competition machines, as compared with the sophisticated types already developed in Great Britain and Europe, were essentially crude pieces of equipment. With but limited fork travel, and solid rear ends, both the Indian Sport Scout and the H-D racing machines, both highly modified in open defiance of the original Class C concept, were but rather poor handling vehicles intended to be manhandled around a dirt track, and broadslided through the turns. The lack of rear springing caused the rear wheel to be airborne much of the time under rough surface conditions, and the foot-operated clutches and wide ratio hand-operated gear change mechanism was not conducive to saving time in a pinch where split second gear changes could spell the difference between defeat and victory.

During the late 1930's, H-D competition in the now universal Class C category was centered on a speed version of their somewhat mediocre 45 cubic inch twin, which was ultimately known as the DLDR ('R' for racing) model. Still cursed by coil ignition, some competitors had, by this time, been fitting proprietary magnetos, which obviated some of the historic difficulties encountered with the age old problem of burned out condensers. In response to much prodding from both enthusiasts and dealers, H-D finally brought out a racing version of the 45 D model in 1941, which was known as the WLR ('R' for racing), or more simply, the 'WR'. Still unable to pry from Tom Sifton his private modifications that had made his own modified DLDR models so formidable, H-D's Engineering Department did its best to come up with their own compromise to challenge the former unassailable position of Indian's Sport Scout. While the new WR was but little different from the former DLDR models in having limited travel forks and a solid rear end, its engine's potency had been substantially increased with improved breathing, high performance cams, and magneto ignition, together with a light pattern clutch and gearbox to save weight. As in the case of the now highly developed Sport Scout, its concept was a continuing violation of the original Class C rules.

In contrast to these Yankee crudities, Mathew's Norton was the identical machine, that, after a decade of refinement, had already won sweeping victories both at home and abroad, for example Harold Daniel's TT victory on a special model in 1938. Its superb road holding qualities offered to serious contestants a well proved engine that was by this time almost unburstable under 200 miles of flat out running. With its spring frame that kept the rear wheel more effectively on the ground, together with its four-speed gearbox, a rider could more effectively mate the rather narrow power band of the engine, running 'on the cam', to whatever racing conditions presented themselves. In addition, the hand-controlled clutch and foot-operated gear change could save many valuable seconds over the

Yankee riders who were still running machines that differed but little from those used on American courses since 1915.

This surprising upset caused President Walter Davidson to bitterly excoriate the AMA Contest Committee for admitting a foreign interloper. The late Charles (Chuck) Billings, then Editor of the *Motorcyclist,* also came under his share of criticism from certain AMA officials for his report in which he admitted, if somewhat grudgingly, that certain advanced (in American eyes) British design features gave Mathews a victory over an extremely grueling course.

The Yankee track racers had now been bested on their own grounds, and technical progress had to be postponed due to World War II.

# Chapter 7

# World War Two

WITH THE OUTBREAK OF THE WAR IN EUROPE IN THE LATE SUMMER OF 1939, President Franklin D.Roosevelt alerted the American people and Congress to the need for preparedness. The ever-widening scope of the war tended to indicate that the United States would be drawn in. He was handicapped by his efforts by certain leaders in Congress who, led by an avowed isolationist, Senator Burton K.Wheeler of Montana, pointed to the long traditional American concept of avoiding entanglement in European affairs. The growing menace of German U-boats and their sinking of large tonnages of Allied shipping brought much sympathy for the plight of Great Britain, however, and Roosevelt was at long last able to persuade Congress to supply the British Navy with 50 of our idle, overage WW I destroyers.

In the Fall of 1939, both American motorcycle factories received contracts to supply military machines to the Allied Forces. Indian had already received an order from the French Army for 5,000 Chief sidecar outfits. Shortly afterwards, both factories each received an order for 5,000 solo military machines from Great Britain since the Coventry area, where the Triumph motorcycle plant was located, had just been leveled by the Luftwaffe.

H-D's answer to this order was a heavy duty utility version of the now venerable 45 inch 'DLD' model. Now designated as the 'WLA' ('A' for Army), it was fitted with 18 inch wheels and 4.00 inch or 4.50 inch section tires and wide clearance D section mudguards to facilitate off-the-road travel with a minimum of mud-clogging. To provide added protection to the underside of the engine cases and transmission, a heavy pressed steel plate with channeled edges was bolted under the frame. This fitting was also provided with a rearward extension on the near side to give further protection to the lower run of the rear chain. A low compression commercial type engine, as fitted to the standard Servi-car was installed and provided with enlarged cooling fins to prevent overheating during prolonged, low-speed bottom gear running. An extra large air cleaner was attached to the carburetor air intake, together with a heavy luggage rack fitted with leather panniers, a rifle boot along the fork legs, ammunition boxes, and other military gear.

With its low compression engine, the highly restrictive air cleaner, and the added weight of the military gear, the rather weighted 'WLA' now had a top speed of a little over 50 mph, together with but feeble powers of acceleration. But with plenty of torque for rough going, and its indestructible clutch and gearbox and traditionally rugged H-D construction, the 'WLA' was ideal for its purpose. As a low-powered machine, the traditional primary chain-shedding weakness was now eliminated, and with no other apparent vices the war model gave exceptionally dependable service under appalling conditions of use with but minimal maintenance.

Following the completion of their contracts with the British, both factories were awarded open-ended contracts by the US Defense Department for military machines, together with official authorization for the acquisition of the necessary supplies of iron, steel, aluminum, and other accessories to complete them. The H-D organization was in a much better position to supply large numbers of military machines than was Indian, whose tooling and production facilities had been allowed to become depleted during the lean sales years of the early 1930's. The H-D management immediately expanded its production facilities, leased additional plant space adjacent to the main Juneau Avenue facilities, and hired additional workers for around-the-clock operation. While the bulk of the production was now 'WLA' models, a limited number of 74 inch and 80 inch big twin sidecar models were also supplied to the armed forces for special services. These differed but little from their former civilian counterparts, being fitted with slightly lowered gear ratios, wide clearance mudguards, and low compression engines. Certain numbers of these were made available to civilian buyers who were able to obtain special government procurement clearance. A limited number of low compression police models were also produced for civilian law enforcement use on the home front. A few 61 inch ohv models were produced on order by the US Navy for Shore Patrol and Coast Guard duties.

The Harley and Davidson families, factory management and production personnel, dealers, and a world wide host of H-D enthusiasts were saddened when on February 7th 1942, H-D's long time President Walter Davidson passed away in his sixty-sixth year. In ill health for several months, his death was attributed to the stresses of overwork due to the company's expanded production for the war effort, together with complications of a liver ailment. His survivors included his wife, Emma, sons Gordon, Walter Junior, and Robert, his brother Arthur, and two sisters, Mrs.Henry W.Marx and Miss Janet Davidson, all of Milwaukee. For all of his adult life, Davidson was vitally concerned with the promotion of H-D motorcycles, first as a consultant in the initial prototype work of his brother Arthur and William S.Harley, and from 1907 as President of the Company after its initial incorporation and formal entrance into the industry. During most of these thirty five years, he was a figure of controversy. Capable of inspiring trust and loyalty in certain company personnel and among its far flung dealership, he was both hated and feared by many who did not see eye-to-eye with his often ruthless manner and arbitrary judgments in managerial decisions. Whatever his personal faults, he became a veritable giant within a long troubled industry. Through the years his role as Company President, both

The WR racing model introduced in the Spring of 1941. It was H-D's answer to the racing Indian Sport Scout. Note the short bottom fork links.

Official US Army photograph of the 45 cu.in. WLA military model. About 89,000 of these machines were eventually produced.

Engine details of a WLA. This restored example was seen at Visalia in 1974.

at its original organization, survival and ultimate success, can never be overstated as he complemented the pioneer engineering efforts of his brother Arthur, and William Harley. While during the early years he established a reputation as a tight-fisted and often hard-hearted executive, at the same moment he insisted that only an honestly conceived and properly built product was worthy of public sale, as long typified in H-D production, and he held unswervingly to these tenets throughout even the most difficult periods of company history.

While his personal holdings of Company stock were said to be substantial, he had diversified his estate by making large investments in other companies. Among these were the Northwestern Mutual Life Insurance Company and the Milwaukee Gas Light Company. He also had substantial holdings in other industrial firms in the Milwaukee area, his total worth being ultimately estimated as between three and five million dollars. Beginning his career as a working class blue collar artisan, certain of his contemporaries have stated that he acquired a certain polish and sophistication as time went by. No little credit for this was attributed to his wife, Emma, who was a woman of culture and talent.

Davidson was not a pioneer motorcyclist in the strict sense, but he quickly became familiar with his brother's and William Harley's prototypes after the decision had been made to incorporate the venture for formal marketing. His subsequent entrance into competition events has already been discussed, and the numerous trophies he won in these early events are still treasured by the present organization as mementos of H-D's earliest days.

In all fairness to Walter Davidson's memory, it must be stated that as President and titular head of the Company, it was quite naturally his role to make both public and inter-company announcements regarding H-D sales and general policy matters. As many of these were to become highly controversial with both the dealers as well as the riders, Walter quite naturally bore the brunt of much criticism. It should, of course, be stressed that all major Company policy matters were exhaustively discussed by the four Founders, and were implemented only after mutual agreement between the Davidsons and William Harley.

The two surviving Founders, together with the families and heirs of William A. and Walter, almost immediately conferred to select a new Chief Executive for the Company. The details of their deliberations were, of course, secret, but the matter has subsequently been the subject of much speculation upon the part of veteran H-D employees. President Walter was survived by three sons, Gordon, Walter Jr., and Robert. While it is a matter of record that the first two were already employed in various capacities within the Company, neither had shown any real interest in assuming managerial

The King himself. Clark Gable and his 1940-1941 EL. The photograph was taken by the late Joe Walker at a Los Angeles motorcycle meet in the Summer of 1942.

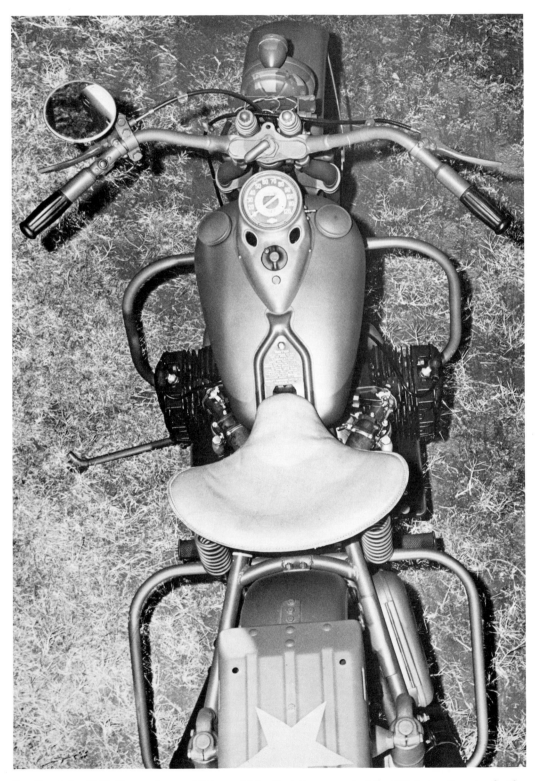

Details of the 1943-44 experimental XA model built at the request of the US Army. It was a frank copy of a utility-type side valve 45 cu.in. BMW used by the German Army. Only 1,000 were ever made. *(George Hays)*.

responsibilities. Robert, the youngest, had already elected to follow a career outside the Company in a field unrelated to motorcycling.

At the same time, the role of William Harley in Company affairs was such that he was already seeking to step down as Chief Engineer, and was in process of grooming his own son, William J., to succeed him. In the light of this fact, it became obvious that his present interests did not lie in the direction of assuming the Presidency of the Company.

Many H-D dealers and enthusiasts speculated whether Arthur Davidson, as one of the original Founders, might now inherit the mantle of Company leadership. In view of the fact that the details of the interfamily discussions were never revealed, a number of former Company employees have offered their own views. Arthur at this time was well over sixty-three years of age, not enjoying the most robust of health. There was also the matter of his drinking problem. Known as an abstainer or an occasional drinker, he periodically went on drinking sprees to return a week or ten days later in disheveled but penitent condition. He continued in his original post as General Sales Manager, where, as reportedly the most personable of the Davidsons, he had garnered a vast circle of loyal friends within H-D's riders and dealer network. Whatever his personal habits, he was shortly to ascend to an equally important post within the domestic motorcycle industry.

The mantle of H-D leadership passed to William Herbert Davidson, the son of the late William A., who was not only a life long motorcycle enthusiast, but held a degree in Business Administration from the University of Wisconsin. He had held various supervisorial and managerial posts within the Company during the between-the-wars period, as well as competing successfully in many competition events, winning the coveted Jack Pine trophy on a modified 'DR' model in 1930.

Another interesting facet of this particular phase of H-D history incidental to the selection of a new President is the fact that William H.'s father, William A., individually held the largest block of Company stock in relation to the other shareholders. This was, of course, now reflected in the position of William H. through his inherited holdings. In any conference within a family-held Company such as H-D, it appears almost inevitable that the stock ownership of the concerned parties affects the voting power. In the absence of any knowledge of the details of the closed deliberations, the whole subject is but a matter of conjecture. While William H. survives today as a retired Chief Executive, he has always refused to comment upon any of these historical proceedings.

During the Fall of the following year, the H-D Company sustained another great loss with the death of William S.Harley in his sixty-third year on September 18th 1943. Noted by his associates to be in a state of increasingly poor health during that summer, he dropped dead of heart failure while sitting at the bar of a local club. As the man almost single-handedly responsible for the development of the original H-D motorcycles, he had remained for many years as a giant within the industry. As a paradox to his conception of the bulk of H-D designs, he was known to relegate their refinement to others within the company who demonstrated their practical mechanical and engineering abilities such as William Ottaway, Arthur Constantine and Joe Petrali. In later years he was seen to withdraw somewhat from the motorcycling sphere, preferring cars to two wheelers. He spent much time in hunting and fishing, as well as his avocation of painting and drawing. A somewhat poetic and introvertive man, he combined the unusual talents of engineering know-how with the abstraction of art. His duties as Chief Engineer were taken over by the veteran William Ottaway, and subsequently relegated to his son, William, who had been his official assistant for the two preceding years.

Indian's long time Sales Manager, James Wright, resigned his position to take a similar position with a manufacturer of machine tools. It is thought that Wright, always a dynamic individual, chaffed at the lack of motorcycle sales activity during the war, and he decided that the critical machine tool sales field, now made vital by war materiel production, offered a more active and lucrative challenge. At a meeting of the AMA's Executive Committee held on January 20th 1944 in the Lexington Hotel in New York City, H-D's Sales Manager Arthur Davidson was named as the succeeding AMA President. It is reported that the Committee was of the opinion that due to the long tenure of office enjoyed by an Indian representative, it was now fitting that an H-D executive ascend to that office. As H-D had for many years enjoyed actual control over the affairs of the AMA, it now had titular control as well. With the ongoing support of long time H-D enthusiast, Secretary-Manager E.C.Smith, AMA control was even more firmly in the grip of H-D.

In the Fall of 1943, United States Army Procurement authorities ordered both factories to produce twin cylinder shaft driven machines based on European design. Apparently greatly impressed with the heavy duty BMW and Zundapp machines employed with much success by Field Marshal Erwin Rommel in his North African campaigns, the US Army considered the domestic development of similar types mandatory to augment this country's already formidable array of motor transport. H-D's Experimental Department's answer was the XA model, a 45 cubic inch horizontally opposed side valve twin with shaft drive and four-speed foot-operated gearbox with hand clutch control. A frank copy of a pre-war utility BMW model, the 'XA' showed much promise as a heavy duty service model, but was

William Hoecker's XA with disc wheels. Only a few of this model were built, and were intended for use in desert terrain. *(Alisha Tamburri).*

marred by lubrication and valve gear problems which could have been corrected if the Army had standardized the model for series production. As it was, the end of the European conflict signalled the transfer of activities to the conflict with the Japanese in the Pacific theater. In the island terrain, the ubiquitous four-wheel drive Jeep was now considered more practical than the motorcycle, and Army orders for the new machines were cancelled after each factory had produced about a thousand examples. Many H-D enthusiasts looked forward to a refined 'XA' being added to the factory's post war line. This was not the case, however, and a couple of hundred civilianized 'XA's remain today in the hands of collectors of antique and special interest motorcycles.

H-D's contribution to the war effort totalled an incredible 88,000 machines. Most of these were of the 'WLA' 45 cubic inch model, and with continually expanded component part production, additional parts for another 30,000 units were on hand by the fall of 1944. For this effort, the Company was awarded not one of the usual Army-Navy 'E' awards for Excellent Service, but two.

A fortuitous side effect of the American motorcycle industry's war production effort was an enhanced public awareness of motorcycling both at home and overseas where the ruggedness of Yankee machines was amply demonstrated. H-D's advantage here was its two-to-one production volume as compared with Indian. Thousands of newly inducted GI's were taught to ride at the various transportation, motor pool, or armoured division training facilities throughout the country. Many of the country's competition stars were utilized as instructors. American Army machines ultimately ended up in nearly every country in the world, along with other types of American military material. Most riders became immediately impressed with the ruggedness of the Milwaukee product as typified in the 'WLA'. Doubtless its necessarily mild performance created a desire in many riders' minds to own a larger and more powerful civilian big twin model.

As is usually the case in such matters, large quantities of hastily produced military equipment never reached the front lines, and motorcycles ordered by the US Army were no exception. With the cancellation of contracts for military machines in the Spring of 1944, thousands of H-D and Indian machines were released for sale on the civilian market. At a government mandated retail price of $450, about 15,000 'WLA's and 6,000 Indian 741's were placed on the market during the Summer of 1945. The shaft drive models from both factories were offered for sale shortly afterwards at $500. Large numbers of Yankee machines were released for public sale in England during the same period. Most of the H-D machines available were 'WLA's'. Some of these had seen limited service in Home Defense or military police assignments, but many were still in their original factory crates at various military depots. Large numbers of these were acquired as surplus by such well known dealers as Marble Arch Motors, Pride & Clarke, and others, as well as by F.H.Warr, the veteran franchised H-D distributor. Most of these 'WLA's' were sold as originally supplied, with military gear intact. Some dealers selling such machines offered the option of civilian specification, stripping them of their military gear and re-finishing them in original factory colors. Many English owners acquiring such machines even went as far as to order civilian type mudguards to replace the rather austere War Department wide clearance type, and Milwaukee obliged by running off an extra supply of such fittings. The once active H-D Owner's Club of Great Britain ordered substantial numbers of such machines, and many were in use until quite recently.

While H-D's war production was phenomenal, the profits accrued were not great, as the machines were produced on a cost-plus basis of about 10% per unit. In addition, the Company was, in the end, not recompensed for the bulk of their spare-part component units that could have accounted for an additional 30,000 'WLA' machines, although the Company was said to have driven a hard bargain with Army purchasing agents for about one half of this parts surplus. In later years, component parts, mostly 'WLA' engines with generators and carburetors, were to come on the civilian market in the mid-1950's at give-away prices. It was at one time possible to acquire such units for $79.50 each.

In the overall sense, it was now apparent to many knowledgeable people within the trade that in the United States, at long last, a new interest in motorcycling was to emerge, and that the sport was now to enjoy a certain modicum of respectability. As a portent of things to come, Alfred Rich Child, H-D's long time Asiatic Distributor, had resigned his position as Manager of the Overseas Reassembly Division of the Lockheed Aircraft Company, which position he had held since the war, and announced that he would shortly import BSA motorcycles from Great Britain for sale on the American market through a newly-formed company based in New Jersey.

# Chapter 8

# Post-War Problems

THE WAR ENDED IN THE SUMMER OF 1945, AND ALTHOUGH THE ALLIES OSTENSIBLY won an overwhelming victory, subsequent events were to prove that while the war had been won, the peace had been lost.

Aside from the political overtones, which were as yet to be revealed, the United States emerged from yet another World War, even greater than the first some two decades before, with its borders unravaged by enemy action and with but minimal human casualties as compared with both its allies and enemies alike. Both the civilian population and the nation's business and industrial leaders at once envisioned that an almost instant and Utopian prosperity would ensue, due to the now immense pentup demand for consumer goods and the belief that the collosal productive might acquired through the war effort could now supply it. Much actual progress was made toward productive conversion to the civilian market during the Fall and Winter of 1945-1946, but other factors were at once to intervene suddenly, seriously curtailing the planned output of consumer goods. With central Europe largely devastated by massive bombing, England prostrate and economically and physically exhausted, and Japan totally annihilated, the United States at once found itself the sole productive nation in a world that was too impoverished to purchase its goods. The US was mindful of the now serious threat of Communism that could well be an attraction to the poverty stricken war-devastated nations, many of which were already well within the Russian sphere following Stalin's duplicity at Yalta.

To counteract this threat, the newly-inaugurated US President, Harry S.Truman, with the backing of majority leaders of the Democratic party in Congress, now proposed that the United States embark on a program of both monetary and industrial aid in the form of vast loans and essential materials for the rebuilding of Europe. Known as the Marshall Plan, it was named for the former US Army Chief of Staff George Catlett Marshall, who was chosen to administer it, and the bulk of the domestic supplies of iron, steel, aluminum and other light metals, machine tooling, synthetic rubber, electrical components, and countless other commodities now under the control of government procurement agencies for shipment overseas. At the same moment, favorable tariff rates were instituted which encouraged the import of foreign goods to be paid for in hard dollars, with which to further strengthen foreign monetary systems.

This massive program, which doubtlessly staved off further Communist advances abroad, brought about great economic hardships at home, where, by this time, most essential civilian goods were in very short supply. The critical transportation industries that supplied railroad rolling stock, automobiles, trucks and critical machine tooling were particularly affected. In order to aid domestic

185

industry as much as possible, essential component materials were allocated to various manufacturers on a quota system, based on their immediate pre-war production.

The American motorcycle industry was at once placed at a critical disadvantage by this state of affairs, as its pre-war production had been minimal. At the same moment, it gave a tremendous advantage to both the overseas motorcycle manufacturers and the growing number of import organizations which came into being to facilitate their sale in the United States.

The sudden dramatic public interest in motorcycles came as a puzzling phenomenon to many old time riders as well as members of the domestic industry, who now noted that trading conditions in the general post-war shortage of goods made for a seller's market. Yet a factual analysis of the situation by both sociologists and economists indicated that this was not surprising. There was presently a vast pent-up demand for luxury and recreational goods, dating back not only to the recent war years, but from the previous decade of the Great Depression. Now that the inevitable post-war prosperity had become a reality, there was plenty of available money for their purchase. Then too, millions of young men, freshly released from the armed forces, sought to make up for the recreational opportunities so long denied them. As far as motorcycling went, countless GI's had been introduced to the sport through service employment, which in turn served to whet their appetites for more luxurious and better performing civilian-type machines. Added to this, the now burgeoning ranks of motorcycle dealers offering new models from overseas made for a greater market penetration through their sheer numbers.

Due to the immediate difficulties in obtaining critical materials, the H-D Company perhaps wisely decided to institute somewhat limited production of their successful pre-war line of models. The top of the line was, of course, the well tried 61 and 74 cubic inch ohv big twins, together with the rugged 80 inch side valver. The venerable 45 twin was still in limited production, with an eye to supplying military and utility machines to their export buyers. The Servi-car was also in production, along with sidecars and package vans. Prices, of course, were greatly advanced, the 61 ohv twin was now retailing at $725 FOB Milwaukee.

Surprisingly enough, the American manufacturers offered no direct competition to the foreign invaders. The H-D 45 was never the sporting mount as compared with the Indian Sport Scout, and the latter had now been dropped from the line by Indian's new President, Ralph B.Rogers, who, while continuing the popular Chief, was planning to introduce a line of lightweight machines, based on continental lines.

In the meantime, the H-D Company was engaged in encouraging a number of its dealers, who had suspended operations due to the hiatus of the war years, to reactivate their franchises, as well as soliciting the acquisition of new dealerships through advertisements placed in both the trade press and various hobby and outdoor magazines. An enhanced factory advertising campaign was also announced through both the pages of the *Enthusiast* and by direct contact with the established dealers.

In spite of production difficulties due to shortages of essential materials, the American motorcycle industry was able to produce about 19,500 units in 1946, according to the US Department of Commerce reports. While this was substantially more than was reported for 1940, the increase was largely due to the enhanced production of scooters, mainly manufactured by the Cushman Motor Company of Lincoln, Nebraska, with lesser numbers produced by Gladding and Salsbury. While both factories strictly enforced their long standing edict against the franchise holders selling other than their own factory's products, it has been noted that they tended to look the other way in the matter of scooters, and substantial numbers of these, mostly Cushmans, were sold by both outlets. As there was still a shortage of available new automobiles due to the material shortages with a consequent high price structure for used cars, the scooter now attracted a growing number of utility riders, as well as schoolboys seeking cheap transportation, as the smallest sized Cushman now retailed for about $150.

At the end of the war, the Cushman concern greatly enlarged its production facilities, and as a result they were now able to keep up with increasing sales. This happy state of affairs, for some H-D dealers at least, came to an abrupt end in the Spring of 1947 when the factory, through its traveling representatives, informed all retailers that henceforth no more Cushman products could be sold through franchised outlets. Several dealers, especially in the larger cities where scooter sales had been brisk, tended at first to ignore this edict. These rebels were at once notified by the factory that any and all orders for H-D machines would be suspended until they complied. A few, who were known to have extensive scooter sales were ordered to certify, with notarized statements, that they had, in fact, officially severed all franchise connections with the Cushman Company.

Various versions of this episode in H-D history have been related to the author by veteran dealers, along with their own personal opinions as to the reason for this official factory mandate. The most popular story is that a group of Cushman's managerial staff visited the H-D factory in the late Winter of 1947. During the course of their tour of the premises, some of them were heard to adversely compare the now somewhat antiquated Milwaukee facility with their own recently-constructed plant in

A 1946-47 'Knucklehead' Dresser. In the restoration, modern plastic panniers have been substituted for the period cowhide bags. (*George Hays*).

Lincoln. Another account has it that with the new lightweight model that H-D was shortly to introduce, which will be subsequently described, H-D's top management now thought it best to remove potential competition for its sales well before its introduction.

Production at Milwaukee now proceeded at a greatly reduced pace, as the Company's material allocations were by necessity based on pre-war production. With a soaring demand for new machines, especially the now popular ohv models, dealers' orders were filled on a quota basis. In spite of production difficulties, the quality and finish of the new machines was excellent. A notable advance was the use of the Parker process in rust-proofing all metal parts most subject to corrosion. The originator of this patented chemical treating process, one Edward Parker, paradoxically enoough began his operations in space leased from the Indian Company in Springfield!

In the meantime, foreign motorcycles, mostly from Great Britain, began appearing on the American market in increasing numbers. By the end of 1946, nearly 10,000 units had been sold. Most of these were imported by organizations formed by the handful of brave entrepreneurs who had the temerity to launch these ventures in the late 1930's, when both the machinations of the established dealers and the sub-rosa disapproval of the AMA had all but strangled their efforts. The most prominent of these were Johnson Motors based in Pasadena, California, who handled Ariel and Triumph, and Alfred Rich Child in New Jersey, who now held the BSA import rights for the United States.

While H-D as yet had no comparable model with which to compete with the British singles, the Company rose to the challenge by inaugurating an accelerated national advertising campaign, and at the same moment increased their efforts to strengthen the morale of their dealership. Factory representatives were instructed to spread the gospel of traditional American motorcycling and the type of machine it typified, as well as emphasizing that it was a patriotic duty of all riders to support the American motorcycle industry. Along with this went a warning to all dealers not to undertake the repair of any foreign machines in their premises, or even sell them tires or lubricants. Another somewhat logical reason advanced for buying American machines was that in their heavyweight configuration they were much more suited to general domestic conditions of use and their longevity was already well proved. While this was true, it did not negate the fact that a horde of new riders were enjoying the lightweight single cylinder machines for casual weekend pleasure riding, and that a new group of feminine enthusiasts were now also coming into the fold. H-D was also somewhat hard pressed to gloss over the fact that not a few long time dealers had deserted Milwaukee to sell the newcomers, sensing not only a new and hopefully more viable market, but also perhaps tiring of the traditional oppressive tactics of H-D's management.

The question of the suitability of the imported machines for typical American riding conditions was well taken, as in many cases they were not. The first British imports were generally 21 cubic inch models that were basically ex-War Department types with civilian finish. These included Ariel, Royal Enfield, BSA, and the 350 cc Triumph twin. The first 500 cc (30.50 cubic inch) models to arrive were side valve Nortons, of North African fame! Their initial retail prices were attractive, first fixed at $585 but soon raised about $100 more. This now relatively modest price, together with their light weight, ease of handling, and above all, their featuring of hand-controlled clutch mechanisms and foot shifted gearboxes found them an immediate welcome from many budding US enthusiasts who could never formerly relate to a 700 pound big twin. In passing, it must also be noted that the imports carried but a nominal import duty of about 8%, while American big twins were still having to contend with a 33% to 50% tariff barrier when exported. Some 9,064 machines were imported in 1946, this figure rising to 15,073 in 1947.

While these figures augured well for a revitalized American motorcycle market, all was not lovely in the garden. While the imports offered the advantages mentioned, together with the capabilities of economical running, their generally initial engine size of 350 cc was scarcely powerful enough to cope with the exigencies of long distance high speed travel. They were particularly prone to failure in the popular motorcycling area of the West and Southwest where high summer temperatures were the rule and where hard riding was the essence of the sport. Then, too, the imports were never designed to stand up to the punishment the average rough-riding Yank was used to giving his machine. Particularly vulnerable were clutches and gearboxes, especially to ex-H-D riders, as the British models required careful application and gentle gear changing if any longevity in use was to be expected. The initial problems were somewhat mitigated when the more powerful 500 cc imports became available in the Spring of 1948. Still no match on the road in high speed travel, the Ariel Red Hunter, the Triumph Speed Twin, and a few others of like size offered at least better longevity. A notable exception was the ohc Norton International, which could give a good account of itself in any sort of going, but, as a high priced machine in low volume production, it was rarely seen.

Another problem for the imports was the weakness of many of their dealers. While many pioneer outlets in the foreign field prospered, too many enthusiasts entered the arena with too little capital and less business experience, and many predictable failures occurred. There was also an ongoing problem with obtaining necessary spare parts. Some dealers were forced to cannibalize new machines to keep favored customers on the road. On the credit side of the ledger, a new market unfolded with the coming availability of utility type lightweight machines for the newsboy rider, such as the James, Excelsior (British) and Francis-Barnett, all powered with proprietary 125 cc Villiers engine-gearbox units. These were later joined by the civilian version of the Royal Enfield 125 cc paratroop machine.

Meanwhile, enjoying at long last a seller's market of enthusiasts' inquiries and a backlog of unfilled orders, many H-D dealers were asking the factory whether or not any middleweight machines with which to compete with the foreign imports might not now be forthcoming. Many were chagrined at the official answer that in view of the current production problems, no new models were contemplated. This position was further amplified by statements, mostly through the factory representatives, that H-D had been producing motorcycles for 45 years, and knew better than anyone else what type of machine suited the American rider. Those dealers who persisted in their inquiries, were told that the venerable 45 model might well be advocated as a sales alternative to the ever-burgeoning imports. This was scarcely a logical answer to veteran dealers, who knew well that this model's 500 pound plus weight and 68 mph top speed was scarcely a challenge to a lower cost Ariel Red Hunter or Triumph Speed Twin whose top speed was 20 mph higher.

On the sporting side, there was now the inevitable collision between the AMA Competition Committee and the dealers in foreign imports, who at once challenged the longstanding ruling mandating a 7.5:1 compression ratio for 30.50 ohv singles when competing against 45 cubic inch side valve engines. The Competition Committee's immediate answer was that for the foreseeable future the present ruling would stand. When pressed for an explanation, the official stand of the management of the AMA now, of course, totally dominated by H-D, was that the AMA and its constituent Competition Committee was totally committed to the interests of the American motorcycling, American riders, and American manufacturers. It was further stated that if foreign machines wished to compete on America's home ground, they must do so on traditional American conditions without reference to foreign precedent. This was a bitter pill for the importers to swallow, as the leading overseas contenders such as the Ariel Red Hunter, Triumph Speed Twin, and Norton International models required at least an 8.5:1 compression ratio to allow them to develop their full power, especially if tuned for competition.

The monotony of the American motorcycling journalistic scene was enlivened in the Spring of

Hollister, California, July 4th, 1947. American motorcycling's Day of Infamy. Here an inebriated reveler on his stripped H-D toasts a Time-Life photographer. *(Time-Life Inc).*

1947 by the launching of a new motorcycle magazine called *Cycle,* which was inaugurated by an enterprising young publisher, Robert E. Peterson, who also had just introduced other motoring publications such as *Motor Trend* and *Hot Rod* to cater to the increasing public interest in automotive progress. The long limpid *Motorcyclist,* which under AMA and H-D domination had traditionally existed as an apologist for the industry, acting principally as its defender, was now challenged by a new publication oriented toward the interests of the consumer. For the first time in the memory of most US motorcyclists, critical evaluations and road tests of currently offered models were actually aired in print.

The domestic answer to this journalistic bombshell was a rather thin magazine, aptly named *American Motorcycling,* launched in Chicago. Heavily backed by both H-D and Indian interests, it emphasized the traditionalist theme of the Yankee big twin and the patriotic obligation to patronize the domestic industry.

In addition, H-D's management sought to strengthen their position by reactivating the regional H-D dealer's associations in various parts of the country, all of which met at least twice a year. Factory representatives constantly impressed upon the dealers the patriotic duty of supporting American products. Practical sales techniques were emphasized in the promotion of accessory sales, where the 45-60% markups were contrasted with the traditional 25% sales markup on the bare machines. This accentuated the 'dresser' theme, where, to customize his machine, the purchaser would add a dualseat, saddle bags, spotlights, and other items which by this time were the style for the typical big twin rider.

H-D was in a most fortunate position in relation to the clubman's market, as the production of the classic Indian Chief had been much curtailed as Indian's new President, Ralph B. Rogers, was preoccupied with the development of two new lightweight models with which he hoped to compete in the market for smaller machines. With the renewed interest in big twin models, the standard clubman's machine was now almost universally a 61 or 74 cubic inch H-D ohv model equipped with windshield, front and rear crash bars, leather saddle bags, a rear carrier for additional luggage, along with whatever extra spotlights and additional chrome gadgets the owner chose to install. This concept was, of course encouraged by the factory, and in any club meeting or semi-private contest, there was inevitably an award for the 'Best Equipped' machine, which could be won by simply loading the model with every available gadget.

Class C racing was somewhat haphazardly revived after the war, and culminated in the first postwar running of the 200 mile Daytona Classic in 1947. Floyd Emde, of San Diego, won the meet handily on a racing Scout, tuned by the inimitable Noel McIntyre, shop foreman of Guy Urquehardt's Indian agency.

An interesting vignette of AMA history emerged from the 1947 Daytona Classic in relation to the barring of a super sports ohc 500 Moto Guzzi from the contest. Its owner, pioneer motorcyclist John Cameron, of Whittier, California, who entered the machine in question, was notified by a member of the AMA Competition Committee that his entry had been disqualified, even though Cameron's entry was accepted before the meet, as required by the rules. Cameron told the author in 1978 that the Moto Guzzi showed such promise during the prerace practice period that the AMA officials were fearful of another foreign victory, such as had occurred with the Norton entry in 1941! Cameron lodged a vociferous protest, but the Committee refused to give him a hearing.

Motorcyclists everywhere, whether clubmen, casual riders, or the new emerging sportsmen favoring imported machinery, were disappointed and chagrined in the Summer of 1947, when a July 4th general clubman's meeting at the village of Hollister, California, was invaded by a group of the so-called 'outlaw' motorcyclists. Over the three day weekend, these worthies terrorized the town, and it took a force of some 500 California Highway Patrol officers, California State Police, and local law enforcement officers to quell the disturbance, and disband the rioters.

The sensational aspects of the incident were at once seized upon by the news media, including *Life* magazine, then the leading news-picture publication, and the roughneck aspects of motorcycling were again emphasized to untold millions of readers. The names of such outlaw clubs as the Booze Fighters, Galloping Gooses, Satan's Sinners, Satan's Daughters, and the Winoes were prominently featured. Dozens of these revelers were arrested for indecent exposure and for relieving themselves on buildings along Hollister's main thoroughfare. The now classic photograph by a *Time-Life* photographer of the drunken rider of a stripped-down 'UL' model brandishing a bottle of beer appeared on the cover of the July 21st issue. The debacle was again aired on its twenty-fifth anniversary when *Life* again featured the picture on its cover in July 1972. Anguished letters from orderly motorcyclists were subsequently printed by *Life* in their 'letters from the readers' section, including one from actor Keenan Wynn and another from *Motorcyclist* Editor Paul Brokaw, deploring the blatant exploitation of the incident. Both declared that of the 4,000 odd motorcyclists present, only about 500 of that number actually caused the trouble, the balance being mostly sober AMA club members. Whatever the actual details, the incident unfortunately labeled the H-D as the outlaw machine of choice.

The so-called roughneck or 'outlaw' element among motorcyclists, while a thorn in the side of clubmen and orderly private riders in pre-war days had ever been a problem, such had previously constituted a minority within a minority, and up to this point had never presented much more than a minor annoyance. The Hollister incident pointed up the fact that certain antisocial elements within the fabric of the nation were now finding within the motorcycle movement a means of expression of protest within the so-called traditional establishment.

The 'outlaw' motorcyclist concept now constituted a fertile field of speculation for psychiatrists and sociologists of the post-war era, who were also studying the effect of certain of the younger elements of the social spectrum who had been dislocated by their participation in the war. Some of these so-called experts averred that these people were motorcyclists who were expressing their revolt against the organized activities of the dealer-sponsored club oriented meetings. Others claimed that certain antisocial individuals had chosen the iconoclastic entity of the motorcycle to express their general emotions of revolt against the formal social structuring of contemporary American life. Whatever the theoretical background to these assumptions, it ultimately transpired that the outlaw adherents in general gravitated to the American heavyweight 'V' twin as their favored mount, with ownership of H-D big twin machines predominating. Adopting stripped machines without windshields, saddle bags, spotlights, or even crash bars, it may well be assumed that their attitude was one of revolt against the big twin 'dresser' favored by clubmen as well as against the now effete middleweight British imports.

Most of the long established H-D dealers refused to countenance the general unwashed outlaw types as customers, so their repair and service needs soon created numbers of small specialist unfranchised shops. Many of these soon became notorious for dealing in stolen machines or pirated parts.

In the Fall of 1947, two updated versions of the ohv 61 and 74 cubic inch big twin models were announced for the 1948 sales year to replace the 'knuckle head' type which had been in production for a decade. While, as ohv machines, the original model had in large part overcome the overheating problems at high speeds that had been an unfortunate attribute of the 74 and 80 cubic inch side valve models, its all-iron cylinder barrel and head had at times evidenced its own overheating problem, especially in hot weather at prolonged high speeds. The problem of oil leaks around the rocker box coverings had never been entirely solved. To correct these faults and produce a cooler running engine, H-D's Engineering Department's answer was the so-called 'pan-head', with an aluminum alloy cylinder head and an hydraulically-controlled lifter in the ohv mechanims. The 'pan-head' description alluded to the skillet-shaped aluminum cover over the valve mechanism.

While the changed configuration was a theoretical improvement, considerable trouble was experienced with the early models. The oil pump, situated low in the crankcase, now had to force the lubricating oil to the top of the cylinder head through a complex labyrinth of oilways. If the oil pressure was not constant for any reason, the hydraulic lifters failed to function properly, causing a variation in the timing sequence. Practical mechanics at once pointed out that the system could be more efficient and reliable if the hydraulic tappets were placed at the bottom of the push rods rather than at the top, and therefore less subject to timing variation if there was a change in oil pressure. After large numbers of dealers and riders reported both rocker arm failure and serious alterations in the normal valve timing sequence, the factory supplied kits of revised parts in hopes of correcting the difficulties.

A feature of this new design was a shaped felt pad fitted into the top of the 'pan' head which was intended to pick up and hold the oil to give added lubrication to the rocker mechanism. In some cases, amateur mechanics failed to replace this felt on reassembly after a valve adjustment. The resultant noise from the increased resonance in the 'pan' from the rockers was said to be ear splitting!

On November 24th 1947, the H-D Company held a general dealers' sales conference in Milwaukee at the Shroeder Hotel, described in the contemporary issues of the *Enthusiast* as the largest meeting of its kind ever held in the Company's history. Dealers from all over the US attended, as well as a number of overseas dealers.

Sales Manager J.C.Kilbert opened the first meeting, and introduced the last surviving Founder, Vice President Arthur Davidson. Davidson spoke at length of the critical economic international situation and its relationship to the ever-growing inflation. Gordon Davidson, the son of the late Walter Davidson, and now Chief of the Production Department, outlined the Company's projected 1948 production schedule. He stated that he hoped to increase the present year's output of about 20,000 machines to 30,000 for the following season. He reported that the Company was currently in process of enhancing its manufacturing facilities and was acquiring additional tooling to meet this projected goal.

Later in the meeting, Arthur Davidson again gave an address, this time emphasizing the company's general sales policies. He warned all dealers that only company built parts, accessories, and factory-supplied lubricants should be handled by the franchised outlets, and that any retailing of the

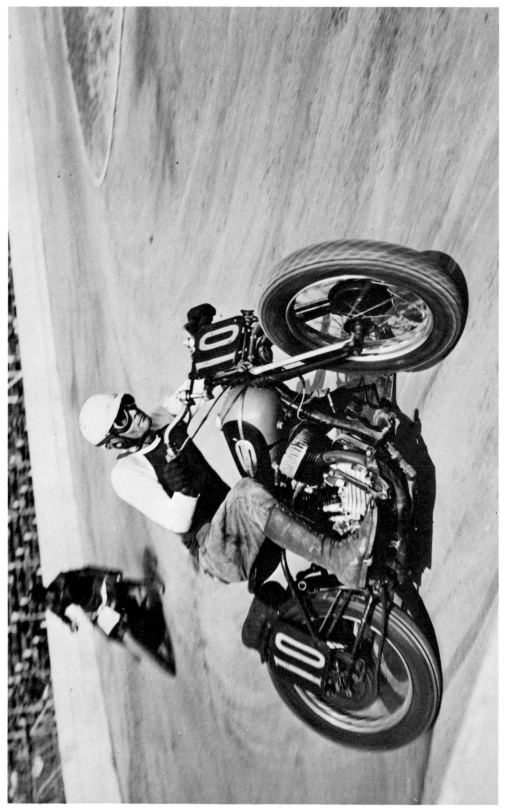

Win Young broadslides at a race on the Lincoln Park oval in 1948. His machine is a DLD with a WR racing engine. *(Robert McGill).*

A study in contrasts. A 1947 Ariel Red Hunter and a 1940 EL go over the jump at Lincoln Park. *(Robert McGill).*

products of other suppliers would result in disciplinary action. He next called attention to the vast display of company-manufactured or supplied accessories on view in a large hall adjacent to the meeting room. He pointed out that the generous 45% dealer markup on these items could greatly enhance their profits, and that buyers of both new and used machines be urged to purchase as many of these items as the traffic would bear. He also stated that as the factory had cut its own costs to dealers to the bone to aid in placing H-D in a competitive position in a growingly critical market, the factory's stake in accessory sales to dealers was now a critical factor in Company economics.

Representatives of the Kilbourne Finance Company spoke at length on the promotion of conditional sales contracts written through its organization to enhance the sale of new and late model used machines. Dealers were also advised to utilize the services of this company to floor larger stocks of showroom machines and informed of the favorable insurance rates offered for the protection of machines sold under the terms of these contracts.

Other factory personnel who addressed the meeting were Service Manager Joseph Ryan, Parts and Accessories Manager Harry Devine, Law Enforcement Sales Manager Frank Egloff, and J.C.Kilbert. Kilbert emphasized the importance of developing commercial sales of Servi-car and package truck sales. He pointed to the enviable sales records in this area racked up by Dudley Perkins of San Francisco, Claude Salmon, of near-by Oakland, and Alfred Rich Child of Japan, who had sold large numbers of these units to commercial establishments in the Bay area in pre-war years.

During an intermission following this stage of the proceedings, Law Enforcement Sales Manager Egloff was seen to be holding conferences with various groups of dealers, urging them to learn whether purchasing specifications written into local municipal, country or state ordinances could be strengthened to continue the mandatory retention of H-D machines. He emphasized that the continuation of this strategy would have the advantage of keeping dealers of foreign machines out of the domestic law enforcement business.

E.C.Smith, Secretary-Manager of the AMA was also on hand to render a report on the current status of that organization. He stated that its membership had grown from 4,650 in 1928 to over 50,000 in 1947, which knowledgeable members of the audience immediately concluded was wildly optimistic. He emphasized that dealer support of the AMA was vital to its continuing success, as well as lauding the H-D Company for its role as its most substantial financial supporter. He also mentioned that continuing rider and dealer support of the *American Motorcycling* magazine would be most helpful for the sales promotion of domestic motorcyles. In conclusion, he again praised the role of H-D in its long support of the AMA, and presented its current President, Arthur Davidson, and sole surviving Founder, with a handsome trophy.

A surprise feature of the meeting was an appearance by Chief Engineer William J.Harley, who outlined briefly the various technical improvements that had been incorporated into the post-war range of H-D models. As this segment of the meeting opened, it was noted that two black-draped objects flanked the rostrum. The mystery was soon dispelled by Harley as he announced the introduction of the first two prototypes of a new 125 cc lightweight model. To be cataloged as the H-D 125, the new 175 pound machine was a startling innovation in contrast to H-D's long preoccupation with heavyweight machines. Of basically simple design, it featured a solid rear frame, the girder forks being sprung with rubber band suspension. To further enhance comfort, 3.25 inch section tires were fitted on both wheels. Experienced members of the audience were quick to note that the engine, with its integral three-speed gear box unit, was a frank copy of the German DKW unit built in Germany from the original Schnurle design shortly before the war. This unit was shortly to be seen again from overseas in the form of the BSA Bantam. Both companies had secured the patents through the Allied acquisition of German assets following the war.

Another surprise feature of the gathering was a train trip to the outskirts of Milwaukee, where President William H.Davidson was on hand to greet the dealers and their guests. He explained that the new 260,000 square foot acquisition had just been purchased from the government and, as a former defense plant, could be readily adapted to motorcycle production. He noted that new tooling and equipment would shortly enhance H-D's output, and that over $3,500,000 was being spent on the project. He also stated that the production of 'WR' racing machines was to be expanded, and hoped that dealers would be quick in sponsoring qualified competition riders to counter the growing challenge of foreign machines in motorcycle sport.

The meeting was, in effect, a challenge by the company in throwing down the gauntlet to foreign competition, and at the same time reaffirming the Company's adherence to American motorcycling tradition by featuring the heavyweight 'V' twin. While the new 125 model was indeed a departure from this tradition, the Company showed no inclination to introduce any new models in the 21 and 30.50 cubic inch categories currently supplied by foreign machines.

Quite naturally the affair was billed by reports in the *Enthusiast* as a love feast, but all was not serene. Many dealers had hoped for an H-D scooter to replace the now-denied Cushman that had been

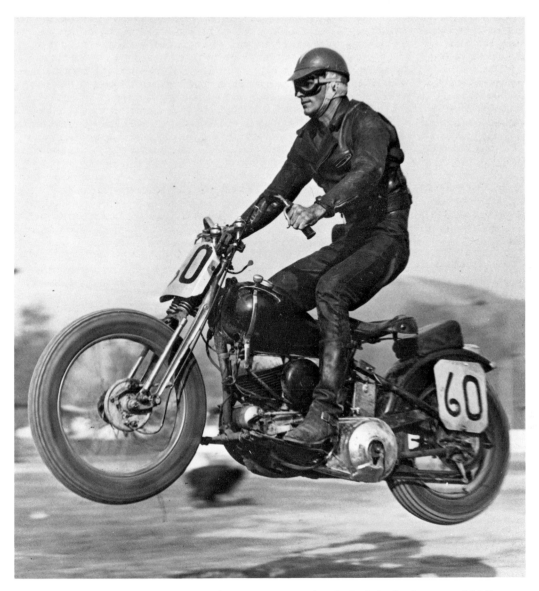

Homer Drown pilots his 1935 VL over the TT course at Lincoln Park in the Summer of 1948.
*(Robert McGill)*.

such a good seller on the utility market. A number were also highly critical of the fact that no new models were planned to fill the 350 cc - 500 cc category featured by their most serious foreign competitors.

The story is often told that a number of veteran dealers, concerned by their inability to compete with foreign machines with H-D's of like category, met privately with Arthur Davidson, to find out whether the Company had plans to offer such models. At the same time, many of the smaller dealers complained that their quota of machine orders was not being filled in the same ratio as was supplied to the dealers in the larger cities and trading areas. Davidson responded to the first query by saying that no new models were planned because at this time the company was not prepared to spend the considerable sum of money required to build such prototypes. He further stated that during the past forty years H-D had built machines best suited to American conditions, and was therefore in a position to know what type of machine was best suited to the American rider. This was the type of machine the Company intended to produce. In response to the second question, Davidson stated that in some cases dealers in the larger trading areas might be given quota preference because their volume sales meant that they were selling proportionately more machines. Put off by the rather arbitrary attitude, some of the dealers next contacted President William H.Davidson, who, it has been alleged, echoed the same sentiments.

In relation to H-D's conservative policy of adhering to their post-war models, John R.Bond, an automotive engineer who later published and edited the prestigious *Road and Track* magazine, offered his own comments on the matter. As an employee in the Company's Engineering Department during 1946 and 1947, he noted that every encouragement was given to the prototype studies of new or innovative motorcycle designs. While H-D's top management showed much interest in such creative projects, nothing was ever done to incorporate any of them into current or subsequent models.

The following spring, the Company did much to reactivate the H-D Dealers Association in the various geographical sections of the country. While still very much alive as organizations, most of them had naturally languished somewhat during the war years. Factory representatives now exhorted the dealers to redouble their sales efforts, and to aid in counteracting the growing threat of intense foreign competition, to emphasize the patriotic theme of patronizing domestic industry as well as harking back to the traditions of American motorcycling in machine selection.

Sales of foreign machines had become substantial. The general motoring public, up to this time often unaware of the availability of foreign makes, was now treated to a new era in motorcycle merchandizing. Some of the well-financed foreign dealers established extensive showrooms in the larger cities, many of which overshadowed the traditionally shabby housing some of the domestic dealers had long suffered. With a generally broad selection of both light and middleweight machines available to them, potential buyers had a welcome range of choice. Then too, the foreign dealers were under no repressive control from either factories or distributors, and were free to not only retail any make of machine, but could offer a diverse group of accessories from any manufacturer as well.

While the foreign machines up to this point had no domestically produced counterpart, the situation changed somewhat when Indian's new President, Ralph B.Rogers, announced that his company was shortly to introduce a new line of light and mediumweight machines. During this period also, the domestic big twins suffered no foreign competition to speak of, as the few that had been produced overseas between the wars, were not reintroduced in the early post-war years. The two exceptions to this were the Ariel Square Four and the Vincent HRD. The former, a somewhat unorthodox design by Edward Turner was, in effect, powered by two vertical twin engines geared to a common crankcase. While the closely grouped cylinders cooled sufficiently for use on the winding lanes in the mild British climate, this configuration was less than satisfactory over the vast distances and high summer temperatures of the West and Southwest US where motorcycling was most popular. To those few Square Four enthusiasts who persisted, the only possible answer was the fitting of a proprietary oil cooler. The Vincent, a massive 61 cubic inch V twin with a rather curious spring frame and dual carburetors, was capable of far out speeds, but was rather temperamental and difficult to keep in tune. This, with its rather weak lower bearing design, was a machine for the enthusiastic mechanic rather than the casual tourist.

On the other side of the coin, the H-D 125 proved to be a sound machine and was generally well received by schoolboys and utility riders, as well as numbers of adult newcomers to the sport. Ruggedly built in the best H-D tradition, its engine proved both more durable and capable of higher performance than the Villiers-engined James, Excelsior (British) and Francis-Barnet lightweights that had been imported in fair numbers. The 125's 47-49 mph top speed was somewhat better than the James's 40-odd, and was far less susceptible to spark plug fouling. About 10,000 H-D 1255's were delivered during the first year.

Great Britain's answer to the Yankee big twins in the speed battle was the enlarging of the classic 500 cc Triumph Speed twin to 649 cc in the new Thunderbird model in 1949. This was soon followed by similar bored out 500's by Norton and BSA. For substantially less retail cost, the British enthusiast now had a machine that could keep up with the Yanks, albeit far less rugged and in need of much tinkering.

It was during this period, when motorcycle journalism was quite naturally expanding with the rising market, that a whole new regiment of aspiring young journalists took to the typewriter. Many of these tried to outdo one another in praise of the now effete imports and in downgrading the native products. As H-D was now the leading producer due to Indian's pre-occupation with some smaller continental-type models, it took most of the brunt of this criticism. Characterized as out of date trucks, crude, overweight, and 'Hawg' like, the Yankee classic was excoriated as an out-of-date dinosaur. This somewhat scurrilous attack was prompted by lack of knowledge and experience of these writers who rushed into print without realizing that they were dealing with two distinct types of machines, having generic origins in separate continents with opposed applications of use.

On the other side of the pond, however, the reaction to the post-war Yankee big twins was reported as most cordial. In a December 1955 issue of the English *Motor Cycling* magazine, published by Temple Press, a road test reported of a 1950 74 cubic inch 'FL' model lent to the staff by a US Army Air Force Sergeant. The author, while commenting on the excessive weight and bulk of the machine, was ecstatic about its effortless high cruising speed, easy starting, and the superlative comfort afforded by the hydraulic fork, softly sprung saddle, and the general air of invincibility engenderd by the large capacity slow turning engine. The conclusion was that the big Yank offered a standard of comfort and enormous power not yet available on the British market.

For the 1949 sales season, H-D enthusiasts were electrified by the announcement that the time tried classic H-D leading link forks were to be replaced on the big twin models by an oil dampened telescopic fork, the first change in H-D suspension in forty years! The new fitting followed the usual telescopic pattern, except that it was, of course, a rather massive fitting. With a wide range of travel, riding comfort was markedly improved, and together with the dampening effect of the time-honored spring seat post and the standard 5 inch section low pressure tires, the effect was such that any present digression into a rear spring frame was entirely unnecessary. Some difficulty was experienced with the earlier models so fitted, however. With soft springs and a long rate of travel, it was possible to spill the machine if a tight turn were made allowing the lower outer end of the standard crash bar to dig into dirt or pavement. The author himself had two narrow escapes from crashing when turning off pavement onto rough desert tracks on a 1950 'FL'. Joe Walker, the local Santa Ana dealer, installed a factory-offered kit that was subsequently developed to slow the rate of oil travel within the fork, which corrected the difficulty. In subsequent sales literature the new models were catalogued as the 'Hydra Glide'.

With the low production of Indian Chiefs in the company's post-war reorganization, the H-D low compression 74 cubic inch 'FL' model became the standard law enforcement machine in the United States, and was widely exported abroad for this use. Its only international competitors in this field were the resurrected BMW opposed twin and the low production copy built in France as the Ratier, neither of which were then produced in any substantial numbers. As a result, probably more Presidents, Prelates, Heads of State, and other dignitaries have ridden with H-D police escort than any other machine! The Police 'FL' was admirably suited to this work, as its low compression engine could be idled for long periods in slow speed traffic work without fouling, yet it could be rapidly accelerated to pursuit speeds as the occasion demanded. While its top speed with full radio and other standard law enforcement equipment was only slightly over 80 mph, this was sufficient during its heyday to overhaul most standard automobiles. Its massive trouble-free drive train and clutch was well suited to standing up to both low speed and start-and-stop usage, and the riders generally commented that its low center of gravity made it very stable and comfortable to ride. A few die-hard municipalities, however, clung to their Indians, mostly through long established tradition, and H-D's Law Enforcement Sales Department was constantly dogging these heretics as a matter of both pride and principle. One of these was the City of New York. Their regiment of pre-war Indian Fours now redundant, they still maintained a vast fleet of Chiefs. The production of this model was terminated in 1953, but some 55 machines were assembled from parts on hand in 1955 by the Tite-Flex Company, the manufacturer of Chiefs since 1951. The purpose of this was to supply these machines to the New York Police Department, whose procurement specifications called for Indian machines. To counter this, H-D assembled two 'FL' models for bidding survey, duly fitted with reversed controls to comply with the left-handed throttle edict, together with a pristine finish in Indian Red Color! This act enraged both the New York Police oficials as well as Tite-Flex, and according to several old timers' accounts, the Atlas Corporation, owner of Tite Flex, filed a patent infringement suit against the H-D Company. The exact outcome of this rather bizarre affair is unknown, but it was long a rumor that H-D paid a substantial sum in damages to Atlas to keep the matter out of court. H-D had the last laugh, however, when the last of New York City's Indians were retired in the late 1950's, and 'FL's' took their place.

By 1950, competition for a now stabilized motorcycle market was keen, with foreign dealers now outnumbering the domestic contingent by a wide margin. While H-D now had a firm grip on both the law enforcement market and the family-oriented club scene, mostly in the Midwest and East, sporting riders and new converts to motorcycling generally preferred the imported machines, particularly in the West and Southwest. The H-D dealers as a group mostly withdrew into their own world, and feigned a haughty disregard for the 'limey' interlopers. Their favorite sales ploy was an appeal to tradition, as well as to the fact that they considered the more lightly constructed overseas offering as flimsily built, particularly in their transmission system. Here they had a point, but a point in common with both the domestic and foreign machines was that they leaked lubricating oil. The imports appeared to shed this fluid from both the engine cases and gearbox, while the Yankees leaked from the ohv mechanism, which even 'panhead' modifications did not entirely cure. One motorcycle journalist was said to have viewed the cumulative problem and stated that an American machine was a motorcycle that weighed 700 pounds, had 63 tail lights that worked, and leaked oil. An imported machine, such as a Triumph, was described as weighing 400 pounds, had one tail light that did not work, and leaked oil! And so the battle raged.

Feeling the marketing pinch, and with a now static dealer representation that made H-D a minority in retail outlets, the Company cast about for other ways to counter the competition. A logical point of attack was the United States tariff system. This allowed, under the Marshall Plan, foreign goods, automobiles, and motorcycles included, a favorable rate of 8%, the hard dollars going to purchase farm products and other commodities. On the other hand, many durable goods produced in the United States, cars and motorcycles included, had to contend with tariff barriers that reached as high as 40%, which all but stifled export trade.

As the majority producer of domestic motorcycles, the H-D Company took the stand that they had a legitimate case for a revision of these policies, and accordingly decided to petition the US Tariff Commission to give substantial protection to the American motorcycle manufacturers. Eric von Gumpert, H-D's veteran Traffic Manager cum Export Manager, was said to have prepared the appropriate briefs, with the assistance of the Company's legal counsel, and accordingly on May 15th 1951, the H-D Motor Company formally petitioned the US Tariff Commission for relief against their foreign competition. In their plea, the Company asked for not only a 40% import duty to be levied on all foreign machines, but also that they be allowed entrance on a quota ratio based on their pre-war shipments, which would in actuality have had the effect of keeping out foreign machines altogether!

In the meantime, the foreign dealers and importers had already formed the British Motorcycle Dealers Association, a rather loosely organized body originally formed to combat the generally hostile policies of the AMA against their products.

When the news of the impending hearings on the tariff matter was relayed to the importers by the Select Senate Committee on Tariffs, the British Motorcycle Dealers Association immediately rose to the challenge. Retaining their own legal counsel, they girded themselves for the forthcoming battle led by one Denis McCormack, then the Triumph importer and President of the group.

The hearings lasted for some three weeks during the month of July, with officials of the H-D Company and their counsel, representatives of the BMDA and their counsel, along with a large group of interested dealers and riders as spectators. Both groups brought examples of their machines to the second floor of the Senate Office Building via the elevator, although it was noted that the full dress 'FLH' was squeezed in with some difficulty.

H-D's counsel presented their case, stating the inequality of the tariff laws currently in force and their effect on the Company. One surprise was H-D's admission that they had suffered serious financial reverses during the post war years, both from impaired production through the mandates of the Marshall Plan, and their non-competitive wage position. H-D, of course, was forced to negotiate with the United Auto Workers local in Milwaukee, while foreign competitors paid on a free-floating scale.

The BMDA presented their case at first through the means of comparing their imports with the domestic product, and pointed to their exhibited machines as being of a size and engine capacity that

The 125 cc 'Hummer' lightweight, H-D's first-ever two-stroke, its engine-gearbox unit was a frank copy of the German DKW.

was not competitive with domestic products, as nothing similar was then being manufactured in the US.

The keynote speech for the importers was not made by counsel, however, but by Alfred Rich Child, longtime H-D representative in the Orient and presently the BSA importer since 1944, with headquarters in New Jersey. Reading from a prepared spech, Child began his remarks with the re-counting of the long established marketing practices of the domestic motorcycle industry. He alluded to the highly restrictive franchise conditions imposed upon retail dealers, initially both by Indian and H-D, and how the latter had carried matters to the point where none of their dealers could handle any products not procured through company courses. He further described how in refusing to allow their dealers to handle other than their own products, they had effectively removed less productive low volume manufacturers from the field. He went on to state that the US manufacturers, H-D in particular, had refused to develop a market for light and middleweight machines, and at the same time had prevented other manufacturers from attempting to serve this market to the detriment of a large potential for machines of broader appeal. He went on to describe the H-D Company as representing an entrenched monopoly that was not only attempting to force on the American market a machine that had but limited popular appeal, but was now attempting to put a segment of American free enterprise out of business by cutting off their source of supply.

Witnesses at the hearing have told the author varying accounts of the proceedings, but all agree that the H-D contingent, headed by President William H.Davidson, sat in stunned silence following Child's testimony. After some minutes, H-D's legal counsel attempted to impeach Child's testimony concerning his reference to the fact that the late William A.Davidson, Vice President in charge of Production, had been born in Scotland. H-D Company publications often stated that all of the four Founders were born in the United States. Child responded that his statements were based on his personal acquaintanceship with the late William A., and he now challenged H-D to produce evidence that William A. had, in fact, been born in Milwaukee.

As the matter was brought up late in the afternoon, the presiding officer called for an adjournment until the next day, and stated that if H-D, through their counsel, wished to pursue this matter, they could do so the next morning. When the hearings resumed the following morning, H-D's counsel did not again allude to the matter, and it was then assumed by those attending the hearings that perhaps in spite of published company 'histories', they could not, or did not, wish to dispute Child's allegations in the matter.

As an aside to the proceedings, several witnesses later told the author that the members of the BMDA were at some pains to restrain the ebullient McCormack from emphasizing the large volume of sales of foreign machines currently being enjoyed by members of that body in fear it might jeopardize their case. After some deliberation, the Senate Committee rejected H-D's case, and in their subsequent written opinion sustained the position of the BMDA in the matter. This was, of course, a bitter pill for the H-D Company to swallow. Not only had the generally monopolistic practices long carried on by both manufacturers been publically exposed, but H-D itself had now to bear the brunt of this long-known but never before publicized aspect of the American motorcycling picture. As matters stood, H-D was now forced to make its own way in the domestic market without any official change in a somewhat disadvantageous position in tariff protection and competition from foreign machines built by low cost labor.

In his reminiscences concerning his role in the affair, Alfred Rich Child told the author in 1979 that while he regretted having to expose to the public the basic tenets of long-established H-D policies, he felt, after some soul searching, that the future of American motorcycling was in serious jeopardy unless a free and unfettered market could be enjoyed by its sales outlets.

American motorcycle sport got underway somewhat haphazardly, as many former competition stars as well as hundreds of thousands of young soldiers were not demobilized until 1946. As previously noted, the rather hastily organized 200 Mile Daytona Classic was won in 1947 by Floyd Emde, on a Sport Scout. H-D took the trophy in 1948, after inducing Emde to leave the Wigwam and enter the contest on a new 'WR'. The 'WR' had become a formidable competitor after Tom Sifton shared his tuning secrets with the factory engineers.

In general, the early post-war period of motorcycle sport can be well described as a time of conflict between the AMA Competition Committee and the riders of foreign machinery as some rather arbitrary rules had been written into the regulations fifteen years before. The long standing edict that ohv machines of 30.50 cubic inch displacement could have no more than a 7.5:1 ratio was at the heart of the controversy, as the popular British machines such as the Ariel Red Hunter, the Triumph Speed Twin, and small numbers of ohc International Nortons had their performance seriously handicapped by this ruling.

In addition, the Competition Committee arbitrarily refused to sanction road racing types of event, such as had long been popular in Europe and England. Some reports had it that the Committee considered road racing on hard surfaces highly dangerous, much more so than the traditional horse track competition. The lack of such courses in the US, and the difficulties in obtaining official support in closing sections of public roads were also cited. Others, mostly competitors favoring foreign machines, were on record as stating that the general design characteristics of the solid framed H-D 45s and Scouts with their minimal rate of front fork travel, were unsuited for use on such circuits and that the AMA did not wish to inaugurate a new competition class for which domestic machines were initially handicapped.

It was during this time that H-D urged both competition riders and dealers sponsoring such contestants, to field as many machines as possible at major racing events. The effect of this was, of course, to 'bury' a budding foreign machine's rider among enough assorted 'DLDR' and 'WR's', making it difficult for them to either win or place. President William H.Davidson had already authorized the assembly of as many new 'WR's' as the Company's meagre material allotments would allow, and dealers and riders were urged to resurrect prewar 'DLDR' models for the use of budding racing enthusiasts. There were also scattered reports of much gamesmanship on the part of allegedly H-D oriented AMA referees in a number of hotly disputed contests where foreign contestants bitterly claimed that wins or places had been unfairly denied them.

In spite of the formidable challenge from overseas, H-D 45s and Sport Scouts continued to do well in competition. The high torque output of the 45 cubic inch side valvers was such that once a rider was able to build up engine revolutions they were more often than not in winning or placing distance. These machines were particularly formidable on the mile or longer courses. The foreign machines were at their best on the shorter quarter or half milers where their nimbleness and ease of control with foot controlled gearbox and hand-operated clutch were telling factors.

Except for the startling British win in 1941, Daytona remained as the American's V twin domain until 1949, when Manx Nortons again entered the fray. Wiry Dick Klamfoth, an eighteen year old farm boy from Groveport, Ohio, placed first, with the 1941 winner, Canada's ace rider Billy Mathews, coming in a close second. For some reason, the AMA Competition Committee had allowed the Manx racers to enter.

It was theorized by some that H-D now had infinite faith in their modified 'WR's', which had made a spectacular showing at the Langhorne, Pennsylvania Classic the year before. Some previous overheating troubles over a long distance were ostensibly cured by fitting larger valves, together with altered port timing. Another surprisingly generous concession was the raising of the traditional 7.5:1 compression ratio for ohv engines to 8:1, this to take place in the 1950 season. On the other hand, the Nortons were forced to fit kick starters, as US contests were still held under the much flouted Class C rules which forbade run-and-bump starting.

For the 1950 Daytona Classic, Norton fielded a team of four, which included Dick Klamfoth, Billy Mathews, Ernie Roccio, and the ex-Indian rider, Bobby Hill. In an all out effort to win, Norton retained the services of the legendary tuner, Francis Beart, who as an independent entrepreneur had already made a name for himself in preparing winning Nortons in England. In addition, Beart had now the assistance of the famous Indian tuner, James Hill, as the Indian Company now distributed a number of British machines through its newly-formed Indian Sales Company.

On the day of the 200 mile main experts event, a huge fleet of H-D's were on hand, together with a smaller contingent of Indian Scouts, six Triumph entrants, which included the indefatigable Ed Kretz, with Jack Horn and Rod Coates. Also included was BSA with an official team of three, headed by Tommy McDermott, who was said to have a very fast machine, together with three additional private entrants on the same make.

When the race was flagged off, Kretz streaked into the lead. At the 20th lap, Kretz was still in front, followed by Klamfoth and Jimmy Phillips on another Triumph. Kretz was sidelined with a slipping clutch, and Mathews then took the lead, with Klamfoth now just behind followed by Bill Tuman on another Norton. Bobby Hill's Norton was unfortunately out of combat, as he had dropped the machine on the north turn and filled his carburetor with sand. Tommy McDermott on his lightning BSA bored through the pack, but was unable to take the lead toward the finish, coming in third behind Billy Mathews who took first, and Klamfoth who was second. Bill Tuman was fourth, with Ernie Roccio seventh, so the contest was clearly a Norton victory.

Klamfoth was again a Norton winner in 1951, coming in first just 20 seconds ahead of teammate Bobby Hill. In 1952, Klamfoth again scored another Norton victory.

No doubt in consequence of these victories, the double knocker style of ohc valve action was now barred from US competition by the AMA, and H-D set about to design a successor to their once formidable 'WR' which was now clearly outclassed. Indian continued its racing representation with its aged Sport Scouts, but without factory help and the nearing demise of the Indian Company, the Redskin's days were numbered.

Interposed between these years of changed US competition activity, H-D people as well as a host

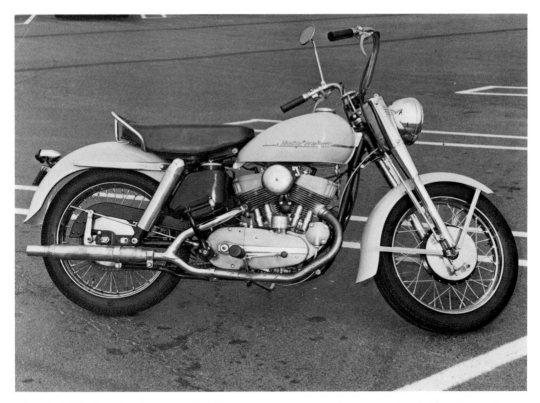

The Model K 45 cu.in. Sportster of 1953. An attempt to combine a traditional side valve engine with modern suspension, it was handicapped by a lack of power.

of other motorcycling enthusiasts were saddened by the untimely death of Arthur Davidson, the last surviving Founder. On the evening of December 30th 1950, Davidson and his wife were returning to their home in suburban Milwaukee. Making a left turn into the driveway, their automobile was struck head-on by a motorist heading in the opposite direction, reportedly traveling at very high speed. The Davidsons were removed from their mangled vehicle and transported to the nearest hospital, but both were dead on arrival.

The career of Arthur Davidson with the H-D Company is almost too well known to bear repeating. Working with William S. Harley, he helped to develop the first prototype machine, and subsequently was almost solely responsible for building H-D's strong dealer organization through the years. A firm believer in advertising, he constantly kept H-D and its activities at the forefront by means of various forms of publicity. Described by contemporaries as the most personable of the Davidson brothers, he nevertheless shared with his late brother, Walter, an almost paranoic antipathy to competitors. With his total dedication to the cause of H-D for all of his adult lifetime, he was no doubt one of the main factors in its survival through the years, and to its successes, even in the very difficult post-World War II years.

As Arthur Davidson's death left the post of Chief Executive of both the AMA and M & ATA vacant, George D. Gilbert of the Baldwin-Duckworth Chain Company of Springfield, Massachusetts, was appointed to fill this position by the joint Board of Directors.

In the meantime, H-D production and sales proceeded apace, though somewhat inhibited by the material restrictions still imposed by the Marshall Plan. With a loyal following of enthusiasts, most of whom would never own another brand of motorcycle, the Company continued to sell all the units it could produce. While foreign machines showed an enviable reception in the Far West and Southwest, they were less popular in the Midwest and East, where the big twin Yank was still the most favored motorcycle. The 125 proved to be a rugged and dependable machine, and sold well to both aspiring young riders and adults entering the game, as well as limited utility users. Before the end of production, the Company was to sell over 100,000 of this model.

In spite of healthy sales on somewhat restricted production, many dealers still complained that the lack of a middleweight model to compete with the imported machines was inhibiting their market penetration. At the same time the Company still imposed their strict policy of allowing dealers to handle only Company supplied products and accessories, this being enforced by the usual eagle-eyed coterie of factory representatives. In the end, some dealers gave up their franchise in favor of foreign products, but there was one notable exception.

Skip Fordyce was a pioneer H-D dealer in Riverside, California, an important motorcycling center since early post-World War I days. As a genial fellow, and the sponsor of a local motorcycle club, he was immensely popular with riders in general, and built up a lucrative business, with the aid of his attractive wife, Ruth, who was also active in Southern California circles of the Motor Maids of America. Noting the growing popularity of middleweight foreign machines, and a legion of sales lost for the lack of an H-D counterpart, Fordyce electrified the nation's H-D community by taking on the franchise for Triumph machines. He was almost at once chastised by both H-D factory representatives and Milwaukee for this heretical defiance of established Company policy. He was also warned that his long-standing and lucrative H-D franchise was now subject to immediate revocation. Fordyce's reply was to reiterate his position in regard to the lack of a suitable middleweight H-D machine in the Southern California market, and informed the Company that he would continue to handle Triumph whether or not the former edict was enforced. While the Company at this point could well have carried out its threat, Fordyce's long popularity and his past impressive H-D sales record prevailed, and H-D's management capitulated, its head bloody, but unbowed.

In commenting on the incident to the author in later years, Fordyce stated that while he was a lifelong H-D enthusiast, he had at long last become disenchanted with the Company's dictatorial policies. With a large establishment to maintain, and faced with the lack of competitive H-D machines in the now popular 500-750 cc class, he saw no other course than to climb on the band-wagon and secure a franchise for a model that was currently much in demand by a broad segment of new enthusiasts.

In his subsequent discussions with H-D's top management, Fordyce stated that he called their attention to the long-standing flouting of the Sherman Anti-Trust and Clayton Acts dealing with the restraint of trade. He further served notice on H-D that he could well successfully institute legal proceedings against them on these grounds should the matter come to the courts.

Following this incident, he recounted that during the course of the matter he received hundreds of long distance telephone calls and letters from long established H-D dealers from all over the country, most of which both encouraged his stand in the matter and offered him their support.

It was now noted that numerous H-D dealers had the temerity to themselves take on franchises for other makes of machines. As a landmark case, the Fordyce episode at long last heralded the end of

H-D's Golden Anniversary Model of 1953. With its 'panhead' engine and solid frame, its direct lineage to the 1936 61E is clearly evident. *(George Hays).*

the Company's death grip on the activities of their dealers. Many of the more bombastic factory representatives, who formerly could enter a dealer's shop and make him quake in his boots, now adopted a less dictatorial and even jovial manner.

While more and more H-D dealers felt free to take on other makes with impunity, Carl's Cycle Service in Minneapolis was not so fortunate. The proprietor at once took on a BSA franchise without factory reprisal. But when he obtained a franchise for the heavy-duty German Zundapp, and equipped a local Shrine drill team which was formerly 100% H-D mounted, with the Teutonic models, the long-suffering H-D Sales Department revoked his franchise!

In the meantime, the factory's Engineering Department was busy developing two new middleweight models, one a racer, the other a roadster. With the devaluation of the British pound, the retail cost of English machines were reduced some 20% and, at the same time, rising material and labor costs at Milwaukee had mandatorily increased the retail price of H-D big twins to over $1,000, a figure some experts solemnly pronounced was more than any enthusiast would pay for any motorcycle.

The new racing machine which was to replace the now outclassed 'WR' was designated as the 'KR'. Taking a lesson from the obvious British successes with their close-ratio, foot-operated, four-speed gearbox and hand clutch, and their rear springing which aided in keeping the rear wheel more in contact with the ground, the new model featured these improvements. However, and what was regarded as a retrograde step by many, the engine itself followed the long hoary traditions of American competition by being a side valve V twin.

While the early 'KR' models did not develop as much power as the 1941-based 'WR', their performance was enhanced by both the new four-speed gearbox and foreign type control system. The engine itself, subjected to critical scrutiny by the now less sychophantic trade press, was described as a 20th century anachronism. With its spread-out combustion chamber necessitated by its side valve configuration, it developed about 56 hp, but it benefitted from a wide open breathing system and the ability to turn out excessive torque at moderate engine revolutions from a mere 6.5:1 compression ratio. Aside from its archaic engine design, the engine and four-speed gearbox were enclosed in a common case in the modern mode, with the disadvantage that the whole required dismantling to repair the latter. The clutch, an H-D innovation after many decades, was the oil-immersed type.

Teething troubles immediately appeared, and early clutch failure accompanied by over-oiling was partially cured by providing a pressure relief system that allowed removal of excess lubricant. Initial competition use showed that the 'KR' neither handled as well or developed as much power as the former 'WR', and much midnight oil was burned in order to stabilize the telescopic fork and swinging arm frame that was in itself a marked innovation in H-D competition machinery.

In order to give the rider the option of varying suspension to suit various types of competition, the spring frame could be replaced with solid units for certain short track events, where the latter proved to be more practical. This option persisted until the mid-1960's when Dick Mann, a brilliant dirt track exponent, demonstrated that his variations of the swinging arm could result in enhanced performance.

The roadster version of the 'K' model proved to be a mid-twentieth century anachronism. Fitted with a mild touring version of the 'KR' engine/gearbox unit, the new model featured a soft acting telescopic front fork and swinging arm rear suspension. In an attempt to provide the best of both worlds, the modern chassis was mated with the identical side valve engine of the 1920 era. The whole concept, it seems, was to hark back to tradition with the engine, yet give a concession to modernization with a softly sprung ride.

While the new model elicited some hope from the assembled dealers at a factory sales meeting where it was unveiled, the ultimate result was disappointing. In its standard tune, the engine developed insufficient power to provide either enough urge for double riding, now the necessary hallmark of a clubman's machine, nor could it satisfactorily haul a sidecar, and no mounting lugs for such fitting were provided. While some impressive road test results were published by the factory, they proved to be inconclusive during actual conditions of use.

The author was provided with a demonstration machine by the late Joseph Walker, pioneer H-D dealer in Santa Ana, California, for his own evaluation. While possessed of adequate acceleration through the gears, the top speed was a disappointing 81 mph, this with the rider well crouched over the fuel tank. At anything over 60 mph, there was simply no acceleration or hill climbing ability left worth noting. In 1955, after disappointing sales, the engine was bored out to 55 cubic inches in an effort to obtain more power. While acceleration through the lower speed ranges was improved, as was the hill climbing ability, the overall results were not up to expectations. The model eventually was superseded by the 57 cubic inch Sportster, of which more later. In the overall sense, the early side valve 'K' models may well be described as the last attempt of America's sole surviving manufacturer to offer a traditional motorcycle in the 45 cubic inch category.

With the offering of the 'K' type, the venerable 45 inch 'D' model was at last laid to rest. Even in its final years, it was still fitted with the traditional leading link girder forks, and its ultimate role appears to have been the basis for the long running three-wheeled Servi-car model, an established favorite for law enforcement parking control in suburban areas and in limited commercial work.

In 1952, a marked concession to modernity was offered in the big twin models with the offering of an optional foot gear shift and hand clutch control as an alternative to the previous traditional system. The latter was effected by the fitting of a spring loaded servi-mechanism that gave positive clutch control with little pressure from the handlebar lever. The traditional system was generally favored for law enforcement use, as it enabled the officers to continue the use of hand signals when engaged in traffic control.

The classic side valve 80 cubic inch model was at long last terminated in 1952. Not seen in the catalogs since 1948, it had been available on special order. Most of the latter models of the series were in use by police units in Mexico and South America where its sterling attributes of both reliability and ease of maintenance were especially appreciated where skilled mechanical services were at a minimum.

In 1952, the hydraulic valve tappet arrangement in the big twins was altered to place the units at the bottom of the push rods rather than at the top, a change that many practical H-D mechanics considered long overdue. This reduced the chronic oil leaks around the rocker boxes to some degree, but enabled the valves to retain their adjustment for a longer period, as well as reducing tappet noise. Further modifications to the cam action and port profiles resulted in a 10% increase in engine power. While this was welcomed by riders in general, most particularly those who favored sidecar units or long distance solo touring, the added surge caused further problems with inherent V-twin vibration characteristics.

For some years the author enjoyed the ownership of a low compression 1950 'FL' model. As a sturdy and dependable machine, it afforded many thousands of miles of pleasant trouble-free travel. Its engine, however, showed an annoying vibration period at speeds between 55 and 60 mph, which represented a very useful rate of travel. A long time H-D enthusiast suggested that an accessory item was available in the form of a short steel forging that could be bolted just ahead of the engine mounts through the twin sidecar stay lugs that were brazed to lower angles of the twin down tubes. A letter of inquiry to the factory, outlining the author's problem, and requesting information on the fitting in question was, in time, answered. On the letterhead of the Engineering Department, the letter stated that H-D machines were not fitted with engines that were subject to vibration, and that therefore the Company did not see fit to include such an accessory in their line of optional merchandise. In the meantime, an old time H-D mechanic and friend of the author, Maury Biggs, procured the fitting in question from some obscure trade supplier, and its installation did much to improve the machine's running characteristics.

During the 1952-1953 sales season, and in celebration of the Company's 50th anniversary, H-D's advertising emphasized its role in the development of 'V-Power', comparing the now classic ohv twin design with the new contemporary fitting of ohv V-8 engines in the current offerings of Ford, General Motors, and Chrysler automobile manufacturers.

In spite of the ever growing threat of foreign competition in the various AMA sporting events now being promoted in enhanced numbers in every part of the country, H-D was able to make an impressive showing during the 1950's and early 1960's. In the initial days of this era, machines tuned by the inimitable Tom Sifton played a decisive role, beginning with Larry Hedrick's sensational 1950 season on his reworked 'WR'. Sifton correctly reasoned that the low weight of the machine could be a telling factor. His judgement was vindicated with the 126 pound Hedrick's many victories on a specially lightened machine on the mile tracks. Following Hedrick's enforced retirement from racing due to injuries sustained in an automobile accident, Sifton's creations next figured prominently in the scintillating career of Joe Leonard, culminating in his Daytona victory in 1958.

In 1954, the AMA Competition Committee instituted a new point system in tabulating the results of individual wins in order to determine the outcome of the National Championship standings. Up to this time, National Championship status was decided by the results of the races held at the famous mile track at Springfield, Illinois, a 'sudden death' type of affair where the winner was crowned National Champion regardless of previous victories. The new system was based on the individual rider's attainment of points earned through his standing in the various Nationals entered during the current season.

The 'K' model racing machine, introduced in 1952, experienced numerous teething troubles, as well as developing noticeably less power than the latest 'WR's' it was designed to replace. This disadvantage was somewhat overshadowed by the fact that, with its option of a sprung rear frame and four-speed gearbox with foot-operated change and hand operated clutch, its rear wheel spent more time in contact with the ground, and the rider could save valuable seconds in its overall control. As usual, Tom Sifton was largely responsible for its later improved performance, but veteran mechanics criticized the complication of the construction of its unit engine case and gearbox castings that

Some of the members of a Mystic Shrine Motorcycle drill team. Many such organizations standardized on H-D FL and FLH machines.

necessitated a complete dismantling of both to make minor adjustments. It was on a Sifton-tuned machine that Joe Leonard of San Jose, California, won the National Championship in 1954. This victory was somewhat tempered by the fact that BSA took all first five places at Daytona.

The administration of the AMA was changed in 1954, when Carl Swenson, President of the Milsco Manufacturing Company of Milwaukee, replaced George D.Gilbert. At the same time, the veteran Secretary-Manager E.C.Smith, retired and was succeeded by Lin Kuchler, who promised a more aggressive role in the management of AMA affairs. He proposed that a firmer policy be instituted regarding the public relations role in the AMA vis a vis media exposure of sanctioned racing events, to give a more prominent role to advertising motorcycle sport. He was actively supported in this by William (Bill) Tuthill, a pioneer motorist and motorcyclist, who was the proprietor of a museum of racing vehicles in Daytona Beach, Florida. Tuthill voiced the opinion of many that the AMA up to this point had not expended enough effort in the public relations sphere in an attempt to gain recognition for motorcycle sport and to put it more prominently in the public eye. Kuchler immediately sought an enhanced budget appropriation from the AMA's Board of Directors for such a program. After a somewhat prolonged discussion, it was later reported that this conservatively-orientated body declined to advance from its historic isolationist position regarding publicizing motorcycle affairs. After numerous futile attempts to change this rather stagnant policy, Kuchler resigned in 1956.

In the Spring of 1954, the so-called 'outlaw' element in motorcycling at long last found its identity in a motion picture released that spring. Entitled 'The Wild One', featuring Marlon Brando, Mary Murphy, Lee Marvin, and Brian Keith, its plot was loosely based on the events at Hollister, as well as somewhat superficially touching upon the iconoclastic self-indulgent philosophy of the 'rebel' motorcyclist. The production was roundly condemned by numbers of the AMA affiliated clubs, some of whom picketed theaters where the film was exhibited. While by this time most of the outlaw riders were centering their interest on heavyweight American V twins, mostly H-D's, the director of the picture charitably mounted some of his actors (some of whom were actually members of bona fide outlaw groups) on a mixed bag of American and English machines. Brando, the anti-hero, rode a pristine Triumph Speed Twin. Much of the antipathy felt by traditional motorcyclists against the outlaws was based on the fact (aside from some of their alleged antisocial actions) that they cut down many of the fine old classic 61E and UH and UHL models that were growing in value each year as long as they remained in original condition.

In spite of losing the Daytona classic when the one time Indian star, Bobby Hill, won on a BSA, Joe Leonard was able to amass enough points in a series of other events to bring a National Championship to the Milwaukee brand.

In 1957, the ill-fated side valve 55 cubic inch 'KH' model was dropped in favor of a new ohv machine that was catalogued as the 'XL' Sportster. This was, in effect, the same machine, with an ohv version of the 'K', but not displacing 57 cubic inches. Critics at once noted that the engine should have been enlarged to the classic 61 cubic inch dimensions as of yore. However, with limited space within the frame, a longer stroked engine would have to be taller to conform to these specifications, and would have necessitated the expense of tooling up for an entirely new model. The new machine was offered in two versions, one a touring type which was in effect a scaled down 'FLH', and a sports type machine that offered magneto ignition. This last was widely heralded as the answer to the need for a middleweight sporting machine. While a weight of about 460 pounds ready for the road made this supposition more or less of a reality, its appeal was somewhat limited by the fact that early examples exhibited high speed steering problems. Starting was also made difficult by the fact that the Edison magneto for some inexplicable reason was not fitted with an impulse coupling. At any rate, the naturally higher performance capabilities of the 'XL' were welcomed enthusiastically by sporting riders, and a new era of H-D model influence was brought into being.

The following year, the venerable 'FL' and 'FLH' models were fitted with rear springing by means of a pair of hydraulically dampened coil springs that supported a pair of swinging arms that had their pivot just behind the seat post. The new model was catalogued as the Duo-glide. Critics at once noted that the forward slanted position of the spring units at once hampered their efficiency. It was also admitted that their more efficient vertical fitting would seriously interfere with the placement of the now traditional saddle bags and/or police radio equipment that had long been carried in paniers on either side of the rear wheel. Had the shock units been placed in the vertical position, this would have created an overwide lateral silhouette. In truth, most big twin enthusiasts had already long been in agreement that with the large section tires, combined with the highly efficient spring seat post, rear springing was not really necessary. On the other hand, it was noted that luggage racks, luggage attachments, carriers and radio equipment fitted to the law enforcement 'FL' models were prone to fracturing after high mileage use. This was attributed to both rear wheel hammer combined with the characteristic vibration syndrome of the V twin engine configuration. The new model was now carried on as the Duo-Glide, and at a weight penalty of some 80 pounds the classic H-D big twin was fitted with rear springing as standard.

A mixed bag of H-D WRs and Manx Nortons duel on the sands of Daytona Beach in 1951.

This general period in time saw an amazing proliferation of motorcycling literature. Numerous articles in the popular motorcycle press saw capsulated histories of various makes, along with other efforts describing historic or especially thrilling race meets and competition events of the past. J.L.Beardsley, a one-time motorcycling reporter of an earlier day, recounted significant sports events, many of them dealing with the Golden Age of dirt and board track racing.

The late Floyd Clymer, who deserted retail motorcycle sales for the publishing business, issued a large number of reprints of early day motorcycle literature in the form of catalogue reprints as well as books on various aspects of the sport. Much of this informative material was abruptly cut off when it was ascertained that he was publishing reprints of foreign works without benefit of royalty payments to the copyright owners. Among these were the classic works of the Nicholson Brothers, of Saskatoon, Canada, on the subject of motorcycle mechanics and speed tuning, and certain other publications from the Temple Press and Iliffe concerns in Great Britain. A large shipment of these works was impounded at the dock just before transshipment to the States through legal action instituted by the companies concerned.

In the late 1950's, motorcycle drag racing became popular, and had its inception in the Southern California area. Long popular in England, where it was known as sprint racing, the contest was actually an acceleration trial where the winner's time, for the short straightaway course, was tabulated at the end of the run in both elapsed time and mph attained at the finish line. Competition was somewhat loosely categorized into classes based on engine displacement, the most spectacular being the larger or unlimited class which included much modified big twin H-D types. With overboring of the cylinders and much stroking, some of these now exceeded 100 cubic inches and put up fantastic times when fueled with blended spirits.

The first H-D dragster of note was built up by Mike Tucker, featuring a more or less standard 'FLH' that was merely stripped and the engine subjected to special tuning. More radical conversions were built by Joe Smith. Other noted special builders were Ken Tipton and Bob George. Tipton is today the proprietor of an extensive shop dealing in speed equipment, and George gained much notoriety with his double engined H-D special which was known as 'The Beast'. Most of the early day motorcycle drag competition centered around a course situation on an old disused airfield at Pomona, where car contests had been held since about 1950.

The design of these dragster machines had profound effect on the early 'outlaw' type of big twin, which was originally merely a stripped standard model with the front mudguard, windshield, crash bars, luggage equipment, and other detail accessories removed, together with the inevitably bobbed rear mudguard.

With the growing scarcity of big twin models, coupled with the fact that the standard 'FL's' and 'FLH's' now had rear springing fitted as standard, small accessory shops offered their own type of specially-made solid frames as substitutes. Many custom designers considered the sprung frame as a spurious luxury, and were probably correct, considering that its added weight reduced overall performance. At the same time, special, small capacity, lightweight fuel and oil tanks and 'banana' type saddles were being manufactured by small specialist firms to fit such frames. The old 'California Bobber' had become the 'California Chopper', inferring that in the lightening process the machine had been 'chopped', and a new era of motorcycling, based on the pre-war 'outlaw' theme was now at hand.

As far as the so called 'outlaws' themselves went, groups of such riders as were organization minded, gathered into formal groups such as the Hell's Angels, and the later Hessians, Satans, Mongols, etc.. These clubs became legally incorporated groups, and stood ready to institute legal action against newspaper reporters, journalists, freelance authors, and publications that aired their doings should they venture to criticize their activities in print.

Many individual riders, however, who favored individually-styled machines, did not elect to join such clubs, but at the same moment favored the life style and leather-dominated dress of the so called 'outlaw' and later joined the collective designation as 'bikers'.

By this time, the biker machine of choice was now almost universally some older model of big twin H-D modified to the owner's liking. A few old Indian Chiefs were 'chopped', together with a few British machines, notably the Triumph Thunderbird. But by 1960, the H-D was the machine of choice for such conversion.

Up to this point in time, both the H-D Company and its dealers continued to ignore the chopper movement. In most cases, H-D still refused to service or overhaul such machines.

In the meantime, the retail outlets continued to expand as growing numbers of enthusiasts secured franchises for foreign machines. If an aspiring dealer had access to sufficient capital, such were relatively easy to acquire. In addition, the importers in most cases were adverse to their franchise holders handling other makes, in contrast with the long established domestic tradition. Not a few of the still numerous Indian dealers acquired franchises for BSA and Triumph after Indian finally phased out production.

As the result, H-D representation dwindled. While the implications of the Fordyce insurrection had by this time stripped the factory of much of its power over the dealers, the majority as dyed-in-the-wool enthusiasts still sold H-D's exclusively. Although Milwaukee still held a strong position in the touring and traditional AMA club organization areas as well as in law enforcement, its monopoly in the latter field was soon to be challenged by BMW.

Almost unnoticed in the November 1959 issue of Floyd Clymer's *CYCLE* magazine, was an advertisement announcing the introduction of the Honda. Proclaimed as an innovation from Japan, it was a small moped-like machine with a 50cc ohc engine that featured, of all things, electric starting. Its challenge to the market was — 'You meet the nicest people on a Honda'.

A group of AMA club riders, with passengers and luggage, move along a desert highway. The FLs and FLHs were the standard US touring machine up until the late 1960s.

In the summer of 1960, H-D's top management entered into negotiations with the Aermacchi concern of Varese, Italy, in regard to the possibility of a merger between the two companies for their mutual benefit. Aermacchi was currently in financial difficulty in competing in the highly competitive motorcycle market in India. H-D was, of course, losing out on a potentially vast segment of the American market from their previously adamant refusal to introduce any middleweight models. The upshot of the matter was that H-D purchased a 50% interest in Aermacchi. This strengthened the latter through an infusion of fresh capital, and at the same time enabled H-D to offer the American buyer a competitively priced middleweight machine that was produced by relatively low cost labor. At the same time, and to strengthen the marketing position of both, an international trading corporation, Aermacchi-Harley-Davidson S.A. was set up in Zug, Switzerland.

The present Aermacchi organization had its origin from a parent company, Aeronautica Macchi S.p.A., of Milan. This had been in existence since its founding in 1912 as S.A. Nieuport Macchi for the manufacture of aircraft. Several interesting and practical designs were produced in limited numbers before WW I. The factory was enlarged in the early 1930's to produce fighter aircraft for Mussolini's air force. Also produced during the between-the-wars era were some highly advanced single seated seaplane types that gave a good account of themselves in the Schneider Cup races.

The factory was destroyed during WW II by bombing. Following its end, the company then established modest facilities in Varese, with plans to produce ground vehicles only. A few light cars were manufactured in 1946, but after experiencing difficulties in material procurement, the management decided to concentrate on two wheelers. Their first effort was a 125 cc scooter-like machine. In 1956, a four-stroke model called the Chimera was added to the line, with the option of either a 175 or 250 cc engine that had the cylinder positioned horizontally. Aermacchi's Chief Engineer, Alfredo Bianchi, was determined to produce good handling machines in the best Italian tradition,

A Club member 'rides the plank' with his FLH 'Dresser' at an AMA Club field meet. *(George Hays).*

and to attain a low center of gravity he frankly copied the long popular Moto Guzzi Falcone and Astore models. The 250 cc machine was also produced as a sport model, and with high lift cams and specially tuned with an 8.5:1 compression ratio could easily top 80 mph. First produced in 1957, it enjoyed rewarding popularity with Italian riders, the model being then known as the Ala Verde. In 1960, its name was appropriately changed to the 'Wisconsin' after H-D entered the picture, and when imported to the States early in 1961 was marketed as the 'Sprint'. In this guise it was fitted with a smaller 2½ gallon fuel tank and sports-type mudguards to conform to the contemporary 'street scrambler' type then popular with US riders.

What with the infusion of fresh capital and enhanced production now scheduled for the US market, Aermacchi next inaugurated an accelerated competition program in Europe which did much to enhance its prestige and resulted in increased sales. During 1962 a limited number of racing 250's were built which made a very good showing in the Belgian and Ulster classics. Aermacchis finished well in the German Grand Prix as well as in other contests in France, Spain, and Finland. Aermacchi next fitted a 350 cc engine with a five-speed gearbox, and on a highly tuned model Renzo Pasolini was able to place third in the FIM 350 cc World Championship in 1966. The noted Kel Carruthers made a good showing on the Isle of Man in 1969, his machine being only 1.4 seconds slower through the Highlander speed trap than the fastest Yamaha 350.

After these successes, Aermacchi next developed an ohc racing special, but H-D's management refused to sanction a continuation of this project due to the ever-mounting expense of fielding a large team of racers. Some factory people have since commented that H-D was already committed to a heavy competition program in the States, and felt that victories at home on Milwaukee-built machines had better advertising value. Aermacchi's top management was equally adamant concerning the importance of maintaining the marque's prestige in Europe, as their racing successes had increased sales. But as Milwaukee held the purse strings, Aermacchi was forced to field a limited number of modified super sports machines that cost less to build and maintain. It then appeared that these machines were entered in various international events to prove their mettle to the public rather than seeking outright wins, the latter course involving vast expense.

In spite of the general good quality and performance of the Sprint, it did not fare too well on the American market. The 250 cc class had never elicited much interest in a country with a traditional pre-occupation with large capacity machines. Then too, the dealer-enthusiasts were largely big twin orientated, and many did not take kindly to either a small capacity machine, especially if it was not made in Milwaukee. What with small volume sales, most dealers stocked only a minimum of spare parts, and some buyers were put off the road for long periods while some essential component was on back order.

As a possible competitor for the ever growing numbers of small Japanese machines that were attracting new riders, H-D introduced a 50 cc model built by Aermacchi, known as the Leggero, in 1965. A well-finished lightweight with good performance for its size in the best Italian tradition, it was somewhat handicapped by the traditionally hard Italian seat. Its low speed handling was somewhat impaired by fitting a wide ratio three-speed gearbox in place of the more usual ratio four-speed type offered by the competition. An improved model bored out to 65 cc was offered two years leter, but sales were disappointing as the dealers generally did not promote the machine locally, in spite of much factory advertising.

The deservedly popular Milwaukee-built 125 which had subsequently been marketed as the 'Hummer' had been updated in 1953 by fitting a soft acting hydraulic fork and enhanced performance was achieved by boring out the engine to 165 cc. Known as the 'Ranger', it was phased out in 1962 in favor of a new 175 cc two-stroke model that powered the 'Pacer', 'Scat', and 'Bobcat' models developed to cover the now popular market for street scrambler and utility type machines. The former 165 cc model was relegated to powering an off-the-road trail type machine without lighting that was designated the 'Super 10'.

While they were soundly built and rugged machines in the best H-D tradition, these models did not fare too well, as by this time the pre-war DKW design had been decisively outclassed by the latterly developed ohc and two-stroke machines from Japan, which now showed fantastic performance in models of like displacement.

The Company entered the scooter market in 1960 with the 'Topper' model, powered with the well proved 165 cc engine that was fitted with a centrifugal clutch. A ruggedly built machine that was easy for a novice rider to control, it was overly heavy for its power. Sales resistance was encountered when it was ascertained that its engine capacity and power development was insufficient for it to legally negotiate the now ever expanding network of high speed freeways. Selling as it did for $600.00, it suffered in comparison with cheaper oriental motorcycles with higher performance. It was ultimately discontinued in 1964.

The 250 cc Sprint enjoyed some mild popularity as a competition machine, as the AMA Competition Committee, at H-D's request, created a special Novice classification for this capacity. As the 250 class had never been taken seriously by Yankee fans, most of the riders went on to large machines when they attained Amateur and Expert status.

H-D racked up an impressive number of competition wins and top placings during the decades of the 50's and 60's, in spite of serious challenges from BSA and Triumph, the principal opponents. The contemporary trade press, its numbers continually augmented by new publications, featured detailed reports of the dozens of AMA-sanctioned events held each season. Even a condensed digest of these usually spectacular events would fill a large volume.

An exhaustive study of the competition scene of this era reveals that H-D's consistent success was based on a composite of a number of factors. By backing a large number of entrants, in most cases the field could be literally blanketed — which could make it more difficult for foreign machines with usually lesser representation to work their way through the pack to a place or win. The long standing AMA competition rules traditionally favoring the Yank machines in the classic horse track courses, was another telling factor. Added to this was the fact that most of the top AMA officials were past middle aged veterans with long years of service in their tenured positions, and by tradition owed first allegiance to that long H-D dominated body. In addition, the accrued point system established by the AMA in 1954 naturally favored the make that could consistently field large groups of entrants in a majority of the sanctioned contests. Points could be thus accumulated by sheer weight of numbers. On the ever critical financial side, H-D seemed consistently willing to pay the expenses and bonuses to a growing number of established stars as well as budding amateurs. While racing could well be charged off to advertising, it involved the expenditure of a great deal of money. Some Company insiders later averred that the resultant depletion of H-D's cash reserves had a significant bearing on later events. Even so, H-D was able to attract both the loyalty and enthusiasm of a number of talented riders during this period, such as Brad Andres, Mark Brelsford, Walt Fulton, Dan Haaby, Mert Lawwill, Joe Leonard, Bart Markel, Fred Nix, Cal Rayborn, and the great Carroll Reseweber.

In 1954, the first year of the AMA point accrual system, H-D's Joe Leonard won the National Championship, with other Milwaukee riders placing behind him. Brad Andres was top man in 1955, with Leonard coming back to head the field in 1956 and 1957. From 1959 through 1961, the great Carroll Reseweber swept the board, and proved to be one of the greatest American riders of all time. A quiet, taciturn individual of unpretentious demeanor, Reseweber's special gift appeared to be not only his uncanny ability to fathom, but to predict ahead of time and execute the tactical maneuvers of competition riding with such finesse as to be almost unbeatable. Knowledgeable observers were quick to note his centaur-like oneness with his machine, as he swept through almost impassable crowds of riders with an agility that left crowds speechless. His best year was 1961, when he won nearly every contest entered. Added to this were the efforts of H-D's Competition Manager, Richard (Dick) O'Brien, who capably oversaw the vast logistical problems of fielding large numbers of riders.

Reseweber's luck and H-D's fabulous era ran out during the fall of 1962. At a practice period for an end-of-season race at Lincoln, Illinois, a very dusty improperly prepared track saw a pile up of riders that ran into an impenetrable cloud of powdered dirt. The debacle saw one rider killed, several seriously injured, and Reseweber, for a time at death's door, sent into a crippling retirement.

# Chapter 9

# A Time of Change

THE MOOD OF THE COUNTRY HAD CHANGED MARKEDLY SINCE THE END OF THE immediate post-war era. The thinking had been that with the war's end, conditions would revert to pre-war social and economic stability, now that the depression was safely passed. But such was not to be the case. The Korean episode was a stark reminder that the Cold War was indeed a reality. While the war had ostensibly been won, it was clear that peace had yet to be attained. What with the general disillusionment, the thinking trend was the preservation of the individual, and old values were abruptly challenged. Personal rebellion was the order of the day. In the search for individual truth, the Haight-Ashbury philosophy of doing ones own 'thing' emerged. With less emphasis on things orthodox, motorcycling as an often iconoclastic release grew in popularity.

By 1960 the motorcycle market had more or less stabilized, with Milwaukee adherents on one hand, and the devotees of British and continental machines on the other. The import dealers maintained a more or less informal coffee clatch club atmosphere, and low pressure selling was the rule where the average customer could be relied on to trade for a new model every other year or so. Harley-Davidson's dealership stood at an estimated 800 outlets, down from the 1,100 odd that serviced the industry when the country lived with but two makes. Assuming a certain hauteur, both the dealers and their customers in most cases withdrew from the other two-wheeled world where Milwaukee was god and H-D was its prophet. Even at this late date, H-D could still count on many middle aged enthusiasts whose experience dated back to the 'J' model days, as well as aging veterans of the belt drive days who would never heretically consider any but the Milwaukee brand. It was almost a cult-like atmosphere, but it was two-pronged. The 'dresser' clubman or Eastern and Midwest clubman were on the one side, and the 'chopper' enthusiast (the term now dignified by the appelation of 'custom') on the other. These were not necessarily outlaw by persuasion, but by those who aped the trend by affecting a cut-down machine, most usually an H-D big twin that sported bobbed mudguards, and without windshield, crash bars, saddle bags, or any other weighty appurtenances. There the matter stood, momentarily uncomplicated by the soon-to-appear invasion from the Orient.

The majority of the custom affectionados were not outlaws in the usual sense, or preoccupied by their unsavory depredations, but rather free thinking Bohemians clothed in leather and iron, who reveled in individualistic freedom and gloried in the macho image.

In spite of this growing trend, modified machines were still unwelcome in most franchised dealerships. Instead, their needs were met by the budding members of back alley mechanics for repair

In 1960, the 125cc 'Hummer' was updated into the 165cc 'Super Ten'.

or overhaul and the burgeoning custom accessory manufacturers who could by this time supply nearly everything needed to build up a modified H-D. The only factory items were engines and gearboxes — more often than not war surplus WLA units that were still available. In other cases the custom machines were built up from aged 61, 74 and 80 cubic inch units salvaged from some worn out or junked standard model. As a paradox, H-D cultivated and encouraged the loyalty of the one cult and ignored, if not discouraged, the preoccupation of the other.

As an aside, a minor but significant market in old model spare parts came into being, this for the benefit of over age or antique H-D's. In contrast to Indian, whose traditional policy had always been 'keep 'em on the road' — H-D's sales policy had always been to promote the new models at the expense of maintaining an older example. For this reason, the continued manufacture of current spare parts generally ceased with the termination of any particular model. With this knowledge in mind, many dealers and enthusiasts stock piled essential spares. This was especially true when the 'J' models were phased out in 1929. What with the initial disenchantment with the new 'VL', most of the existing stocks of 'J' parts at the factory were quickly sold to dealers. In addition, and in later years, small specialized firms and individuals began fabricating such hard-to-get items as primary and secondary chain cases, tool boxes, and other sheet metal items.

In the meantime, new converts to motorcycling were being attracted to the advanced designs of the 50 cc and 90 cc moped type machines soon traded up to larger displacement models. Honda was soon joined by Suzuki and Yamaha, who offered a line of small but high performance two-stroke models. This market was further expanded by the entrance of Bridgestone and Kawasaki. Honda next cannily capitalized on the growing interest in larger machines with the introduction of the high performance 250 cc Hawk, together with the 305 cc Dream model that was offered for the benefit of the tourist. Sales were enhanced not only by the high quality of these machines, but with their adoption of electric starting — a heretofore unheard of luxury in two wheelers. Another bonus was their general propensity to be oil tight, a condition generally not experienced with traditional American and British machines. A further telling factor was the reasonable price of the Japanese imports due to their low labor costs which augmented their ability to attain high volume production.

William J. Harley, Walter C. Davidson, and William H. Davidson inspect the first shipment of cycles from Aermacchi Harley-Davidson. The motorcycles are 1961 Sprints.

It was during this period that the use of plastics material in industry to replace certain metal fabrications of higher production cost came into being. In line with this trend, H-D acquired 60% of the stock of the nearby Tomahawk Boat Company, who were presently producing moulded plastics pleasure boats. Boat production continued, along with an augmented line of plastics bodies for the Servi-car, windshields, saddle bags, and other parts. Boat manufacture was carried on until 1965.

In addition, H-D expanded its activities in the manufacture of golf carts, both gasoline and electric powered. The former were fitted with the Dyna-start mechanism. A short time later a line of industrial carriers and in-plant trucks were added to the line. The bodies for these were moulded in plastics, being fabricated in the Tomahawk plant.

Three-wheeled golf carts and utility trucks, manufactured in the Tomahawk Plant. Most models offered the option of either gasoline or electric power.

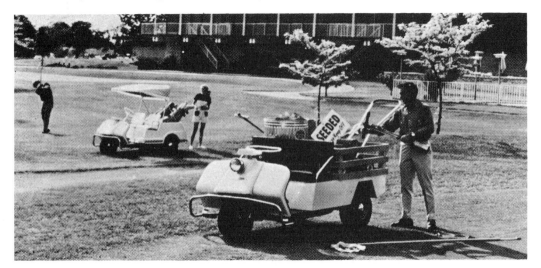

In the Spring of 1962, a new trade publication called *Cycle World* was launched by Joe Parkhurst, who was both its Publisher and Editor. Parkhurst's endeavor was orientated toward the offering of a more sophisticated journal than had heretofore been seen in the field. Featured were in-depth articles with technical aspects of motorcycle engineering. Also emphasized were searching evaluations of new models as they appeared, along with comprehensive road tests by members of the staff, who were experienced riders. Parkhurst's efforts were generally well received by both the trade and consumers, as his efforts were directed toward the interests of the latter.

An early road test featured the latest H-D 'FLH' model. While noting its generally high quality of manufacture, the tester commented on a number of minor faults, such as a certain heaviness in the gear shift mechanism, heavy steering at low speed, and its now inadequate braking capabilities.

An evaluation of the Sportster resulted in the report that its steering capabilities were somewhat vague when put into a tight turn. Other observations concerned hard starting and critical engine vibration at certain speeds.

In addition, Parkhurst commented editorially on the evergreen question of AMA policies. Taking a strong stand on its undemocratic structure and its long domination by Milwaukee, he called for at least better liaison between its trade management and the ordinary rider. He also commented on the often arbitrary stand taken by the Competition Committee in regard to their control of contestants.

Such frank revelations could scarcely endear Parkhurst to H-D's top management, and it was later alleged that the thinking in Milwaukee was that *Cycle World* was anti H-D. There were several subsequent icy confrontations between representatives of the two organizations when by chance they encountered each other at various trade shows. Parkhurst ultimately offered Milwaukee an olive branch in the Summer of 1964. In an editorial appearing in the July issue, he stated that the magazine and its management were definitely not anti-H-D, nor had it any axe to grind in regard to any make of machine. He restated the magazine's objective policy in regard to quality of product that the industry was producing, and that his main thrust was in promoting the best interests of both the sport and the industry.

Reportedly somewhat mollified, H-D continued to purchase limited advertising space in *Cycle World,* and ill will between the two subsided until a few years later when further controversies relating to AMA policies were aired in the magazine.

H-D volume of sales, as noted in Standard and Poor's Corporation Index reports, rose from $16,390,000 in 1958 to $30,560,000 in 1965. This was not a real increase however, when the ever-rising inflationary factor was taken into consideration, and profits during this period did not increase. As it was now estimated that H-D was currently enjoying but 6% of the retail market, its overall position was precarious at best. It was now painfully apparent that the Company had to review its marketing position, and in any case, required an infusion of new capital. It was accordingly decided that the Company now go public, and for the first time in its history its stock was offered for general sale. The exact details of what next transpired are somewhat clouded. While data regarding the matter was released to Standard & Poor, other individuals have rendered conflicting accounts of the matter.

The M-50 Sport.

William G.Davidson in 1969. He shortly afterwards abandoned the formal role as a Corporate Executive and took to the highways of America to personally contact motorcyclists of all persuasions.

According to the former, there were ultimately 1,780 shareholders. On the other hand, and in a rare interview granted to motorcycle journalist Tony Hogg by President William Davidson, the latter stated that there were but 300 shareholders. It is definitely known, however, that of the 53% of the voting shares outstanding, over fifty members of the Harley and Davidson family held this majority. These consisted of not only the direct heirs of the Founders, but also cousins and relatives by marriage, as well as the shareholding estates of deceased members.

A subsequent report of the matter from Standard & Poor, the originally offered 300,000 $20.00 par shares were converted to $5.00 par shares, raising the total to 1,200,000 shares. A group of Wall Street brokers headed by Robert W.Baird & Company, next offered 101,898 shares, 75,000 of which were new financing, priced at $14.75 per share on May 27 1965. The following year a new offering was placed on the market by the Baird group that consisted of 101,543 shares of which 85,000 were new financing, at $18.00 per share, the offering being advertised in the Wall Street Journal on April 4 1966.

In 1965, the 'FL' and 'FLH' Duo Glide models were fitted with electric starting, a somewhat belated gesture in competition with most of the Japanese models which had in some cases been so fitted since 1960. Many veteran enthusiasts at once decried this move as unnecessary, as what with refined field coil ignition systems, starting up the big twins had never been difficult if the correct drill was followed. A starting system from an outside supplier who also had recently developed a similar type for large outboard marine engines was adapted, the whole electrical system being converted to twelve volts. An embarrassing sequel to the introduction of this new model, now cataloged as the Electra Glide, was the fact that the starting system was susceptible to shorting out in wet weather. A new system hurriedly developed in conjunction with the Homelight Corporation resulted in a dependable unit. What with an added 75 pound weight penalty, the already heavy machine's braking capabilities were impaired, as the contact areas had not been increased in some years. To cope with this and the weight of the rear springing, the hp of the engine was increased from 52 to 65. Some riders claimed that the increase in power through modified cam action and increased compression ratios resulted in more severe vibration at certain speeds. Another problem was that the increase in power put undue stress on the main bearings, and it was reported that this traditionally trouble-free item of H-D design was now in some cases prone to failure. The problem was later remedied with the fitting of a larger diameter crank pin. A final difficulty was that the increased power put added stresses on the drive train, so that the standard pattern chain was sometimes subject to breakage. This matter was solved when the suppliers fabricated a heavier chain with larger rollers. In spite of these minor faults, the big twins continued to attract their usual quota of long time enthusiasts. The refined police models were still in strong demand, foreign machines up to this time having made but few inroads into H-D's long traditional market. What with rising prices, however, some government purchasing agents were now complaining that the motorcycles were costing substantially more than the heavy duty 'export' model sedans that for some years had been favorites for long distance highway patrol duties.

Somewhere in the Arizona desert. A relaxed tourist on an FLH slakes his thirst while under way. *(David Rose)*.

A serious problem was noted in handling and steering regarding the new Electra Glide models used by the California State Highway Patrol in the Spring of 1967. The State Highway Department had recently cut longitudinal rain grooves on many of the freeway routes on the theory that they aided in reducing the risk of skidding in wet weather. While this practice obviously did not affect the stability of cars, it was rightly hailed as a hazard to motorcyclists, as in some cases it caused the front wheel to oscillate. There were several serious crashes sustained by Patrol Officers taking part in high speed pursuits. It was ultimately ascertained that the oscillation of the front wheel combined with the lack of rigidity in the lower portion of the spring frame units caused a whipping effect that rendered the machines unmanageable at high speed. Factory representatives were hastily dispatched to California to seek a solution to the problem. In the meantime, a private owner, Johnny Eagles of Orange, a highly skilled mechanic and motorcycle engineer, already had an answer to the problem. He theorized that if gussets were welded horizontally along the lower ends of the standing part of the frame, the resultant increase in rigidity could eliminate the vibration. His suggestion was relayed to the factory by Santa Ana dealer Joe Walker, and subsequent models soon appeared with this modification, which cured the trouble.

To cater to the long-standing American interest in high powered motorcycles, a new challenge from Great Britain was forthcoming in the form of beefed up vertical twins. Matchless, Norton, BSA, and Triumph were now offering 650 cc and 750 cc versions of their classic 500 cc models. Offered as an alternative to H-D's growingly popular H-D 833 cc Sportster, they provided high performance at very competitive prices. In spite of the fact that these big machines often leaked oil, suffered from chronic clutch and gearbox problems, and featured tooth-loosening vibration, stalwart young speed enthusiasts bought them in large numbers. Some of these were soon appearing as much modified 'choppers'.

In spite of this competition, H-D carried bravely on. The Sportster was proving to be a popular seller among younger riders who preferred a more agile mount than the 'FL' and 'FLH' models, and were growingly providing a new outlet for customizing. Both the 'Muscle Bike' imports as well as the Sportster came under criticism for their uncertain steering on rough or winding roads, the straight-line point-to-point travel offered by the freeways appeared to obviate the real need for such niceties for the average American enthusiast. An important source of added cash flow to the Company were the golf carts and industrial trucks. The Tomahawk plant's production capacity was augmented for their accelerated assembly, with the aid of the additional capital secured from the stock sales.

In spite of the somewhat sober financial outlook, H-D continued to support a vigorous competition program under the continuing management of Dick O'Brien. Bart Markel followed the great Carroll Reseweber in 1962 to win the National Championship. Roger Reiman took the honors in 1964, with Markel to return as the victor in 1965 and 1966. Ralph White won the Daytona Classic in 1963, with Reiman, who had already taken top honors there in 1961, returning to win again for Milwaukee in 1964 and 1965.

In the meantime, interest in custom machines was growing. Weird and wonderful examples were by this time being featured at cycle shows, and many trade fairs were now featuring custom entries. A new magazine *Street Chopper,* catered for this growing interest, along with other occasional news stand publications of lesser magnitude. The once miniscule custom parts suppliers were now expanding their activities to more commanding proportions, and counterfeit H-D parts were being manufactured in larger quantities. While the retail cost of these were often inordinately high due to low production, bikers put off by the hostile attitude of many of H-D's franchised dealers toward their patronage in most cases overcame this cost differential.

The sedate Servi-car was now somewhat surprisingly coming to the attention of the customizers. A few of these three wheelers had lately come into use for hauling the beer and sleeping bags on group picnics and weekend outings. Iconoclastic designs were soon seen to be fitted in place of the usual box body, such as ornate rickshaw structures or even decorated outhouses.

Custom sidecar bodies also were receiving their fair share of attention. On more than one occasion, the author has noted burial caskets mounted on a more or less standard chassis, the leather and Levi-clad passenger ensconced within the tufted taffeta lining!

In tune with the times, Hollywood favored biker interest by producing motion pictures on this theme. Established stars such as Jack Nicholson, Peter Fonda, John Cassavetes, and Joe Namath were featured in a number of these productions which came to be known in the trade as 'Bikers'. Bona fide custom enthusiasts and biker club members usually were hired either as bit players or to fill in an authentic background.

All in all, the once strong cult-like fervor of H-D enthusiasts of other days was now part and parcel of the biker image. Often a source of embarrassment to both long established dealers and factory alike, H-D was by this time the basis for a custom-cult of its own.

The ultimate in dedication to Milwaukee. A pair of MMA members display their H-D tattoos. *(David Rose).*

In spite of added capitalization and an intensified advertising program, H-D's share of the growing motorcycle market remained more or less static. Top management's next decision was to attempt the sale of the Company to a strong conglomerate. With heavy resources of both capital and extensive advertising capacity, it was hoped that such a sale could infuse new life into the Company. Apparently at this point, H-D's top management was fearful of actual bankruptcy. The financial losses of such an eventuality were enormous, both to the proliferated H-D family group as well as the

The Jammers Company display a part of their ware in an advertisement in *Iron Horse* magazine.

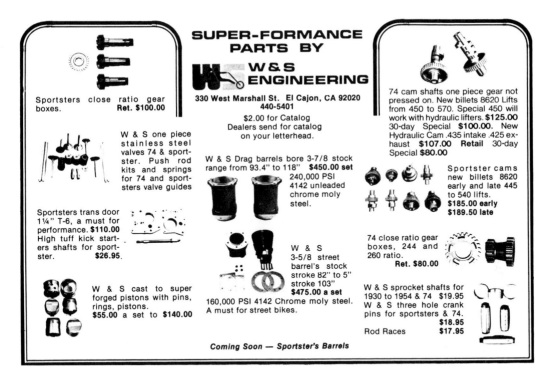

W & S Engineering offer custom-built Sportster parts in an advertisement in *Super Cycle*.

numerous stockholders, many of whom had ventured their life savings. Accordingly, in the Fall and Winter of 1967 and 1968, feelers were put out on Wall Street in an effort to entice firms dealing in registered stocks to consider what H-D liked to term a 'merger'.

It was shortly following these efforts that two giant conglomerates expressed interest through their top management in acquiring H-D. One of them was Bangor Punta, the other, the American Machine and Foundry Company. The adversary proceedings between these two concerns in the forthcoming battle over which of them was to purchase the assets of the venerable Milwaukee Company now forms one of the most complex financial stories ever to be noted in the domestic motorcycle industry.

The Bangor Punta concern, with headquarters at 405 Park Avenue in New York City, was originally known as the Punta Alegro up until 1960. It came into being shortly after WW I, the parent company being the Bangor and Aroostock Railroad, a feeder line which carried mostly farm produce from the interior of Maine. Its Directors acquired additional capital shortly thereafter, and amalgamated with the Punta Alegro organization that owned and operated sugar processing plants in Cuba. As time went on, its holdings were expanded to include leisure time products, such as pleasure boats, camping equipment, emblematic jewelry, fire arms, public security, energy systems, process engineering equipment, fashion fabrics, agribusiness and transportation, to name the most prominent. The total assets of B-P at that time totaled well over $267,000,000 according to reports of Standard & Poor and Moody's Corporation Indexes.

In an ongoing expansion, B-P acquired the Waukesha Engine Company of Milwaukee, a pioneer firm who manufactured gasoline and diesel engines for automotive and industrial uses. David W. Wallace, B-P President, and Nicholas M. Salgo, majority stockholder and Chairman of the Board of Directors, were reported as being most anxious to acquire H-D, not only for the motorcycles, but for the golf carts to augment their present line of leisure products. It was noted that the carts made up about 18% of H-D's current production.

At this point in time B-P already held 28,450 shares of H-D stock, recently purchased, it was reported, from groups of small private owners. It was also alleged that some of the shares had been purchased from dissident members of H-D families who were not interested in the motorcycle business, and wished to cash out their holdings as the Company was now in less than sound condition.

The American Machine and Foundry Company was formerly known as the American Car and Foundry Company, and had been organized in the earlier years of the century to manufacture railroad rolling stock, heavy machinery, and also owned a yacht building and marine engine business known as the New York Yacht, Launch, and Engine Company. In later years it gradually expanded its holdings to include companies building electrical products, bakery equipment, tobacco processing machinery, oil and gas products, and diversified industrial products, recreational products, such as bicycles, rubber goods and bowling products. Its total assets, noted at the time of its initial negotiations with H-D, amounted to $433,567,000.

Also incidental to the proposed sale of H-D's assets was the public declaration of its current financial condition, along with the names of its Board of Directors. This latter named William H.Davidson, President, Secretary-Treasury O.P.Resech, together with Board members A.H.Davidson, J.A.Davidson, R.J.Davidson, W.C.Davidson, W.H.Davidson, J.E.Harley, W.J.Harley, O.P.Resech, and A.W.Williams.

It was also revealed that during the past fiscal year, H-D had purchased from the Eck Foundries, Inc. of Milwaukee, $966,334 worth of raw materials, forgings and castings. An interesting revelation was that William H.Davidson, Walter C.Davidson, and Robert J.Davidson, were listed as Directors of the Eck Company, together with holdings owned by the estates of the deceased Arthur H. and Gordon M.Davidson. It was stated that the Davidson holdings amounted to 43% of Eck's outstanding stock. Some former H-D employees have alleged that at one time or another, the Davidsons actually owned a controlling interest in Eck, but in any case, their holdings gave them convenient control of a critical source of supply for H-D's manufacturing operation. Also significant was the fact that an Eck representative held a seat on the Board of Directors of the AMA.

Other facts revealed were that as of September 30th, 1968 H-D was represented by 650 retail dealers throughout the US and Canada, who were supervised by 23 factory supervisors. During the past five years, 80% of H-D sales were of the larger Sportster and FL-FLH models, an area where foreign competition was less effective. At that date, H-D had approximately 1,700 employees, the production force being represented by unions, the salaried managerial force being non-union. The Company's source of income was listed as the sales of domestically produced motorcycles, the sales of motorcycles imported from Harley-Davidson Aermacchi, the sales of golf carts and industrial trucks, and the profits from a finance organization and an insurance company operated for the benefit of both dealers and customers. A significant item also was that H-D's export sales, outside the US and Canada, now amounted to but 3% of the total production.

On the financial side, it was noted that on $43,000,000 worth of gross sales in 1968, the net profit after taxes was but $1,176,000. While H-D was still in the black, its profit margin was becoming dangerously thin.

AMF's interest in acquiring H-D was essentially that of B-P, namely to augment their respective lines of sporting and recreational equipment. AMF's position in the matter was strengthened by the

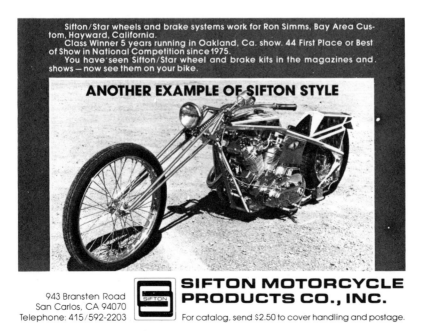

Tom Sifton, the Patriarch of H-D tuners, offers his wares in an advertisement in *Easy Rider.*

An original type of five-speed transmission adaptable to all 1936-1979 H-D big twins from Little John Ltd., of Denver, Colorado.

Chairman of its Board of Directors who was also President of the Company, Rodney C. Gott, who had not only been a motorcyclist but was an H-D enthusiast as well. AMF's offer was to purchase H-D on the basis of a merger, in which they not only would acquire the H-D families' controlling interest, but would give the balance of the stockholders one and one half shares of AMF common stock on a tax free exchange. According to information on the matter contained in their offer, AMF would retain the present H-D management, allow them to continue to control and supervise their dealerships, as well as allowing them to be responsible for the development of future models.

To advise both the H-D Company and its stockholders in the matter, H-D retained the Robert Baird organization, reportedly for a fee of $100,000. During the course of the negotiations, AMF's initial offer had been to offer 1.23 shares of their stock in trade, but in learning of B-P's accelerated purchase of H-D shares, they subsequently raised their offer.

It was then noted in various issues of the Wall Street Journal that B-P had acquired 28,450 shares of H-D stock in over-the-counter trading during the latter part of September, 1968, and on through November 8. The first 9,000 shares were pruchased at $25.00 each on September 20th. The following week its purchase of another 7,800 shares saw its price rise to $25.75. During the week ending October 18th, 10,000 more shares were pruchased at $29.75. On the week ending November 8, 850 additional shares were purchased at $30.00.

In the meantime, H-D's management had already informed its stockholders by letter that it favored the proposed merger with AMF. This communication stated that H-D's Board of Directors had already approved a 'letter of intent' to consumate a tax free merger with that Company. Despite this announcement, on October 31 B-P gave notice of a tender offer to acquire at least 150,000 shares of H-D stock at $40.00 per share, net to the sellers. On November 14th, B-P increased its offer to $42.50, and on November 19th withdrew the limitation on the number of shares it agreed to purchase and to acquire any and all shares tendered. The total value of all H-D shares held by B-P now stood at $770,950. B-P's strategy of course was to purchase as many shares as was possible in order to gain the voting rights.

In the meantime, H-D's management continued to communicate with the outstanding shareholders by means of form letters signed by William Davidson, urging that they consider accepting AMF's offer, and advising against dealing with B-P. The main consideration was, the letters stated, that the proposed merger with AMF would involve a tax-free exchange which would not be the case with B-P. What was not mentioned, but subsequently alleged, was that AMF's Rodney C. Gott had assured William Davidson personally that the former would retain the present company management intact and would allow H-D continuing control over their dealership. It was also alleged that if B-P got control of H-D, that it might well put it on the market for sale to others if a profit could be realized.

In rebuttal, B-P issued an open letter in the *Milwaukee Sentinal*, stating their own case in the matter, as H-D had refused to provide them with a list of H-D stockholders for direct communication. This statement, in the form of a full page advertisement, called attention to the fact that AMF had

## Phase 3 of America Belt Drives

Phase 3 and Uniroyal combine motorcycle and rubber technology for the finest belt drive available. The new high performance SUPER 8 belt is 60% stronger than previous timing belts. The pulleys are fully machined from billets (not castings) of high strength 6061-T6 aluminum alloy. A perfect mating is provided between the pulley and the belt. Engine shaft inserts are also precision machined from 4130 chromemoly — the ideal super combination for strength and light weight where it is most needed. The SUPER 8 is 60% lighter than the stock chain drive and will outlast a stock unit many times over.

**Super 8**

**74**

**Sportster**

STOCKING AUTHORIZED JAMMER DEALERS FOR YOUR AREA See Page (129)

In addition a SUPER 8:
- Needs no lubrication
- Reduces noise
- Eliminates drive train vibration by 75%
- Increases top speed
- Increases all around performance
- Provides a quicker horsepower transfer to the rear wheel
- Does not stretch due to wear
- Needs no break-in
- Bonneville and dragstrip proven

Only! $2.25 or You can now call toll free 1-800-423-2633 to order a catalog & get the name of your nearest Jammer dealer (See Order Blank on Page 129)

**JAMMER'S HANDBOOK**

**74 Belt Drive Open Primary.** This unit is designed with the stroker in mind. It has ample margin of safety for big inch "killer motors". It is an open unit — that is, it is not intended for an enclosed primary cover. Accessories to enhance the appearance and safety of this unit are also shown.

143060 '74 Belt Drive Open Primary. 1937-1954. 195.00
143061 '74 Belt Drive Open Primary. 1955-1978. 195.00

**74 Belt Drive Closed Primary.** This unit is designed for a closed installation. It will comfortably fit within all 74 primary covers, aluminum or steel. It too is amply strong to withstand the power of the big inch stroker motor.

143062 '74 Belt Drive Closed Primary. 1937-1954. 175.00
143063 '74 Belt Drive Closed Primary. 1955-1964. 175.00
143064 '74 Belt Drive Closed Primary. 1965-1978. 175.00

**74 Belt Drive — Electric Start.** An electric start application, this unit can be installed in either an open or closed unit. Design concessions permitting the installation, dictated the use of smaller pulleys. Although the gear ratio remains the same as the other units, this unit is not recommended for big inch motors due to higher pulley speeds; it is more than capable of handling 74 horsepower.

143065 '74 Belt Drive Closed Primary, Electric Start, 1965-1969. 200.00
143066 '74 Belt Drive Closed Primary, Electric Start, 1970-1978. 200.00

**Sportster Belt Drives** These units are designed to fit easil, within stock primary covers, aluminum or steel. They are capable of delivering high horsepower loads without fear of failure. Three models are available, differing only in clutch pulley configuration, depending on the model/year requirements. Electric-start units are available.

143067 Sportster Belt Drive. 1957-1968. 175.00
143068 Sportster Belt Drive. 1969-1970. 175.00
143069 Sportster Belt Drive. 1971-1976. 175.00
143070 Sportster Belt Drive. 1977-1978. 175.00
143071 Sportster Belt Drive. Electric Start. 1967-1970. 200.00
143072 Sportster Belt Drive. Electric Start. 1971-1976. 200.00
143073 Sportster Belt Drive. Electric Start. 1977-1978. 200.00

**Belts** The Super 8 belt wieghs only nine ounces, but it will outlast the primary chain for five times. Designed and engineered by Uniroyal. Fiberglass and steel cord reinforced.

143081 74 Belt, closed primary & electric start. 22.00
143082 74 Belt, open primary 22.00
143083 Sportster Belts, all models. 22.00

Jammers offer their own version of a custom primary belt drive in the advertising section of *Super Cycle*.

recently declared a loss of $12,547,000 applicable to its common stock through losses sustained incidental to their bowling equipment manufacture. This loss, according to B-P, amounted to 74 cents against each outstanding share, which H-D stockholders would have to assume.

Another allegation was that the $1.35 dividend on AMF shares was substantially less than the $1.80 dividend on the B-P stock which figured in the exchange.

B-P's statement furthermore called attention to the fact that the proposed AMF merger, the equity per share of H-D's stockholders would decrease from $23.03 to $14.13, a loss of 38%. On the other hand, if H-D merged with B-P, the per equity per share would increase 100%, or so they alleged.

Finally, H-D's retention of the Robert W.Baird group was challenged on the grounds that the latter was prejudiced in favor of H-D through their past dealings, together with the fact that they were scheduled to receive a $100,000 fee for their service.

The actual monetary value of B-P's offer would amount in the end to approximately $23,650,000.

According to notices mailed to stockholders, a meeting was scheduled for December 17 1968, at the Milwaukee Athletic Club, stating that the former would be urged to vote for the merger with AMF.

On December 16 B-P, through their legal counsel, filed suit in Superior Court against AMF and H-D, pleading that the two companies had not acted in the best interests of their stockholders in their proposed merger, and also cited that in their opinion, certain regulations of the US Securities and Exchange Commission had been violated.

The next round of this complex battle was that B-P filed notice that they would drop their lawsuit if AMF would increase their offer to H-D stockholders. Ultimately, the actual per share offer of AMF rose to about $42.00.

In the end, the H-D stockholders, both from management's urgings and an increase in their

Various types of custom frame offered by Jammers.

New stock custom-cast engine cases for H-D big twins offered by S.T.D. Engineering.

offer, caused the latter to accept AMF's bid, with but token opposition. While the whole affair had been responsible for much controversy and uncertainty among many of the stockholders, in the end it was actually of great benefit. In the bidding against each other, AMF and B-P had driven the value of the stock much higher than it would have been under more normal circumstances. The author has interviewed a number of one time shareholders such as present or retired dealers, as well as others outside the industry who in some cases held substantial blocks of shares. As many of them had originally purchased them at $6.00 or $7.00 per share, the ultimate increase to $43.00 had enabled them to profit handsomely.

The course of the proceedings was widely reported in such leading financial papers as the *Wall Street Journal* and *Barron's*, as well as enjoying exhaustive coverage in the local Milwaukee press. Other leading newspapers such as the *New York Times* and the *Los Angeles Times* also featured comprehensive coverage. The events were widely followed by interested motorcyclists, as this was the first time in Company history that any financial details of H-D's transactions had ever been aired. It was ultimately noted that AMF exchanged 877,671 shares of its common stock, valued at approximately $21,650,000 for all of the assets of H-D.

AMF formally took over the H-D Company in January, 1969. As anticipated, there were no substantial changes in the managerial staff. William H.Davidson remained in office as President, and the present Board of Directors all retained their position. William J.Harley, Vice President in charge of Engineering, John Harley, Parts and Accessories Manager, O.P.Resech, Secretary-Treasurer, carried on as before. The third generation Davidsons were represented by William H's two sons, John A. and William G., the latter in the Design Department. Vice President in charge of Sales, Walter G.Davidson, resigned shortly to pursue other business interests outside the Company.

AMF at once launched an intensive advertising campaign, stressing their line of leisure time products, with H-D prominently featured. A sales blitz in the Pacific Northwest on behalf of their snow-mobiles, ran into difficulties however. The firms of Moore and Pierre, Inc., Kellogg Sales and Service, Inc., and Joe's Snowmobiles, all of Spokane, Washington, filed suit in Federal District Court in Spokane against AMF and H-D as a subsidary. Asking $35,000,000 in damages, the plaintiffs charged that AMF had breached their franchise agreements and monopolized the sale and distribution of AMF products by setting up competing outlets within the plaintiff's areas of trade. The matter was settled through negotiations between the opposing counsels before the matter came to trial.

At the annual meeting of the Board of Directors of AMA held in Anaheim, California, during the month of February, William M.(Bill) Bagnall, editor and publisher of the *Motorcyclist* was elected President, succeeding William E.Kennedy, a sales executive of the Rex Chain Belt Company of Milwaukee who had held the office since 1965.

In a self-congratulatory editorial announcing the event, Bagnall pledged that he would exert his best effort for the best interests of both the AMA and for motorcycling. In recounting the names of his predecessors, he concurred in the traditional H-D mandate in omitting the name of the AMA's first president, one-time Indian dealer, Douglas Hobart.

And so it was that H-D, sixty eight years after the first prototype motorcycle built by its two founders, saw the light of day, now joined the ranks of the many family-owned business concerns that were lately merging with vast conglomerates.

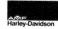
An official warning from AMF H-D in a current accessory catalog against the use of non-factory replacement parts.

The 'Topper' scooter, marketed briefly after 1960. It was fitted with the 165cc engine and a centrifical clutch.

The 'Super Ten' as the 'Ranger', an off-the-road machine without lighting. First produced in 1962.

The M-50 Moped.     227

William Hoecker's 1965 175 cc 'Bobcat'. This is typical of the other two-stroke Pacer and Scat models. *(Alisha Tamburri)*.

Mark King's beautifully restored 1969 883 cc Sportster. *(Alisha Tamburri)*.

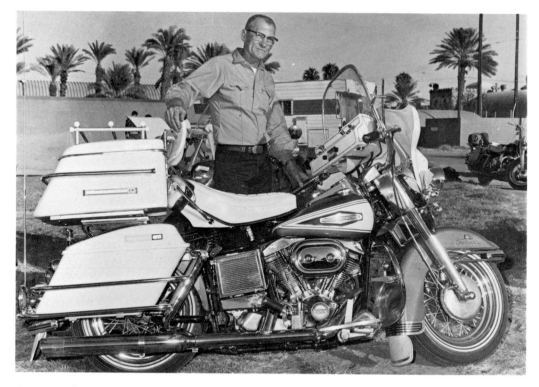

A super Full Dress touring FLH. *(George Hays).*

Stuntman 'Slide' Sommers puts his 1971 1,000 cc Sportster through its paces. *(George Hays).*

The great Cal Rayborn caught by the cameraman in a split-second manoever. *(H-D Motor Company)*.

Coming out of the north turn. A typical dirt track race somewhere in Middle America.

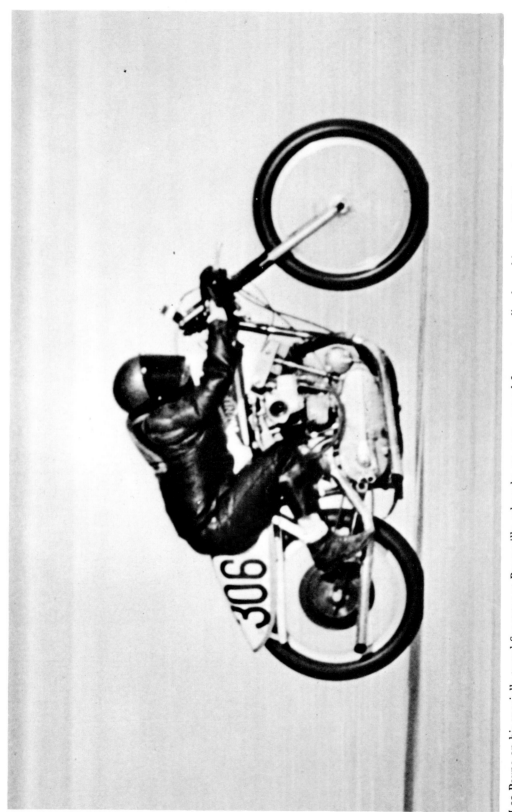

Leo Payne on his specially-tuned Sportster at Bonneville, where he set a new record for unstreamlined machines at 182.89 mph.

William Herbert Davidson,
the second Chief Executive
of H-D. He served from
1942 through 1973, when
he retired.

William J.Harley shortly before his death in 1971.

William G.Davidson as a youthful enduro
contestant in 1962.

233

The XR-750, officially launched in the Spring of 1970. It is offered in both road racing or dirt track models with options as to suspension systems and gear ratios. It is a formidable contender on the dirt track at this writing.

The Dirt Track version of the XR-750. *(AMF-Harley Davidson).*

The extended fork syndrome. A group of customized H-Ds sporting varying styles of front suspension, as seen at the Visalia CAMA Rally in 1972. *(George Hays).*

A group of MMA club
members at their
annual Santa Claus
Rally, Christmas,
1972. *(David Rose)*.

MMA Club members
on their much
modified H-Ds. *(David
Rose)*.

A group of MMA
members display their
diverse ideas on
customizing along
Santa Monica
Boulevard.

235

A futuristic power rickshaw based on the Model G Servi-car. *(George Hays).*

A Servi-car much modified and fitted with a large V-8 car engine. *(David Rose).*

# Chapter 10

# A New Era

THE FIRST ACT OF H-D'S TOP MANAGEMENT FOLLOWING THE AMF TAKEOVER WAS to assure both dealers and owners that all present Company personnel were to remain, and that traditional H-D policies would be carried on as usual. It was emphasized that with an infusion of fresh capital, H-D's line of products would shortly be expanded. It was also pointed out that an updated advertising and marketing campaign would soon be forthcoming from AMF's vast expertise.

This reassurance was to allay the fears of many enthusiasts that motorcycle production might be suspended in favor of other products. At the same time, the output of the gasoline and electric golf carts and three-wheeled industrial trucks were expanded to enhance the AMF's position in the leisure time field.

While these pronouncements had a calming effect outside the factory, the situation in some cases was less than happy within it. It is reported that many of the Company's large group of veteran employees not only resented the change, but took exception to a group of AMF liaison people who were now ensconced in the factory. Some veteran dealers have reported that, in their opinion, this resentment in some cases resulted in downright sabotage efforts on the part of certain of the production staff. It was noted that on occasion new machines received had been obviously maladjusted, or had certain vital parts missing. Following various reports on these incidents, the factory immediately instituted a tightened quality control, both on final assembly and inspection of finished machines, and the difficulty was soon overcome.

H-D's competition program was carried on uninterruptedly during the merger negotiations. The inimitable Cal Rayborn took the checkered flag at Daytona in 1968, the first rider to top the magic century mark at 101.29 mph average, his KR running faultlessly the whole distance. Roger Reiman's KR broke the AMA Time Trial record in a contest held at the same meet at an incredible 149.08 mph. This remarkable speed was notable for its being attained with an engine type that differed but little in principle from the 1916 example of side valve design first introduced by Indian's Charles B.Franklin.

1968 was a banner year for H-D's modern Wrecking Crew. Of a total of twenty three Nationals entered, H-D took eighteen first places. Cal Rayborn went on after his Daytona victory to seven straight wins on the National circuit.

In spite of the success of the much redesigned racing K, which had formed the backbone of H-D's competition efforts since the mid-1950's, it was now obvious that its days were numbered. Modern highly sophisticated designs from the Orient were already making their appearance in competition, and the Engineering Department rightly concluded that it had already wrung the last possible horsepower out of a long ancient design.

The overall design of the new racer, provisionally designated as the XR-750, closely followed that of the last K's in having the double loop frame that had been adapted in 1967. The rear swinging arm was secured against lateral movement by a pair of massive pre-loaded Timken bearings. Ceriani forks and Girling dampened rear units took care of the suspension. In a break with tradition, the 45 cubic inch engine was fitted with overhead valves, and in essence was a sleeved-down 833 cc Sportster unit. This design featured a bore/stroke ratio of 3.005 x 3.291 inch, with high domed pistons and large valves. With a cam action that emphasized long duration with moderate ramp action, a rather broad power band between 4800-7800 rpm was attained. The maximum torque output at 6200 rpm showed 62 hp.

Anticipating the time required to build and test the new machine, H-D petitioned the AMA Competition Committee in October 1969, to sanction a new Class C design that featured ohv. That Milwaukee dominated body at once complied, but stipulated that at least 200 examples be produced before a final clearance could be granted. H-D at once protested this ruling, as the production department did not consider enough models could be assembled before the opening of the 1970 season. The Committee was adamant, however, as the 200 unit mandate had long been previously employed to keep the more exotic foreign models out of US competition. It was thought that if an exception was now made in favor of H-D, who had instigated the original ruling in the first place, additional ill feeling would be heightened within an already somewhat tense situation.

The new model was first exposed to public view at a trade show held in early Spring of 1970, held in conjunction with a meet at the Astrodome. Prototype tests had already been conducted the preceding January at Daytona by both Cal Rayborn and Roger Reiman. Both reported that the XR handled as well, if not better, than the last KR models.

In the Fall of 1969, a new television series gave a sympathetic treatment to the sport of motorcycling in general, and H-D in particular with the showing of 'Along Came Bronson'. Initially a two-hour motion picture starring Michael Parks and Bonnie Bedelia, it was subsequently made into a series production. The theme was that of a knight-errant rider who traveled the California coast, and his interaction with various people met along the way. An MGM-TV Production produced by Robert

The 1978 XLCR-1000 Cafe Racer. *(AMF-Harley-Davidson).*

The 1979 FXE 1200 Super Glide. *(AMF-Harley-Davidson)*.

H.Justman and Robert Sabaroff, in association with NBC Television in New York, it featured exceptional cinematography by the late Ray Flin.

The actual logistics of the feature were under the direction of the one time noted desert Enduro rider, Bud Ekins, who built a special sidecar outfit with a seat over the front wheel to facilitate closeup shots of the motorcyclists involved. Parks, as the leading man, rode a new Sportster which, along with the other machines involved in various episodes, were maintained by Ekins. The latter for some years, has been supplying motorcycles and riders as well as stunt men for various Hollywood productions.

In 1969, a new Sprint model was forthcoming from Aermacchi with an improved 350 cc engine. The first 250 cc Sprint model introduced in 1961 had evoked only mild interest, for reasons already mentioned. Some favorable publicity regarding it had been forthcoming in 1965, when a torpedo type streamliner powered with a tuned engine and piloted by George Roeder attained a speed of 177.22 mph on the Bonneville Salt Flats. Sprint fans noted that the enlarged engine gave better all around performance, especially in hill climbing. It also benefitted from recent technology incorporated into its design as the result of Aermacchi's active competition program in Europe. It was offered in both Sports and Street Scrambler versions.

During the late 1960's the growing conflict between riders with an interest in road racing and the Competition Committee of the AMA came to a head. The controversy had centered around the participation of AMA-licensed contestants in events that were not officially sanctioned by the AMA. This type of competition had long been an anathema to the latter body, as neither H-D or Indian had ever produced machines that were well suited to other than horse track competition. In fact, such events had been actively discouraged ever since the mid-1930's when a few foreign machines with a race-bred background, such as Norton, made a few successful appearances on the American sporting scene.

In the post-war years, however, with the increasing number of foreign machines, riders of such, by sheer weight of numbers, had instigated a series of road racing events which were, of course, not AMA sanctioned and were at once classed as 'outlaw' by that body.

In defense of their interest, several small groups of road racing enthusiasts organized their associations, the more prominent being Motorcycle Racers Incorporated (MRI) and the American Association of Motorcycle Road Racers (AAMRR). Matters came to a head when two well-known riders ran afoul of the AMA Competition Committee. Dick Mann, who currently held the number two position in the Nationals, competed in a road race at Pepperwell, Massachusetts, and was promptly

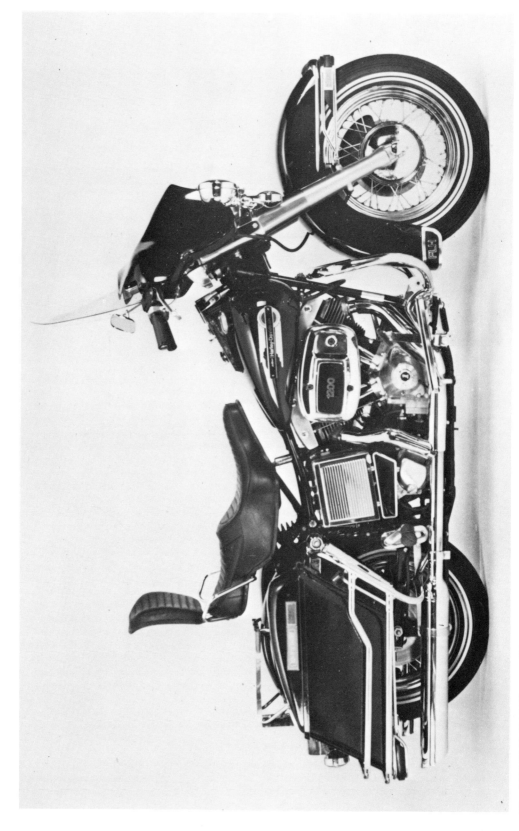

The 1979 FLH 1200 Electra Glide. (*AMF-Harley-Davidson*)

The 1979 FLH with optional frame-mounted seat. *(AMF-Harley-Davidson).*

suspended by the AMA for competing in an unsanctioned event. Privateer Gordon Jennings, a motor-cycle journalist as well as being a competitor of note, entered a road race at Indianapolis, with the same result. Both protested that no AMA sanctioned races were being held during the weekend of their alleged transgressions, and both pointed out that they had been loyal supporters of the AMA for some years previously. During the well publicized discussions of the matter between various prominent competition riders, as well as trade representatives, much of it in *Cycle World,* many agreed that the AMA was acting in a most arbitrary manner in branding as 'outlaw' a segment of the sport which was by this time attracting increasing interest among motorcyclists as well as spectators. As a result, many people within both the sport and the trade became very bitter against the AMA generally.

The matter was exhaustively discussed in *Cycle World* by Assistant Editor Ivan J. Wagar. He pointed out that if the AMA could not see its way clear to sanction types of competition events that catered to broader public interests, it was then logical that other organizations would come into being that could provide them. He mentioned that for too long the AMA had existed as a small private club, dominated by H-D and a small circle of their satellite suppliers. He further questioned the long standing head-in-the-sand attitude of the AMA in neglecting the best interest of riders in general. He also pointed out that it was a real economic necessity that professional riders be allowed to compete in indoor short track races that were currently being held during the winter season when sanctioned AMA events were not forthcoming. The public airing of the matter was later to have much bearing on the coming reorganization of the AMA hierarchy.

In the Fall of 1970, H-D introduced a new model based on the classic FL that both startled the club type 'dresser' rider and delighted the ever growing number of custom enthusiasts. Cataloged as the 'Super Glide', the new machine was basically a stripped 'FL', without electric starting, was fitted with Ceriani-type forks, foot pegs in place of foot boards, and was most definitely not intended for a windshield, saddle bags, a myriad of spotlights, or any of the other excrescences that had long been traditional for the Yankee big twin rider.

Some factory personnel have reported that its creator, William G. Davidson, the elder son of President William H., now in the Company's Design Department, had been working out its details in various prototypes ever since 1967. It was also reported that he was an early advocate of the introduction of a new type of machine that would have an appeal to the sports-hobbyist market. As a friendly and gregarious individual combining an artistic flair with a strong background in engineering, William G. shortly, as we shall see, turned H-D products from its long antecedents of being rooted to formal traditions. A college graduate with an engineering degree, his main interest has been in creative design. For some years after graduation he had been associated with the noted Brook Stevens, and after joining the Company, set about the updating of H-D's traditional styling. Adopting the appelation 'Willie G.' to distinguish himself from his grandfather, William A. and his father, he was soon to put aside the sartorial splendor of the traditional conservative executive. Donning the leather and Levis of the biker, he was to now sally forth on the highways and beer bars to mingle freely with the riders of the custom-chopper cult. It is reported that marketing personnel within the AMF liaison group encouraged Willie G. in his endeavor. It was now quite obvious that H-D's former austere detachment from the desires of a large segment of their enthusiasts had not only lost sales, but had driven them to trade with the custom equipment manufacturers whose sales volume was now measured by millions.

AMF-H-D expanded their advertising activities, and in slick Madison Avenue style, couched its appeal in new generation language. A new identifying logo was adopted: a broad ribboned number '1', which carried a simulation of an American flag, together with the slogan 'The All-American Freedom Machine'. The '1' no doubt was meant to refer to H-D's recent victories in the big Nationals, with the emphasis that H-D was an all-American product. The term 'freedom' was an apt reference to the freedom of self-expression that motorcycling can provide.

The Harley and Davidson families and dealers and enthusiasts everywhere were saddened by the news on August 23 1971, that William J. Harley had died in his 59th year. He had been reported as having been in ill health for some months previously, a condition, according to some allegations by Company associates, that was aggravated by his excessive consumption of alcohol. As the son of the real father of H-D, he had literally grown up in the Juneau Avenue factory. Starting at the bottom in the Shipping Department at the behest of his father, who saw to it that he learned every phase of H-D production, he was by 1957, a Vice President and head of the Engineering Department. Not the least of his practical education, in addition to his college degree, was the ongoing tutelage from his father and others on the staff such as William Ottaway and Hank Syvertson who had enjoyed years of practical experience in both theory as well as trial and error.

Harley is described as being cautious and conservative in his outlook on engineering matters, innovations being introduced only after prolonged and careful analysis. His first original design was his adaptation of the well proved German DKW 125 cc engine-gear unit to produce the first ever H-D lightweight — the 125 Hummer. This was later modified to evolve the 165 cc Teleglide and later

Pacer, Scat, and Bobcat models. His most noted design was, of course, the Model K Sportster. As a rather curious mixture of traditional and modern that was greeted with mixed emotions by H-D enthusiasts, it was later to become, with modern refinements, one of the most popular on-going models the Company ever produced. A lifelong motorcycle enthusiast, Harley grew up in the 'J' and 'Peashooter' eras, and as a young man conducted much of the road testing and practical evealuation of the 61E and continuing 'EL' series.

In later years he was President and a Director of the Aermacchi operation after its management was reorganized following its acquisition by H-D. He was also the Chairman of H-D's Swiss international marketing affiliate. The President of Italy presented him with the Order of Merit, an honor historically accorded to Nationals of foreign countries who contributed to Italy's economic and social betterment. In addition, he had served the usual tours of duty by the H-D family members as a Director of the AMA and the M & ATA.

In projecting production for a hoped-for enhanced sales volume, AMF-H-D's top management decided to move the main assembly procedures from Milwaukee to York, Pennsylvania. It was decided that the now antiquated multi-story Juneau Avenue complex with its somewht haphazard production facilities could not be economicially converted to modern computerized production methods.

The York facility is a single story 800,000 square foot building that was built during World War II as a defense plant. It was acquired by AMF in 1964, and converted for the manufacture of certain of the Company's leisure time products. In adapting it to motorcycle manufacture, a 1,000 foot main assembly line was laid out, with component part assemblies feeding into it at appropriate intervals.

It was decided to retain the Milwaukee plant to manufacture engine and transmission assemblies. These are completed to the testing stage and then shipped to York where the balance of the motorcycle components are made. The Juneau Avenue plant was then closed to the public, guided tours no longer being featured, and the famous museum was placed in storage.

Situated in a park-like setting in scenic rural Pennsylvania, its surrounding 232 acres are a part of its rolling hills and wooded streams. A substantial adjacent labor pool from the former AMF operation formed the nucleus of the present production staff. It is also suggested that there is in York a more harmonious labor situation as the area is not as heavily unionized as is the case in Milwaukee. In 1979, it was reported that the average wage paid to general production personnel was $6.00 per hour.

A noted feature of the present operation is the simulated road test of completed machines. This is an indoor operation with the machine being clamped over a set of movable rollers. A series of some twenty-eight tests including braking, acceleration, accessory functions, and engine performance at various speeds.

Guided tours for the benefit of the general public are conducted twice daily. Attendants inform the visitors that present production averages 300 machines per day, one new model coming off the line every nineteen minutes. The Publicity Department recently announced that yearly production is presently 50,000 units per year, the Company shipping only on firm dealer orders. This revelation is a far cry from the earlier days of the American industry when actual production was a carefully guarded secret.

Shortly after the AMF takeover, President Rodney C.Gott retired as Company President. Since that time, he has taken a personal interest in the H-D museum, which has moved from Milwaukee and now occupies a separate portion of the York plant. Featured are not only the treasured collection of past models, but exhibits of new machines and cutaway part models are on display. The new Exhibit is now appropriately named the Rodney C.Gott Museum. Custom enthusiasts complain, however, that no examples of this type are currently displayed.

Shortly after the inauguration of the expanded production facilities, the Company announced the offering of the most comprehensive line of models in H-D's history. Five two-stroke models from Aermacchi added a welcome dimension to market penetration. The X-90 was a portable small-wheeled minibike weighing but 126 pounds, equipped with lighting to make it street legal. The Z-90 was fitted with the same engine-gearbox unit and was of the street scrambler type. The SR-100 was a high clearance motocross model with long travel suspension and a specially tuned 100 cc engine. To enhance its rather narrow power band, it was fitted with a five-speed gearbox. The largest model was the TX-125, a street scrambler with a slightly enlarged 'SR' type engine. These two models were subsequently refined and carried forward as the Baja and Rapido, respectively, and for their size exhibited an amazing power output.

Two updated 350 cc Sprint models filled the middleweight category. The SX-350 was a trials machine with knobby tires and a new five-speed transmission The SS-350 was similar, except that it was fitted as a street machine. A heavier frame with twin down tubes steadied the steering, in answer to reports that the frames of earlier models were prone to flexing.

The Sportster was entirely redesigned, with a longer, taller, and heavier frame which now accommodated a new engine that was of 61 cubic inches. It was offered in two models, the XLCH-1000    243 being a sports type, the XL-1000 a touring model with electric starting. The former versions had been alluded to in review and test descriptions as being somewhat indeterminate; as if the designers were not sure whether the Sportsters were a scaled-down FL or a sports model in their own right. The new models were now most definitely not orientated toward the 'dresser' category. The fitting of an electric starter to the XL model countered objections in some quarters that the machines could be hard starters.

The classic FL models featured an improved oiling system and hydraulic brake controls which somewhat enhanced their recent lack of stopping power. A couple of seasons later, disc brakes were added, which did much to modernize this now ancient design. Detail updating of trim and color motifs were executed by Willie G.. Featured were new plastic windshield fairings and streamlined luggage carriers catering to the interest of the tourist — the FL's traditional customer.

The XR-750 racer was offered as two distinct models. One was a dirt track machine, with a choice of gear ratios and suspension systems to suit the individual rider. The other was a road racer, with an enveloping forward fairing and a streamlined tail section. It was advertised as being capable of 160 mph with an improved aluminum engine.

The Super Glide as a stripped down FL was fitted with Ceriani pattern forks of the Sportster, and was designated as the FX-1200, the forerunner of a coming line of X models. As road tested by *Cycle World,* it was noted that it exhibited all of the long familiar FL running characteristics as a somewhat heavy steering ponderous machine with the usual 'clunk' shifting gearbox. The tester noted that the big slow turning engine gave the traditional high torque urge at moderate rpm for a comfortable cruising speed of 70 mph without excessive vibration. A surprising 47 mph fuel consumption at moderate speeds was also claimed. Noting its design concession to the now familiar custom chopper type, the FX was hailed as heralding a new era in contrast to the historic conservative H-D tradition, and was characterized as an 'institutionalized chopper'. A subsequent option in later models was an electric starter, which caused some raised eyebrows among custom enthusiasts as somewhat denegrating its macho image.

Along with the introduction of the new model, the custom accessory businesses that continued to cumulatively offer the possibilities of the individual building a complete machine continued to flourish. This condition was now mandatory, due to the growing scarcity of old H-D's that could be converted.

The 1979 XLH 1000 Hugger. *(AMF-Harley-Davidson).*

A new trend in customizing was the emergence in the late 1960's and early 1970's of the extended fork. Some unknown experimenter extended the fork legs to produce a somewhat reared back and rakish appearance. As subsequent enthusiasts began outdoing each other in raising the front end, the next step was to increase the rake of the head lug. This not only allowed the fitting of even more extended forks, but became mandatory to maintain a semblance of stability. In the beginning of this trend, a rake of about 45% was established at the expense and complication of altering the standard frame. The custom manufacturers almost immediately entered the field with special frames, mostly of the rigid type with the rake already built in, and often with the option of several lug angles. The earliest extended forks were usually pre-1948 girder types that had been extended by welding in additional tubing. The custom manufacturers designed their own types as original fabrications of various lengths and patterns. Some were based on the original H-D design; others were based on the British girder models with single compression springs. In most cases special front wheels were required. These were usually of 21 inch diameter with 3 inch section tires. Most were fitted with brakes to make them street legal, some being of the internal expanding type inside the hub.

The extended fork posed problems in steering and handling, and were often downright hazardous when negotiating tight turns. As the chopper was generally a straight line freeway machine, such was not too critical if the rider came to a near shut down when rounding a curve or turning into a right angle turn.

Willie G.'s subsequent custom-based models featured extended forks, but without the extreme rake or length as the early originals. Most of the current sports types have a 33% to 35% rake. With careful balancing, stability and cornering appears satisfactory.

A significant event in H-D history occurred in 1973, when President William H. Davidson announced that he would retire from active service on September 30th. With his retirement, he rang down a curtain of some forty five years of continuous participation in company affairs. Officially joining the Company in 1928, he became a member of the Board of Directors in 1931. He was also elected Vice-President in 1937, following the death of his father, William A., in 1937. With the death of his uncle, Walter C., in 1942, he became President. With a lifelong dedication to H-D's cause he was also an enthusiastic motorcyclist. He won the 1930 Jack Pine Enduro, a very tough course laid out in a primitive area in northern Michigan. In his elevation to the ultimate position of Company leadership, he was considered well qualified through both education and experience. It is also suggested that his

The 1980 FXEF 80 Fatbob Super Glide. *(AMF-Harley-Davidson)*.

position within the managerial hierarchy was much strengthened by the fact that through inheritance from his father he controlled the largest individual block of Company stock.

In addition to his substantial H-D share holdings, he was also involved in a number of outside business interests. Among these were his interests in the Seventh District Federal Reserve Bank in Chicago, and the Eck Foundry in Milwaukee. He was also active in civic affairs, such as the United Fund, and was also appointed as a member of the Economic Development Division of the State of Wisconsin. Also long active in Boy Scout work, he was awarded membership in the order of the Silver Beaver for his volunteer work in that organization.

A man of sophistication and refinement, he was more suave and diplomatic as President than his more bombastic uncle. Yet he could be forceful and adamant if occasion required. Following his retirement, he was reported to have incorporated a substantial portion of his holdings into the Harley-Davidson Foundation, the usual income tax saving ploy of large corporate holders.

In later years he was known to have relented in the somewhat restrained reserve that H-D always exhibited toward the trade press, and granted several personal interviews. In the ever controversial question regarding H-D's historic domination of the AMA, Davidson stated quite frankly that that body could never have survived its 1925 financial crisis had not the Company elected to underwrite its financial requirements. In the matter of the long time preoccupation of the AMA toward the 45 cubic inch side valve engine, he also stated that it was the only machine for many years available for competition. Had the AMA not emphasized such a readily available stock model as the basis for a competition machine, then any sort of motorcycle competition during the lean years of the late 1920's and early 1930's would have been non-existent. As far as the restrictive rule on the compression ratio maximum enforced on the 500 cc ohv imported machines that caused so much controversy after WW II, Davidson was reported as stating that the AMA did not think it was obligated to completely obliterate all chances of the domestic products competing against imported machines.

As an interesting aside to these comments, Davidson's sentiments in the matter were echoed from a rather surprising source. In 1948, Steve Lancefield, the noted British speed tuner, stated in an

The 1980 XLH 1000 Sportster. *(AMF-Harley-Davidson)*.

The 1980 FXE 1200 Super Glide. *(AMF-Harley-Davidson).*

interview published in *Motor Cycle* that in his opinion the AMA rules were equitable to the point that British machines, even though of differing design, had a fair chance to compete. He further stated that while the AMA was protecting its own side valve machines, the British had been protecting their own type of machine by banning the fitting of superchargers and the use of special fuels. This restrictive attitude was placed in force after Georg Meier had won the Isle of Man TT with a supercharged BMW.

Shortly after assuming office, President Willie G. faced H-D's problem of increasing competition from the Japanese manufacturers. At this point they were seriously challenging the FL models in both the touring and law enforcement fields with large high powered machines whose sophisticated design and high performance capabilities far overshadowed the venerable American classic. What with high volume production and low cost labor, their selling prices were far and away lower. In the matter of law enforcement, the FL Police model had for nearly four decades been the unchallenged choice for this work throughout the United States and even foreign countries, in spite of the Oriental advances in later years. Then there was the matter of the restrictive purchasing specification ordinances that had been built into many municipal charters. What with the development of special police machines by Honda and Kawasaki that could be sold for less than half the cost of the FL, it was inevitable that many government bodies simply repealed these restrictions and purchased whole fleets of Oriental machines. An official in the Purchasing Department of the California State Highway Patrol was coincidentally noted as saying that with ever-growing inflation, the Department could now buy two Police Model Dodge Polaras for the price of one H-D!

In the face of this trend, it was most fortunate that at long last H-D had turned to the custom-type machines. Sales of the Super Glide and Sportster boomed, as many long suffering devotees of the custom-chopper cult who could not afford the cash price of buying all the component parts of such a machine through the accessory outlets could now seek an H-D outlet that could sell such a machine new on time payments.

In the Fall of 1973, the governing body of the AMA was reorganized. The change had been gradual over the preceding two or three years, mostly through the pressure of splinter groups of

The 1980 FLH Classic with sidecar. *(AMF-Harley-Davidson).*

The 1980 FXS 80 Low Rider. *(AMF-Harley-Davidson).*

competition riders who rebelled against the arbitrary AMA Competition Committee's ruling concerning events of public interest which they refused to sanction. As spectator interest in road racing was growing, pressure for the recognition of such was also growing from within the trade itself. California's District 37, one of the most active groups in the country, was threatening to secede from the AMA, as were a number of New England Clubs. Splinter organizations of professional riders were already promoting races for the benefit of former AMA licensed riders who had lost interest from traditional horse track competition.

The AMA Executive Committee was now expanded from eight to ten members, bringing in some new blood. The next step was to vote the AMA as an FIM affiliate, which would now allow certain US race meets to count on points for the International Championships. Formula 750 events held in the US could now also be a part of the FIM calendar. After some prolonged negotiations, the AMA's petition to the FIM was accepted, and the International Six Days Trial was next scheduled to be held in the New England, Berkshire. This was a notable step in international motorcycle competition relations, and marked the first time since 1923 that American motorcycling had returned to the fold of the international body.

In commenting on the reorganization of the AMA in an editorial in the November 1973 issue of *Cycle World,* Associate Editor Ivan J.Wagar, long a crusader for a modernized AMA, stated that at long last the latter was no longer a private club dominated by H-D and a small clique of their suppliers, but was now more truly representative of a broad spectrum of both trade and rider interest.

The number of AMA Executive Board members was increased from eight to ten and later twelve members. Its makeup now included representatives from *Cycle World* and *Cycle Sport* magazines, as well as from Kawasaki, Suzuki, and Yamaha. New trade suppliers once excluded from the AMA Board were now included. The incoming President, J.R.Kelley, head of KK Motorcycle Supply, who now succeeded William Bagnall, pledged that the new AMA would henceforth attempt to serve the interests of all people interested in motorcycling, whether trade, competition riders, or more casual private owners.

In a succeeding editorial in *Cycle World,* Ivan Wagar complimented the H-D contingent for gracefully relinquishing their former majority positions on the AMA Board in order that the AMA could now proceed in a more democratic manner. He noted that John Davidson retained his seat as the H-D representative, and that John Harley agreed to retain his position s AMA Secretary. He further

The 1980 FXWG Wide Glide. *(AMF-Harley-Davidson).*

The 1980 FLT Tour Glide. (*AMF-Harley-Davidson*).

mentioned that the new Board harbored no ill will toward long time AMA Competition officials such as Aub Le Bard, Pete Coleman, Walt Fulton, or Earl Flanders, and that their many years of dedication to the cause of motorcycling was deeply appreciated.

What with the broadened representation within the AMA, retail dealers for the Japanese imports now urged their old customers as well s the buyers of new machines, to join the AMA as private riders, and private representation increased accordingly.

As an aside to this long overdue revamping of the AMA, its effectiveness for the benefit of motorcycling in general has greatly increased up to the point of this writing. Private rider and owner representation has lately been increased by the institution of a Rider Council drawn from private members within the geographical AMA Districts. A special committee has been formed to counteract the ignorant and often misguided efforts of certain state and national legislators to penalize motorcycle riders by ill-advised restrictive local or national legislation detrimental to the sport. This committee has successfully challenged certain restrictive ordinances banning motorcycle riding in certain public parks and scenic recreation areas laid down by short sighted municipal and state law enforcement bodies. It has also successfully challenged such ridiculous laws that have safety belts to secure the rider to the motorcycle, or a motorcycle design that steers from the rear wheel!

While the acceptance of H-D's new custom type models was rewarding, the production of counterfeit H-D parts by independent suppliers was increasing. This proliferation reached the point that the Company recently ran paid advertising columns in biker magazines decrying the use of counterfeit H-D parts and stating that their accuracy of manufacture and measurement tolerances were open to question. What effect this warning may have had on this market is not clearly known, but it is still possible to obtain such important items as engine cases, cylinder barrels, and special transmssions from outside suppliers.

A recent innovation from certain accessory manufacturers has been the development of a primary belt drive unit with which to combat the age old V twin vibration problem. These feature a spring loaded pulley that is attached to the engine shaft, the power being taken to a specially fabricated clutch pulley via a flat armoured rubber belt. While the 98% efficiency of the more usual chain drive is not retained, many users claim that its fitting makes the H-D one of the smoothest machines on the road!

As an aside from the custom-chopper movement, the sidecar outfit and the three-wheeler have also received their share of attention. Some sidecar bodies attached to customized machines are more often than not a somewhat bizarre adaptation of some other object.

Another and more sophisticated type of three wheeler has been the custom tricycle. These are usually based on the rear portion of a standard VW that is grafted on to the front fork and single front wheel of a motorcycle, usually H-D components. Some of these have been designed with either a standard or extended rake. The more exotic examples are fitted with either reworked VW engines for enhanced performance, or even Porsche engines, which makes them very fast indeed.

The custom-chopper-biker movement, and the later H-D enthusiast interested in the more recent custom type factory machines, have been well served in the journalastic sense during recent years. The earlier publications were *Street Chopper* and *Custom Chopper*. These magazines gave further impetus to the movement by forming a media for the exchange of ideas and the dissemination of technical knowledge dealing with the usual eccentricities of the H-D engines and the conversion of standard machines. While some of the data has dealt with the customizing of British or Japanese machines, the bulk of the interest has been focused on H-D. They have also had much to do with promoting the popularity of trade fairs and shows devoted to customized machines, with heavy subsidies from the various accessory manufacturers who exhibit their wares. To attract private entrants, prizes are usually given for both the most unusual designs and mechanical excellence.

Three more recent magazines in the field are *Supercycle, Easyrider* and *Iron Horse*. Both vigorously promote the free swinging biker life style as being fanatically pro H-D. Deriding the Oriental imports as 'rice grinders' or 'rice mills', they stress the patriotic necessity for buying an American product that is rich in American two-wheeled tradition. An interesting advocation of the big V twin machine is that it offers 'safe' power, in contrast to the 'dangerous' power of the late-model Japanese superbikes. While admitting the fantastic top speeds of the latter are far and away above those of the H-D, they suggest that the low down torque capabilities of the latter offer more effective performance at 'safer' and more satisfying speeds.

Featured also in these blunt but sophisticated and effectively written publications are in-depth articles dealing with technical and design subjects, repair and overhaul outlines. Also noted are highly explicit articles dealing with various sexual mores, together with eye-catching nude female figure studies, and in-mail beauty contests featuring photographs of the readers "Ol' Ladies".

Not the least of their emphasis is for individual biker freedom. They support the free thinking policies of the loosely-organized Modified Motorcycle Association (MMA) as well as ABATE, another group who campaigns against restrictive laws against motorcyclists, and most particularly, compulsory helmet laws.

Another interesting activity is the conducting of a lonely hearts club for the benefit of brother bikers, who for various reasons are presently incarcerated in the nation's prisons.

Aside from their cult-like devotion to the ongoing cause of H-D, they heartily support the present open-door policy extended to bikers by the present management. Willie G. gives frequent interviews on present and future design projections. His popularity is enhanced by his sponsorship of an annual H-D show held at Daytona in conjunction with the traditional race meet. Both new machines from the factory and a custom show of private machines are featured.

Added to the above broad coverage, there are articles on legal methods of avoiding police harrassment of bikers, and suggested methods of legally defending oneself against unwarranted search or seizure of either person or possessions.

A recent expression of the ultimate in H-D enthusiasm occurred in California in the Fall of 1978. Westminster dealer James Wismer hosted a Sunday picnic for his customers and fellow riders in a nearby recreational area of Orange County. At the height of the festivities, guests were invited to participate in the destruction of a still viable Honda 175, sledge hammers for this purpose being provided by Wismer.

In 1979, the top management decided to terminate sales of the Aermacchi light and middleweight models. While generally good quality machines, and possessed of good performance, especially the 100 cc Baja and 125 cc Rapido models, a sufficient penetration of the market had never been attained. In spite of much advertising, the motorcycling public never seriously equated H-D with small machines, and the mass market was in the hands of the Japanese importers whose dealer representation for such was much more extensive. Then too, H-D was the traditional purveyor of big twins, where both enthusiasts and the dealers themselves had their principal area of interest. AMF-H-D subsequently sold their interest in Aermacchi, the import of their products being terminated in August.

Another recent change in the Company was the elevation of one Gus Davis to the Presidency. A dedicated motorcycle enthusiast, he possessed a strong background in sales and marketing. In taking over the Company's executive position, he freed Willie G. to concentrate on design matters and his continuing personal public relations campaign with riders and owners.

H-D's present models comprise a wide range of heavyweight chopper custom type machines. The

The 1980 FXB Sturgis. *(AMF-Harley-Davidson).*

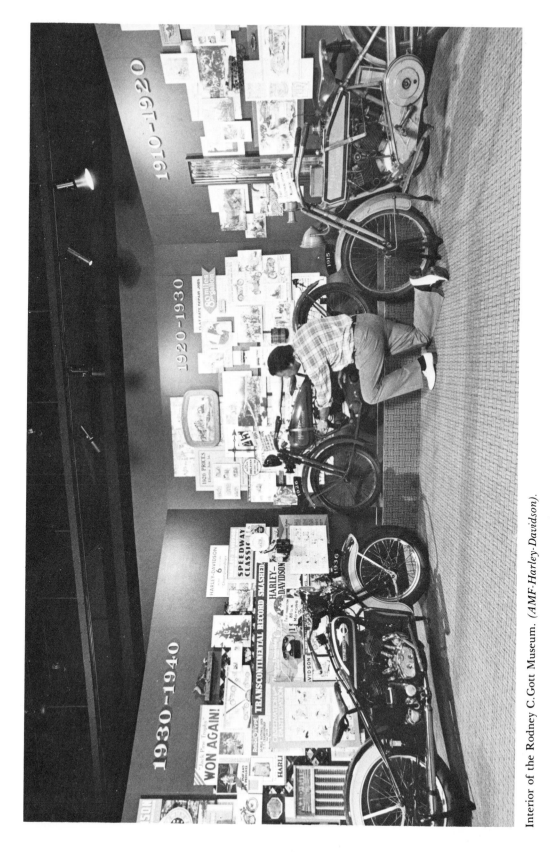

Interior of the Rodney C. Gott Museum. *(AMF-Harley-Davidson).*

XLH-1000 Sportster is available in various finishes with either conventional or spoked magnesium alloy wheels as an option. The FX-1200 series based on the former FL models include the Super Glide, Fat Bob, Roadster, Low Rider and Wide Glide models.

The 74 cubic inch Electra Glide is retained as the Anniversary Classic model, and is available with an 80 cubic inch engine. A plastic bodied sidecar is also offered. The recent 80 cubic inch engine is also offered in several of the 'FX' models.

An innovative model for 1980 is the Sturgis, which features a belt drive arrangement for both primary and secondary transmission. Named after a well known Black Hills rally, it takes another leaf from the custom accessory manufacturers for incorporation into a new factory offering. The armoured rubber belts were developed in co-operation with the Gates Rubber Company, and are stated to be capable of lasting as long as a set of conventional chains. In a *Supercycle* road test, the riders were enthusiastic about the lack of V twin vibration and the quietness of the machine.

An interesting new model for 1980 is the FLT, an entirely new machine fitted with the 80 cubic inch engine, intended for the tourist. V twin vibration is at long last recognized, its interaction now being characterized as 'drive train feedback'. The engine mounts are padded with rubber blocks, and do much to isolate engine vibration from the frame and handlebars. The steering has been lightened considerably by fitting the head lug behind the steering head. It has been suggested that the spacious engine area behind the twin downtubes might well accommodate another type of engine, rumors of which have been about for some time. While a very innovative design, early examples have been troubled by detachment of the rear wheel sprocket, as well as problems in the chain lubrication system. Late in 1980 the Company recalled certain of these models to remedy the defects. There have been unsubstantiated reports that both Fiat and Ferrari have been approached by AMF-H-D regarding the production of engines adaptable to the big twin frames.

In the matter of ultimately replacing the traditional V twin, it has often been stated that loyal H-D fans would never accept other than the traditional power plant. This also applies to the classic H-D design concept.

This last concept was well illustrated with the introduction of the XLCR-1000 Cafe Racer model in 1977. The standard Sportster engine and gearbox were fitted to a lightweight Continental-type space frame, of quite different pattern than the standard H-D type. It was fitted with a new style one-piece fuel tank, dropped handlebars, a small plastic forward fairing, along with a streamlined tail piece — all in the modern Cafe Racing styling.

While of somewhat stylish appearance, the light frame appeared to be insufficiently rigid to cope with V twin vibration, and the machine shook badly. The author was treated to a brief test ride by an acquaintance who had just run-in a 1978 model. It was immediately noted that the left front down tube was fractured just below the head lug. When queried about when this condition was to be repaired, the startling answer was that the machine rode and handled so much better in its present state, that no repair was contemplated! The machine, in the eyes of many, did not even look like an H-D, and after two seasons of rather disappointing sales, the model was discontinued.

H-D's recent competition successes with the XR-750 cc racer have been gratifying. As always, the high torque capabilities of the V twin have been at their best on the dirt. What with the added power from the new ohv engine, this characteristic had made the XR almost invincible on mile and half mile tracks. The current Champion is Jay Springsteen.

The XR has not fared as well as a road racer at Daytona, however. While developing adequate power for its type, the long antiquated V twin design simply cannot stand up to the high revolutions of the more sophisticated and latterly developed foreign machinery. What with multiple carburetion, overhead camshafts, and 10,000-15,000 rpm capabilities, the XR is here outclassed. Honda won Daytona in 1970, and during ensuing seasons Yamaha has swept the board with its highly developed two-strokes.

Competition Manager Dick O'Brien reportedly requested funds for the possible development of a new engine design, but apparently AMF has decided to maintain the V twin in its traditional sphere, and refused to allocate the required money.

H-D has run into some problems with the Environmental Protection Agency in the matter of polution, as the V twin is characteristically a 'dirty' engine in the matter of exhaust emissions. The recent fitting of solid state ignition has somewhat alleviated the trouble.

In the search for economies in manufacture, some machines have fitted Hitachi ignition systems, and Keihin and Mikuni carburetors from Japan. In some recent models, certain engine castings have also been obtained from the same source. In spite of this, H-D's Publicity Department has been successful in maintaining H-D's image as the All-American machine!

In line with H-D's unfortunate high cost situation in comparison to that of Oriental makes, several petitions for tariff relief and inquiries into charges that the Japanese are guilty of 'dumping' models at artificially low prices on the domestic market have gone unanswered.

H-D's export market has, of course, been all but made redundant by the Japanese monopoly of the world's markets. A few overseas enthusiasts persist, however, and apparently will ride no other make. A few machines are imported into Great Britain by the veteran F.H.Warr concern. Through some past minor disagreements, the Warr organization refuses to deal with AMF, and persists in communicating through Milwaukee. Richard Child, the son of H-D pioneer rider-dealer Alfred Rich Child, is still H-D's importer for Japan. As a paradox to its world wide domination of the industry, a few Japanese enthusiasts continue their American allegiance, and Child orders several hundred machines each year. Due to the high import duty, only the most wealthy of Oriental riders can continue their loyalty.

A great source of wonderment to any serious motorcycle historian is the continuing mystique of H-D through the years. During past years when the industry suffered hard times, and H-D's position was both tenuous and difficult, its management sometimes erascable, and its general policies the despair of both dealers and customers alike, there was alsways a hard core of riders who would accept no other make. The venerable 'Js', the disaster ridden 'VLs', and heavyweight 'ELs', 'FLs' and 'FLHs' have all had their devoted generations.

In spite of the continuing controversy amongst past and present motorcycle riders, dealers, motorcycle journalists and historians regarding the various aspects of Harley-Davidson history, one salient fact remains. Whatever the policies of the Company, it was able to survive and even prosper during some very difficult years. When all the other domestic manufacturers had ceased production, Harley-Davidson carried on.

The modernized Company in some manner has been able to shrewdly capitalize on this cult-like fervor from H-D's traditional past. While today penetrating new markets in the new generation, the latest models already have an appeal to tradition, and the old and the new is personified by the 1916 style H-D decals on the tanksides.

Nothing else has ever ridden or handled like a large American V twin. With a rather heavy clutch action and a ponderously clunking gearbox, the machine proceeds down the road with tractor-like chuffing that implies invincibility. They shake, yes, but then you are all the more conscious of that throbbing power, and their seeming indestructibility.

While the new range of machines has been well received generally by a growing generation of enthusiasts, certain of the Company's later design concepts have come under criticism by more experienced riders who had previously owned older models. Some have stated that some of the H-D's traditional ruggedness and high quality of manufacture has been lately sacrificed in the interests of lowering production costs. Instances are cited where the walls of alloy castings in the gearbox as well as the engine cases are being made up with considerably less thickness than before. There has also been some adverse comment on the recent quality of the paint finish.

The matter is probably best summed up through the following conversation overheard in a dealer's showroom. A young man of obvious technical knowledge was discussing the merits of the big V twin with the proprietor. While admitting the ruggedness of the overall design, he questioned the efficiency of the V twin engine. The dealer listened in silence until the young man finally ran out of words. Then he stated simply and succinctly — "Well, either you like a Harley, or you don't ... "

As we go to press, two significant events have occurred in the H-D saga which may well have lasting effects upon the future history of the Company. Yamaha has recently offered two heavyweight V twin models, the design of which is most definitely based on traditional American lines. One is of 750cc displacement, and features a shaft drive. The other is a bored out 850cc version which has a final chain drive enclosed in an oil lubricated case. The engines are of advanced design, featuring 75 degree configuration with ohc activated valve gear. With the wide angle of the cylinders, a very smooth running and almost vibrationless engine is the result, which shows a very high torque output.

The latest available domestic motorcycle marketing statistics indicate that of the over 1000cc class of heavyweight machine, examples of which are currently offered in the US by Honda, Kawasaki, Suzuki, and Yamaha, as well as by H-D, the latter concern has over the past two sales seasons produced 31% of this market. What with this fairly substantial penetration of the heavyweight, or 'hog' market, to employ popular trade vernacular, it now appears that the Japanese manufacturers consider, in Yamaha's thinking at least, that the present state of H-D's sales warrants an attempt at competing within this category.

As Yamaha's new models are most sophisticated, with their compact layout, it may well be that H-D's longtime monopoly in this field will be seriously challenged. To achieve compact dimensions, the new Orientals have eliminated the front down tube by the simple expedient of bolting the head of the front cylinder just below the head lug. An attractively clean aspect is effected by utilizing Draper-type cantilever rear springing, where the chainstays are hinged behind the gearbox, the springing being effected by a large oil dampened coil spring that is positioned underneath the saddle, quite similar to the system last seen in the once popular Vincent HRD heavyweights.

The AMF-H-D Assembly Plant at York, Pennsylvania. *(AMF-Harley-Davidson)*.

The other somewhat surprising occurrence is that it has recently been learned that AMF is now willing to sell its H-D division to that operation's management team.

This information has just been noted in the February 27th and 28th 1981 issues of the *Milwaukee Sentinel*, as well as in the March 3rd, 1981 issue of the *Milwaukee Journal*.

In the copyrighted article in the Journal, the Staff Business Editor, Dave Beal, sums up the events leading up to the situation, together with an analysis of the recent relationships between H-D and AMF.

A few years preceding AMF's purchase of H-D in 1969, the former had been in process of acquiring leisure time products such as sporting goods, power boats, snowmobiles, golf carts, and other related items which came to include H-D as a part of its sports-acquisition program. In the mid and later 1970s, AMF began shifting its diversification toward more industrial type holdings, such as an oilwell servicing concern in Texas, and an industrial filtration complex in Connecticut. Most of their substantial capital became diverted to these and other related activities.

In the meantime, the H-D Division had prospered through the substantial infusion of AMF capital, the lack of which had been ultimately responsible for their original management to seek conglomerate affiliation in the first place, after their position on the domestic market had seriously deteriorated.

However, H-D's profits had never been outstanding, with $13,000,000 netted on $275,000,000 in sales for 1979, and $12,000,000 on $289,000,000 for 1980. It was this somewhat slim 8% profit margin that probably precluded AMF's top management's decision not to allow the H-D Division any extra funds for developing new competition machinery or for prototype work on new models with which to update their now ancient designs.

H-D's principals, currently engaged in negotiating with AMF, include present members of the H-D Division's management team, such as Board Chairman John Davidson, a grandson of Founder William A.Davidson and a son of former President William H., along with his brother and H-D Designer William G., Charles K.Thompson, Division President, and Vaughn L.Beals, Jr, Vice President. At an indicated purchase price of $80,000,000, the group are said to be currently raising funds from bank loans, Company stock holdings, as well as possibly from William H., who is still stated to be concerned with the ongoing future of the Company. Other members from H-D's current management are rumoured to be involved, but at this writing have not yet been identified.

In an interview with David Beal, John Davidson and Thompson gave two principal reasons for their proposed purchase of H-D. First they called attention to AMF's change of conglomerate direction. Secondly, they cited their own recent managerial successes in keeping H-D within a profitable situation. They point out that as a possible autonomous firm following their proposed acquisition,    257

H-D can now be brought into a more competitive position within the industry, without the more usual constant preoccupation of providing dividends for the parent company's stockholders.

They also emphasize that a strong asset is the continuing loyalty of a large dealer organization, many of whom have already expressed elation at the prospect of H-D again reverting to family owner-ship.

The Milwaukee operation presently consists of the original 1920 complex, along with the Tomahawk plant in a Milwaukee suburb. At present, about 2100 production workers, along with another 1,800 in the Butler assembly plant, comprise the assembly force. They plan to reinstall all manufacturing activities in Milwaukee, the Company's ancestral home.

While the proposed new owners refused to divulge any of their rumoured long term plans for H-D's future, they did indicate that the Company might develop new models within the middleweight range in competition with the Japanese, where they now hold dominance.

Some critics have pointed out that giving up the Butler plant in favor of a total return to Mil-waukee could pose production problems, as AMF's first move following H-D acquisition was to move the assembly procedures to the more modern Butler complex.

At the moment, and on the credit side of the ledger, the prospective new owners have several advantages. A centralized management of dedicated motorcycle enthusiasts could quite naturally have a more cohesive and single minded approach in the promotion of the product. While recent H-D profits have been only modest, the operation is at least solvent, with consequent facilitation of finan-cing and credit backing from suppliers. Perhaps their best asset is their still substantial dealer represen-tation, most of whom are almost fanatically loyal to the cause, together with the host of rider-enthusiasts who would ride no other machine.

Whatever the potential road blocks, H-D's future in the proposed new situation seems secure. As the Company now prepares to enter its ninth decade, a new and prosperous future may well be down the road.

# Appendix 1

# The Excelsior Motorcycle

THE EXCELSIOR MOTORCYCLE WAS A DISTINCT MAKE OF MACHINE THAT WAS produced independently of any other. Its brief history is included here as it was significant in its survival through 1931, as was its role as the smaller of the so called 'Big Three' manufacturers that formed the bulk of domestic motorcycle production during the pioneer and vintage periods. Many of Excelsior's activities and some of the men responsible for certain of the designs were at one time or another connected with both Harley-Davidson and Indian.

The make had its beginning sometime early in 1905 in connection with a small manufacturing company in Chicago, Illinois. What fragmentary information is available indicates that it was founded by a small group of early day motorcycle enthusiasts who were impressed with the design efforts of one Walther Heckscher, a French-Jewish mechanic with some engineering background. He had gained some prior experience in Europe at the turn of the century with early variations of the engine designs of De Dion and Bouton.

Heckscher, who in the early 1900's was most probably unaware of the prototype experiments of Harley and Davidson, had independently arrived at the same conclusions: namely that the conversion of standard heavyweight roadster pedal cycles to motorcycles by the simple expedient of fitting an engine and driving mechanism did not result in a satisfactorily rugged machine. It was during this period that he built at least three prototypes from the ground up, with more substantial components that were infinitely superior to the many bicycle conversions already being marketed, this being the 'clip on' era.

Heckscher's ultimate effort followed the then standard design with a De Dion type single cylinder engine fitted into a diamond-type frame. The fuel tank was carried above, between the twin top tubes, with cannister type containers carrying the ignition batteries, tools, and lubricating oil, clipped to the frame in various positions. The single-speed drive via a flat belt and pulleys was fitted with the then standard belt tensioning device that also served as a primitive clutch, a spring loaded pulley activated by a handle. The standard bicycle pedaling gear was retained to afford both initial starting and braking power, with a coaster hub in the rear wheel. The substantial frame carried a loop at its lower forward end to accommodate the engine cases, and was further distinguished by a spring fork with twin fixed and movable legs in a parallel position, to which the wheel axle was fitted in a leading link configuration. The machine was built of substantial materials, and Heckscher's version of the now familiar De Dion engine proved more rugged and reliable than many of its contemporaries.

Using his prototype as a demonstrator, Heckscher attracted the interest of a small group of enthusiasts who were able to raise sufficient capital for him to set up production facilities in a small machine shop in Chicago's South Side. But with limited funds and with almost no sales or marketing facilities, the infant company, whose name is now forgotten, was only able to build and sell about sixty machines during 1905 and 1906, most of them in the immediate area.

It was during this period that Ignatz Schwinn was considering motorcycle manufacture as a sideline. A German immigrant bicycle mechanic, he had founded a growingly successful manufacturing concern in that city during the world wide boom in the then newly-developed safety bicycle. In casting about for a suitable design, the story goes that he quite by chance discovered Heckscher's somewhat ineffectual efforts to produce what was proving to be a satisfactory machine. Already it had gained a measure of recognition in the Chicago area. The upshot of the matter was that Schwinn offered to purchase the manufacturing rights and to engage Heckscher to oversee production.

The deal was consummated early in 1907, the first 300 or so machines being assembled as originally produced, the only visable change being the name 'Excelsior', selected by Schwinn, painted in script on the tank sides. Extensive advertising of the new product, along with its inclusion into the franchises of selected members of the already far flung dealer organization soon made the Excelsior a prominent make within the now rapidly expanding domestic motorcycle industry. From what fragmentary information is available, Heckscher remained with Schwinn but a short time, then resigning and fading into history. The reason for this is unknown, except that the somewhat eccentric Schwinn was remembered as a difficult man to get along with.

Schwinn's small engineering staff refined the machine further, which underwent expanded production during 1908 and 1909. Sales were now extended into Schwinn's vast export market, with outlets in Europe, Africa, and Australasia.

In 1910, a 50 cu.in. V twin model with mechanical inlet valves, in the so-called 'pocket valve' configuration was offered to compliment the original single cylinder model, which somewhere along

The first Excelsior 30.50 cu.in. belt drive single. These early 1907 models were identical to the 1906 machines as designed by Walther Heckscher. *(Antique Motorcycle Club of America)*.

The first Excelsior twins offered for 1910 and 1911 were of 50 cu.in. displacement, and had single geared belt drive. This example is owned by George Twine. *(Antique Motorcycle Club of America)*.

the line had its engine size adjusted to conform to the international half liter 30.50 cu.in. displacement. The twin was also a belt driver with parallel leg leading link suspension, but featured a heavier frame.

The two model range was continued through 1911, and in 1912, the engine size of the twin was increased to the now standard 61 cu.in. displacement. The Company was now actively supporting competition, this being the era of the wooden 'motordromes' that were being built along the lines of the similar 'velodromes' that had been catering for bicycle racing. It was during this year that a limited production close-coupled racing machine was offered for public sale at the bargain price of $250.00. Its performance was comparable to similar models now being offered by Indian, Thor, Flying Merkel, and a few others who were supplying machines for this growingly popular spectator sport. The Excelsior became a formidable contender in racing circles, with Lee Humiston being the first rider to break the magic 100 mph speed barrier on December 30, 1913, at the mile board oval at Playa Del Ray, a resort suburb of Los Angeles. Humiston went on in the opening months of 1913 to establish a number of records that stood for several years thereafter.

In 1913, the single was dropped from the line, production being concentrated on the 61 cu.in. twin which, as a roadster model, was now fitted with all-chain drive, but was single geared with a clutch mounted on a countershaft just behind the engine. In 1914, a two-speed version was also

The 1912-1914 Excelsior twins were of 61 cu.in. displacement, and featured single gear chain drive with an Eclipse type clutch. This 1912 model was restored by AMC Founder Ted Hodgdon. *(Antique Motorcycle Club of America).*

offered, with a planetary gearset. Both machines were now fitted with heavier fork, the suspension being effected by a quarter eliptic scroll-ended leaf spring almost identical to that already used by Indian.

In 1915, a three-speed model was offered in place of the two-speeder, this with the now standard sliding gear transmission and clutch that was also introduced this season by Harley-Davidson, Indian, and other leading makes. In addition, a new two-stroke ultra-lightweight model was also introduced. This was a rather crude looking machine with a 250 cc engine, somewhat like the contemporary English Villiers, with single geared flat belt drive. It featured a cylindrical fuel tank clipped under the single top tube, with a cartridge-type spring fork activated by a horizontal coil spring fitted to the top of the head lug. While possessed of somewhat limited performance, it was a transportation bargain at a price of $125.00.

During the 1914 competition season, Excelsior's rivals, Harley-Davidson and Indian, had developed more potent speed machinery, and a new designer was engaged to improve engine performance.

J.A.'Jock' McNeil was a recent immigrant from Scotland who had already gained a measure of racing fame as both a rider and practical engineer. He had made a name for himself with a series of machines of his own design that appeared at various board track meets fitted with 61 cu.in. '90 bore' V twins then being marketed as proprietory units by J.A.Prestwich in England. In addition, McNeil was

Excelsior's first excursion into the lightweight field was in 1914, with a single geared 250 cc belt drive model. An improved two speeder was offered in 1915, as shown here. A smooth running machine, its very mild performance attracted few buyers. It was withdrawn from the line the following year. *(Excelsior Motor Company)*.

Excelsior's famous short-coupled racing model was first offered in 1914, and was based on the factory model ridden by Lee Humiston for the first 100 mph record made in December, 1913. Its performance was later improved by J.A.McNeil, who originated the 'Big Valve' configuration that was later a standard feature of all Excelsior twins. *(Excelsior Motor Company)*.

The famous 17-3 model that was in production from 1915 through 1919, with but detail improvements. It featured a three-speed gearbox, electric lighting, and a gracefully streamlined fuel tank, the first of its kind in the United States. *(Excelsior Motor Company)*.

actively engaged in engineering work for other private owners. He was also retained by the Joerns Manufacturing Company of Minneapolis, Minnesota, to refine the very advanced 61 cu.in. overhead camshaft Cyclone designed by Walter Strand, which was then suffering from numerous teething troubles. McNeil's efforts enabled their riders to rack up some sensational wins during the 1915 and 1916 seasons, after which the company foundered due to inept management and financial problems.

McNeil's efforts on behalf of Excelsior resulted in the famous 'Big Valve' model, featuring valve diameters of 2 1/8 inch which greatly improved induction and exhaust porting, adding some 30% to their power output. This new engine was next added to the roadster line as an option, but became standard the following year, albeit in somewhat detuned form.

Competition riders gaining further laurels for Excelsior during this period included Carl Goudy, 263 his lesser known brother, Bill, Lee Creviston, Bill Leuders, Roy Artley, Bob Perry, Joe Wolters, and later, Maldwyn Jones, an already established star for his past performances on Flying Merkels and Harleys. In the Fall of 1915, Carl Goudy made a sensational win at the 300 mile race at the Maywood, Chicago oval.

For 1915, the 61 inch twin had its appearance enhanced with the fitting of a handsomely contoured fuel tank, a marked improvement of the more usual slab sided types of the competition. The overall appearance of these models was such that one would not look out of place when compared with the domestically-produced models of two decades later.

Excelsior machines were always handsomely finished, with rich pearl gray paintwork highlighted by maroon tank panels outlined in gold striping and gold lettering on the name transfers. Scarlet pinstriping in the form of small arrows extended along the fork tubes, and small control parts as well as the cylinder barrels were nickel plated. For the 1917 season, and through 1919, the paint finish was changed to military olive drab, but retaining the maroon tank motif.

An outstanding model was the 17-E for 1916, which featured deeper sectioned mudguards, with full valances on the front wheel. An all-electric model with a Nidco lighting system was offered, although many experienced motorcyclists still preferred the well-proved acetylene Solar system with the gas tank fitted on a bracket over the handlebar lugs. Many law enforcement bodies were now specifying Excelsior big twins, whose utility had been enhanced during the last two seasons by a line of sidecars.

Excelsior machines were also purchased in limited numbers by the War Department, and gave good service both during General Pershing's 1916 Mexican campaign, as well as during overseas operations in World War I. These later models were subject to continuing detail improvement, along with a strengthened clutch and drive train.

The lightweight model was continued by 1916 in two versions, the original single gear, along with a two-speed model that was fitted with a two-speed sliding-dog type transmission integral with the engine, the final drive still being by flat belt. Selling for an increased price of $140.00, its already mild performance was somewhat hampered by its now increased weight. Never an overpopular seller in an age when the heavyweight V twin was the favored American motorcycle, it was not reintroduced for 1917.

Excelsiors were never produced in large numbers, even though the make was now established as a member of the 'Big Three', along with Harley-Davidson and Indian. In 1912, the Company announced that 40,000 machines were then on the road, both at home and overseas. In 1919, it was stated that 100,000 Excelsiors had been marketed, with substantial numbers going to export.

In the immediate post-war continuance of long distance record breaking, Wells Bennett, the enthusiastic Portland, Oregon, Excelsior dealer, bested the 1915 Three Flag record made by

The 17-C model as updated in 1920 by Arthur Lemon. Henderson Four forks were fitted to rationalize production, but many enthusiasts felt that their heavier pattern upset the handling. A few 74 cu.in. models were built in 1921. With the emphasis on Henderson production, less than 300 of these machines were produced between 1920 and 1924. *(Antique Motorcycle Club of America)*.

The first Super-X 45 cu.in. model introduced late in 1925, which was designed by Arthur Constantine with some help from Joe Petrali. The engine and gearbox unit had been designed in 1924 as a proposed new Harley-Davidson Model, but now appeared with modified Henderson cycle parts. A front brake was fitted in 1928. *(Excelsior Motor Company)*.

Cannonball Baker on an Indian, this being the run from the Canadian border to Tijuana, Mexico. In the seesaw running of this course by other makes, Bennett set up new times in this event during 1918 and 1919. In 1920, he won the Los Angeles 'sealed top gear' run to Bakersfield, with a time not equaled until years later.

Another noted Excelsior star of this era was Roy Artley, who rode a racing 'Big Valve' at Los Angeles's famed Ascot Speedway during 1918 and 1919. Artley had previously represented the marque during the famous Southwestern Desert Races held annually, except for the war years, between Los Angeles and the hazardous roads to Phoenix, Arizona.

Following the Armistice, McNeil designed a new racing engine for Excelsior based on the former Cyclone design, featuring overhead camshafts. As an all-ball bearing motor, with many advanced features, it proved to turn out fantastic power. The racing shop assembled about a dozen engines, one of which was fitted to a standard track machine which factory rider Bob Perry had shipped to Los Angeles for testing on the Ascot Speedway. On January 2nd 1920, Perry was killed when the machine went out of control in a power slide and through the fence. The story goes that Schwinn, who had long considered Perry as a son, in his grief destroyed the remaining engines. There appears to be some doubt concerning the validity of this fact, however, as team members Wells Bennett, Joe Wolter, as well as Jock McNeil as a private entrant, continued to race the cammers on the West coast. Another

265

private owner, Waldo Korn, was also known to compete on a cammer, for which he had a spare engine.

As a footnote to this affair, cammers based on the original design were built in small numbers by the Reading Standard concern, who had purchased moulds to make the engine castings from the now defunct Cyclone concern. The Company suspended production in 1922 due to financial difficulties, and after an abortive attempt at reorganization in 1924, finally expired for good.

As Schwinn had now made the decision to suspend official factory support, private entrants still riding Excelsior machines fared less well than did Harley and Indian riders who still enjoyed factory sponsorship.

In 1917, Schwinn purchased the manufacturing rights to the Henderson four, and took on its originator, William Henderson, together with his brother, Thomas, and Arthur Lemon, who was the former's engineering protege. Following a series of disagreements with Schwinn over the latter's insistence on changing the Henderson's basic design, William and his brother resigned, to organize the Ace Motor Company, with Lemon remaining to become chief of Excelsior's Engineering Department. The Ace venture figured in the complex metamorphosis of the original Henderson design through the Ace period and on to the development of the Indian four, which history has already been exhaustively explored in the Author's companion work on the Indian motorcycle entitled *The Iron Redskin* (G.T.Foulis/Haynes Publishing Group).

The new Chief Designer, Arthur Lemon, updated the twin for 1920. The traditional pearl gray finish was now a dark blue, matching that of the four cylinder Henderson which had carried this color since its acquisition from the original designer. The twin was now fitted with the same fork as the Henderson, which was of trailing link type with forward curving fixed legs and activated by an enclosed oil dampened coil spring.

As the four had been a popular seller, the factory now concentrated most of its efforts to its production, and according to the best available information, only about 300 twins were assembled between 1920 and 1924, many of which were exported. In 1921, a 74 cu.in. version was built in small numbers, intended for sidecar and commercial work.

In 1922, Arthur Lemon was able to convince Schwinn that official company sponsorship of competition should be reinstated. He proposed the development of the 21 cu.in. class, which was admittedly safer for the riders than either the 61 or 30.50 cu.in. classes. Schwinn finally acquiesed, and two lightweight competition machines were built. These were ridden by Paul Anderson, a highly skilled rider, and Maldwyn Jones, a one time Flying Merkel and H-D exponent. AMA President Douglas Hobart, a one time Indian employee, inveigled the Contest Committee to sanction the new lightweight Class, and incurred the wrath of Harley-Davidson as that company at the time had no comparable machinery.

In 1922, Maldwyn Jones had considerable success in hill climbing, entering a 74 cu.in. twin in numerous events, together with Eddie Ryan, the enthusiastic San Pedro, California, Excelsior dealer.

Arthur Constantine, an automotive engineer who had been employed by Harley-Davidson since 1920, resigned from that Company late in 1924, and immediately joined Excelsior. He brought with him his design for a then new class of middleweight motorcycle with a 45 cu.in. engine, which he had developed while in H-D employ, but which had been rejected by H-D's top management. Constantine was able to sell Schwinn the idea of putting it into production. In its final form, however, it utilized certain Henderson components, such as frame members and fuel tank, in the interests of rationalized production. Cataloged as the 'Super-X', as a high performance machine of moderate weight and reasonable selling price, it became immediately popular, within the limitations of the then stagnant domestic market.

During the prototype development of the Super-X, the youthful Joe Petrali joined Excelsior's Engineering Department. With an already established competition reputation which was augmented by his legendary skills in speed tuning, he was able to convince Schwinn that he could contribute much to the Company's design progress. Petrali was also anxious to work with Constantine, for whom he had great admiration.

With Schwinn's somewhat grudging approval, about a dozen racing versions of the Super X were assembled, having close-coupled frames and blanked off gearboxes to conform to the current rules mandating direct drive for track and speedway work. A factory-sponsored racing team which, in addition to Petrali, included Charles 'Red' Wolverton, Bill Minnick, and Bob Sirkegian, together with some private participation by Jock McNeil, hung up a series of notable victories. Petrali also racked up a number of notable records at the board oval at Altoona, Pennsylvania, during 1926 and 1927.

At Schwinn's suggestion, Constantine updated both the Super-X and Henderson for the 1929 sales season, resulting in resurrecting of his original 45 cu.in. design. With its bulbous fuel tank and general appearance it now followed Harley Davidson lines, as well as the new four 'K' models which had a new pocket valve type 80 cu.in. engine. During the two previous years, Excelsior's interest in the

The last Super-X model, produced between 1929 and 1931, as updated by Arthur Constantine. It bore a distinct resemblance to contemporary H-D machines. The machine shown is a 1930 Sports Model, with enlarged porting and extra cylinder finning. Owned and restored by Dewey Bonkrud. (*Alisha Tamburri*).

21 cu.in. class waned, as what with his racing activities, Petrali had not had the time or opportunity for development.

The factory also built a few ohv hill climb specials, with which both Petrali and Gene Rhyne won a number of National Championships. Interest in the Super-X was enhanced with the optional offering of a 61 cu.in. version. Its overall appearance was unchanged, and the increased displacement was effected by enlarging the cylinder dimensions.

The Company suspended all motorcycle production in the late Spring of 1931, the reason given by Schwinn being the now worsening worldwide economic depression. Another, and perhaps more obscure reason, was the technical failure of a number of the 1931 Hendersons due to the fitting of inferior electric components in order to cut production costs. A limited number of both models were assembled from parts on hand during the summer of 1931, an activity which finally came to a halt in the Fall. Most components still on hand passed to the hands of the Ballack Company, also of Chicago, who continued to supply Henderson and Super X enthusiasts for many years thereafter. The great Cortland Street plant was now wholly given over to bicycles.

Petrali now joined Harley Davidson, and was for some years their only professional rider, as well as making important contributions to their technical progress. Constantine went on to engage in free-lance industrial engineering projects, and was for some years associated with the Bendix organization. In 1945, he became a consultant for Indian, in a program that attempted to salvage their ill-fated Torque based lightweight motorcycles.

There was much consternation on the part of Super X and Henderson enthusiasts when the news of suspension of production was announced, but domestic motorcycle sales were in the doldroms, and the exigencies of the depression were such that both Indian and Harley-Davidson were hard pressed to keep afloat.

Both models were never produced in other than limited numbers, and never enjoyed extensive dealer representation. As in the case of their competition, a large portion of the output went to the export field, and when world markets declined, Excelsior's now limited domestic sales could not sustain economic production.

The demise of Excelsior represented the end of a motorcycling era in the United States, which had begun with such promise in the early years of the century. For the ensuing two decades, American motorcycling dwindled to become a very minor entity on the domestic transportation scene.

# Appendix 2

# A General Guide to the Descriptive Designation of Harley-Davidson Models.

**A GENERAL GUIDE TO THE DESCRIPTIVE DESIGNATION OF HARLEY-DAVIDSON MODELS**

| Year | Piston displacement | Type of engine | Model name or popular name | Factory designation |
|------|------|------|------|------|
| 1903 | 26 cu.in | De Dion Bouton atmospheric inlet valve | none | inconsistent numbering under 2500 |
| 1904-1918 | 35 cu.in | as above until 1910. Pocket valve type thereafter | Silent Gray Fellow | 5-35, 9A, 9B, 9E |
| 1909-1952 | 61 cu.in | 4 stroke type pocket valve to 1929. Side valve 1930 to 1936. Ohv 1937 onward | Sixty-One | F, FE, J, JE, JD, 61E, E, EL, JH, JDH |
| 1919-1922 | 37 cu.in | Horizontally-opposed side valve 4 stroke | Sport Twin | W, WJ |
| 1922- | 74 cu.in | Pocket valve to 1929 Side valve 1930-1936 Ohv onward | Seventy Four Hydra-Glide, Duo-Glide Electra-Glide Super-Glide | J, JD, JE F, FD, FE, V, VL, VLH U, UL, FL, FLH, FX, FXE |
| 1926-1934 | 21 cu.in | Side valve single Ohv single | Peashooter | A, AA B, BA |
| 1929-1934 | 30.50 cu.in | Side valve single | Baby-Harley | C, CM |
| 1929-1955 | 45 cu.in | Side valve V twin | Forty-five | D, DL, DLD, R, RL, RLD, WL, WLD, K |

| 1932-1974 | 45 cu.in | Side valve V twin | Servicar | G, GE |
|---|---|---|---|---|
| 1936-1947 | 80 cu.in | Side valve V twin | Eighty | VLH, UH, UHL |
| 1942-1943 | 45 cu.in | Side valve flat twin | H-D-BMW | XA |
| 1947-1953 | 125 cc | Two-stroke single cylinder | 125 | M-125, S, ST |
| 1953-1962 | 165 cc | Two-stroke single cylinder | 165 | M-165-BTF |
| 1955-1958 | 125 cc | Single cylinder two-stroke | Hummer | B |
| 1955-1956 | 45 cu.in | Side valve V twin | Sportster | KH |
| 1957 | 55 cu.in. | Side valve V twin | Sportster | KH |
| 1955-1971 | 57 cu.in | Ohv V twin | Sportster | XL, XLH, XLCH |
| 1961-1966 | 175 cc | Single cylinder two-stroke | Pacer, Scat Bobcat | BT, BTU, BTH |
| 1961-1969 | 250 cc | Single cylinder ohv four stroke inclined cylinder | Sprint | C, H, SS |
| 1965-1967 | 50 cc | Single cylinder two-stroke | 50, Leggero | M-50 |
| 1967-1972 | 65 cc | Single cylinder two-stroke | 65, Leggero | M-65 |
| 1968-1979 | 125 cc | Single cylinder two-stroke | Rapido | ML, MLS, SS, STX |
| 1969-1979 | 125 cc, 175 cc 250 cc | Single cylinder two-stroke | | SS, SX |
| 1969-1976 | 350 cc | Single cylinder ohv four-stroke inclined cylinder | Sprint | SS, SX |
| 1971-1977 | 100 cc | Single cylinder two-stroke | Baja | MSR |
| 1971- | 61 cu.in | Four stroke V twin | Sportster | XL-XLCH |

## MODEL DESIGNATION OF HARLEY-DAVIDSON MOTORCYCLES FROM 1908 THROUGH 1929

| Year | Model | Twin or single belt or chain drive | | Ignition | NACC hp rating | Motor numbers (left base of cylinders) |
|---|---|---|---|---|---|---|
| 1908 | 4 | single | belt | battery | 3.90 | Under 2500 |
| 1909 | 5 | single | belt | battery | 4.34 | |
| 1909 | 5A | single | belt | battery | 4.34 | All 1909 numbers |
| 1909 | 5B | single | belt | battery | 4.34 | 2500 to 4200 |
| 1909 | 5C | single | belt | magneto | 4.34 | Models 5B-5C 26in. wheels |
| 1910 | 6 | single | belt | battery | 4.34 | All 1910 numbers |
| 1910 | 6A | single | belt | magneto | 4.34 | 4200 to 7600 |
| 1910 | 6B | single | belt | battery | 4.34 | |
| 1910 | 6C | single | belt | magneto | 4.34 | |
| 1911 | 7 | single | belt | battery | 4.34 | All 1911 numbers |
| 1911 | 7A | single | belt | magneto | 4.34 | 7600 to 10,000 and are |
| 1911 | 7B | single | belt | battery | 4.34 | followed by letter A |
| 1911 | 7C | single | belt | magneto | 4.34 | models 7B and 7C |
| 1911 | 7D | twin | belt | magneto | 7.20 | have 26in. wheels |
| 1912 | 8 | single | belt | battery | 4.34 | |
| 1912 | 8A | single | belt | magneto | 4.34 | All 1912 numbers 10,000 |
| 1912 | 8D | twin | belt | magneto | 7.20 | and up followed by AB, |
| 1912 | 8E | twin | chain | magneto | 8.68 | BA, or B |
| 1913 | 9A | single | belt | magneto | 4.34 | 10,000 up with letter C |
| 1913 | 9B | single | chain | magneto | 4.34 | 10,000 up with letter D |
| 1913 | 9E | twin | chain | magneto | 8.68 | 10,000 up with letter E |
| 1913 | 9G | twin | chain | magneto | 8.68 | 10,000 up with letter E Forecar truck letter E |

| Year | Model | Cyls. | Drive | Ignition | NACC hp | Motor numbers |
|---|---|---|---|---|---|---|
| 1914 | 10A | single | belt | magneto | 4.34 | number with letter CF |
| 1914 | 10B | single | chain | magneto | 4.34 | number DG or G single speed |
| 1914 | 10C | single | chain | magneto | 4.34 | number DG or G two speed |
| 1914 | 10E | twin | chain | magneto | 8.68 | number EH or H single speed |
| 1914 | 10F | twin | chain | magneto | 8.68 | number EH or H two speed |
| 1914 | 10G | twin | chain | magneto | 8.68 | number EH or H two speed fore car |
| 1915 | 11B | single | chain | magneto | 4.34 | number with J single speed |
| 1915 | 11C | single | chain | magneto | 4.34 | number with J two speed |
| 1915 | 11E | twin | chain | magneto | 8.68 | number with K single speed |
| 1915 | 11F | twin | chain | magneto | 8.68 | number with K three speed |
| 1915 | 11G | twin | chain | magneto | 8.68 | number with K fore car |
| 1915 | 11H | twin | chain | generator | 8.68 | number with LT single speed |
| 1915 | 11J | twin | chain | generator | 8.68 | number with LK three speed |
| 1916 | 16B | single | chain | magneto | 4.34 | number with L single speed |
| 1916 | 16C | single | chain | magneto | 4.34 | number with L three speed |
| 1916 | 16E | twin | chain | magneto | 8.68 | number with M single speed |
| 1916 | 16F | twin | chain | magneto | 8.68 | number with M three speed |
| 1916 | 16J | twin | chain | generator | 8.68 | number with LM three speed |
| 1917 | 17B | single | chain | magneto | 4.34 | number with 17S single speed |
| 1917 | 17C | single | chain | magneto | 4.34 | number with 17S three speed |
| 1917 | 17E | twin | chain | magneto | 8.68 | number with 17T single speed |
| 1917 | 17F | twin | chain | magneto | 8.68 | number with 17T three speed |
| 1917 | 17J | twin | chain | generator | 8.68 | number with L 17T three speed |
| 1918 | 18B | single | chain | magneto | 4.34 | number with 18S single speed |
| 1918 | 18C | single | chain | magneto | 4.34 | number with 18S three speed |
| 1918 | 18E | twin | chain | magneto | 8.68 | number with 18T single speed |
| 1918 | 18F | twin | chain | magneto | 8.68 | number with 18T three speed |
| 1918 | 18J | twin | chain | generator | 8.68 | number with L18T three speed |

'J' type single cylinder models were discontinued after 1918, but a few models were assembled to special order during 1918-1919, presumably from left-over spare parts. These were unsequentially numbered, as were about 26 machines assembled during 1920.

All models were fitted with 28in. wheels, except as noted, from 1903 through 1918.

Engine numbers between 1903 through 1907 were under 2500, but were not sequentially numbered.

Belt drive singles were discontinued after 1914, but a few more were assembled during 1915 and 1916, presumably to special order and made from left over spare parts. These were unsequentially numbered.

| Year | Model | Cyls. | Ignition | NACC hp rating | Motor numbers (left base of cylinders) |
|---|---|---|---|---|---|
| 1919 | 19F | twin | magneto | 8.68 | number preceded by 19T or 19A three speed |
| 1919 | 19J | twin | magneto generator | 8.68 | number preceded by L19T or L19A three speed |
| 1920 | 20F | twin | magneto | 8.68 | number preceded by 20T three speed |
| 1920 | 20J | twin | generator | 8.68 | number preceded by L20T three speed |
| 1921 | 21F | twin | magneto | 8.68 | number preceded by 21F three speed |
| 1921 | 21FD | twin | magneto | 9.50 | number preceded by 21F three speed |
| 1921 | 21J | twin | generator | 8.68 | number preceded by 21J three speed |
| 1921 | 21JD | twin | generator | 9.50 | number preceded by 21JD three speed |
| 1922 | 22F | twin | magneto | 8.68 | number preceded by 22F three speed |
| 1922 | 22FD | twin | magneto | 9.50 | number preceded by 22FD three speed |
| 1922 | 22J | twin | generator | 8.68 | number preceded by 22J three speed |
| 1922 | 22JD | twin | generator | 9.50 | number preceded by 22JD three speed |
| 1923 | 23F | twin | magneto | 8.68 | number preceded by 23F three speed |
| 1923 | 23FD | twin | magneto | 9.50 | number preceded by 23FD three speed |
| 1923 | 23J | twin | generator | 8.68 | number preceded by 23J three speed |
| 1923 | 23JD | twin | generator | 9.50 | number preceded by 23JD three speed |

The 9.50 hp designation beginning in the Fall of 1921 indicates the 74 cu.in. motor. The 61 cu.in. was bored out from 3 5/16in. to 3 7/16in.

The 37 cu.in. opposed twin cylinder 'Sport Twin' model manufactured from the Spring of 1919 through the Fall of 1922 had the engine number prefix 'M' for the magneto-equipped model, and 'MJ' for the electrically-equipped machines that were fitted with head and tail lights. The numbers ran from 100 through 8000, but were not in sequential order.

A limited number of these machines were assembled in 1923 and 1924 for export, principally to England and Australasia, where the model had enjoyed a better acceptance than it received in the United States. The prefix on these engines was either 'E' or 'EX'. The numbers were at random.

| Year | Model | Cyl. | Ignition | Comp. | Description |
|------|-------|------|----------|-------|-------------|
| 1924 | 24FE | twin | magneto | 8.68 | number preceded by 24FE three speed. Aluminum pistons |
| 1924 | 24FD | twin | magneto | 9.50 | number preceded by 24FD three speed. Cast iron pistons |
| 1924 | 24FDCA | twin | magneto | 9.50 | number preceded by 24FDCA three speed. Aluminum pistons |
| 1924 | 24 FDCB | twin | magneto | 9.50 | number preceded by 24FDCB three speed. Iron alloy pistons |
| 1924 | 24JE | twin | generator | 8.68 | number preceded by 24JE three speed. Aluminum pistons |
| 1924 | 24JD | twin | generator | 9.50 | number preceded by 24JD three speed. Cast iron pistons |
| 1924 | 24JDCA | twin | generator | 9.50 | number preceded by 24JDCA three speed. Aluminum pistons |
| 1924 | 24JDCB | twin | generator | 9.50 | number preceded by 24JDCB three speed. Iron alloy pistons |
| 1925 | 25FE | twin | magneto | 8.68 | number preceded by 25FE three speed |
| 1925 | 25FECB | twin | magneto | 9.50 | number preceded by 25FECB three speed |
| 1925 | 25JE | twin | generator | 8.68 | number preceded by 25JE three speed |
| 1925 | 25JDCB | twin | generator | 9.50 | number preceded by 25JDCB three speed |

All above 1925 models had iron alloy pistons

| Year | Model | Cyl. | Ignition | Comp. | Description |
|------|-------|------|----------|-------|-------------|
| 1926 | 26F | twin | magneto | 8.68 | number preceded by 26F |
| 1926 | 26FD | twin | magneto | 9.50 | number preceded by 26FD |
| 1926 | 26J | twin | generator | 8.68 | number preceded by 26J |
| 1926 | 26JD | twin | generator | 9.50 | number preceded by 26JD |

All above 1926 models had iron alloy pistons

| Year | Model | Cyl. | Ignition | Comp. | Description |
|------|-------|------|----------|-------|-------------|
| 1927 | 27F | twin | magneto | 8.68 | number preceded by 27F |
| 1927 | 27FD | twin | magneto | 9.50 | number preceded by 27FD |
| 1927 | 27J | twin | generator | 8.68 | number preceded by 27J |
| 1927 | 27JD | twin | generator | 9.50 | number preceded by 27JD |

All above 1927 models had iron alloy pistons

| Year | Model | Cyl. | Ignition | Comp. | Description |
|------|-------|------|----------|-------|-------------|
| 1928 | 28F | twin | magneto | 8.68 | number preceded by 28F. Iron alloy pistons |
| 1928 | 28FD | twin | magneto | 9.50 | number preceded by 28FD. Iron alloy pistons |
| 1928 | 28J | twin | generator | 8.68 | number preceded by 28J. Iron alloy pistons |
| 1928 | 28JD | twin | generator | 9.50 | number preceded by 28JD. Iron alloy pistons |
| 1928 | 28JXL | twin | generator | 8.68 | number preceded by 28JXL. Dow metal pistons |
| 1928 | 28JDXL | twin | generator | 9.50 | number preceded by 28JDXL. Dow metal pistons |
| 1928 | 28JDH | twin | generator | 9.50 | number preceded by 28JDH Twin Cam. Dow metal pistons |
| 1929 | 29D | twin | generator | 6.05 | number preceded by 29D. Side valves. Dow metal pistons |
| 1929 | 29F | twin | magneto | 8.68 | number preceded by 29F. Iron alloy pistons |
| 1929 | 29FD | twin | magneto | 9.50 | number preceded by 29FD. Iron alloy pistons |
| 1929 | 29J | twin | generator | 8.68 | number preceded by 29J. Iron alloy pistons |
| 1929 | 29JD | twin | generator | 9.50 | number preceded by 29JD. Iron alloy pistons |
| 1929 | 29JDH | twin | generator | 9.50 | number preceded by 29JDH Twin Cam. Dow metal pistons. |
| 1929 | 29JDL | twin | generator | 9.50 | number preceded by 29JDL. Dow metal pistons |

The JDH twin cam, or 'Two Cam' models had distinctive engine cases that were not interchangeable with the standard single cam models

## MODEL DESIGNATION OF SINGLE CYLINDER MODELS — 1926 THROUGH 1937

| | | | | |
|---|---|---|---|---|
| 1926 & 1927 | Model A | magneto | 3.31 hp | number preceded by A, side valves. Iron alloy pistons |
| 1926 & 1927 | Model AA | magneto | 3.31 hp | number preceded by AA, oh valves. Aluminum pistons |
| 1926 & 1927 | Model B | generator | 3.31 hp | number preceded by B, side valves. Iron alloy pistons |
| 1926 & 1927 | Model BA | generator | 3.31 hp | number preceded by BA, oh valves. Aluminum pistons |

The A, AA, and B and BA Models were of 21 cu.in. displacement.

| | | | | |
|---|---|---|---|---|
| 1928 & 1929 | Model C | generator | 5.50 hp | number preceded by C, iron alloy pistons |
| 1928 & 1929 | Model CM | magneto | 5.50 hp | number preceded by CM, aluminum pistons |

The C and CM models were of 30.50 cu.in. displacement.

The magneto-equipped 21 cu.in. export model was designated as AAE, and was fitted with handlebar clutch control, foot pegs, and flat-type bars. The battery-equipped export model was as above, cataloged as BAE.

The standard 21 cu.in. single first offered in 1926 had a wheelbase of 56½in. and weighed about 280 lb. The later versions had 2in. less wheelbase with a shorter and somewhat more bulbous fuel tank.

The 1926 and 1927 models were fitted with 3;30x20in. clincher tires.

The 1928 and later models were fitted with 3;30x19in. drop center tires.

The Model C 30.50 cu.in. single first cataloged in late 1928 weighed about 365 lb. and had a 57½in. wheelbase. The tires were 4.00x18in. drop center.

In the Fall of 1931, the Model C shared the same chassis with the newly updated 45 cu.in. twin. Its weight was now about 430 lb.

The competition 21 cu.in. 'Peashooter' was designated as the Model S. Its wheelbase varied from 52 to 54in. and it weighed about 190 lb. Its specially-built ohv engine featured pressure oil feed to all bearings except the wrist pin, and had a sodium-cooled exhaust valve. Two port cylinder heads were optional. The Model SA had an optional barrel-type carburetor. Tires sizes were 28x2¼ clincher.

The competition 30.50 cu.in. model of 1934 was designated as the CAC, and was fitted with oh valves. Designed for alcohol fuel only, it had a 14½:1 compression ratio, and was said to develop 45 hp at 6,800 rpm. Optional tire sizes were 28x2⅜ in. clincher or drop center. Total weight was about 230 lb.

A 21 cu.in. side valve stationary industrial engine was offered briefly in 1931, designated Model CG. It had a stub shaft on both sides of the crankcase.

## MODEL DESIGNATION OF 45 cu.in TWIN-CYLINDER MACHINES 1928 THROUGH 1952

In regard to the model designation of the 45 cubic inch side valve models, there are some discrepancies in descriptive nomenclature. As introduced to the line late in 1928, they were provisionally cataloged as the 'R' models. Later designation from the best available information is as follows:

| | | |
|---|---|---|
| D | Low Compression | 1929-30-31 |
| DL | High Compression | |
| DLD | High Compression | 'Sports Special Solo'. It was fitted with a 74 inch twin carburetor, large intake manifold and one extra plate in the clutch. |
| R | Low Compression | This was the 1932-36 series, with the generator changed to horizontal type, and featured large diameter valves. |
| RL | High Compression | |
| RLD | High Speed Model | |

273

| W | Low Compression | This was the 1937-51 series, with circulating oil system, cooling fins on engine cases, and had the same fuel tank halves as the '61 E'. |
| WL | High Compression | |
| WLD | High Speed Model | |
| WLDD | | Introduced in April 1939, as the 'WLD Special'. Had deep finned aluminum cylinder heads and larger cylinder finning. In 1940 its designation was returned to 'WLD'. |
| WLDR | | Racing model introduced in 1940 This was usually known as the 'WR' |
| WR | | Racing models. A few ohv machines were built as road racers for use in Europe, as well as factory-owned hill climb machines. |

## MODEL DESIGNATION OF HARLEY-DAVIDSON SIDECARS FROM 1915 THROUGH 1925

(These units were all supplied by the Rogers Company)

| Code | Year | Model | Frame number |
|------|------|-------|--------------|
| | 1915 | 11 L | 100 L to 3500 L |
| | 1916 | 16 L | 3500 L up |
| | 1917 | 17 L | numbers preceded by 17 L |
| | 1918 | 18 L | numbers preceded by 18 L |
| | 1919 | 19 L | numbers preceded by 19 L |
| Jenny | 1920 | 20 L | |
| Joy | 1920 | 20 QL | |
| Meadow | 1921 | 21 L | The frame numbers on all |
| Mimic | 1921 | 21 LR | models from 1920 through |
| Mister | 1921 | 21 QL | 1925 were preceded by |
| Pen | 1922 | 22 L | these symbols. They were |
| Pie | 1922 | 22 LR | stamped on either the top |
| Plot | 1922 | 22 QT | or the rear of the back axle |
| Purity | 1923 | 23 LT | tube. |
| Puritan | 1923 | 23 QT | |
| Repand | 1924 | 24 LT | |
| Rescue | 1924 | 24 QT | |
| Slant | 1925 | 25 LT | |
| Slash | 1925 | 25 QT | |

Sidecar units offered after 1925 were manufactured by Harley-Davidson, and their frame numbers and symbols were non-sequential. Body styles were identical from 1926 through 1930. Models offered from 1931 through 1939 had a lowered chassis and more streamlined bodies.

Model U or V is a generator-equipped 74 cu.in. with standard compression ratio
Model U, VL or VLD is a generator-equipped 74 cu.in. with high compression
Model E refers to the 61 cu.in. ohv medium compression
Model EL refers to the 61 cu.in. ohv high compression
VLH or U to H 80 cu.in. high compression
VHS or UHS 80 cu.in. medium compression.

The letter C used in conjunction with models F, J, JD, or V indicates a heavy-duty low compression commercial type motor, generally fitted to sidecar or package truck models

The foregoing data has been compiled from extensive model designation published at various times in factory literature, and it must be emphasized that there are many discrepancies between it and the model and engine numbers of actual machines. In some instances the engine numbers are out of sequence in many machines produced through the years, and sometimes the letter designations follow an inconsistent pattern.

Old machines are often found to have been altered or updated with the fitting of later type parts. Similar engines fitted to like models then naturally show differing numbering. Most early engines as overhauled were fitted with aluminum or Dow metal pistons in place of the original cast iron type.

This data can therefore be used only as a general guide.

## COMPETITION RECORDS FROM 1919 THROUGH 1950

| Record | Name | Machine | Track or Course | Date | Time | MPH |
|--------|------|---------|-----------------|------|------|-----|
| **Board Track — Solo—Class A—61 cu.in. motors** | | | | | | |
| 1 mile | Jim Davis | IND | Beverly Hills, Cal. | Apr 17, '22 | :32.53 | 110.67 |
| 5 mile | M.L.Fredericks | IND | Salem, N.H. | Sep 18, '26 | 2:37.60 | 114.21 |
| 10 mile | Joe Petrali | H-D | Laurel, Md. | Sep 7, '25 | 5:23.80 | 111.18 |
| 20 mile | Jim Davis | H-D | Fresno, Cal. | Oct 2, '25 | 11:50.60 | 101.32 |
| 25 mile | Joe Petrali | H-D | Laurel, Md. | Sep 7, '25 | 14:08.40 | 106.07 |
| 50 mile | Otto Walker | H-D | Fresno, Cal. | Feb 22, '21 | 29:34.60 | 101.44 |
| 100 mile | Joe Petrali | H-D | Altoona, Pa. | Jul 4, '25 | 59:47.20 | 100.36 |
| **Board Track — Side Car — Class A — 61 cu.in. motors** | | | | | | |
| 10 mile | Sam Riddle | IND | Sheepshead Bay, N.Y. | Oct 11, '19 | 8:15.60 | 72.64 |
| 25 mile | F.J.Scott | IND | Altoona, Pa. | Jul 4 '25 | 18:35.40 | 80.68 |
| 50 mile | Bill Minnick | H-D | Altoona, Pa. | Jul 4 '25 | 37:34.20 | 79.85 |
| **1 Mile Dirt Track — Solo — Class A — 61 cu.in. motors** | | | | | | |
| 1 mile | Ralph Hepburn | IND | San Luis Obispo, Cal. | Nov 5, '22 | :39.60 | 90.91 |
| 5 mile | Ralph Hepburn | IND | San Luis Obispo, Cal. | Nov 5, '22 | 3:26.20 | 87.29 |
| 10 mile | Ralph Hepburn | IND | San Luis Obispo, Cal. | Nov 5, '22 | 6:59.80 | 85.76 |
| 25 mile | Ralph Hepburn | IND | San Luis Obispo, Cal. | Nov 5, '22 | 18:02.00 | 83.11 |
| 50 mile | Fred Ludlow | H-D | Syracuse, N.Y. | Sep 19, '21 | 38:52.13 | 77.19 |
| 200 mile | Ralph Hepburn | H-D | Dodge City, Kan. | Jul 4, '21 | 137:54.00 | 87.02 |
| 300 mile | Ralph Hepburn | H-D | Dodge City, Kan. | Jul 4, '21 | 210:03.00 | 85.69 |
| **1 Mile Dirt Track — Solo — Class A — 30.50 cu.in. motors** | | | | | | |
| 1 mile | John Seymour | IND | Syracuse, N.Y. | Sep 19, '25 | :44.20 | 81.26 |
| 5 mile | John Seymour | IND | Syracuse, N.Y. | Sep 19, '25 | 3:43.76 | 80.45 |
| 8 mile | Jim Davis | H-D | Syracuse, N.Y. | Sep 13, '24 | 5:59.39 | 80.14 |
| 10 mile | John Seymour | IND | Syracuse, N.Y. | Sep 19, '25 | 7:30.04 | 80.00 |
| 15 mile | John Seymour | IND | Syracuse, N.Y. | Sep 19, '25 | 11:19.60 | 79.45 |
| 20 mile | Paul Anderson | IND | Syracuse, N.Y. | Sep 13, '24 | 15:07.80 | 79.33 |
| 25 mile | John Seymour | IND | Syracuse, N.Y. | Sep 19, '25 | 19:15.65 | 77.91 |
| **1 Mile Dirt Track — Solo — Class A — 21.35 cu.in. motors** | | | | | | |
| 5 mile | Miny Waln | IND | Bakersfield, Cal. | Apr 12, '31 | 3:34.60 | 83.88 |
| 10 mile | Joe Petrali | H-D | Syracuse, N.Y. | Aug 31, '35 | 7:20.90 | 81.65 |
| 15 mile | Joe Petrali | H-D | Syracuse, N.Y. | Aug 31, '35 | 11:10.85 | 80.50 |
| 20 mile | Curly Fredericks | IND | Syracuse, N.Y. | Aug 31, '29 | 15:21.40 | 78.14 |
| 25 mile | Joe Petrali | H-D | Syracuse, N.Y. | Aug 31, '35 | 18:44.52 | 80.11 |
| **1 Mile Dirt Track — Side Car — Class A** | | | | | | |
| 1 mile | Floyd Dreyer | IND | Toledo, O. | Aug 14, '21 | :51.60 | 69.77 |
| 5 mile | Ralph Hepburn | H-D | Syracuse, N.Y. | Sep 13, '24 | 4:04.31 | 73.68 |
| 10 mile | F.J.Scott | IND | Toledo, O. | Jul 26, '24 | 8:25.00 | 71.29 |
| 25 mile | Floyd Dreyer | IND | Toledo, O. | Aug 14, '21 | 21:47.00 | 69.18 |
| **½ Mile Dirt Track — Solo — Class A — 30.50 cu.in. motors** | | | | | | |
| 1 mile | John Seymour | IND | Winchester, Ind. | Jul 22, '23 | :54.00 | 66.67 |
| 3 mile | Otto Pechar | IND | Torrington, Conn. | May 30, '25 | 2:46.40 | 64.89 |
| 5 mile | John Seymour | IND | Winchester, Ind. | Jul 18, '23 | 4:39.40 | 64.41 |
| 10 mile | Paul Anderson | EXC | Winchester, Ind. | May 18, '23 | 9:39.00 | 62.18 |

275

**½ Mile Dirt Track — Solo — Class A — 21.35 cu.in. motors**

| | | | | | | |
|---|---|---|---|---|---|---|
| 3 mile | Tuffy Jacobs | IND | Ascot Speedway | Apr 27, '30 | 2:30.40 | 71.79 |
| 5 mile | Joe Petrali | H-D | Hamilton Speedway | Jun 21, '31 | 4:18.08 | 69.75 |
| 10 mile | Joe Petrali | H-D | Hamilton Speedway | Jun 21, '31 | 8:35.20 | 69.88 |

**½ Mile Dirt Track — Side Car — Class A**

| | | | | | | |
|---|---|---|---|---|---|---|
| 1 mile | Lester Foote | H-D | Greeley, Colo. | Sep 16, '20 | 1:13.60 | 48.91 |
| 5 mile | Bill Minnick | H-D | Frederick, Md. | May 30, '24 | 5:34.00 | 56.89 |
| 10 mile | Floyd Dreyer | IND | Pittsburgh, Pa. | Oct 10, '21 | 11:11.20 | 53.64 |

**Non-Competitive Board Track Records — Solo — Class A — 45 cu.in.**

| | | | | | | |
|---|---|---|---|---|---|---|
| 1 mile | Joe Petrali | S-X | Altoona, Pa. | Jul 2, '26 | :33.44 | 107.65 |
| 5 mile | Joe Petrali | S-X | Altoona, Pa. | Jul 2, '26 | 2:53.70 | 103.60 |
| 10 mile | Joe Petrali | S-X | Altoona, Pa. | Jul 2, '26 | 5:57.50 | 100.70 |

**Straightaway — Solo — Class A — 40 cu.in. motors**

| | | | | | | |
|---|---|---|---|---|---|---|
| 1 mile | Bobbie Turner | TRI | Daytona Beach, Fla. | Feb 19, '51 | :27.88 | 129.24 |

**Straightaway — Solo — Class A — 61 cu.in. motors**

| | | | | | | |
|---|---|---|---|---|---|---|
| 1 mile | Rollie Free | VIN | Bonneville, Utah | Sep 11, '50 | :22.99 | 156.58 |

**Straightaway — Solo — Class A — 30.50 cu.in. motors**

| | | | | | | |
|---|---|---|---|---|---|---|
| 1 kilo | John Seymour | IND | Daytona Beach, Fla. | Jan 12, '26 | :19.34 | 112.63 |

**24 Hour Record**

| | | | | | |
|---|---|---|---|---|---|
| | Fred Hamm | H-D | Muroc Dry Lake, Cal. | Apr 8, '37 | 1825.2 miles | 76.05 |

**1 Mile Dirt Track — Solo — Class C — 45 cu.in. motors**

| | | | | | | |
|---|---|---|---|---|---|---|
| 5 mile | Larry Hedrick | H-D | Springfield, Ill. | Aug 20, '50 | 3:39.11 | 82.15 |
| 8 mile | Art Hafer | IND | Milwaukee, Wis. | Aug 25, '40 | 6:00.58 | 79.87 |
| 10 mile | Kenneth Eggers | H-D | Springfield, Ill. | Aug 20, '50 | 7:17.06 | 84.66 |
| 15 mile | Larry Hedrick | H-D | Milwaukee, Wis. | Aug 26, '50 | 10:50.72 | 82.99 |
| 20 mile | Horace Travis | H-D | Du Quoin, Ill. | Sep 4, '49 | 14:41.98 | 81.52 |
| 25 mile | Larry Hedrick | H-D | Springfield, Ill. | Aug 20, '50 | 18:01.71 | 83.20 |
| 50 mile | Lester Hillbish | IND | Syracuse, N.Y. | Aug 26, '39 | 39:15.59 | 76.42 |

**½ Mile Dirt Track — Solo — Class C — 45 cu.in. motors**

| | | | | | | |
|---|---|---|---|---|---|---|
| 3 mile | Bill Miller | H-D | Richmond, Va. | May 29, '49 | 2:49.38 | 63.76 |
| 5 mile | Bobby Hill | IND | Jacksonville, Fla. | May 8, '49 | 4:39.38 | 64.43 |
| 7 mile | Paul Albrecht | H-D | Shreveport, La. | Oct 29, '50 | 6:48.40 | 61.74 |
| 8 mile | Johnny Butterfield | H-D | Richmond, Va. | Oct 1, '50 | 7:30.34 | 63.95 |
| 10 mile | Paul Albrecht | H-D | Richmond, Va. | May 29, '49 | 9:15.35 | 64.82 |

**Dirt Track Speedway — Solo — Class C — 45 cu.in. motors**

| | | | | | | |
|---|---|---|---|---|---|---|
| 100 mile | Jimmy Chann | H-D | Langhorne, Pa. | Sep 4, '49 | 68:53.45 | 87.09 |
| 200 mile | Louis Guanella | H-D | Oakland, Cal. | Oct 27, '40 | 141:45.55 | 84.64 |

**Straightaway — Solo — Class C — One Mile**

| | | | | | | |
|---|---|---|---|---|---|---|
| 40cu.in. | Bobbie Turner | TRI | Daytona Beach, Fla. | Feb 20, '51 | :30.43 | 118.40 |
| 45cu.in. | Fred Ludlow | IND | Bonneville, Utah | Sep 25, '38 | :31.27 | 115.12 |
| 74cu.in. | Fred Ludlow | IND | Bonneville, Utah | Sep 25, '38 | :29.81 | 120.74 |

The above record tabulations, incomplete through the years shown, were compiled from contemporary trade and sports reports. They differ markedly from the official AMA records as published in later years. After H-D came into control of the AMA after the mid-1920s, it was alleged by some that many of the earlier tabulations were altered, and in some cases records attained by other makes of machines were deleted, or the results changed.

Most of the early records tabulated when American motorcycle sport was under the auspices of the Federation of American Motorcyclists, from 1909 through 1920-21, were lost during the organization period of the AMA. The only source of these today are the fragmentary data available from that published in contemporary trade publications.

# Bibliography

Publications and photographs publicly circulated by the Harley-Davidson Motorcycle Company

The Archives of the Hendee Manufacturing Company
The Archives of the Indian Motocycle Company
The US National Museum, Department of Transportation
The United States Congressional Record
The United States Department of Commerce
The Reports of the United States Senate Select Committee on Tariffs
The United States Department of Justice, Bureau of Prisons
The Federal District Court, Denver, Colorado
The Superior Court of Cook County
The Superior Court of Monroe County
The Detroit Public Library
The Milwaukee Public Library
The Los Angeles County Public Library
Bibliotica Nationale, Mexico City, Republic of Mexico
Motor Cycle Cavalcade, by Ixion (Canon B.H.Davies), Iliffe
Vintage Motorcycles, by James Sheldon, Batsford
The World's Motorcycles, by Erwin Tragatsch, Temple Press
Motorcycles, by Victor Page
Vintage Motorcycling, by M.A.Bull
The Golden Age of the Fours, by Theodore Hodgdon, Bagnall
The Story of the TT, by G.S.Davison
Standard & Poor's Corporation Index
Moody's Corporation Index
Barron's Weekly
The Motor Cycle
Motor Cycling
The Motorcyclist
Motorcycling Illustrated
The Western Motorcyclist and Bicyclist
Cycle World
Cycle
Custom Chopper
Street Chopper

Iron Horse
Supercycle
Automotive Illustrated
Motor Age
The World's Automobiles, by G.N.Georgano
The New York Times
The Los Angeles Times
The Milwaukee Journal
The Milwaukee Sentinal
The Wall Street Journal
The Journal of the Antique Motorcycle Club
The Official Journal of the Vintage Motor Cycle Club
The Journal of the Classic and Antique Motorcycle Club
Robert W.Baird & Co., Incorporated
The First Boston Company
The Atlas Corporation
The Baldwin Chain Company
E.I. duPont De Nemours
Delco, Incorporated
The Firestone Tire & Rubber Company
Bangor Punta Incorporated
American Machine & Foundry Company
The Goodyear Tire & Rubber Company
The Wisconsin Historical Society

# Index

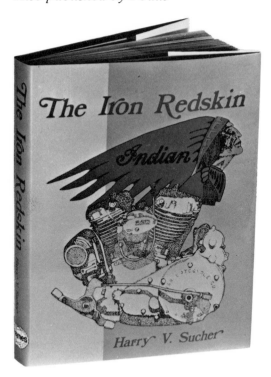

Indian is a Magic name in Motorcycling. Its mention brings back nostalgic memories of the rich red machines with flamboyant bold striping, lithe of appearance, and, seemingly even at rest, poised for flight. Its distinctive trademark was the staccato bark of its high revving, side valve engine. This was joined in later years by the quiet hum of the smooth-running four cylinder models which could assume a lightning burst of acceleration and an impudent snarl at a touch of the throttle. The cadences of both were to echo through nearly every country of the world.

THE IRON REDSKIN is a vast work which took many thousands of hours to compile, yet it is one of the most readable and interesting histories ever to be published. Because the Indian motorcycle was manufactured during some of the most exciting and changing years of America's history, much of that excitement and change comes through, albeit carried on the saddle of a motorcycle. It is pure motorcycling history told with the pace and grace of a classic V-twin, Indian Style!

FOULIS is a name associated with publishing for over 400 years. The Haynes Publishing Group, of which G. T. Foulis Limited is part, are the World's largest publishers of motoring and motorcycling books, including the range of Haynes Owners Workshop Manuals for cars and motorcycles. For further details please contact the address shown on the title page.